Trapped in Poverty?

On both sides of the Atlantic there has been a fierce debate about the causes of and remedies for poverty. Are people with low earning-power excluded from mainstream society, or do they marginalise themselves by expecting too much and contributing too little? Is there an underclass, and if so is it a product of structural inequalities or of individuals' moral shortcomings?

This book provides a detailed study of how couples with children in low-income households make decisions about employment and claiming benefits. It shows how they account for their moves in and out of the labour market, and between employment and self-employment. It challenges both views of poor people – as passive victims and as deviant opportunists – by demonstrating how they adopt an ethic of hard work and family responsibility, but 'bend the rules' of the benefit system to fit them better to current employment conditions.

Trapped in Poverty? provides a wealth of new empirical data, and a cogent theoretical analysis of labour-market decisions in the context of household, kinship and community. Direct and accessible in style, it is a valuable contribution to the study of poverty, employment, social relations and economic and social rationality. It will be a sourcebook for students in a wide range of social science subjects.

Bill Jordan is Reader in Social Studies at Sheffield University. **Simon James** is Senior Lecturer in Economics at Exeter University. **Helen Kay** is Researcher for the Scottish Office. **Marcus Redley** is Research Assistant at Exeter University.

Trapped in Poverty?
Labour-market decisions in low-income households

Bill Jordan, Simon James, Helen Kay and Marcus Redley

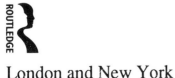

London and New York

First published 1992 by Routledge
11 New Fetter Lane, London EC4P 4EE

Simultaneously published in the USA and Canada
by Routledge
a division of Routledge, Chapman and Hall, Inc.
29 West 35th Street, New York, NY 10001

© 1992 Bill Jordan, Simon James, Helen Kay, Marcus Redley
Typeset by LaserScript Limited, Mitcham, Surrey
Printed and bound in Great Britain by
Billings & Sons Limited, Worcester

British Library Cataloguing in Publication Data
Trapped in poverty?: labour-market decision in low-income households.
  1. Great Britain. Low-income persons. Employment
  I. Jordan, Bill *1941*–
  331.540941

ISBN 0–415–06867–3

Library of Congress Cataloging-in-Publication Data
Trapped in poverty?: labour-market decision in low income housholds/
Bill Jordan . . . [et al.].
    p. cm.
Includes bibliographical references and index.
  ISBN 0–415–06867–3
  1. Poor – Employment – Great Britain Case studies. 2. Labor
market – Great Britain – Case studies. 3. Work and family – Great
Britain – Case studies. I. Jordan, Bill, 1941–   .
HD5765.A6T73   1992
306.3′6 – dc20   91-10046
                                                              CIP

Contents

Acknowledgements

The authors wish to thank the Economic and Social Research Council (ESRC) for the award (grant number GOG 232446) under which this research study was carried out.

We are also very grateful to Janet Finch, Jan Pahl, Jan Otto Andersson and Liselotte Wohlgenannt for helpful comments on parts of an earlier draft. Special thanks are due to Gill Watson for accuracy and stamina in typing the drafts and final text of the book, and to Elaine Harrison for skilled transcription of the interview tapes.

1 Introduction

This book provides a detailed study of how men and women in low-income households with children decide what work to do, at what wages, for what hours, and with what prospects. It shows how they account for their moves in and out of the labour market, relating such changes to job security, pay, income tax, benefits, family responsibilities, spending patterns and other factors. It also analyses how each partner's decisions relate to the other's, and the sense in which they follow a joint 'strategy'.

We started out to study how poor people describe their experience of the unemployment and poverty traps. The research focused on one deprived neighbourhood, and investigated moves between employment, unemployment and self-employment in a fragmented, casualised labour market. We were interested in finding out whether any one feature distinguished households in which there was one or more adult in more-or-less continuous employment from those in which employment was intermittent, and those in which no one had been employed for many years. We wanted to see what they said about the incentives and disincentives associated with income tax and benefits, and how they made choices about paid and unpaid work roles.

We found that this investigation took us into some very controversial and contested territory. It raised thorny issues both at the methodological and theoretical level, and at the level of interpretation and policy implications. One theoretical problem was central and inescapable. Our research method was intentionally interdisciplinary because we wanted to look at poor people's accounts with open minds, to see whether there were issues that had been missed by all the disciplines. However, there was no easy way that an interdisciplinary approach to these accounts could bridge the gulf between rival social science paradigms. In particular, the paradigm of economic individualism (rational choice, the calculative pursuit of interests according to consistent preferences) increasingly represents an explanatory model for all the social sciences: it is challenged in fundamental ways by theories which emphasise the ethical, group, community and societal factors which influence human decisions. We had no alternative but to address these theoretical issues head on.

This was not because we have a preference for theoretical over empirical work: on the contrary, we were originally motivated by the remarkable lack of hard data on a subject over which there was so much pontification. However, we were led into these issues by the respondents themselves. First, they framed their answers to our questions about their employment decisions less in calculative, economistic terms than in terms of their roles in the family, and hence their responsibilities towards each other (providing income, caring for the children, etc.). Their interview responses demanded to be analysed as accounts of what they did to fulfil the moral requirements of being partners and parents – and also members of kinship and friendship networks, and a close-knit local community. But this did not exclude calculation or quantified economic reasoning about how to maximise household income from paid work (official and unofficial) and benefits. Rather, it meant that such reasoning – about how to get the most from the labour market and the benefits system – was firmly located in a discourse about mutual responsibility, partnership and membership. Hence all economic decisions – keeping a steady job, working for cash 'on the side', fitting in work hours with children's needs, or refusing low-paid employment – were justified in terms of the standards expected of partners and parents (and, to a secondary extent, of kin, neighbours or residents of their estate).

The empirical findings of the study contained pitfalls of a different kind. Like other researchers, we found that poor people described snares and complexities in the benefits system, and experienced the delays caused by an overstretched administration: this often left them very short of cash, got them into debt, or provided a disincentive to taking low-paid, part-time or short-term work. Our research was done after the reforms of the social security system, implemented in April 1988: it showed that – for couples such as those in our study – the government's policies for improving incentives were failing, because they failed to take account of such factors.

But we also found that two-thirds of these households described times when they did undeclared work for cash while claiming benefits, or supplemented low wages by doing cash jobs that were not declared to the Inland Revenue. Such evidence could easily be pounced upon, taken out of context, and used rather irresponsibly in political debates about 'dependence', 'demoralisation' and the 'underclass'. Although we have been careful to show how these respondents describe and justify such practices – in terms of the workings of the tax-benefit system, which they see as otherwise unfairly constraining their attempts to cover family expenditure – there is still a danger that our research will be misused, on this point in particular.

Hence the two controversial aspects of the research are linked. On the one hand, we have produced very detailed new evidence about how poor people make their decisions, in the face of current employment conditions, wages, and tax-benefit systems. These include important findings about how they bend the rules of the latter. However, their rule-bending cannot be properly understood solely in a context of economic opportunism. On the contrary, it is justified by them as required by their moral responsibilities to their families. In the process of tracing in detail the way in which these interviewees combine moral and economic reasoning, we believe that we have developed important new insights into the relationship between these aspects of modern social relations. We also think that our analysis allows us to come up with a new theory of household decision-making which relates employment to household roles and household expenditure. Finally, we make some careful and qualified recommendations about policy for the tax-benefit system.

The plan of the book is as follows: we start by showing the relationship between our research interviews and the theoretical debate about low-income households and the labour market; then we describe our methodological problems and how we resolved them; after this we present our analysis of the interviews and our conclusions.

Our starting point (Chapter 2) is the widely differing theories about poor people's employment decisions offered by the major social science disciplines. Economists treat these as instances of choices made under constraint, and try to model the effects of tax and benefits changes on the behaviour of household members. Sociologists emphasise the influence of social norms and roles and the effects of structural relationships. Social policy analysts point to the way benefits systems shape the attitudes and life chances of the poor, but argue over whether they are 'encouraged to be dependent' or 'excluded from economic participation'.

In Chapter 3, we explain why we chose to use a research method based on interviews and qualitative analysis. We became convinced at an early stage that in order to start exploring this area, a statistical, survey approach was not appropriate. The aim was to find out, from their own accounts, how men and women described changes in their employment situations, how men's changes affected women's and *vice versa*, how they fitted their employment hours together, and whether they described a poverty or an unemployment trap. We make it clear that this study, by using in-depth interviews, attempts to generate theory on decision-making that captures the respondents' diverse and sometimes contradictory accounts of their household and personal choices. Unlike surveys based on statistically designed samples, the validity of our research rests upon the quality of our theorising of all our data, including apparently deviant cases. It is only when this stage of the investigation has been completed that quantitative methods may be used to test the generalisability of our findings.

We also explain in Chapter 3 how we chose our sample of thirty-six two-parent households with dependent children. These were all people living on an outer-city council estate which has one of the highest profiles for social deprivation in southern England. But they were not all claiming benefit, and in only eleven households was there no adult in paid work. We also interviewed seven lone parents with dependent children for purposes of comparison. The aim was to look at how people with similar access to the labour market moved between employment, self-employment and unemployment, and for this purpose our sample of people, including some in each of these employment statuses, but all from a *poor neighbourhood*, seems well suited to generate theory and hypotheses.

In Chapter 4, we analyse the accounts of their employment decisions given by the men in these households. They adopted the role of 'bread-winner' – self-respecting worker and provider of family income – in their versions, even when they had experienced long periods of unemployment. Indeed, only two interviewees had not been unemployed in the 1980s, and only twelve of the men currently had regular, full-time, long-term jobs. All the rest could be classified as 'irregulars', moving in and out of various short-term employments, government training schemes or self-employment. In all, twenty-three men – including some of those in regular full-time work – told the interviewer that they did 'cash jobs' that they did not declare to the tax or benefit authorities.

There were some marked differences between the accounts of the 'regulars' and those of the 'irregulars'. The former emphasised job security: they greatly feared redundancy and having to resort to the benefits system. The latter (two-thirds of the men) were far more sanguine about job changes and periods of claiming, describing the kind of judgement that is needed to be a 'breadwinner' in a casualised, fragmented labour market, including the recognition of employments that were unacceptable because of low pay. Their criticisms of the benefits system focused on delays and unreliability in its administration, and pressures to take short-term or low-paid work which they saw as inconsistent with their roles as providers of family income. Conversely, undeclared cash work was described as a better way of meeting household expenses during periods when no acceptable employment was available, or there was insufficient work for the self-employed.

In line with these criticisms, irregular workers described a 'vicious circle', caused by interaction between the prevalence of short-term low-paid or part-time work and a benefits system where administrative proce-dures related to regular full-time jobs. This was how they described the 'unemployment trap', and they used undeclared cash work as a way of breaking out of it. When in work, irregulars (like regulars) tried to increase their earnings through overtime hours, and saw themselves as penalised by a system which made them ineligible for family credit if they earned more in this way. Some argued that those who worked less hours, or did not work at all, were eligible for family credit or income support: hence the benefits system was seen as rewarding idleness, while the tax system punished hard work. This way of describing the 'poverty trap' has some important implications for policy.

In Chapter 5 we turn to the accounts of the women. Their descriptions of their labour-market decisions started from the perception of their role as having primary responsibility for child care. Hence their important contribution to household income had to be consistent with the welfare of their children: they had to 'fit in' employment with this and other domestic responsibilities.

The problems of 'fitting it all in' were particularly marked for those women whose partners were irregular workers. In line with findings from other studies, the female interviewees explained that it was not 'worth it' to continue their employment when these women were in part-time jobs. Hence they withdrew from the regular labour market when their partners were claiming income support.

The women respondents described in detail the child-care arrangements that were necessary to allow them to take available employment (often working early in the morning or later in the evening) involving partners, kin and friends. These hours were shaped by tax considerations, since employers had designed them to minimise their liability for National Insurance Contributions. However, some women who had the option to increase their hours chose not to do so, having calculated that the return would be very small because of the impact of tax.

These findings confirm the econometric and survey work on married women, which suggests that they are more sensitive to tax and benefit factors than men are. Women's sensitivity to these constraints and disincentives must be seen alongside their sensitivity to other – in many cases more influential – factors which affect their labour supply behaviour. Above all, these women respondents give primacy to child-care responsibilities because this is the norm among their network of female kin and friends. They are socialised and sustained in this role by the network, which in turn enables them to contribute to family income from employment that is vital to the standard of living of the household. Their accounts show how they balance all these factors in their employment decision-making.

In our sample, four of the women were in full-time employment, and one of these had a partner doing no paid work, and caring for the children. Yet these women, too, constructed themselves primarily as responsible for child care and unpaid domestic work, and saw the help they got from partners as exceptional – 'he's one in a million'.

In Chapter 6, we analyse the joint interviews with both partners. It was not possible to interview all couples jointly, mainly because of the tensions which surfaced in the individual interviews. In particular, where clashes of interest between the man and the woman emerged, or accounts of the same events and decisions were widely divergent, or contentious issues were clearly not being discussed, joint interviews were evaded by the couple, or not pressed by the interviewer.

The respondents made it clear that their norm for decision-making was 'jointness' – 'discussion' leading to agreement. However, it emerged that this did not refer to decisions over men's employment, and that discussions over women's employment centred on child care and other practical arrangements. Our analysis shows that joint decision-making concerned issues of *expenditure*, not employment, and that once couples had decided how much to spend (on regular weekly outgoings and 'extras' like clothing and leisure items) they then made work decisions independently. Hence we question the concept of a 'household work strategy', preferring that of a 'household income strategy'. We go on to demonstrate that there were three such strategies recognisable among these households. The first relied on one partner's full-time employment (twelve men and two women) for regular weekly expenditures and the other's (usually part-time) earnings for 'extras'. The second involved one or both partners in irregular work to provide household income, but relied on benefits to support the family and cover costs when such periods were interrupted. The third relied on benefits for income to cover regular weekly expenditure, and undeclared cash work for 'extras'.

In Chapter 7, we address the issue of whether the roles of men and women, as displayed in the respondents' accounts, can be described as 'rational', given their situation. This involves a critique of the concept of 'rationality' in rational choice theory. We argue that norms can only be explained in terms of collective interests, and can be seen as rational in these terms. We go on to show how these households' roles, norms and decision-making processes are related to their kinship and friendship networks in this close-knit community, where the majority had close kin living nearby, and friends played an important part in finding work and assisting in child care.

We also consider the respondents' accounts of their community, and their decision-making over house purchase. Among those buying or planning to buy their houses, liking for their neighbourhood and neighbours, having kin nearby, fear of privatisation of the council's housing stock, and the desire to protect their investment of time and energy in home improvements (usually done with relatives or friends, and often during a period of unemployment), were the main reasons given for this choice. Buying their house was described as giving a stake in the community, and securing the support of their network.

The interviewees described house purchase as requiring both partners to do paid work, and that this was often onerous in the short run. They did not describe it as a move towards individualism or (except in two cases) as part of a plan to leave the area. They were mainly concerned to protect their position in the community and the culture with which they were familiar, and where they got support and a sense of membership.

Chapter 8 analyses the interviews with lone parents, and shows that only one of them had been in full-time work since having sole responsibility for children, but all placed a high value on employment (including voluntary work) as providing a 'break' from the home. They described the powerful disincentive effects of the benefits system in relation to full-time employment, and especially over the costs of child care.

In Chapter 9, we address the issue of how the rules and administration of benefits and income taxation influence the roles and norms governing these couples' decisions. We show how the 'social forms' available to them are derived from official power and knowledge, both in their accounts of autonomy and constraints. Finally we return to the question of whether these households are trapped in poverty. We contrast four of the couples in our study. A man in regular employment who has just moved into the household of a single parent mother of one child, who now expects a second: he wants to increase his overtime, but if he does so they will not be eligible for family credit, even after the birth of the new baby. A couple who are planning to increase their working hours in order to buy their council house, and who already scarcely see each other because of the demands of their employments: they are not eligible for family credit, and see this as a 'trap'. A couple with six children, in which the man is an irregular self-employed worker, but where the woman has just given up her part-time job in a café after a row with the supervisor: soon afterwards he started to claim income support. And a couple, both unemployed, who are in trouble with the benefit authorities over their claim: he says his choice is between 'taking a chance' on doing undeclared cash work, or stealing and being sent to prison. Which of these, if any, is trapped in poverty?

We examine the similarities and differences between these couples' accounts, and consider their relevance for the theoretical and policy debates about poverty. We consider how our qualitative study relates to policy proposals, and draw attention to features of these accounts that indicate how modest changes in the tax-benefit system would make it more compatible with the actual labour-market conditions faced by our respondents.

Throughout all the chapters, repeated references are made (by the interviewees and in our analysis) to the systems of income taxation and social security benefits. The interviews took place in late 1988 and early 1989, when the reforms introduced by the 1986 Social Security Act had just been implemented, and the names of certain benefits were changed. This is confusing. For instance, interviewees sometimes talk about family income supplement, which was replaced by family credit in 1988; or about supplementary benefit, which was replaced by income support at the same time. The danger of misunderstanding is compounded by the modern printing convention of starting these names with lower case letters. The reader should be cautioned that certain terms – 'budgeting loans' for example – are technical, and refer to the benefits system. Hence we think it is helpful to provide a background guide to the system, as it operated then (it has been changed in several ways since). We debated at some length on where in the book to locate such a guide: one possibility was to put it here, at the end of the introductory chapter. However, we eventually decided to put it at the end, as an appendix (Appendix 1). Those not at all familiar with the main principles and terms used in British income taxation and social security benefits are advised to read it before embarking on the substantive chapters of the research itself. Those with a working knowledge of the systems can use it as a reference section, for information about the details of the situation in late 1988 to mid-1989.

Another point should be made before embarking on our account of the research. Throughout the text we have used quotations from tape recorded interviews with members of households in the study neighbourhood. In order to link parts of the same interviews, and partners to each other, we have given each person a pseudonym. The surnames chosen are those of British rivers, on the grounds that few real surnames are taken from river names. A list of these names, linking them with the occupations of the partners at the time of interview, and the number and ages of their children, is given in Appendix 2. Also in this list are the pseudonymous first names of the couple and their children which we have given them where they refer to each other in the parts of the interviews quoted.

TRANSCRIPT CONVENTIONS

In all quotations from interviews, ... denotes a pause; [...] denotes the omission of a short passage from the transcript. The number in brackets denotes the page in the transcript.

2 Contested territory

This study focuses on a small area of decision-making which stands at the crossroads of several academic disciplines and ideological traditions. Like many such locations, it is fiercely disputed territory – a battleground which inspires far more bellicose words and warlike postures than its size or character would seem to warrant. It is, as it were, of strategic importance for economics, sociology, psychology and social policy, but also for the major political movements of the day: currently a zone for mobilisation and tactical advance on the right; for fortification and protective defence on the left.

As more befits the real dimensions of this area, our study is small-scale and rather humble: it involved only one research worker, for a period of 16 months. She (Helen Kay) interviewed thirty-six couples with children living on the most deprived council estate in Exeter, a city of some 90,000 inhabitants in south-west England. She asked them about their choice of employment, at what pay, for what hours, and with what prospects of training and promotion; she invited them to talk about changes in jobs or hours that had occurred in recent years, to explain what they hoped to achieve by these changes, and how they worked out in practice. She tape recorded her separate interviews with both partners and (where possible) with both together; she also talked to seven single parents for comparison. At the end of the interviews, where these had not already been discussed, she inquired about income tax and social security benefits – how, if at all, these had influenced their decisions. The recordings were then transcribed and analysed: in a preliminary way by the interviewer, and comprehensively by a newly appointed research worker (Marcus Redley). Both analysts had trained in qualitative methods.

The main reason why this apparently innocent exercise touches on so much controversy is that these people were all poor. They had all at some time claimed benefits, and many were currently claiming – almost one-third were households in which no one was in employment, and another nine were in receipt of family credit. Of those in work, thirteen had been claiming income support by virtue of unemployment during the past year. So these were people at the bottom end of the labour market, mostly in irregular, low-paid, insecure and unprotected employment or self-employment, who frequently or continuously resorted to 'targeted' (income-tested) benefits to sustain their households at subsistence levels.

In the population as a whole, households like these are quite few. In May 1988 (the year the research study began) there were, in Great Britain, 473,000 claimants of income support by virtue of unemployment who were 'heads' of couple households of whom some 392,000 had dependent children;[1] and 176,000 claimants of family credit.[2] It is estimated that perhaps another 200–250,000 would have qualified for family credit if they had claimed; by 1989, the numbers claiming had risen to 285,000.[3] So the couples we interviewed were examples (not necessarily typical examples, as we acknowledge in Chapter 3) of some 7–800,000 households, forming about 14 per cent of all couples with dependent children, who in turn form 44 per cent of all couples. These in turn form 28 per cent of all the 19,492,000 households in Great Britain.[4]

Yet the significance given to these people's behaviour is out of all proportion to the size of the group, and they have been the focus of attention from legislators, philosophers (political and moral) and social scientists since the late Middle Ages. The first Poor Law statute (1597) stated in its preamble that 'a great number of poor people are become wanderers, idle and loose, which is a source of infinite inconvenience', and gave powers for 'rogues and vagabonds' to be punished or put to work.[5] One hundred years later, John Locke thought that unemployment was the result of 'some defect in ... ability or honesty', and that the increase in the number of paupers, and the cost of maintaining them, was the consequence not of lack of work but of 'the relaxation of discipline and the corruption of manners'; beggars should be conscripted into the armed services or sent to houses of correction.[6] Bernard Mandeville, writing in 1728, thought that just as the poor 'ought to be kept from starving, so they should receive nothing worth saving.... Those that get their living by their daily labour ... have nothing to stir them up to be serviceable but their wants which it is prudence to relieve but folly to cure'.[7] Thomas Malthus, writing in 1798, was even more severe about the labouring poor who 'live from hand to mouth'. 'Even when they have an opportunity of saving they seldom exercise it; but all that is beyond their present necessities goes, generally speaking, to the ale-house. The poor-laws of England may therefore be said to diminish both the power and the will to save, among the common people.'.[8] In the 1880s, Herbert Spencer denounced the idleness he saw in London, and attributed it to excessive state intervention. Idlers 'are simply good-for-nothings, who in one way or another live on the good-for-somethings – vagrants and sots, criminals and those on the way to crime, youths who are burdens on hard-worked parents, men who appropriate the wages of their wives, fellows who share the gains of prostitutes; and then, less visible and less numerous, there is a corresponding class of women'.[9]

But it was not only liberals like all these who feared the poor, or bemoaned their lack of the industrious virtues. Karl Marx wrote of 'the lowest sediment of the relative surplus population (which) dwells in the sphere of pauperism', including the 'actual lumpen proletariat' – 'vagabonds, criminals, prostitutes' -- as well as 'the demoralised, the ragged, and those unable to work, chiefly people who succumb to their incapacity for adaptation'.[10] Trotsky, while still a close colleague of Lenin's and a leading Bolshevik, argued that 'love of work is not at all an inborn characteristic: it is created by economic pressure and social education. One may even say that man is a fairly lazy animal.... We (are for) regulated labour on the basis of an economic plan, obligatory for the whole population and consequently compulsory for each worker in the country'.[11]

These judgemental and prescriptive views of what poor people *should* do have many modern counterparts. There has never been a shortage of politicians and commentators to tell them of their obligations to society at large, and particularly to those who pay taxes for their support. What is more, poor people themselves are denunciatory and moralistic about those (always others) who exploit the system or avoid work. In our study, the interviewees took an almost Spencerian view of idleness; like Marx, they said that there was a lumpen element, which gave their community a bad name, was unreliable and feckless; and if they might have baulked at a Trotskyesque solution to this problem, they were Lockean in their condemnation of such behaviour, and thought it should not go unpunished.

However, concern about the working habits of the poor has moved beyond the realms of opinion and judgement, and entered the sphere of social scientific investigation. At the outset, we will briefly review the main theoretical explanations of decision-making in low-income households, to set out the rival claims of academic disciplines over the analysis and prediction of these choices.

THEORETICAL ISSUES

Lurking behind these disputes is a fundamental theoretical issue in the social sciences. The most powerful and persuasive theories to emerge in the 1980s have been based on rational choice theory and game theory, which derive ultimately from microeconomic analysis. Actors (individuals or collectivities) are treated as seeking to maximise utility in the face of various kinds of constraints, by choosing according to a consistent set of preferences. This analytic method has been adopted over an ever-wider field of social studies, being used to explain household relations, class divisions, the evolution of political institutions and international power systems.[12] In its popular forms, it has come to be the taken-for-granted basis of the policies of the market-minded governments which dominated British and American politics in the period, and which claim credit for over-throwing the regimes of Eastern Europe, and fatally weakening the Soviet regime.

Against this formidable and coherent body of ideas is set a stubborn resistance from those who insist that no such analysis can do justice to the moral and social elements which are an inescapable feature of all human relationships. Though far less theoretically coherent, and often still under-developed, this school of thought insists that actions of community, membership and sharing are essential to the understanding of social units, from households to societies, and that concepts such as justice, equality and deomocracy, derived ultimately from ethics and politics, are therefore as necessary for the analysis of social phenomena as those of preference and self-interest.[13] Furthermore, this tradition insists that rational choice and game theoretical explanations of non-economic behaviour and institutions are fatally flawed – that they are vacuous, reductionist or tautological.[14]

This fundamental dispute has haunted every aspect of our study. On the one hand, our interviewees' choices – to take paid work or stay at home, for example – could be seen as rational responses to the set of opportunities and constraints (wage and benefit levels, needs of children, child-care facilities, etc.) that confronted them. Certainly they often described them in these terms. Mr Derwent works night shifts loading vegetables into lorries:

Q: How many nights a week?
Mr Derwent: Well I could work 6 if I wanted to, ah, I used to, but our place has been taken over, see, so we've been moved over to the other depot. They shut down one, but mainly I work 5 nights – and Friday night is overtime, so ... I can't work Friday 'cause Rachel [wife] works on a Friday. So usually I go into work soon as Rachel comes home. I start work at about midnight on Friday and work through till morning.

(Mr Derwent, 12)

There are hundreds of such passages in our interviews, showing the respondents using a discourse of economic decision-making under constraint to explain their past or present behaviour. However, often in the very same speech-episode, or soon afterwards, they then account for their actions in rather different terms, using a rhetoric of 'what is right', of 'fairness', or of loyalty to others. Slightly later, Mr Derwent is explaining why he does not claim family credit by sending in five low wage slips, and then go back to working overtime, while receiving the benefit for the next 6 months.

> ''Cause in the trade I am at the moment it's related to seasons so at the moment it's winter, it's a quiet time ... because if I wanted to ... see it would be the ideal time to work flat week and I could perhaps make the claims, but then in the summer the hours go up so you could get your money coming in then. That ... in a sense ... that's ah ... fraud i'n'it, I mean, you'm cheating the system really, aren't you? When you do that. I i'n' no conman like that [laughs].'

> (Mr Derwent, 24)

Here Mr Derwent seems to be saying that economic logic would recommend him to make the claim, which would probably be legally justifiable, but that he feels it would not be consistent with his sense of fair play. He says elsewhere that he thinks the *system* is wrong that allows someone who chooses to work less to claim the benefit, while he is ineligible if he chooses to work more. These are judgements – which Mr Derwent acknowledges to be contestable – that appeal to quite different standards to legitimate his behaviour.

Our study provides a rich source of data on how poor people deploy these two discourses, of economic rationality and of morality, in justifying their choices. However, if we are to go beyond a mere display about how these are deployed (for example, which questions evoke which kinds of vocabulary of motivation) we have to address more fundamental questions about social relations and social institutions. One of the most controversial parts of our study concerns the widespread practice of doing cash work while claiming benefits. How is this to be explained? The respondents themselves account for much of it in terms of the benefit system: irregular workers are penalised for taking short-term employment because of a 2–3 week delay before receiving benefit when the job comes to an end. In one sense, therefore, they are responding 'rationally' to the constraints of a fragmented labour market and an overstretched, complex benefits system. Yet behind their accounts of doing undeclared cash jobs is an implicit or explicit appeal against the unfairness of the present benefits system. Furthermore, those who do such work distinguish between legitimate and illegitimate behaviour in this category. One currently unemployed man and his wife both describe doing undeclared cash work, but define limits on it. He had been doing some roofing work with travellers.

'Well, I just turned 'em away, about 2 weeks ago 'cause ... what, um ... what it is, see, they, us was down Torquay and ... there was a little extension roof and what it was, it was a elderly woman and instead of charging her what I would have charged the elderly woman and what ... 20 quid to do it, they charged her 140 pound which I disagreed with, see. And I just told them if they didn't give the money back to the woman I wouldn't work for them again and I, which I haven't; they come down and I said no 'cause I don't, I don't agree with, you know, cheating elderly women. Which was wrong.'

(Mr Bow, 8)

His wife has done undeclared work in the past, and resents the fact that they have now had their benefits reduced because of an 'overpayment'; she feels aggrieved.

'Well one of my friends, right, honest to God, she's fiddling left, right and centre; she's been doing it now for 3, 4 years – fiddling left, right and centre – and honestly she gets in her house 350 pound a week clear. And it just annoys you. Where they can stop our money when they feels like it and we're not doing nothing wrong.'

(Mrs Bow, 20)

These passages, with their references to moral standards embedded in an account of endemic illegality, raise important issues about motivation, deviance and social control. They suggest that the analysis of the black economy in terms of detection, deterrence and disincentives is far too simple: but they also undermine a good many of the Poverty Lobby's pieties about the extent of 'fraud'.

In any attempt to understand the underlying social relations revealed by these accounts, the division of labour between men and women is of fundamental importance. Here again, some of the reasoning used by interviewees is straightforwardly economistic. Mr Wye has been unemployed for 3 years, and his wife has a full-time job as a warehouse manager. He explains that:

'Women can get more secure jobs than blokes. They, they take 'em on for so long and then ... they'm up the road so ... we decided to go that way.'

(Mr Wye, 15)

Yet Mr Wye still defines himself as a worker and a provider, and Mrs Wye still sees her first responsibility as to care for the children. Furthermore, although Mr Wye's comment is probably as true for many of the other couples in our sample, Mr and Mrs Wye are the only household in which the woman has a regular full-time job and the man stays at home full-time doing child care. This raises intriguing questions about the gendered role division which is characteristic of the estate. Is it a 'rational' response to past or present labour-market conditions, or a relic of traditional working-class culture? Does it reflect power differentials between men and women or wage differentials? Is it in the process of changing, and if so what effect will this have on the close kinship ties that are so clearly part of the estate's social system?

Domestic and caregiving work is itself subjected to a dual analysis by some of our interviewees. Mrs Ribble starts her interview about work as follows:

Q: Do you have a job at the moment?
Mrs Ribble: Yep. Well I'm a housewife and a mother; that's good enough for me [laughs].
Q: Unpaid job?
Mrs Ribble: Well no I don't think like that. I, I do get paid [laughs].
Q: Do you?
Mrs Ribble: My husband pays me [laughs]. Mind you if, if you really wanna go into details then I'm a cook; I'm a chef; I'm a nurse [laughs] I'm a teacher [...] I mean ... on that programme [...] the other day when they were saying about all the, all the different jobs that a mother does, you know ... there's a woman that stays at home then [...] and they worked out to be over 200 pound that they should be paid for all the different jobs they do – I don't get half as much as that [laughs].

(Mrs Ribble, 1)

Yet, later in the same interview, Mrs Ribble makes it clear that she and her husband agree that their son's needs come first, and that she would interrupt a conversation with the Queen to attend to him, because a child always has priority. Does her role as full-time mother reflect this value statement, or Mr Ribble's equally strongly expressed view that the man should be the provider, and the woman should not take paid work until the children reach school age?

The rhetoric of fairness in the division of labour between spouses is quite widely employed in our respondents' accounts. Mrs Tamar is a full-time machinist, and has worked for the company for over 20 years; Mr Tamar is in his mid-40s, has a heart condition for which he was recently in hospital, and works nights for an engineering firm. Her job is secure, his is not. She likes work, and says that even if she had loads of money she would still like to work part time or even full time; he adds that his would be for the companionship, not the money. He dislikes his present job. Then the following exchange occurs:

Mr Tamar: But it's not right for a man to deliberately get his-self out of work just to stay home ... you know, and let his wife go to work and bring in most of the money. I don't think that's right. If your marriage is based on a 50–50 then ... you both should work. If the wife can't work it's diff, different matter altogether [...]

Q: So it's all right for a wife to live off her husband but not for a husband to live off a wife?

Mr Tamar: Yeah. Yeah, I quite agree with that. The man should never live off a woman. I don't think so anyway. Probably that's a different attitude than most, than most blokes but but that's my attitude: a man should never live off a woman.

Q: Would you go along with that?

Mrs Tamar: [pause] I don't know really ... I s'pose ... it all depends ... What money a woman's got I s'pose ...

Mr Tamar: Yeah, but if a man deliberately puts his-self out of work; if I put myself deliberately out of work it's not right for me to depend on you to bring the wages home every week is it?

Mrs Tamar: Oh no.

Mr Tamar: That's what I [indistinct] ... But if a man ... is ill and he can't work it's ... probably that is different ...

(Mr and Mrs Tamar, 42–3)

This kind of moral reasoning about fair shares of work – paid and unpaid – goes on in several of the interviews, but, as in this one, within a very clear division of gender roles over primary responsibility for paid and unpaid work. The man's obligation to do paid work is binding, the woman's elective; in the case of unpaid work the reverse is the case. Fair distributions are then negotiated within this overall framework. But can the framework itself be explained in terms of rational choice theory (or a game-theoretical account) of household formation?

Like the relationship between economic and moral reasoning, that between paid and unpaid work is complex and contested. Mr Wye talks about working for £50 a week for a friend as a labourer because they had been around together for many years, then working part-time at the hospital, but eventually giving that up because it interferes with his commitment to a sports team. It turns out that he is paid to captain the team and act as manager and fixtures secretary. Asked about whether his pay for this is reasonable he replies:

> 'Ah ... yeah, I s'pose it's not bad, I mean I, I don't necessarily do it for the money, I do it because I enjoy it, but I think it's about 50 pound a year.'

(Mr Wye, 12)

Many men speak of getting help from kin and friends in making structural improvements to their houses. Mr Ribble describes major alterations that he has made to his, with help from workmates; he in turn helps them with theirs. He and his wife say that they could not afford to fit a new bathroom if they had to pay for the labour involved, but this is supplied free. Even the materials are bartered between his mates at work, all of whom are sub-contract building workers. They explain that the system is not organised on economic, but on reciprocal principles.

> Mrs Ribble: I mean, they don't sort of keep up and score, you know. I mean Gordon might come out and borrow, say, three things in one week and he might just go and like, borrow the one, you know what I mean. I mean there's no equivalent to it [...] But they sort of ... seem to even it out.

(Mr and Mrs Ribble, 73)

This sounds like a classic example of 'generalised reciprocity' – part of a system of what Sahlins calls 'stone-age economics',[15] which is characterised by 'sharing without reckoning', and which many sociologists now regard as being the prerogative of the domestic sphere, and of female kinship networks in particular.[16] Yet Mr and Mrs Ribble have a fairly precise notion of how much money they are saving through this way of doing things: Mr Ribble estimates that it would have cost him £200 to pay another plumber to do what his friend Eric did for nothing.

Very few interviewees make comparisons between their standards of living and those of better-off people in Exeter or elsewhere, yet one or two comments indicate that they are not unaware of disparities. Mrs Torridge has just lost her part-time job, and is in the process of separating from her husband: she is critical of the benefits system, and particularly of the delay in the payment of family credit, which will effectively keep her out of the labour market. Like other respondents, she does not object to income taxation, but points out that the burdens are unfairly shared out between rich and poor.

> 'But I don't, I don't agree with the way that people who are earning a lot of money seem to pay ... pay ... you know, not much more tax than the

people who are on low income ... because I think that's unfair, really. I mean they probably do less hours than the people that's working and they seem to get a helluva lot more money for it.'

(Mrs Torridge, 26)

Here Mrs Torridge shows that she is aware of the shift in income taxation off the rich and on to people on lower earnings, and criticises it from the perspective of equity in relation to economic effort – the rich do not merit their favourable tax treatment in comparison with those who work harder. Her brother adds that the economic theory that influenced the Conservative government works very much to the advantage of people who are well off.

So the discourse displayed in our study interviews parallels the theoretical debates in the social sciences, and sets us some formidable puzzles. Above all, we are required to try to disentangle those elements in their decision-making processes which can be explained in terms of the pursuit of individual or household utility, and those which are better accounted for in terms of moral, social or political factors which escape that form of analysis. This in turn raises another set of theoretical issues, concerned with how specific decisions are located in longer-term plans and projects.

STRATEGIES

One element of convergence between economic and sociological theory in recent years has been in the widespread adoption of *strategic analysis* in the latter.[17] This can in itself be seen as an example of the colonisation of the social sciences by rational choice and game theory, since these provide the theoretical underpinnings of, for instance, Elster's analytic Marxism[18] and much sociological writing on industrial relations[19] and the behaviour patterns of economic groups.[20] However, strategic analysis has also been adopted in an attempt to address theoretical problems of structure and action,[21] though this in turn gives rise to new problems over the analysis of power, rationality and structural constraints.[22]

The notion of a strategy implies that individuals or collectivities pursue their interests over time by reference to a set of long-term goals or purposes. A game-theoretical analysis of strategy implies that actors know the rules of the game, the opportunities for gaining advantage from the choices they make, and any possibilities for co-operation as well as competition in pursuit of their interests.[23] One objection to such analyses is that they take no account of issues of power: the strategy of one individual or group may be to limit the choices or strategic opportunities of others.[24] However, it may be possible to construct a theory which overcomes these and other criticisms over issues of structural constraints,[25] by analysing a number of different levels at which strategic games are being played. Thus, for example, the ruling elite's strategy for maintaining and extending its means of rule will include the passing of laws and regulations on economic life, taxation and social security benefits. These state powerholders are uniquely able to make the rules under which the collectivities of civil society play,[26] but rulers' strategies are themselves related to power games involving capital, labour and other nation states.[27] Employers in turn follow strategies – for example over labour utilisation[28] – which define the choices open to workers: a strategy for flexibility leads to less regular full-time and more casual and part-time employment. At each level, a game can be postulated, and a strategic analysis devised, which in turn explains the rules under which actors at the next level are constrained to play, and the limits on their choices.

However, when we get down to the level of individuals and households the difficulties and ambiguities of this method of analysis emerge. Most households are made up of couples with or without 'dependants'. The rules under which couples play a 'household game' are set by the actors in a large number of higher-level games: the state-power game, the capital-labour game, and arguably the gender game – the societal struggle between a coalition or interest group made up of men, and another made up of women.[29] Thus if households as collectivities are seen as playing a game of 'getting by' in the economy – as is suggested, for instance, in R. E. Pahl's notion of 'household strategies'[30] – this implies that men and women co-operate to achieve what is in their collective interests as members of a household. However, if account is taken of the very different choices open to men and women in the structures of employment, wages, tax allowances and benefits, then individuals may be seen as following gender-specific strategies – as many feminist writers have suggested.[31]

This last point is of particular relevance to our study. The notion of a household strategy offers a tempting way out of the theoretical dilemmas outlined in the previous section, because it suggests that couples might co-operate according to the moral standards of membership, sharing and fairness, while participating in the outside economy in accordance with the requirements of rational choice.[32] There was certainly some evidence in our interviews of respondents perceiving themselves as team players in an economic game, where the rules were made by powerful actors in a higher-level game. Mrs Clyde is a part-time café worker; her husband has recently been sacked from his job, and suffered a suspension, followed by a penalty cut, for 13 weeks, in the family's income support while this was being investigated and as a result of the benefit authorities' decision. Mrs Clyde sees the reduction in their benefits as an attack on the whole household's subsistence.

'they decided that they'd suspend our money. Now the government says you need 70 something pounds to live on but they ... they worked our money out and they took another 13 pound so I think it was – 13 pound something it was – away from us 'cause he lost his job. And with my money they used to send us 20 pound a fortnight [...] I mean we're still fighting the appeal now.'

(Mrs Clyde, 11)

She is furious that the state can – as she sees it arbitrarily – deprive herself and her husband, their children and their dog of food on these grounds, and points out the contradiction between the authorities requiring her to look after her children and feed them properly, and denying her the means to do so. In all this, she seems to describe the household as an economic unit, striving to get by under rules made by state powerholders. Mr Wye talks about how the structure of the labour market for unskilled men in combination with the benefit system causes disharmony in the household unit.

'Yes I thinks so, that's actually where the tension sets in, and then you think well bloody hell it's a waste of time you know, 'cause you're going for 6 months, laid off, back up there, sign on, 3 weeks with no money. And then having to go down, knock on the door of the social every 5 minutes. And that's where the tension starts. I mean I think that's where a lot of people can actually split up with, you know [indistinct] the aggro of trying to sort it out.'

(Mr Wye, 8)

This seems to imply a potentially co-operative household unit disrupted by the structural constraints imposed by employers' and governments' strategies. Certainly there are a great many references to 'joint decisions' in the accounts, implying some sort of 'household strategy', or at least collective purpose by the couples. Mrs Ribble is particularly emphatic on this point.

'Oh yeah, we share everything. I mean um ... and everything's ... if we buy anything for the house it's a joint decision.'

(Mrs Ribble, 13–14)

But this is not the whole story. Some women's accounts make it clear that they do not see their employment decisions as congruent with those of their partners. Mrs Nene has stuck at her job in the box factory, where she has recently been promoted to supervisor. She describes the constraints on her as being different from those on her husband, a motorcycle mechanic, who expects to enjoy his work, and would not stick a job he disliked.

'If he wanted to change his job he would come home and say, well I'm changing my job, and that would be it. I mean, it don't matter what I would say – it wouldn't make any difference [...] His theory is if you don't like it you don't do it, so if he's gone from one job to the other, he's just come home and he's said, well I've got a job ... somewhere else and that's it.'

(Mrs Nene, 35)

Mrs Nene says immediately after this that he has chosen worse-paid work which he has preferred, whereas she works for the household income.

'Well that's why I had to go back to work: because the motorbikes don't pay so ... So I went back to work and that ... that sorted that out [...] I s'pose if I'd a forced him enough but ... he might have stuck it at something he didn't like so ... he's awful to live with ... awful ... Yeah. He really does, you know, moan, moan, moan about it if he doesn't like doing it.'

(Mrs Nene, 36)

This does not sound much like a household work strategy, even though Mr and Mrs Nene are a close and co-operative couple over unpaid domestic tasks, and he gives her a good deal of practical support, for example with transport to her employment. Many other women's descriptions of job decisions suggest that they make their choices independently of their husbands, and that they explain them in terms which do not fit the household work strategy theory. This is fully discussed in Chapters 5 and 6, where we argue that women's decisions are framed in terms of child-care responsibilities, providing income for certain expenditures, and their personal needs – for a 'break', for stimulation and company.

Another essential feature of strategic analysis is that the actions at issue must be planned within a broadly predictable environment;[33] some have argued that planning should also be comprehensive, coherent, long term and conscious.[34] As we have already seen, the men in our study do not regard the labour market for male labour in their sector as predictable. Only twelve of the men have regular full-time jobs.[35] Even these show much preoccupation with the insecurity of their position. Three of them work for local authorities, and fear that privatisation will cause redundancy or make their jobs less secure. The rest stay in what are low-paid jobs with often inconvenient working hours for fear of the unpredictability of the casualised, fragmented labour market that has developed, with its mosaic of short-term contracts, cash work and 'self-employment'. Mr Avon has worked for a farm foodstuffs firm for 15 years; his present earnings are £122 per week. He does not feel secure.

'They turn round and say, right, if orders don't pick up then they'll cut you down to a, to a 3 day week. Well that'd be alright but you, you get

3 days out there and you, that means you gotta into town and go dole for 2 days [...] When I first went out there 15 year ago we had 96 working and there ... on 3 shifts. Now there's 2 shifts with 10 blokes.'

(Mr Avon, 20)

All the other twenty-four men are irregular workers, and eleven of them were unemployed at the time of the interview. This has important implications for their partners. Although demand for female labour appeared more buoyant than for male, married women's employment took the form of part-time work: only four women in our sample had full-time jobs. Thus in those households where the man was in and out of work, the woman found herself in a position where all but £5 of her earnings were deducted from the household's income support benefits. Most gave up their employment at such times, which meant that they too were irregular in their working patterns. This extreme unpredictability for two-thirds of our households casts further doubt on the concept of a household labour strategy.

However, this does not imply that we reject strategic analysis in our understanding of the study's data. There is evidence of planning and long-term purposes in our interviewees' accounts, and some of this is done on a household basis. The theoretical issue is how to analyse the way in which different kinds of planning – by individuals, households and groups of kin or friends – relate to each other. For instance, what is the relationship between a household's method of budgeting for expenditure on the long-term project of purchasing their council house, and the systems of mutual assistance over structural alterations to houses that was described in the previous section by Mr Ribble? This is a specially intriguing example, since our interviewees give quite detailed information about how they plan expenditure, trying to cover their anticipated outgoings, and hence using an economic vocabulary, whereas the mutual help given in home improvements is described in terms of generalised reciprocity and sharing between kin and friends.

ECONOMIC THEORY AND ECONOMETRIC MODELLING

In order to locate these issues more clearly in the theoretical literature, the rest of this chapter will be devoted to a brief sketch of the economic, sociological and social policy literature on the subject of labour-market decisions in households like the ones in our study. What we want to show in each case is the kind of understanding of these decisions developed in each discipline, and the particular theories and models that have been advanced. We will also show how our respondents demonstrate some awareness of the issues addressed in these theories in talking about their actions. The aim of these sections is not the traditional 'literature review' (this would be a book in itself), but a kind of map of the very contrasting theoretical discourses of these three disciplines – their assumptions, structures and methods – with which our own analysis must be linked.

The most general characteristic that is common to all economic theories and models is that people are economisers in the broadest sense – that they buy cheap and sell dear, to maximise utility in the face of various kinds of constraints (on resources, time, energy, etc.). In neoclassical microeconomics, these actors are individuals making rational choices, according to consistent preferences. In labour-market decisions, their preferences are conventionally divided between certain quantities of work time, yielding an income from earnings, and leisure time, for relaxation and consumption. However, this simple picture is immediately complicated by two factors: first, some work (for example housework and care given to children) is unpaid; second, some people who do no paid work may qualify for various kinds of benefits, if they can establish that they are legitimately unemployed, sick, disabled or handicapped.

To date, few economic theorists have addressed these complications; their assumptions have tended to exclude unpaid work, and to oversimplify the nature of benefits by failing to take account of official systems for testing the legitimacy of claims. The two complications are linked, since unpaid houseworkers are not eligible to claim in their own right if they are members of couple households, but they are allowed to claim as responsible for the care of dependent children if they live alone and have little or no other financial support.

The state is therefore not neutral about preferences for 'work' and 'leisure'. In all modern societies, employment for a substantial part of the week is seen as a desirable situation for most adults below a certain age. Until 1989, in the centrally planned economies of the USSR and Eastern Europe, employment did not necessarily imply much work, nor was it conspicuously well rewarded; but even if the general rule of these regimes was 'you pretend to work, we pretend to pay', those whom the state regarded as voluntarily unemployed were likely to find themselves undergoing compulsory retraining, imprisonment or psychiatric hospitalisation. In the developed market economies of the West, non-employment is a perfectly respectable status for people with property incomes, and their spouses and adult offspring (from the Royal family to those who can sell their houses in south-east England and move to the periphery with their capital gains); however, the state takes a very different view of people with no such income, who claim benefits without being able to establish the proper credentials. So choosing a lot of leisure is not a permitted option, unless one has already acquired the means of subsistence, or convinced officials that one is incapable of doing so.

The state's keenness to promote employment – motivated by all kinds of political, moral and economic concerns which will be discussed later – leads to various official measures, from extensive and expensive provision of state-guaranteed jobs (as in the Soviet Union), to more *ad hoc* schemes for temporary state-financed training or employment (as recently in Britain), subsidies to individuals for child care and transport (as in Canada), compulsory public-sector work (as in some states of the USA), and various forms of exclusion or disqualification from benefits. The British experience of the 1980s has been one of moving sharply away from policies for state support of employment, towards all the other expedients, and especially (at the end of the decade) the final one of disqualification. High levels of officially recorded unemployment (about 14 per cent of the workforce) were reached in the middle of the 1980s, but these declined by the end of the decade to levels slightly above those prevailing 10 years earlier. Labour-market statistics suggest that policies for excluding or disqualifying claimants were much more successful than policies for stimulating employment and self-employment, especially for adult males.[36]

Microeconomic theory on labour-market decisions takes account of benefits for people who are out of work, but no account of official attitudes towards the unemployed. It treats people as choosing between work and leisure at a given wage and benefit rate as if the latter were a lump-sum grant for choosing a very high proportion of leisure, which is withdrawn as soon as a certain amount of work is performed. In practice, of course, claiming such benefits is strenuous, time-consuming and hazardous – it has costs of its own, which are different from those encountered in employment, but sometimes quite as arduous. Here is how our respondents described the process:

'they were 3 weeks late sending our money so we didn't have no money for the, 3 weeks, we didn't have a penny from them and then they cocked it all up ...'

(Mrs Parrett, 11)

'Supplementary say I'm allowed 40 pound a week; now with that 40 pound being suspended I get 25 ... and that's suspended for 6 months; once 6 months is up I'm supposed to get all the arrears back again but it never does work out like that.'

(Mr Itchen, 2)

'we've applied for everything, you know. They won't tell you what you can apply for [...] so he [husband] has gone back in and he says he's going to sit there until they give him something, you know.'

(Mrs Cam, 1)

Similarly, income-tested benefits for those in work, like family credit, are not simply tapered supplements that attach themselves automatically to certain wage rates, according to the size of the claimant's family. They, too, are benefits rather grudgingly given by a state which is zealous in requiring the low-paid worker to prove that he or she is really as poor as stated, by accumulating and posting five pay slips for scrutiny. This often involves a period of privation in which the worker is a good deal worse off than he or she was when receiving unemployment benefit or income support.[37] For an explanation of the mechanics and consequences of claiming family credit, see Appendix 1.

Furthermore, current microeconomic theorists have paid scant attention to the complexities of unpaid work. Some of this has economic value (either because of saving consumption costs, or because it adds value to assets); this makes a considerable difference to calculations of utility, and hence to preferences. (For instance, one of the authors has worked out that his 'wage' for improving his house by means of his unskilled unpaid labour is at least 100 times higher (during a year of moderate house price inflation) than his 'wage' for writing books.) Such calculations clearly influenced some of our respondents, to judge by their answers to questions about employment decisions at certain points in their working lives.

On the other hand, some potential workers (mostly women) are constrained by unpaid work which they or others regard as their duty. However much they might prefer to do paid work, their role in the household requires them to take responsibilities which are far from leisurely, and which do not leave time or energy for employment. At the very least, if they see these duties as being primarily theirs, they must arrange their paid work so as to 'fit in' with their unpaid responsibilities – as with Mrs Stour, who used to work as a school cleaner.

'... during the summer holiday you see, when they're on their long break, I could either take, take her with me or ... I'd go before she was out of bed and she wouldn't even know I'd been, and I'd be back again, you know. I'd probably go at about 6 o'clock in the morning or something like that and leave her with Arnold (husband) and back again, you know, before she even got out of bed, so that suited me.'

(Mrs Stour, 3)

Economic analysis has tried to take account of this issue. Until recently, most theories and models treated the couple relationship as a complete harmony of interests; the analysis of labour–supply decisions started from a joint utility function that depended on total family consumption and on each spouse's 'leisure'. In other words, choices over paid work were treated as choices of a single actor (the household) rather than the outcome of interaction between the couple; and men's 'leisure' time was treated as identical with women's, despite known differences in their unpaid work duties. However, in a pioneering paper in 1968, Leuthold – looking at labour-market decisions by poor people – proposed a model in which each partner maximises an independent utility function, given the labour supply of the other; the labour supply of each contains that of the other as an explanatory variable. In order to reach an equilibrium, each partner adjusts his or her labour supply until their decisions are mutually consistent.[38]

In the last few years, a series of attempts have been made to capture this same idea in econometric models to be tested against large-scale samples of employment behaviour by couples.[39] Kooreman and Kapteyn apply a game-theoretical approach to household labour participation – the household becomes the arena for a 'co-operation game' between the partners over how much paid work each is to do.[40] Grift and Siegers, trying to account for low rates of female employment in Holland, develop a model in which men and women have different utility functions, based on estimates of their bargaining power in the household.[41] Using data from Dutch labour surveys in 1985 on couples who were both in paid work, they found that the relative weight the husband attached to household income was about 1.5 times the relative weight the wife attached to household income, and that both spouses attached a larger weight to their own 'leisure' than to the 'leisure' of their partners. However, when the sample included working husbands with wives doing no paid work, the man attached a slightly greater weight to his partner's 'leisure' than his own.[42] They conclude that, when there are children present, this reflects the fact that women predominantly pay the time costs of their care, and men the money costs.[43]

A more radical use of rational choice and games theory is made by Alan Carling.[44] He considers why couples form households at all, as well as how they divide paid and unpaid labour. In his model, each individual has to do enough paid work to get a certain income, and a certain amount of unpaid work to care for themselves, but their wage rates vary: under what circumstances will they form couples? Under typical microeconomic assumptions they will do so if and only if both parties gain from the exchange of paid and unpaid work, such that the partner with the higher wage rate can earn more by increasing labour-market supply, and 'subcontracting' unpaid work to the lower earner, at a 'wage' which is higher than the latter would get in open employment. Which households are formable, and in what combinations (breadwinner, dual earner or divided labour) will depend on the time and money needed for survival through both kinds of labour, and the partners' wage rates, but a wage differential is a necessary condition for any household to form, and if there is a correlation between wage rates and gender, then women will do a disproportionate share of the unpaid work, and a greater total amount of all the work (paid and unpaid) done by the partners.

Such models are often criticised because their assumptions (such as a notional 'wage' for unpaid work) are unrealistic, or because partners do not apply such economic logic to the division of household roles. Yet we have already seen (p. 15) that Mrs Ribble does talk of her 'pay' for her many skills as a mother and housewife. Furthermore Mr Wye, who looks after the children while his wife works full time as a warehouse manager, says quite specifically that he will not return to employment unless he can earn more than she does. So the model proposed by Carling finds some echoes in the accounts of the decisions given by our interviewees. However, our analysis must also explain why no woman other than Mrs Ribble refers to the idea of 'pay' for care or housework, and why the practice of swapping roles does not arise in other households – and particularly in those (such as the Plyms and the Derwents) where the wife earned more than the husband before they had children (see pp. 155–6).

We will return to these models in the chapter on decision-making in the household (Chapter 6). They offer some possible explanations of the behaviour of poor couples under rather simple assumptions about the economy and the constraints they face. However, another application of microeconomic theory is the construction of much more complex models of these choices, which incorporate the detailed impact of income taxation and the complex benefits system in the structure of incentives and disincentives.

One approach to this model-building is to draw up budget lines which show the relationship between net income and effort.[45] If this is represented graphically, the vertical axis measures income and the horizontal axis 'leisure' time; if the individual pays no taxes and receives no benefits, and there is a single wage rate then the budget line is straight, and its steepness is determined by the wage rate. Income taxation changes the slope of the line, and with tax allowances on the first part of earnings and increases in the tax rate at higher levels, kinks in the slope appear. The introduction of a range of universal and targeted benefits produces such phenomena as an income support plateau with (for childless couples) a trough for those with very low wage rates at the end of it.[46] As a result, the budget line ceases to look like a ski lift, and takes on the aspect of an Alpine ski jump, with several very hard landing places.

This type of analysis is very much favoured both by officials and politicians analysing labour-supply incentives, and by critics of the system (from left and right). However, it is of little use in predicting actual behaviour. For example, in 1987 Michael Beenstock and his associates reported on an exhaustive project for constructing a model on budget lines, and testing it against data from the 1978 and 1981 Family Expenditure Surveys (FES) on male hours of work. They concluded that their results 'on the whole provide little or no support for the hypotheses [developed from the model] ... by wage rates, family or tenure types'.[47] They speculated that individuals might have no choice about what jobs to take or hours to work, because of high unemployment and demand for labour in the form of fixed 'full-time' hours, that workers may have been ignorant about their budget lines, and that FES data may be inaccurate (some households spent a good deal more than they said they earned). However, the general conclusion was that the model (which performed even less well for women), though informative about constraints facing couples, had little predictive value, either in relation to the disincentives confronting the unemployed, or the incentives for others to work long hours.[48] Our data on undeclared cash work (Chapter 4) and on household income strategies (Chapter 6) provide important insights into these aspects.

Another approach is to try to devise structural models of labour-supply behaviour which take account of such labour-market features as fixed costs and search costs – this has been applied to the study of women's employment patterns in particular, because of the range of their working hours and their known sensitivity to tax and benefit factors.[49] These models increasingly use structural theoretical restrictions in order to identify parameters necessary to conduct policy and welfare analysis, but at some cost in terms of theory consistency. In spite of the complexity of the tax-benefit system, four-fifths of married women currently in the UK labour market merely pay income tax and National Insurance Contributions at a constant rate and over a wide range of possible wage rate and hours of work combinations.[50] Yet in spite of this fairly straightforward set of budget constraints, the actual distribution of hours worked by married women is very peculiar, with alternating troughs and peaks between hours, and spikes at 20 and between 35 and 40 hours.[51] This suggests that demand side factors are very influential on these patterns. The women interviewees in our study who worked part-time described their choices of hours as made within fixed packages, determined by employers. Some had no choice at all. Mrs Torridge found her hours cut from 38 to 20 with no warning.

'I worked ... from 8 till 1 Monday, Tuesday, Wednesday and Friday and that was 46.25, and then I had ... That, that was for about 5 months and then I went to the Saturday one and then it was 83 pound ... so it wa'n't too bad; it was 2.45 an hour, ... but when he cut that 18 hours off there was just no way I could afford to live on 46 pound again ...'

(Mrs Torridge, 14)

Taken together, the results of microeconomic theorising and econometric modelling are rather less impressive in explaining labour-supply decisions than the mathematical precision of the methods or the complexity of the modelling would lead a lay person to anticipate. Although at the macro-level the effects of changes in taxes and benefits on behaviour can be fairly well predicted, and although new models are now enabling econometricians and others to identify individual patterns more accurately,[52] it is by no means clear whether these are well captured within the theories economists advance, or well understood in terms of their assumptions and models. For example, as Carling points out, his rational choice analysis predicts that, given a rigid gender-related wage differential, partners will adopt some version of a patriarchal division of labour; but exactly the same prediction could be made from sociological role theory.[53] Furthermore, the economic model would go on to predict that where the woman does have a higher wage rate than her male partner, role reversal should occur. However, empirical research has shown that this is extremely rare[54] and in our study there was only one such case (Mr and Mrs Wye).

This leads to a consideration of a very different tradition of economic theorising, though one which has also been influenced by rational choice and game theory – the Marxist school, and specifically its Elsterian manifestation[55] which might best be called Rational Marxism. A number of writers, including Van Parijs and Carling, have analysed household relations in terms of the ability of a coalition or 'class' (in this case men) to exploit and dominate another (women) by virtue of their possession of an asset (maleness) conferring advantages – in power and income – under existing social relations. Van Parijs suggests that gender can be recognised as a new dimension of exploitation and domination in contemporary society,[56] while Carling argues that the exploitation of women by men in households, under conventional economic assumptions within his rational choice model, can be demonstrated by Roemer-style methods (if assets were shared out equally, it would be in women's interests to withdraw from households).[57]

All this is an important corrective to the other two traditions. However, there is a central problem about this analysis of the gendered division of labour which is of considerable relevance to our study. The 'class' position of women cannot be deduced from a consideration of household relations alone; these must be set alongside all other social relations, to determine whether a coalition of women have an interest in changing the rules under which power and income are distributed in households (by means of a thought experiment involving a Roemerian game). Jordan has argued that, if 'job assets' and other forms of property are included in this analysis, most women have an interest (as members, albeit subordinate and disadvantaged ones, of job-rich, property-owning households) in joining a coalition of such *households* (men, women and young adults) against the members of households with no job-holder and no property ('jobs' here means secure, adequately paid employment for at least one member of the household, usually the male 'head'). This being so, even though most women may be exploited and dominated in terms of household relations, they none the less have an interest in retaining the meta-rules governing social relations, since these are based on a coalition of property owners of which they are part, against a property-less underclass.[58]

Clearly most of the couples in our study belong to the latter 'class' – the men as much as the women. This raises an important issue about the oppression suffered by the women we interviewed. Was it primarily their oppression as *women* which was at issue (their unequal share of unpaid work, unequal access to paid work, unequal proportion of household resources, etc.) or was it the oppression that they shared with their partners, as members of an excluded underclass, without access to job security, property ownership, savings, pensions, and so on?[59] And was a different analysis required for those few women (Mrs Rother, Mrs Stour) whose husbands had relatively better-paid secure jobs, and who were buying their own houses? We will address this issue when we deal with household decision-making in Chapter 6.

SOCIOLOGICAL THEORY AND RESEARCH

This discussion of class leads us naturally into the second relevant theoretical discipline for our study – sociology. In recent years this somewhat beleagured subject (the pet hate of many British government ministers and high-profile intellectuals of the right) has been experiencing something of an identity crisis. Its territory has to some extent been colonised by economic theory, both of the rational choice and the econometric modelling varieties, and this has influenced its methods. Indeed, practitioners of sociology might be represented as having polarised themselves between those who imitate the methodology of economics, either by using game-theoretical or statistical model-building approaches, and those who are much influenced by the regulation school of historical analysis – Michel Foucault and his followers. Critics might argue that a discipline made up of economists' manqués and historians' manqués is doomed to an early extinction.

Yet despite the disproportionate number of theorists in British sociology departments, there is still a fairly healthy community of sophisticated empirical researchers, and of thinkers willing to apply critical methods to practical and policy issues.[60] It is within these branches of sociology that we wish to locate our study, though clearly theory from both rational choice and regulation school literature is of relevance to the overall analysis of our findings, and particularly to the analysis of the social relations in which the couples' lives were lived.

For the sake of clarity, it is best to start with the work of those sociologists who have been most affected by neoclassical microeconomic theory. The work of Gary Becker on family and economy has been particularly influential, and has stimulated sociological theory and research. Becker focused on individuals as bargain-hunters in all spheres of their social relations, making their optimising choices within constraints as much in personal as in economic transactions, calculating the costs and benefits of decisions, and changing preferences in response to altered pay-offs. Where actions benefit others (as in domestic altruism) it is either because of their non-material benefits, or because the actor includes the other's utility function in his or her own. Becker uses 'exchange theory' to analyse partner selection,[61] marital relations, the relationship between domestic and market behaviour[62] and divorce,[63] and his approach has been followed by a whole school of theorists and researchers.

The main sociological modification to this economic model has been to analyse the *structural* constraints on individual choices, in terms of roles as structural positions with differing opportunities and rules.[64] Here 'contract theory' is introduced, making the parallel between employment structures which encourage continuity, retraining and career planning (through efficiency wages, severance pay rights, pensions and fringe benefits, etc.), and implicit marriage contracts, involving investments of emotional and material resources in a specific relationship.[65] These in turn affect the choices open to individuals, and their relative power in bargaining games.[66] In this way, the 'new structuralist' sociologists are able to use a unified theoretical framework for analysing household and employment decisions, taking account of structural gender factors.

One paradoxical conclusion from this approach is that, whereas in the labour market high investment in training and knowledge is correlated with job security and male power, in the household high relationship-specific investment by women in family and home leads to powerlessness and bargaining disadvantage.[67] Because household power depends on access to options outside the relationship, and assets gained in the economy, women's bargaining position deteriorates as their benefits within the relationship exceed what they could get outside it; since they stand to lose so much, they are more willing to compromise or back down. This analysis complements Jordan's account of gender assets, quoted in the previous section. In our study, women's commitment to family and child care clearly put them at this kind of disadvantage in bargaining over access to employment.

This was particularly obvious in the case of women with several children or who had another child after a long gap – such as Mrs Severn, whose elder daughter is 20. She did part-time shop work when the elder daughter went to school, but has withdrawn from the labour market on the birth of her baby (now aged nearly 2). She misses work – 'always glance through the papers [...] in case there's anything which would fit in [...] maybe evenings or during the day' – but cannot rely on her husband to help with child care. The weakness of her position is obvious in the following exchange in their joint interview which occurs soon after Mr Severn has emphasised how low his wife's wages would be likely to be.

Mr Severn:	So I, I would have to come home and she would have to get an evening job of some sort.
Q:	Right. Would you welcome that change or would that be quite difficult to organise?
Mr Severn:	Well it ...
Mrs Severn:	I could cope with it after a while; might cause a bit of a ... [child interrupts]
Mr Severn:	Well it, yeah ...
Mrs Severn:	... friction ... [laughs]
Mr Severn:	I, I think it, it would be ... On the long-term effect it would be a bit of a bind um because, you know, often I ... as I said before ... sometimes I don't finish jobs ... on ... I mean ... finished off before half past 5 tonight ... um ... and you know that is early [...] on occasions um I had a lot of work to do and I, I could use ah, ah, working on an hour or so, it would be a real nuisance to, to have to come home.

(Mr and Mrs Severn, 32–3)

This also links with Marxist and feminist theory about household relations. What these have in common is their analyses in terms of structural power; where they differ is that the former give theoretical priority to economic relations, whereas some of the latter argue that ideas about the public domain of the economy need to be radically adapted to take account of the personalised relations of the household. Marxist theories emphasise the complementary character of capitalist production and family reproduction, and how the latter can only be fully understood in terms of the former; they also stress the ideological justifications that have been used to uphold traditional divisions of domestic labour.[68] Feminists emphasise women's dependence and power disadvantage and, while acknowledging that this is rooted in men's structural advantages within the economy, consider that patriarchal domestic relations require a separate and particular analysis, which takes detailed account of care responsibilities and the dynamics of interpersonal obligations in the family.

In order to move beyond an analysis of women's oppression and into an account of how decisions are made in households, feminist theory must show the specific factors which influence women's behaviour in the domestic context, and how this relates to wider economic relations. In recent years a great deal of study has been made of women's choices over caregiving – both of children and of other relatives – and how such decisions are framed.[69] In an impressive synthesis of work on kinship obligations (excluding child care and marital relationships), Janet Finch analyses these within a framework of 'normative guidelines', requiring judgement and negotiation skills for their detailed interpretation.[70] Following Giddens[71] and Abrams,[72] she argues for an interactive model of the social order, in which such moral decisions are intrinsically contestable, and guidelines often conflict with each other, and provide general criteria for reasoning about what is right and wrong in particular circumstances.[73] This view of moral reasoning has been characterised as typically female, and is well suited to dealing with situations in which it is important to include and protect others.[74] However, this form of morality involves public standards, sustained by conversations and debates inside and outside the family, and justifying actions according to shared understanding of the right thing to do.

There are many examples of this kind of reasoning in the women's accounts of their employment decisions in our study. Seeing themselves as primary caregivers for their children, they were also involved with their mothers, sisters and neighbours in various kinds of reciprocal arrangements over care and assistance which required constant negotiation to sustain a long-term equilibrium (not always successfully achieved). However, this whole system of obligations and mutual support was located in a network with shared understanding of men's and women's roles which reflected traditional gender identities and divisions. Other studies have confirmed that – particularly in low-income areas – women's access to employment depends heavily on their social networks for information and support, but that the requirement to fit in with family responsibilities requires frequent withdrawals from employment, damages long-term prospects for better earnings, and reinforces their structural disadvantages.[75]

These factors are clearly reflected in studies of women's position in the labour market. Both historical research[76] and analyses of surveys[77] indicate the designation of certain occupations and roles as female, and the consequences in terms of pay and career structure for women of this form of labour-market segmentation. There is massive evidence of women's over-representation in secondary labour markets,[78] in part-time work,[79] and in home working;[80] of persistence of gender-related differentials in pay, promotion and trade union protection;[81] and of work done by women being classified as 'unskilled', even where it requires more training than 'skilled' work done by men.[82]

The employment histories of the women we interviewed reflected these features of the British labour market, as will be shown in Chapter 5. However, those of their partners were by no means characterised by security, regularity, adequacy of pay, union representation or any of the features of the primary labour market. Indeed, they were histories which provide graphic evidence of the restructuring of unskilled and semi-skilled employment, its casualisation, fragmentation and 'South Africanisation'.[83] Whereas the women's accounts seemed to take for granted the fact that much of the work on offer to them was part-time, involved unsocial hours, and very low pay, the men's accounts reflected an awareness of the deterioration of their position in their segment of the market, in the face of global economic forces, government policy and local competitive practices. Largely deserted by labour organisations, their interests scarcely advanced by the Labour Party, and increasingly unprotected by the welfare state's major schemes (such as National Insurance), these men were in a situation (as part of the secondary labour market) which had some things in common with their partners'.

The male interviewees were well aware of this change in their sector of the labour market.

''cause most of the firms now are just taking on self-employed labourers and um [indistinct] now. Saves on redundancy and all that sort of thing. So really you got to have your own transport. But they don't pay travelling time whatever [...] All self-employed now. Very, very rare you get anybody on the books.'

(Mr Parrett, 19–20)

Yet their own construction of their situation, and the decision-making processes to which it gave rise, was very different from those of their partners. Their economic and social self-identification as workers and providers – 'breadwinners' – was unshaken by the transformations in their labour-market constraints, as were their perceptions of women's roles as family carers.[84] The paradoxes of this dissonance between role and reality will be examined in Chapter 5.

The most ambitious British study of the relationship between employment and household roles in recent years was Ray Pahl's *Divisions of Labour*, which analysed the results of an extensive and intensive study of families in the Isle of Sheppey.[85] Starting from theories about the growth of informal work (much of it with economic value, such as do-it-yourself home improvement) and the substitution of capital-intensive 'self-provisioning' for paid employment in such activities as transport, laundry services and entertainment (increased use of cars, washing machines and television/videos),[86] he looked at household 'strategies' for 'getting by' through paid and unpaid activities, and for changing patterns in these strategies in the face of economic recession in the early 1980s.[87] Contrary to his original hypothesis, Pahl found little informal work among poor people, and much among the better-off; the former lacked resources for tools and materials for home improvements or do-it-yourself car maintenance, for instance, whereas multi-earner households could organise themselves and finance a great deal of such activity. He concluded that a polarisation was occurring between these two kinds of households: those with two or more earners gained access to owner-occupied housing, and resources for 'self-provisioning'; but there was a minority of no-earner households in rented accommodation with no such informal opportunities.[88] Pahl concluded that the gulf between these two types of household was widening in the early 1980s, and survey evidence has tended to bear this out.[89]

Our study, though by no means an attempt to replicate Pahl's work, brings fresh evidence on the same areas. Among these poor households, we found very little sign of the 'strategies' he identified; employment was too irregular and unpredictable to allow the planned approach to decisions over labour supply that such a terminology implies. If these couples followed an implicit strategy, it was an 'income strategy' rather than an employment strategy – an endeavour to plan household expenditure and devise ways of covering both basic expenses and irregular 'extras'. In this, they made tactical or strategic use of social security benefits, often ignoring regulations, for example by doing undeclared cash work while claiming income support. In Chapter 7 we consider possible similarities between these and the strategies adopted by poor people in certain Third World countries.[90]

Furthermore, it was not the case in our study that informal work was negatively correlated with unemployment; rather, several men said that they had improved their homes (some in major structural ways) while unemployed, and a few had actually given up employment to do so. This kind of do-it-yourself work usually *preceded* any decision to purchase their council houses; indeed, some gave as a reason for wanting to buy that they wished to protect the investment they had made by improving the council's property. But this was not the only kind of 'self-provisioning' that went on. Several households in our study kept considerable numbers of dogs, birds and fish, and said that they increased the time they spent on breeding or hunting during periods of unemployment, and the income that they derived from selling the results of these endeavours. One transaction occurs during an interview: Mr Humber has just lost his job, and is worried about his rising mortgage repayment. There is a knock on the door as he is discussing this. On returning he explains that his mate Acker had said

"'Now you ain't working see, you have to ... flog off all your fish." That's the thing. He said it'd pay half me mortgage. I said: "I wish it would."'

(Mr Humber, 31)

Taken together with the work done for cash which was not declared to the benefit authorities, this combination of home improvements (for themselves and for family or neighbours) and animal breeding and selling amounted to a considerable volume of 'informal' activity. We are carrying out a similar study of better-off households' decision-making for comparison with this one, which will provide further evidence relating to Pahl's findings. It may well be that the unstructured, relaxed pace of our interview methods allowed respondents to provide more details on these aspects of their lives. (Even so, some were willing to talk about undeclared cash work only when the tape recorder was switched off.)

There have, of course, been many other sociological studies, using qualitative methods, of decision-making in low-income households. Several of these have noted the part played by the conditions surrounding benefits in constraining the labour-supply choices of women. Bell and McKee noted that in Kidderminster only wives with well-paid or long-established jobs maintained them after their husbands became unemployed; by contrast, women doing temporary, casual or informal work withdrew from it, or postponed further employment.[91] Similarly, Morris found that in South Wales wives of redundant steel workers frequently experienced redundancy soon after their husbands. In both studies, the response of a wife taking a full-time job following her husband's loss of his job was very rare[92] – yet economic analysis would predict that this would happen quite often. In our study, there was only one such example, and this 'role reversal' occurred only after the man had been unemployed for some years. Our analysis of men's and women's accounts suggests that this is because of the persistence of the breadwinner–family carer role division, rather than a result of labour-market conditions.

The study most similar to our own is Millar, Cooke and McLaughlin's qualitative research on couples in which the man was unemployed at the time of being interviewed; their overall findings, on the effects of the benefits system in particular, are consistent with ours.[93] The main difference in the two studies is that only a minority of our households contained an unemployed man. We were keen to analyse the responses of people who were currently in work (though the great majority had experienced unemployment quite recently), and to look at what took them back into the labour market as well as what kept them out. We found that this allowed instructive comparisons: for example, between a small group of men who stayed in regular employment in spite of bad pay and conditions out of fear of unemployment; a larger one of men who had frequent changes of work, interspersed with periods of claiming or working on government training schemes; a group who had opted for self-employment, justifying it mainly in terms of autonomy and self-respect; and a group who were longer-term unemployed, who regarded the work available as unacceptably badly paid. These distinctions will be elaborated in Chapter 4.

SOCIAL POLICY ANALYSIS AND PRESCRIPTION

The research evidence on poor couples' labour-supply behaviour takes little time to be processed into social policy analysis and prescription; yet the products of this processing are extremely diverse. On the one hand both survey and small-scale studies are turned into theory or models, relating to tax and benefit disincentives; on the other recommendations for policy change, often global in scope, are manufactured and debated. Two factors in the 1980s stimulated the latter type of literature – the Fowler Reforms of the British social security system, and the penetration of the US underclass debate into British politics and social policy studies.

Because of the highly ideological tone of much of the latter category, our study is at risk of being turned into some form of offensive weaponry in this war of words. In particular, some of our findings – notably those about undeclared work for cash, the unemployment and poverty traps, and the functioning of the benefits system – are potentially explosive, and we have no way of controlling into whose hands they fall, or how they are used. Already, in giving papers on our preliminary findings from the data, we have witnessed the excitement and controversy that is provoked, and the fires of battle that are fuelled.

It is therefore important to start this section with an acknowledgement of the ideological construction of poor people in much social policy literature.

Although ostensibly about the perversities of the tax-benefits system's incentives, this debate really pivots on rival accounts of who poor people are and what motivates their actions. Market-minded theorists construct them as opportunistic rational egoists, whose utility functions favour leisure, and who will always exploit any chance to cheat the system, if they can avoid detection. Starting from these economistic assumptions, they then go on to try to eliminate incentives for claiming, and increase those for employment, sometimes elaborating these technical measures with lurid accounts of the moral depravity or social degeneration which follow from the existing structure. Welfare-minded theorists construct the poor as victims who have been marginalised from the mainstream, both economically and socially, because of their inability to get regular work or adequate wages. They go on to show how the tax-benefit system reinforces this exclusion, and further victimises them, by denying them an adequate income or access to valued goods. In all this, poor people are portrayed as passive and penalised, systematically disadvantaged by public policies, despite their best efforts to contribute to society. By contrast with both these views, our analysis is based on poor people's own accounts of themselves as active, resilient and fully involved in the mainstream of their own community, whose lifestyle they prefer to those of other, more affluent neighbourhoods. While their accounts contain much suffering and privation, and a good deal of conflict with employers and officials, they also convey much energy and excitement, in contrast with the drab picture which is standard in poverty literature.

Although British government policy in the 1980s was dominated by the market-minded approach to poverty, the analysis and theory on which this was based came mainly from the United States. Studies there suggested that factors such as lack of skills, low educational achievement and membership of ethnic minority groups were not the important ones in whether claimants came off welfare benefits and returned to work;[94] single parents were found to be able to arrange their own child care if they were keen to find employment, the age of children not being a significant factor in their 'escape rates'.[95] Conversely, research on unemployment found that claimants sought jobs with higher pay than they had earned previously, and were unwilling to travel more than 20 miles to work or to move house.[96] Studies claimed to have discovered groups with 'pathological instability in holding jobs',[97] and excessive expectations of earnings (especially among young black people).[98] These findings influenced the introduction of 'work-fare' programmes – increased requirements on claimants to take available employment or training, or do public service work for benefits – which in turn have impressed British ministers and officials.

The rhetoric of market-minded politicians and newspaper editors was familiar to our interviewees: it was occasionally adopted by them. Mr Thames, who is doing low-paid work, legitimates the fact that his partner, Ms Otter, still claims income support as a single parent on the grounds that he is an occasional visitor; he also says that he has 'worked a fiddle' in a previous job. However he does not believe that people should be paid unemployment benefits without a strict test of their willingness to work.

> 'there should be some sort of system ... where ... um ... you should be ... um ... interviewed for a job before you signed on [...] it would take [...] a lot of these people who don't want a job off, off the dole because if they didn't wanna, if they didn't wanna work then they shouldn't get paid. I mean I've heard quite a lot of people saying well I've ... why should I work when I can get money for nothing ...'
>
> (Ms Otter and Mr Thames, 10)

By contrast, British social policy literature still overwhelmingly reflects the welfare-minded school, with its strong links with the Labour Party and the Child Poverty Action Group. The dominant influence of Peter Townsend in the two previous decades[99] is carried forward by writers like Bradshaw,[100] Walker,[101] Lister,[102] Piachaud,[103] and Bennett.[104] Both in their development of tax-benefit models and in their detailed critiques of the workings of benefits systems, they have focused on the traps and penalties that constrain the poor and deny them the opportunities available to the majority in an affluent yet unequal society. Yet, as we shall show from our data, poor people seldom construct their world in these terms. Although many recognised the 'vicious circle' of the unemployment trap, caused by low wages, irregular work and pressure from benefits authorities, most were willing to 'have a go' at breaking out of this, either by taking whatever employment was available, or by doing undeclared work for cash, or both. Similarly, they saw the poverty trap in terms of an unfair penalisation of hard work, rather than a ceiling on their earning potential. In all this, their accounts of themselves were of people far more active, resourceful and involved than the welfare-minded texts would suggest. Yet they took for granted the existence of social security payments as an important protection against the insecurity and exploitation of the labour market, and resented the attempt to drive them into unchosen employment by benefit cuts and the threat of benefit withdrawals. So their construction of themselves was more market-orientated and economically activist than the picture drawn of them by the welfare school, and more welfare-orientated than the market school aspires to make them.

A third, small but influential, strand of policy analysis is concerned with the integration of income taxation and social security benefits as a way of reducing perverse incentives, and increasing labour supply by poor people. The Institute for Fiscal Studies (IFS) has developed its own tax-benefit model, and produced a stream of literature on reform of the system.[105] An alternative model has been developed by Atkinson and his colleagues, which is associated with the investigation of a Basic Income approach to integration.[106] The somewhat esoteric debate between the IFS Negative Income Tax prescriptions (*post hoc* additions to or subtractions from *household* earnings, resulting in a kind of universal income-testing and taxing system) and the Basic Income Research Group's emphasis on individuals' entitlement to a guaranteed, unconditional sum *before* they enter the labour market or the household, which is then withdrawn through the tax system[107] has important implications for poor couples, which will be discussed in the conclusions (Chapter 9).

In addition to these general analyses, there have been a number of specific studies of relevance to ours. Mack and Lansley carried out a national survey in 1985, in an attempt to establish an agreed acceptable minimum standard of living, by getting a cross-section of the population to say which items from a list they regarded as necessities for all members of British society.[108] They then surveyed claimants of what was then supplementary benefit, to find which of these items they went without, and reached the conclusion that the rates of benefit at that time were inadequate for the consensual minimum standard of living, especially for unemployed claimant couples with children.

In a detailed follow-up to this survey, Bradshaw and Holmes studied sixty-seven unemployed claimants in couple households with two dependent children in Tyne and Wear.[109] The couples kept detailed records of their income, expenditure and living standards. They found them living on a restricted diet, lacking essential items of clothing, spending much time at home and unable to afford travel to leisure facilities; about half had a telephone and less than a quarter a car, compared with 80 per cent of the population who own both. Only three households had more than £100 in savings, and the average debt was £440, involving repayments of 11 per cent of their average incomes. Seven men and three women had undeclared earnings at an average of about £20 per week. The authors concluded that 'the lives of these families, and perhaps most seriously the lives of the children in them, are marked by the unrelieved struggle to manage, with dreary diets and drab clothing. They also suffer what amounts to cultural imprisonment in their home in our society in which getting out with money to spend on recreation and leisure is normal at every other income level.... Clearly the level of benefits is not enough to allow ordinary families to share in conventional living standards'.[110] This very detailed survey confirmed other studies which suggested that the poor were excluded from mainstream living standards, and had a low quality of life.[111]

The difficulty with research which focuses on unemployed claimants is that it does not address the issue of how these particular households come to be in this situation while many of their neighbours are not. This leaves open the possibility that their poverty is a consequence of choices they have made, of mistaken expectations of employment, of bad management or disorganisation. Although there is little British research to settle the issue, market-minded analysts use the American studies already quoted to attack the assumptions behind this approach, and argue that the benefits system itself is an important cause of a phenomenon which should be interpreted as pauperism rather than poverty.

While a wide range of authors now accept that there is an underclass of poor people in Britain and the United States,[112] the policy implications of this are fiercely contested. From the USA, the dominant view has become one of hawkishness: either benefits should be cut to make welfare dependence less attractive, or much more rigorous requirement should be made of claimants, so that they can be *forced* to be reintegrated into society. The first alternative is associated with Charles Murray, who argues that generous benefits sap initiative and self-sufficiency, reward incompetence and bestow the means for easy idleness.[113] Murray visited Britain in 1989, as 'a visitor from a plague area come to see whether the disease is spreading' and announced that he had found the same phenomena here: the British underclass 'is characterised by drugs, casual violence, petty crime, illegitimate children, homelessness, work avoidance and contempt for conventional values.... The underclass spawns illegitimate children without a care for tomorrow and feeds on a crime rate which rivals the United States in property offences'.[114] He argued that such behaviour could infect the respectable poor, spreading from a minority of deviants to become the cultural norm, unless the state's support of this lifestyle was removed.

This style of addressing the issues makes it clear that poor people's labour-supply behaviour has become as much a question of moral and political philosophy as of technical social administration. Hence the new literature on poverty increasingly includes references to citizenship and social obligation rather than simply to perverse incentives or the adequacy of benefits. The intellectual construction of the poor thus moves away from the details of their income and consumption, and towards their identity and status.

One of the most influential works in this revival of the classical tradition is Lawrence Mead's *Beyond Entitlement: The Social Obligations of Citizenship*.[115] Taking very seriously the problem of the underclass as excluded from economic participation and the moral mainstream, he argues that their reintegration requires active policies for re-education, work train-ing and the inculcation of appropriate personal discipline. Hence officials should see it as part of their duty to make benefits far more conditional, and to place obligations on them that require the changes necessary to get them off welfare. He argues:

> work has become increasingly elective, and unemployment voluntary, because workers commonly have other sources of income, including government programmes.... Non-work is most serious among the dis-advantaged. There are a number of competing explanations, but which-ever we choose, public authority seems indispensible to solutions. For the non-dependent non-work may not pose a public issue. For the dependent, however, government probably must enforce work as a condition of support if it wants to advance integration. For recipients, work must be viewed, not as an expression of self-interest, but as an obligation owed to society. At the same time, to fulfil this obligation would permit the poor a kind of freedom that government benefits alone never can.[116]

Following this logic, John Moore justified the changes in the 1989 Social Security Act by arguing that every available employment – no matter how dirty, low-paid or unpleasant – is an opportunity to gain self-respect and independence, and state officials should require the unemployed to take such opportunities, for the sake of their own best potential, and the good of the whole community.[117] Hence it was justifiable for claimants to be required not only to answer detailed questions about their availability for employment, but also to keep records of their job search and the steps they had taken to find work. Yet this view is not without its attractions for theorists on the left; for example, Raymond Plant has pointed out that in Sweden there is an obligation to take employment, within a system of generous benefits and minimum wages. Provided that 'full employment' were achieved, 'what would be wrong with making an able-bodied person's own benefits depend on a stringent availability-for-work-or-training-test?'[118] Similarly, Esam, Good and Middleton argued that, in their socialist social security proposal, a condition for receiving benefit would be willing-ness to take a 'suitable' job.[119]

The great question, of course, is what constitutes 'full employment' and a 'suitable' job. Britain is not Sweden: there is no minimum wage, benefits are low and workers enjoy less protection than in most West European countries. Hence the majority of writers in the debate about citizenship have argued that any such policies must be accompanied by *either* a greatly improved supply of training and job opportunities, *or* a better structure of income protection.[120] Others still contend that citizenship – a concept implying membership and shared rights and obligations – cannot be linked with such specific requirements, which fall on the poor but not on those with property incomes.[121] Proponents of the Basic Income approach to poverty prevention suggest that this measure would improve both security and incentives for excluded groups, without the necessity for increased state surveillance and coercion.

One couple in our study take up this argument in similar terms: Mr and Mrs Frome, neither of whom have been in the labour market for 9 years. Mrs Frome suggests that rather than being more 'targeted' and more conditional, benefits should be more universal and have more generous earnings rules, treating people of working age at least as generously as pensioners.

> 'But I think there should be a system where ... yes you can earn, you know, 30 pounds or 40 pounds a week ... without it affecting your, your social security. And I think they'd probably find then ... that a high, that a lot of fiddling would stop ...'
>
> (Mrs Frome, 10)

These debates are taking place in all the developed market economies, and will no doubt soon envelop Eastern Europe and the Soviet Union. They raise fundamental issues about the connections between income and work, and between employment and citizenship, in the wake of the structural changes which have overtaken these economies. They reflect the extent to which social policy rests on political and moral values which are once again highly contested. In this sense, the technical literature on the labour-supply behaviour of the poor cannot be understood in isolation from its ideological underpinnings.

The respondents were not unaware of these issues and political debates. They saw that employment in their segment of the labour market had been restructured to their disadvantage, and some talked wistfully about the past, when jobs were more reliable and plentiful. They recognised the traps and pitfalls in the benefits system, but most did not regard them as insurmountable; they also recognised that some claimants cheated the system, or used it for deviant purposes, but always attributed these actions to others. Their own accounts reflected a way of steering a course between the constraints of the labour market and the benefits system which was proactive in its search for opportunities, but prudent in trying to keep a fallback position. In doing this, they constructed a justification for breaches in the rules surrounding the tax-benefit system, which might be seen as a kind of post-industrial version of the social rights of citizenship that existed before the economic changes of the 1980s.

In our policy recommendations at the end of the book, we try to extrapolate from their accounts a reformed tax-benefit system which might better meet their needs, and improve labour supply. This is a risky enterprise, given the size and particular situation of our sample. Even so, it seems worth attempting, since we are well aware that if we do not do so, others will – and in directions that would not necessarily be consistent with our respondents' views.

CONCLUSIONS

Our study was chosen to generate hypotheses and develop theory in a field which is highly contested, both in terms of theoretical issues, and in terms of the politics of employment, welfare and citizenship. In this chapter we have sketched in the debates within and between academic disciplines, and in the wider political arena, and shown how these manifested themselves in interview data. We are not required to look 'through' our respondents' words to discover these issues: they display awareness of them, and give their accounts of how they resolve – for instance – conflicts between economic and moral reasoning, or issues about disincentives. Indeed, one feature of their accounts of labour-market decisions is the rhetorical skill with which they describe complex motives in an interview situation.

The challenge of our study's data is therefore to make the methodological links between our interviewees' accounts and the economic, sociological and policy questions we were addressing, by establishing the status of this form of research, and the way in which inferences can be drawn from it. We need to make the epistemological links between economic and social theory and the utterances of these particular people, living on this estate in Exeter. This is necessarily quite a large and complex task, and will be the subject of the next chapter.

REFERENCES

1 Department of Social Security, *Social Security Statistics, 1989*, HMSO, 1990, Table 37.13, p. 356. This is necessarily an estimate, because the statistics merely record the total number of dependent children (783,000) without saying how many couples had such children in their households. The figure given is arrived at by dividing the number of children by 2, which is just over the average number of children in households containing dependent children in Great Britain (1.8).
2 ibid., Table 33.02, p. 231.
3 HMSO, *Social Trends*, 20, 1990, HMSO, 1990, Table 5.7, p. 89.
4 *Social Trends*, 1990, Table 2.4, p. 36.
5 Poor Law Act, 1597, preamble.
6 John Locke, Board of Trade Papers, Journal B, 1697, pp. 242–326, quoted in H. R. Fox Bourne, *The Life of John Locke*, King, 1876, pp. 377–87.
7 Bernard de Mandeville, *The Fable of the Bees* (1728) Clarendon Press, (reprint) pp. 212–13.

8 Thomas Malthus, *First Essay on Population* (1798), Macmillan, 1966, Ch. V, pp. 86–7.

9 Herbert Spencer, *The Man versus the State* (1884), Penguin, 1969, p. 82.

10 Karl Marx, *Capital*, Vol. 1 (1867), Penguin, 1976, p. 797.

11 Leon Trotsky, 'Terrorism and Communism' (1920), quoted in Baruch Knei Paz, *The Social and Political Thought of Leon Trotsky*, Clarendon Press, 1978, pp. 264–6.

12 See for example Gary S. Becker, *A Treatise on the Family*, Harvard University Press, 1981; John E. Roemer, *A General Theory of Exploitation and Class*, Harvard University Press, 1982; Abram de Swaan, *In Care of the State: Health Care, Education and Welfare in Europe and the USA in the Modern Era*, Policy, 1988; Eric Jones, *The European Miracle: Environments, Economics and Geopolitics in the History of Europe and Asia*, Cambridge University Press, 1981.

13 See for example Amital Etzioni, *The Moral Dimension: Towards a New Economics*, Free Press, 1988; Robert N. Bellah, Richard Madsen, William M. Sullivan, Ann Swidler and Steven M. Tipton, *Habits of the Heart*, University of California Press, 1985; Janet Finch, *Family Obligations and Social Change*, Polity, 1989; Martin Hollis, *The Cunning of Reason*, Cambridge University Press, 1987; Bill Jordan, *The Common Good: Citizenship, Morality and Self-Interest*, Blackwell, 1989.

14 Iain Hampsher-Monk, 'Prices as Descriptions: Reasons as Explanations', Paper given to Seminar on Culture and Social Change, Exeter University, 10 November 1990.

15 Marshall Sahlins, *Stone Age Economics*, Tavistock, 1974, Ch. 5.

16 Finch, *Family Obligations and Social Change*, Ch. 7.

17 Graham Crow, 'The Use of the Concept of "Strategy" in Recent Sociological Literature', *Sociology*, Vol. 23, No. 1, 1989, pp. 1–24.

18 Jon Elster (ed.), *Rational Choice*, Blackwell, 1986; Jon Elster, 'Further Thoughts on Marxism, Functionalism and Game Theory', in J. Roemer (ed.), *Analytical Marxism*, Cambridge University Press, 1986, pp. 202–20.

19 M. Buroway, *Manufacturing Consent*, University of Chicago Press, 1979.

20 R. Jenkins, 'Ethnic Minorities in Business: A Research Agenda', in R. Ward and R. Jenkins (eds), *Ethnic Communities in Business*, Cambridge University Press, 1984, pp. 231–38; J. H. Gilligan, 'The Rural Labour Process: A Case Study of a Cornish Town', in T. Bradley and P. Lowe (eds), *Locality and Rurality*, Geo Books, 1984, pp. 91–112.

21 Anthony Giddens, *Central Problems in Social Theory*, Macmillan, 1979, Ch. 2.

22 Crow, 'The Use of the Concept of "Strategy"'.

23 Robert Axelrod, *The Evolution of Co-operation*, Basic Books, 1984.

24 F. Parkin (ed.), *The Social Analysis of Class Structure*, Tavistock, 1974.

25 Anthony Giddens, *The Constitution of Society*, Polity, 1984, pp. 288–9.

26 Michael Mann, 'Ruling Class Strategies and Citizenship', *Sociology*, Vol. 21, 1987, pp. 339–54.

27 De Swaan, *In Care of the State*.

28 J. Atkinson and N. Meager, *Changing Working Patterns: How Companies Achieve Flexibility to Meet New Needs*, National Economic Development Organisation, 1986.

29 Alan Carling, *Social Division*, Verso, 1991.

30 R. E. Pahl, *Divisions of Labour*, Blackwell, 1984.

31 S. Yeandle, *Women's Working Lives*, Tavistock, 1984; J. Finch, *Married to the Job*, Allen & Unwin, 1983.

32 Bill Jordan, *Rethinking Welfare*, Blackwell, 1987, Ch. 1.

33 Crow, 'The Use of the Concept of "Strategy"', p. 2.

34 S. Wood and J. Kelly, 'Taylorism, Responsible Autonomy and Management Strategy', in S. Wood (ed.), *The Degradation of Work?*, Hutchinson, 1982, pp. 74–89.

35 Compare Jane Millar, Kenneth Cooke and Eithne McLaughlin, 'The Employment Lottery: Risk and Social Security Benefits', *Policy and Politics*, Vol. 17, No. 1, 1989, pp. 75–81.

36 According to the Department of Employment's *Employment Gazette*, see p. 279.

37 Ian Walker, 'The Effects of Income Support Measures on the Labour Market Behaviour of Lone Mothers', *Fiscal Studies*, Vol. 11, No. 2, 1990, pp. 55–75.

38 J. H. Leuthold, 'An Empirical Study of Formula Income Transfers and the Work Decisions of the Poor', *Journal of Human Resources*, Vol. 3, 1968.

39 J. S. Ashworth and D. T. Ulph, 'Household Models', in C.V. Brown (ed.), *Taxation and Labour Supply*, Allen & Unwin, 1981; Tim Barmby, 'Pareto Optimal Household Labour Supply', Paper presented at EMRU/Labour Study Group Conference, Loughborough University, 9 July 1990.

40 P. Kooreman and A. Kapteyn, 'Estimation of a Game Theoretic Model of Household Labour Supply', *Research Memorandum 180*, Department of Economics, Tilburg University, Netherlands, 1985.

41 Yolanda K. Grift and Jacques J. Siegers, 'An Individual Utility – Household Budget Constraint Model for Dutch Couples', Paper presented at EMRU/Labour Economics Study Group, Loughborough University, 9 July 1990.

42 ibid., p. 11.

43 ibid., p. 10.

44 Alan Carling, 'Rational Choice and Social Division', Paper presented at the British Sociological Association Conference, University of Surrey, 3 April 1990; and *Social Division*, Verso, 1991, Chs 11 and 12.

45 Models of the tax-benefits system using Family Expenditure Survey data include C. Morris and A. Dilnot, 'Modelling Replacement Rates', *Institute for Fiscal Studies Working Paper No. 40*, 1984, and A. B. Atkinson, J. Gomulka, J. Micklewright and N. Rau, 'Unemployment Benefit Duration and Incentives in Britain', *Journal of Public Economics*, Vol. 23, 1984, pp. 3–26. Models using hypothetical families based on average attributes include A. P. L. Minford, D. H. Davies, D. Peel and A. Sprague, *Unemployment: Cause and Cure*, Martin Robertson, 1983; models of the social security system to evaluate marginal tax rates include J. Bradshaw, *Equity and Family Incomes: An Analysis of Current Tax and Benefit Policy*, Study Commission on the Family, Occasional Paper No. 5, November 1980; A. N. Dilnot, J. A. Kay and C. N. Morris, *The Reform of Social Security*, Clarendon Press, 1984; models using budget lines to evaluate net income over a range of working hours include D. M. Egginton, 'Case Studies of Labour Supply Incentives and Budget Lines', in M. Beenstock and Associates, *Work, Welfare and Taxation: A Study of Labour Supply Incentives in the UK*, Allen & Unwin, 1987.

46 Michael Beenstock and Michael Barber, 'The New Social Security System' in Beenstock and Associates, *Work Welfare and Taxation*, pp. 245–6.

47 D. M. Egginton, 'An Informal Empirical Analysis of Labour Supply Decisions in the UK', in Beenstock and Associates, *Work, Welfare and Taxation*, p. 164.

48 Michael Beenstock, 'Conclusions and Overview', in Beenstock and Associates, *Work, Welfare and Taxation*, p. 261.

49 Richard Blundell, 'Evaluating Structural Microeconometric Models of Labour Supply', Paper presented to the EMRU/Labour Market Study Group Conference, Loughborough University, 11 July 1990.

50 ibid., p. 17.

51 ibid., p. 18.

52 For example, A. B. Atkinson and Holly Sutherland, *Tax-Benefit Models*, Suntory International Centre Occasional Paper No. 10, London School of Economics, 1988; A. B. Atkinson, *Institutional Features of Unemployment Insurance and the Working of the Labour Market*, Welfare State Programme, Suntory International Centre, Discussion Paper WSP50, 1990.

53 Carling, *Social Division*.

54 Susan McRae, *Cross-Class Families: A Study of Wives' Occupational Superiority*, Clarendon Press, 1986.

55 Jon Elster, *An Introduction to Karl Marx*, Cambridge University Press, 1986.

56 Philippe Van Parijs, 'A Revolution in Class Theory', *Politics and Society*, Vol. 15, No. 4, 1987, pp. 453–82.

57 John E. Roemer, *A General Theory of Exploitation and Class*, Harvard University Press, 1982.

58 Bill Jordan, *The Common Good: Citizenship, Morality and Self-Interest*, Blackwell, 1989.

59 The same issue is raised by Valerie Walkerdine and Helen Lucey, *Democracy in the Kitchen*, Virago, 1989.

60 For a discussion of the relationship between theoretical and applied sociology see Martin Bulmer, 'Successful Applications of Sociology: Can Britain Learn from Abroad?', Paper given at BSA Conference on Sociology in Action, Plymouth, 20 March 1989; and Martin Bulmer, 'The Prospects for Applied Sociology', *British Journal of Sociology*, Vol. 29, No. 1, 1978, pp. 128–35.

61 Gary S. Becker, *A Treatise on the Family*.

62 Gary S. Becker, 'Altruism in the Family and Selfishness in the Market Place', *Economica*, Vol. 48, 1981, pp. 1–15.

63 Gary S. Becker, Elisabeth M. Landes and Robert T. Michael, 'An Economic Analysis of Marital Instability', *Journal of Political Economy*, Vol. 85, 1977, pp. 1141–87.

64 'Exchange theorists begin with the self-interested actor faced with the problem of choice. They assume that the working out of these choices will generate social structures. But the reverse is equally plausible. Social structure – particularly the distribution of power in society – determines not only the terms of exchange in a relationship, but the interests of actors too.... Structures shape behaviour and attitudes in such ways as to fit the prevailing options'. (John Wilson, *Social Theory*, Prentice Hall, 1983, p. 97).

65 Paula England and George Farkas, *Households, Employment and Gender: A Social Economic and Demographic View*, Aldine de Grayter, 1986, Ch. 2.

66 John Scanzoni, 'A Historical Perspective on Husband–Wife Bargaining Power and Marital Dissolution', in G. Levinger and O. Moles (eds), *Divorce and Separation*, Basic Books, 1979, pp. 20–36; and 'Social Processes and

Power in Families', in W. R. Burr, R. Hill, F. I. Nye and I. L. Reiss (eds), *Contemporary Theories about the Family*, Free Press, 1979.

67 Howard Raiffa, *The Art and Science of Negotiation*, Harvard University Press, 1982; England and Farkas, *Household, Employment and Gender* p. 56.

68 C. Middleton, 'Sexual Inequality and Stratification Theory', in F. Parkin (ed.), *The Social Analysis of Class Structure*; Paul Close, 'Family Form and Economic Production', in Paul Close and Rosemary Collins (eds), *Family and Economy in Modern Society*, Macmillan, 1985, pp. 9–48; Linda Murgatroyd, '*The Production of People and Domestic Labour Revisited*', ibid., pp. 49–62.

69 See for example Clare Ungerson, *Policy is Personal: Sex, Gender and Informal Care*, Tavistock, 1987; Hilary Land and Hilary Rose, 'Compulsory Altruism for Some or an Altruistic Society for All?' in P. Bean, J. Ferris and D. Wagner (eds), *In Defence of Welfare*, Tavistock, 1985; J. Lewis and B. Meredith, *Daughters Who Care*, Routledge, 1988.

70 Finch, *Family Obligations and Social Change*, especially Chs 6–9.

71 Giddens, *Central Problems in Social Theory*.

72 Philip Abrams, *Historical Sociology*, Open Books, 1982.

73 Bill Jordan, *Social Work in an Unjust Society*, Harvester Wheatsheaf, 1990, Ch. 5.

74 Carole Gilligan, *In a Different Voice: Psychological Theory and Women's Development*, Harvard University Press, 1982; N. Noddings, *Caring: A Feminine Approach to Ethics and Moral Education*, University of California Press, 1984.

75 Judith Chaney, 'Returning to Work', in Close and Collins, *Family and Economy in Modern Society*, pp. 162–73.

76 Chris Middleton, 'The Familiar Fate of *Famulae*: Gender Divisions in the History of Wage Labour', and Maxine Berg, 'Women's Work, Mechanisation and the Early Phases of Industrialisation in England', in R. E. Pahl (ed.), *On Work: Historical, Comparative and Theoretical Approaches*, Blackwell, 1988, pp. 21–47 and 61–94.

77 Kate Purcell, 'Gender and the Experience of Employment', and Shirley Dex, 'Gender and the Labour Market', in Duncan Gallie (ed.) *Employment in Britain*, Blackwell, 1988, pp. 157–86 and 281–309.

78 Shirley Dex, *The Sexual Division of Work*, Wheatsheaf, 1985; Jean Martin and Ceridwen Roberts, *Women and Employment: A Lifetime Perspective*, Office of Population Studies and Censuses/Department of Employment, 1984.

79 Catherine Hakim, 'Occupational Segregation', Research Paper No. 9, Department of Employment, 1979; J. Harvey, 'New Technology and Gender Division of Labour', in G. Lee and R. Loveridge, *The Manufacture of Disadvantage*, Open University Press, 1987; S. Berger and M. J. Piore, *Dualism and Discontinuity in Industrial Societies*, Cambridge University Press, 1980; V. Beechey and T. Perkins, 'Conceptualising Part-time Work', in B. Roberts, R. Finnegan and D. Gallie (eds), *New Approaches to Economic Life*, Manchester University Press, 1985.

80 Catherine Hakim, 'Homeworking in Britain', in Pahl (ed.) *On Work*, pp. 609–32; 'Homework and Outwork: National Estimates from Two Surveys', *Employment Gazette*, Vol. 92, No. 1, 1984, pp. 7–12.

81 David Winchester, 'Sectoral Change and Trade-Union Organisation', in Gallie (ed.), *Employment in Britain*, pp. 493–518.

82 Pahl, *Divisions of Labour*, p. 174.

83 André Gorz, 'Comment on Bill Jordan', Paper given at Conference on The Ethical Foundations for a Basic Income, Louvain la Neuve, Belgium, 2 September 1989.

84 W. L. Slocum and F. I. Nye, 'Provider and Housekeeper Roles', in F. I. Nye (ed.), *Role Structure and Analysis of the Family*, Sage, 1976.

85 Pahl, *Divisions of Labour*.

86 J. I. Gershuny, *Social Innovation and the Division of Labour*, Oxford University Press, 1983; J. I. Gershuny and I. D. Miles, *The New Service Economy: The Transformation of Employment in Industrial Societies*, Pinter, 1983.

87 Pahl, *Divisions of Labour*, Ch. 8.

88 ibid., pp. 250–3.

89 *General Household Survey*, 1983, Table 7.17, p. 115; Michael Kell and Jane Wright, 'Benefits and the Labour Supply of Women Married to Unemployed Men', *Economic Journal*, Vol. 100, No. 399, 1990, pp. 119–26.

90 See for example Keith Hart, 'Informal Income Opportunities and Urban Employment in Ghana', *Journal of Modern African Studies*, Vol. 11, No. 3, 1973, pp. 61–89.

91 C. Bell and L. McKee, 'Marital and Family Relations in Times of Male Unemployment', in B. Roberts, R. Finnegan and D. Gallie (eds), *New Approaches to Economic Life*, Manchester University Press, 1985.

92 Lydia Morris, 'Renegotiation of the Domestic Division of Labour', in Roberts, Finnegan and Gallie (eds), *New Approaches to Economic Life*.

93 Jane Millar, Kenneth Cooke and Eithne McLaughlin, 'The Employment Lottery: Risk and Social Security Benefits', Eithne McLaughlin, Jane Millar and Kenneth Cooke, *Work and Welfare Benefits*, Gower, 1989.

94 Judith Mayo, *Work and Welfare: Employment and Employability of Women in the AFDC Program*, Community and Family Study Center, University of Chicago, 1975; Leonard Goodwin, 'What has been Learned from the Work Incentive Programme and Related Experiences: A Review of Research and Policy Implications', Office of Research and Development, Employment and Training Administration, US Department of Labor, 1977; Jesse E. Gordon, 'WIN Research: A Review of the Findings', in Charles D. Garvin *et al.* (eds), *The Work Incentive Experience*, Allanheld Osmun, 1978, Ch. 3.

95 Mary Jo Bane and David T. Ellwood, 'The Dynamics of Dependence: The Routes to Self-Sufficiency', Department of Health and Human Services, Urban Systems Research and Engineering, June 1983; Dorothy Herbert, 'Child Care', in Garvin *et al.*, *The Work Incentive Experience*, Ch. 10.

96 Martin Feldstein and James Poterba, 'Unemployment Insurance and Reservation Wages', Working paper No. 1011, National Bureau of Economic Research, July 1982; Carl Rosenfeld, 'Job Search of the Unemployed, May, 1976', *Monthly Labour Review*, 100, No. 11, November 1977, pp. 39–42.

97 Robert E. Hall, 'Why is the Unemployment Rate so High at Full Employment?', *Brookings Papers on Economic Activity*, No. 3, 1970, pp. 369–402.

98 Richard B. Freeman and Harry J. Holzer, 'Young Blacks and Jobs – What We Now Know', *The Public Interest*, No. 78, 1985, pp. 27–30.

99 Peter Townsend, *Poverty in the United Kingdom*, Penguin, 1979.

100 Jonathan Bradshaw and Jane Morgan, *Budgeting on Benefits*, Centre for Family Policy Studies, 1987; J. Bradshaw, J. Morgan and D. Mitchell,

'Evaluating Adequacy: The Potential of Budget Standards', *Journal of Social Policy*, Vol. 16, No. 2, 1987, pp. 165–81.

101 Carole Walker and Alan Walker, *The Growing Divide*, CPAG, 1987.

102 Ruth Lister and Berth Lakhani, *A Great Retreat from Fairness*, CPAG, 1987; Ruth Lister, 'Social Security: The Real Challenge', CPAG Poverty Pamphlet No. 38, 1978.

103 David Piachaud, *Round About 50 Hours a Week*, CPAG, 1984; 'The Dole', Centre for Labour Economics Discussion Paper, 1981.

104 Fran Bennett, *Your Social Security: Know Your Rights: The Questions and the Answers*, Penguin, 1982.

105 A. Dilnot, J. Kay and N. Morris, *The Reform of Social Security* Clarendon Press, 1984.

106 A. B. Atkinson, *Poverty and Social Security*, Harvester Wheatsheaf, 1989; Tony Walter, *Basic Income: Freedom from Poverty, Freedom to Work*, Marian Boyars, 1988.

107 Hermione Parker, *Instead of the Dole: An Enquiry into Integration of the Tax and Benefit Systems*, Routledge, 1989.

108 Joanna Mack and Stewart Lansley, *Poor Britain*, Allen & Unwin, 1985.

109 Jonathan Bradshaw and Hilary Holmes, *Living on the Edge: A Study of the Living Standards of Families on Benefit in Tyne and Wear*, Tyneside CPAG, 1989.

110 ibid., pp. 138–9.

111 M. Noble, G. Smith, J. Payne and J. Roberts, *The Other Oxford: Preliminary Report of a Survey of Low Income Households in Oxford*, Department of Social and Administrative Studies, Oxford University, 1987; P. Townsend, P. Phillimore and A. Beattie, *Health and Deprivation: Inequality and the North*, Croom Helm, 1988.

112 Ken Auletta, *The Underclass*, Random House, 1982; Michael Harrington, *The New American Poverty*, Rinehart & Winston, 1984; Frances Fox Piven and Richard Cloward, *The New Class War: Reagan's Attack on the Welfare State and its Consequences*, Parthenon, 1982; Frank Field, *Losing Out*, Blackwell, 1989; Ralf Dahrendorf, *The Underclass and the Future of Britain*, Tenth Annual Lecture, St George's House, Windsor Castle, 27 April 1989; Paddy Ashdown, *Citizens' Britain: A Radical Agenda for the 1990s*, Fourth Estate, 1989. For a critique of the use of the term, see J. MacNicol, 'In Pursuit of the Underclass', *Journal of Social Policy*, Vol. 16, No. 3, 1987.

113 Charles Murray, *Losing Ground: American Social Policy 1950–1980*, Basic Books, 1984.

114 Charles Murray, 'Underclass', *Sunday Times*, 26 November 1989.

115 Lawrence Mead, *Beyond Entitlement: The Social Obligations of Citizenship*, Free Press, 1986.

116 ibid., pp. 69–70.

117 John Moore, Secretary of State for Health and Social Security, speech during the second reading of the Social Security Bill, 1989, *Hansard*, House of Commons, 10 January 1989, Vol. 714.

118 Raymond Plant, 'The Fairness of Workfare', *The Times*, 16 August 1988. See also his *Citizenship, Rights and Socialism*, Fabian Society, 1988.

119 P. Esam, R. Good and R. Middleton, *Who's To Benefit?*, Verso, 1985, p. 55.

120 For example, Ruth Lister, *The Exclusive Society: Citizenship and the Poor*, CPAG, 1990.

121 Ralf Dahrendorf, 'Liberty and Socialism', *New Democrat*, December 1988; Bill Jordan, *The Common Good*, Chs 5 and 6.

3 The study, the people and the methods

So far we have explained why the study of labour-market decisions in low-income households raises such thorny and bitterly contested theoretical issues. In this chapter we will set out how we came to do our research, to find our sample and to choose the methods of analysis we used. The first section will describe the background to the research, and how we planned to do it; the second will describe some of the problems and pitfalls we experienced; and the third how we chose our eventual method of analysis and interpretation.

It was precisely because of the complex issues within and between the social science disciplines that our interdisciplinary team – Simon James (an economist), Bill Jordan (a social policy analyst) and Helen Kay (a sociologist) – came together and chose to do a study in this field. We had all done work on labour markets, and Simon James had conducted research on tax issues, while Bill Jordan had written on the benefit system. We had all become aware that there was no in-depth, qualitative British study on how members of poor households decided what work to do, at what wages, for what hours, and how these decisions were affected by tax and benefit considerations.

However, the very issues which we were choosing to study arose for us too. As a small team – more like a household than a working group in terms of size – we had to make decisions about our roles and relationships, and how we could most effectively and productively co-operate. As academics with different knowledge and skills, employed on different terms (one full-time, one part-time, and one specifically to do the research for this project), we had to find a fair division of tasks, as well as a rigorous interdisciplinary research methodology.

In this sense, our team's situation paralleled that of the households we were studying. When we interviewed members of their households, individually and together, we were asking them to give accounts of how they worked – how they decided what to do, and how they co-operated. In this chapter, we aim to give our account of our working methods and co-operation – to tell our story in a convincing way that will give the study a creditable standing in the research community.

As with the couples in their joint interviews, we must also say how our work fitted together. It is not just that we had different roles in the work of the team: we also came from different disciplines, each with its own language and theoretical framework. The respondents displayed rhetorical forms in which they accounted for their actions as individuals and as partners – though some found the latter too difficult, and avoided joint interviews. We had to construct a common language and shared concepts in which to clarify and justify our findings.

This process took time. Although there were essential areas of agreement and common purpose from the start of our co-operation, differences and disagreements, arising from our roles and theoretical antecedents, persisted within the context of co-operation. Shared understandings emerged gradually, rather than arriving in a flash of light. We struggled to understand the data, rather than reaching a quick consensus that provided the key to our analysis. We did not find answers in existing theory – we had to do this work ourselves.

To do justice to this process, we have tried to find a way of writing this chapter that reflects the struggle as well as the outcome, and that tells how our debates and disagreements eventually led to a shared methodology and analysis. In particular, this requires us to tell the story of the research in a coherent and comprehensible manner, yet one which allows the different voices of the team to be heard. For this purpose, the three original members of the team and Marcus Redley have all contributed separate accounts of the process, which include some of their individual experiences and feelings at the time, and Bill Jordan, as the main writer for the team, has drawn on these in constructing our joint account. As we shall see in Chapter 6, this procedure is rather different from the one used by the couples in their joint interviews, but it mirrors our understanding of joint accounts – that they seek to give morally adequate versions of co-operative decision-making and behaviour, while acknowledging the differences in roles and skills between members, and the disagreements and conflicts which are part of any such process. Above all, this chapter acknowledges the essential basis of our analysis – that there is not a single 'objective' account of such decisions and actions, but that actors' versions give rise to accounts which reveal the underlying structure of relations.

Clearly this also links closely with the theoretical issues discussed at the beginning of the first chapter. In our analysis of the interviewees' accounts, and the account we give of our research, we have to show how the calculative decision-making of self-interest meshes with the social–moral processes of sharing and co-operation. Our methodology must establish epistemological links both with economic theory and with social theory, and show the links between them.

As we shall argue in this chapter, the methods of qualitative analysis of actors' accounts provide a suitable framework for these tasks, and allow us to demonstrate the hypotheses that emerge from the study. Qualitative methods allow us to draw out from the interviews the background assumptions about roles and responsibilities which underpin the interviewees' accounts, the dynamics of household relationships, and the mechanics of decision-making. They enable us to construct a theory of the strategies for labour-market participation and household expenditure which are pursued in their households.

We will argue that the accounts themselves are constructed in terms of social–moral relations between men and women in households, and present individuals and couples as making calculative, economic decisions in certain spheres. Hence the overriding rhetorical mode of their descriptions of choices and actions is moral, though the values and beliefs that inform this are seldom spelt out. Our methodology enables us to develop theory about how economic calculation is deployed within the moral framework of the accounts, and how this reflects the structure and dynamics of local social relations.

THE BACKGROUND AND PLANNING OF THE STUDY

In 1985–6, the government's programme for reforming the social security system spawned a large number of publications and conferences – many of which were as concerned with what the government had excluded from its package of reforms as the proposals themselves.[1] In particular, although the Green Paper *Reform of Social Security* discussed work incentives and disincentives from tax-benefit interaction in one crucial section, income taxation was not considered in the measures recommended. This omission was widely criticised, yet a weakness of the case made by the critics themselves was the absence of any detailed, qualitative study of the 'poverty trap' – the impact of income taxation and means-tested benefits withdrawal on the work behaviour of low-income households.

Helen Kay, a sociologist experienced in qualitative methods, who was then faculty research assistant at Exeter University, and concerned with initiating collaborative interdisciplinary research, discussed the possibility of such a study with Simon James and Bill Jordan. The faculty was persuaded to give her two days a week working on a preliminary study, both to address theoretical issues and to undertake some interviewing. This was completed by June 1986, but an application for funding from the

University was turned down. It was not until April 1987 that a favourable response from the Economic and Social Research Council (ESRC) was obtained, but the funding itself was not forthcoming until September 1988. During this period, Helen Kay's temporary contract with Exeter University ended, and because of resource restrictions was not renewed: she worked on various other projects, and then accepted the post of research assistant for this study – a rather different status, and hence one that made for a different team dynamic from the preliminary study experience.

The project was to be an exploratory study – we started with no hypotheses to test and no model to compare. We wanted to find out how people framed their labour-market decisions, without imposing our academic or commonsense assumptions on interviewees' discourse. However, we chose this field of study because of the theoretical and policy issues it raised, and hence if such issues arose in an interview, Helen Kay guided the discussion into our areas of particular interest. Our ideal was to get as close as possible to understanding how people thought about their decisions, and to pick up ambiguities and conflicts in their accounts of household decision-making. Hence we could not use a standardised questionnaire with its built-in assumptions and requirements of hypotheses to be tested. The only way to explore people's reasoning about the labour market was to ask them to tell their story and to say how they made sense of the options open to them.

This method of qualitative research requires a lot of time – one to two hours to interview each partner, followed by a joint interview of a similar length, and much longer to transcribe, code and interpret these hours of recorded speech. With limited time and funds we could study in depth only a small number of people – but enough to be able to develop some well-informed hypotheses which could hopefully be tested for their generalisability subsequently on a larger population in a later study.

From our preliminary study, which included both poor and better-off households, we suspected that there might be major differences in decision-making processes between income groups. Because our starting point was the current social security reform process (the substance of which was about to be implemented in April 1988), we decided to limit the first project to the investigation of labour-market decisions in low-income households, stating our intention of tackling a similar study of higher-income households at a later date. (In fact, a further ESRC grant was forthcoming, and this project began in April 1990.)

One of the first problems was to define 'low-income household'. Should we define 'low income' in terms of the main income provider or the whole household income? What if members did not know each other's earnings? We knew from our preliminary study that many households had frequent changes of income depending on the current labour-market status of members. We also knew that recruiting interviewees required tact, and that filter questions about income could result in rejection. But above all, a study of labour-market decisions needed to leave open the possiblity that some households *escaped* (temporarily or permanently) from poverty, rather than selecting only those who were currently poor.[2] To choose people who declared a low income would be to beg the most interesting question about the poverty trap – how much of a trap is it? In these circumstances it seemed more appropriate to interview willing couples in an area where the majority of households were known to have a low income.

We consulted the city planning department, and decided to conduct the interviews in one easily defined area of Exeter which had the lowest socio-economic profile, and some local notoriety as the 'least desirable' council estate. This impression of poverty was confirmed by consulting the Jarman Index, which revealed a very high level of social and economic deprivation by the standards of southern Britain.[3] By restricting the study to this area, we expected to be interviewing households which had experienced poverty in the 1980s, even if they were not currently poor – and this was borne out by our data, since all but two of them had claimed benefits through unemployment in the past ten years. This geographical focus also meant that interviewees had similar access to public transport and perhaps to the local labour market.

From the start, we were aware that respondents would interpret, edit and alter their own constructed biographies, to make sense of their past actions and decisions: we did not seek to check details in order to get a 'true' version. We wanted to hear their own accounts of what work they chose, for what hours, at what pay, and with what prospects of training or promotion, and to find out what mention they made of tax or benefits considerations in describing their motives for decisions.

Our preliminary study indicated that interviewees made their labour-market decisions as individuals, though women took account of family constraints. For the main study we planned to interview male and female partners individually and later together. We wanted to look at individual reconstructions, to find out what reference was made to discussions between partners, and then in the follow-up joint interviews we hoped to trace how these decisions fitted into the course of household events, and whether couples were able to construct a joint version without damaging their individual interpretations of past events.

We planned three in-depth interviews with forty two-parent households with dependent children (the largest single group in the poverty statistics, and the main target of the recent social security reforms). We hoped to draw interviewees from several categories – regular and irregular workers; employed, self-employed and unemployed workers; tenants and mortgagors; people with and without training and qualifications; households with pre-school and school age children – but the final choice of comparative categories would depend on the analysis and interpretation of the interview data.

The interviews were to be tape recorded, transcribed and photocopied so that each member of the team would keep in touch with the research process of interviewing and analysis. The audio-typist, Elaine Harrison, used considerable sociological sensitivity and skill in producing the transcriptions of the tapes, and contributed valuably to team discussions – for example the significance of pauses, interruptions and 'background noises' from children and animals. We planned to analyse the data into cultural domains, using respondents' own concepts to identify emerging themes,[4] and follow this up by using cognitive mapping to lay out the process whereby individuals link up their concepts,[5] as this method would facilitate the generation of theory and provide a means of focusing discussion within the team.

THE AREA AND THE SAMPLE

In one sense, Exeter is not the obvious place to study poverty. In a survey conducted by a Scottish University Geography Department during the period of our research, it emerged as having the highest quality of life among the medium-sized cities of the British Isles, with its favourable climate combining with good educational and recreational services, moderate house prices and pleasant environment. Its unemployment rate was around the national average throughout the 1980s; never having industrialised, Exeter was not prone to post-industrial restructuring. All but two of its top ten employers are in the public sector, and all but one are service organisations.

Yet, other features of Exeter to make it an appropriate location for the study. Low-paid service occupations are overrepresented in its economy, as are women in its labour force. The polarisation of incomes and job security which has become a feature of the British economy is exaggerated by the influx of middle-aged people from the south-east of England, bringing with them large capital sums which allow them to corner the housing market, and small occupational pensions to supplement their earnings, and hence allow them to accept low wage rates without experiencing poverty. Above all, the high profile of deprivation on our study estate revealed in the Jarman Scales indicated that it was a suitable district in which to investigate how the 1980s' changes in the labour market and the benefit system had affected people with low earning power and little employment security.

The estate lies some 1½ miles to the south of the city centre, and was constructed in the interwar period. It consists mainly of two- and three-bedroomed semi-detached houses, many of which are in quite a poor state of repair, but which have large gardens, and a more generous sense of space than many modern dwellings. The estate is divided in half by a broad thoroughfare, on or near which stand shops, school and community centre, and which is encircled by a number of radial roads, each with smaller cul-de-sacs fanning out from them. Although somewhat bleak in grey weather, the area is lively and sociable in character, and when the sun shines the first impression is of children and adults alike enjoying the open spaces on or near the estate, for conversation, play and pleasantries.

Most residents have strong local connections, and there are many large families, with two or three generations of tenants. However, there is a minority from outside the south-west, including small numbers from overseas (such as students from abroad): the relevance of this community structure for our study will be analysed in Chapter 7.

In order to check whether the widely-held view of the estate as an undesirable place to live is reflected in length of council housing tenure, we conducted a survey of the Exeter City Council's housing department's record cards for properties on three estates, the one in our study, the most popular in terms of applications from would-be tenants (Stoke Hill), and one of intermediate popularity (St Thomas).[6] We sampled every sixth house in every street on the estate, eliminated flats from each sample, and recorded changes of tenant since 1980, the date the present tenant moved in, and the date the house was sold if it had been purchased by the tenant. The average numbers of move per house since 1980 were as follows:

Stoke Hill	0.36
St Thomas	0.58
Study Estate	1.02

The average length of time the current tenant had been in the study estate's survey sample houses was 9 years 3 months. The average for the sample of interview respondents was 6 years. This difference reflected the fact that our interviewees (all of whom had children) were at the younger end of the age range of tenants on the estate. It also showed that they were likely to be representative of this age group, in terms of their period of tenure.

The social characteristics of the study estate were also evidenced in the data on house sales. In our survey sample of properties, we found that none of the houses on the study estate had been sold before 1980, compared with 13 per cent in Stoke Hill; only 11 per cent had been sold on the study estate between 1980 and 1987, compared with 26 per cent in Stoke Hill. But in 1988–9, the period of the study, another 9 per cent of the study estate's houses were sold – a considerable quickening of the pace of house sales – and a further 22 per cent in Stoke Hill.

The reasons why house sales on the study estate quickened in the 1980s will be discussed in Chapter 7. But one of our strong early impressions of the estate was that – contrary to the view expressed by outsiders – the people living there liked it, and for the most part liked each other. Indeed our interviewees gave liking the area, and community support, as reasons for buying or wanting to buy their council houses. For example:

'(We been here for) 15 and a half years, we been. It's nice here. I mean a lot of people won't come here 'cause it's got a very bad reputation [estate's name] and some of them ... I mean you used to have problems out here in the street, used to have the police out here midnight, you know, and various things [indistinct] they fight [...] Never a dull moment round here. But you've got all that view out the back and I was born in the country, and you think to yourself, well, you've lived here all this time, and we've done it up and that, you're not going to move from here, so ...'

(Mrs Kennet, 14)

'I'd hate to leave here; I don't wanna go up and live on Nob Hill. Do you know what I mean? ... Ah, that doesn't appeal to me. Love it here. I'm content to stay here until my kids are off my hands, and then perhaps we'll get a one-bedroom bungalow or something like that ... [indistinct] if you can look that far ahead. But I like it here, friends are here, I've no intention ... I mean, I could be made ... I could get promotion and go right up the scale tomorrow [...] but I'd live here. Do you follow me?'

(Mr Rother, 71–2)

'No, 'cause I like it here. I don't care what anybody's got to say about [estate's name]. I've never had any problems with it. I was born here – in [estate's name] – and I like it. I mean all this ruffian stuff what goes on, I mean, I don't see any of it, so ... no, I wouldn't move away.'

(Mrs Nene, 9)

These accounts of housing decisions emphasise that the community is close-knit despite its reputation, and supportive in its networks of friends and kin. The same aspects emerge in accounts of labour-market decisions, particularly those of women managing their child-care commitments (see Chapters 5 and 6).

Little store was set on privacy, 'keeping oneself to oneself' or minding one's own business in the respondents' accounts. On the contrary, many interviewees claimed insider's knowledge of the ways of the estate and what went on beyond the purview of the outside world, and especially of the eyes and ears of the state's officialdom. As we shall see, although many acknowledged that they had broken rules on benefits or tax liability, they justified this within a story about the inequities or inefficiencies of these systems, in combination with labour-market constraints. They also differentiated their own behaviour from that of others on the estate, or legitimated it in terms of the prevalence of such actions. For example:

'You know, boy down the road ... might say, like, oh my mate wants his house decorating and ... he'll say to someone else, oh his mate wants his house decorating and he'll say, oh I know somebody, and just gets passed around, you know, and it ... sometimes it comes to you, sometimes they go to somebody else [...] I can guarantee there's loads of people doin' it, you know, there's hundreds of people doing these jobs on the side and all that.'

(Mr Itchen, 6–7)

One of the issues to be disentangled in our analysis is therefore how individual decisions are located and legitimated in this web of community, and how accounts given to a researcher in a domestic context (in people's houses, and relating to their household roles) are woven into this wider context of a network of friendship and kinship, which is clearly significant for men and women on the estate.

Helen Kay had already done some interviewing on the estate in the preliminary study, so she had some familiarity with the area. Initially she set out to contact suitable couples through a number of community agencies.

1.   *Health visitors*: She spoke to a number of health visitors about their work in the area and asked each to provide the names and addresses of two families willing to take part in the study. Six families were contacted and four agreed to take part, but one later withdrew.

2.   *Community worker*: She spent one afternoon with the community worker with special responsibility for the under-5s talking about the nursery and her role. She provided the contact with one family.

3.   *Open learning centre*: She met the co-ordinator of this Centre and talked of her work and objectives. Two women attending the Centre agreed to be interviewed.

4.   *Mother and children club*: For the first three months of the project she dropped in most Thursdays to the Club which caters for women with

young children; six families were contacted through the Club. However, she felt increasingly uncomfortable about contacting families in this way for a number of reasons. Firstly the majority of women attending the Club were single-parent mothers whose family life sometimes included a man living in their household; it was therefore inappropriate to ask whether they were one of a couple before asking them to take part in the study. We have included in the analysis a small number of women who were contacted through the Club and who were living as single parents at the time of interview. (These are not included in the sample of thirty-six couples, and are included for comparison: for our analysis of these interviews see Chapter 8.) However, it became important to develop other means of contacting households which included a male partner.

5. *Community Centre*: Helen Kay met many of the people involved in running the Centre who were willing to talk about their role in the community. She attended four bingo sessions which provided interesting and useful background data and introductions by a key contact to two willing interviewees.

After 3 months Helen Kay had made sixteen contacts and had become increasingly involved in the pressures, tensions and ethical issues of meeting household members, gaining their consent, negotiating the co-operation of their partners, and carrying through the set of three interviews as planned. By this stage it was apparent that individuals had strong feelings about their labour-market experiences, and that the issues raised by the research became extremely sensitive when we tried to place them within a household context. Even in relatively harmonious, co-operative couples there were tensions and no-go areas. For example, Mr Rother, a local authority worker (now foreman) for the past 23 years, was not prepared to disclose his earnings to Helen Kay.

Q:	Can I ask you how much you earn?
Mr Rother:	No, no, not really. [laughs]
Q:	Obviously we don't tell anybody else. It's only so we can compare ...
Mr Rother:	My wife ... my wife don't even know.
Q:	Oh.
Mr Rother:	I tells her within a few figures, like, but, that, you know, that's, it isn't, I mean ... we're, we ... she's sort of one that, as long as she got enough to put back so much every week for so many things and ...

(Mr Rother, 24)

Mrs Avon, married to a regular worker, resented not being eligible for family credit: she sees her husband's wages as low.

'No, he doesn't earn a big wage: his wage is very low – very low wage. But we just can't get it; we can't even get a rent rebate.'

(Mrs Avon, 11)

But Mr Avon insists that his earnings (as a shift worker in a farm foodstuffs firm) are – at £122 per week – among the best in Exeter, and that his wife has grown used to a degree of luxury. He gives her £50 or £55 a week for housekeeping, but he pays the rent and the television rental.

'I'm not ... ah blowing me own trumpet sort of thing but ... when Sandra, then San ... money's concerned, Sandra ... don't pay noth, don't pay hardly anything: she, she lives like the queen in one respect, 'cause ... like I say, she don't pay no bills; all she ... she pays, she buys the television licence ... right, which is once a year, and she pays for the childrens' insurance ...'

(Mr Avon, 40)

In other households, one partner would participate enthusiastically in the research interview, but engaging with the other (usually the man) proved problematic. Mrs Bure, who was not in paid employment, talked articulately about her past labour-market experiences and about claiming family credit. However, when Helen Kay returned by appointment to see Mr Bure, she received a different reception. Here is an extract from her research notes.

20.9.88. 7 p.m. Called to interview Mr Bure. Mrs B. opened the door, saying her husband had just arrived home, and anyway did not want to be interviewed. She started to put on her coat saying that she was on her way out to get some chips for his tea.

I said I would come back on another night, perhaps when he was not so tired etc., gradually moving into the sitting room and peeping round the door. Husband sat on floor by fire, stripped to the waist, looking very tired. Wife 'explains' that he is always in a bad mood when he first comes in – she seems to be half apologetic, half anxiously protecting him from me. Baby lying on the floor with bottle, saying nothing, being ignored by rest of family. Toddler watching everyone, making asides, full of energy and interest. Father looks at toddler proudly. Wife seems strangely incompetent, uncertain. [Saying 'go away' but allowing me to come into the sitting room, following her.] Husband agrees to interview Friday 6 p.m. before they go shopping at 6.30.

The individual interview with Mr Bure was done as arranged, but this is Helen Kay's record the following month.

> 20.10.88. Called to do joint interview. Mrs Bure answered the door – husband eating his tea, just home from work 7.15 p.m. Mrs Bure said he was very tired as he was working 12 hour shifts, and intended to do so till Christmas. She was 'fed up', stuck with the children all day. She said her husband was not interested in doing another interview, he was tired and grumpy. I suggested Saturday a.m. but Mrs Bure said they did things with the children Saturday morning and 'he' went to play football in the afternoon. 'What did I want to talk about anyway?' 'I heard about your work and then about your husband's work. I would like to ask you about how work and family fit together.' 'Well they don't, do they? That's the point. He's too tired anyway – it's a long day.' (In the event, no joint interview took place.)

In other households there were covert or disguised disagreements between the partners which made the practical arrangements for doing a tape recorded interview difficult. In principle, the individual interviews should have been conducted without the other partner being present, in practice this was often impossible, as space, family requirements or the needs of children meant that only one room was available for the adults of the household. Sometimes the other partner interjected comments: on other occasions the interviewee was discomforted by the other's presence, and took the opportunity of a temporary absence from the room to make a comment about this, or lower their voice so as not to be overheard. Mr Calder is talking about this preference for self-employment over his present regular but boring work as a lorry driver – but his wife disapproves of irregular hours and earnings.

> 'But I'd like to work for myself, I'd like ... a little van and do sort of express parcels, things like that, you know, [indistinct, whispering] she's dead against it, self-employed ... she's not too keen on it at all, so ...'
>
> (Mr Calder, 29)

Overt conflict was rare, but some men were rather overbearing towards the interviewer, their partners, or both. Mr Cam, an irregular worker currently driving a roadsweeper, has a loud voice and is quite voluble. He and his wife describe past disagreements between them in their joint interview.

Mrs Cam:	No he was going to leave me.
Mr Cam:	Well it got the stage where the marriage wa'n' really working out. [indistinct] [laughs]
Mrs Cam:	[laughs] Excuse me, I'll just turn the immersion off.

Mr Cam: ... you know, the ah so what used to get me is the doors slamming, you know. The [indistinct – also tape jumps] [laughs] you can always tell when Lucy's upset because everything goes bang ...

Mrs Cam: [laughs] That ... This is on tape dear. [laughs]

Mr Cam: ... cupboard doors ... Don't care if it is on tape or no we – I always ... [indistinct – coughing]

Mrs Cam: Edit out the worse bits. [laughs]

(Mr and Mrs Cam, 44)

Mr Exe who has been unemployed for 4½ years intervenes frequently in his wife's individual interview, in such a way as to disqualify her account, eventually silencing her altogether.

Q: Have you thought about getting, trying for a job?

Mrs Exe: Ah, yeah. [indistinct] ... Me husband said it ... yeah, I was gonna go for work, but me husband says wa'n' worth it, di'n' you Gary?

Mr Exe: Well 't'i'n' i'n'it?

Mrs Exe: Ah ... ah ...

Mr Exe: Unless you can get what you want ...

Mrs Exe: Ah ... ah ...

Mr Exe: ... in wages ... it ... it's a waste of time going back i'n'it?

Mrs Exe: Yeah. [indistinct – child talking] That's it, yeah.

(Mrs Exe, 12)

Other households were more intangibly uncomfortable for Helen Kay, who felt conscious of her outsider status as references were made to family events – some of them quite anxiety-provoking – in explanations, or in asides to others present. Mr Dart has been unemployed for 9 years, and is under pressure from the benefit authorities to take a job. The house is untidy, and there are other people present each time she calls. (In retrospect, Helen Kay is conscious of intruding on this household, and their anxiety to present themselves creditably – they thought at first she was a health visitor.) The baby is well dressed; Mrs Dart says she attends the child development centre with her daughter aged 3, who 'just speaks her own language'. On the second visit, the following are extracts from the research notes:

18.10.88: Mr and Mrs Dart at home with Mr Dart's brother, another brother (?) and two children, Monica (3) and Martin (4 months) ... [Mr and Mrs Dart] were quick to tell me that the baby had a bump on his head and they had told the health visitor right away because everybody would think it was Charlie, Mr Dart's brother, who had done it because he had been in trouble before for child abuse, but they knew he would not touch any children now, and certainly not their children. Charlie sat passively in the chair whilst they told me this ... Charlie works on the fairground at the moment ... There was a news item about house burglary and Mr and Mrs Dart teased Charlie saying, 'I wonder who would know about that?'

At about this stage in the fieldwork, Helen Kay felt close to abandoning the research design in the face of these difficulties. Reflecting on the interviews, she was aware that in some cases the conflict of interest between couples had not been articulated in the individual interviews, and their withdrawal from further participation in the research may well have signified their wish to continue their pattern of avoidance of direct discussion (Mr and Mrs Bure). On the other hand, in a few cases she had made the decision not to proceed with the third interview in households where there was evidence that the conflict had recently been overt and expressed in marital violence (Mr and Mrs Exe). In still other instances, when it seemed that a couple might withdraw from the project if left to reflect on the issues, she reacted by allowing, or encouraging, the individual interview(s) to run on into a joint interview. Although this allowed some discussion of the issues between the couple on tape, it did not give the researchers the opportunity to consider which issues needed to be explored further in the joint interview, and was in some ways an avoidance of the ethical issues of this kind of research.

In particular, Helen Kay was aware of the penetrative nature of the questions, the deep feelings involved in decision-making and the conflicts of interests between partners over their respective decisions. There was no way to prepare respondents for these aspects of the interview experience – how emotionally involved they would become in their accounts, the hurts, humiliations and frustrations they would describe, or the way in which the interview process could highlight or even heighten conflict. She came to doubt whether the respondents could be said to give 'informed consent' to take part in the research.[7]

In the next section we will describe the issues over coding, interpreting and communicating our findings, which were already emerging at this middle stage of the fieldwork. However, to conclude this section on the sample and how it was gathered, Helen Kay used door-knocking as the method of finding the rest of our respondents, using a local household directory. Thus about half of our sample was gathered in this way. The eventual composition, in terms of employment statuses, was as follows:

Table 3.1 The families' employment status

Husband and wife both employed	18
Husband and wife both unemployed	10
Husband employed, wife unemployed	7
Husband unemployed, wife employed	1
Total	36

Table 3.2 The husbands' employment

Unemployed	11	Supervisor (café)	1
Metal finisher	1	Foreman	1
Bus driver	1	Warehouseman	2
Gardener	1	Plasterer	1
Stonemason (trainee)	1	Shop manager	1
Civil servant (clerical)	1	Road sweeper/driver	1
Car valeter	1	Painter/decorator	2
Driver (lorry, van)	2	Mechanic (motorcycle)	1
Meat cutter	1	Labourer	3
Sign-writer/labourer	1	Machinist	1
Security guard	1		

Table 3.3 The wives' employment

Housewife	17	Machinist	2
Cleaner	6	Warehouse manager	1
Caterer	3	Factory supervisor	1
Shop assistant	2	Chambermaid	1
Shelf-filler	2	Care assistant	1

COMMUNICATING, CODING AND INTERPRETING

So far in this chapter we have described how we planned the research, selected the sample and carried out the interviews. The rest of the chapter is about how we discussed the data in the team, talked about it with colleagues at academic conferences, and attempted to code, interpret and analyse it. However, the central issue can be very simply stated. Given that our respondents were thirty-six non-statistically selected couples living on this estate, what can lengthy tape recorded interviews tell us about labour-market decisions in poor households that has relevance to the empirical knowledge and theoretical explanations of the phenomena outlined in the opening chapter? Given that what we did was to listen to these people's stories about their recent employment histories, and ask a few questions about issues of interest in our study, without checking the accuracy or veracity of their accounts, and often leaving details on earnings, dates and events vague and contested, what weight should these stories carry, and how can our analysis of them contribute to the social science and political debates on this subject?

It is not our intention to rehearse here the details of the historical feud between quantitative and qualitative methods of research. Fortunately, there is some evidence of peace breaking out in this lengthy and wasteful war.[8] Both methodologies can contribute importantly to an understanding of issues such as these, and there are ways of linking them in a middle ground, in which large-scale survey evidence is used to test hypotheses generated through case studies, and theory from qualitative research modifies the assumptions incorporated into statistical models. The long-term aim of our project is to move from a case-study to a survey approach, and from the local to the national, once our data have been fully analysed. So the main point of this section is not to try to discredit survey and statistical methods, but to establish what can be learnt from qualitative studies such as ours.

In any social science research, the findings consist of a presentation of data in some reasonably coherent form, and inferences from the data about the wider social phenomena that are being investigated. Survey research gives rise to statistical data, and the inferences from them are required to be theory neutral, and to associate phenomena in terms of correlations with variables. Even very strong statistical correlations do not have the explanatory status of 'causes', and their claims to validity depend on the representativeness of their samples.[9] These methods are highly appropriate to the investigation of aspects of human life which are public, quantified and generalised, and especially those on which official statistics are regularly gathered. They are much less appropriate for investigating activities which are unstructured, experiential and difficult to quantify,[10] for issues around which ideas and facts are seldom articulated or recorded,[11] or for others where the participants have reasons for concealing their activities from the official gaze. Furthermore, statistical methods deal with deviant cases by means of a 'standard error' procedure, which precludes an explanation that accounts for the exceptional or extreme.

Qualitative methods have the obverse advantages. They allow investigation in the nooks and crannies of social life,[12] as well as in the rather wide open expanses of unstructured, unmeasured, unrecorded activity and in-activity which characterise much human existence. But their claims to validity rest on the adequacy of their underlying theories, on the ability of the analysis to provide a logical or causal account which explains the data – all of the data, including the apparently deviant or exceptional examples – in a convincing way.[13] The subject for study is chosen because it seems to exemplify a particular theoretical issue, and the analysis should provide a theory which specifies the necessary conditions for a phenomenon's occurrence.[14]

In our study, the theoretical issues at stake were the ones outlined in the previous chapter. How did these couples decide the quantities of paid and unpaid work done by each partner? Did they calculate their net gain in household income (allowing for tax and national insurance deductions, benefit withdrawals, travel and child-care costs) before deciding whether to take a low-paid job? Did they recognise a poverty or unemployment trap, and if so what did they do about it? Which features of the labour market and the tax-benefit system, and what interactions between them, did they describe as influencing their decisions and how?

Here we had poor people's accounts, in research interviews, of exactly these decisions, how they made them, and which factors they took into consideration. We had their retrospective reconstructions of their actions, and their attempts to justify them to the interviewer, by reference to features (real or imagined) of their personal, family, community and economic circumstances – the contested theoretical issues we wanted to study.

Our task now was to analyse and interpret our data, and present our findings to others. However, this could be done in several different ways. Were we to read the interviews as biased reports of an objective 'real' world – a positivist approach? Alternatively, were we to read them as poor people's subjective experiences of employment and claiming? Were we to analyse them purely as interviewees' descriptions of 'their' worlds? Or alternatively again, we could produce an ethnomethodological demonstration of how some poor people 'do an interview',[15] or present them as instances of social group interpretive repertoires,[16] or as an exposure of the meta-linguistic rules of conversational sequencing,[17] On pp. 73–9 of this chapter we describe how we eventually decided to carry out our analysis, in the face of these dilemmas – to read the transcribed tapes as situated accounts of poverty in a research interview, revealing the moral framework of social relations on the estate. But at this stage, while aware of the alternatives, we were still seeking a method which could use these accounts to develop a theory to explain the decisions our respondents described – a convincing version of how these individuals' stories related to the wider world of economy and society.

We were, of course, conscious of certain general principles that governed the interpretation of all such data, and should guide our methods of analysing and communicating these accounts to the wider academic community. To be convincing, our analysis must be a coherent, preferably an elegant, theoretical explanation of decision-making, refined by (rather than blunted by) the anomalous or extreme examples in our sample. Second, it must draw on and preferably develop theory from this and other fields: for instance, it might exemplify, modify or falsify economic theories of household exchange, or sociological theories of work strategies. Third, it must move beyond the micro-level of individual and household decisions, to explain wider social relations – for example, the role of poor people in Thatcher's Britain – and to contribute to policy debates, such as the one about workfare and incentives. Fourth, it should be imaginative in its ability to make connections with other studies from quite different fields, such as Third World evidence on informal work and income strategies in poor households. Fifth, it must subject itself to attempted falsification, by trying to distinguish necessary from sufficient conditions for phenomena, by considering deviant cases, and by providing whatever quantified evidence is available, but above all by investigating rival explanations of the same data.

However, such a process of analysis and interpretation took place within a particular context – the research team, within the University or centre, and as part of the wider academic community. The issues raised by the research reverberated within the team, exaggerating existing tensions over unequal power, status and rewards, and the gendered division of labour. Some of the problems already described generated feelings of isolation from her colleagues in Helen Kay, and the experience of a gap between 'theory' (what University based academics 'do') and 'practice' (the work of the research assistant in the field).[18]

Here it is necessary to consider the relationship between the structure of social relations in the University and the team on the one hand, and in Exeter and wider British society on the other, and the kind of knowledge our study was trying to produce. Modern sociological theory, under the influence of Michel Foucault and of feminism, has grappled with issues of structure, knowledge and power, and as we experienced conflicts within and beyond the team, we came to recognise the phenomena analysed in these theoretical works, and to draw on them to move forward from the difficulties we encountered.

Like other academic disciplines, sociology has been concerned to produce objective knowledge, by means of a method free from political or personal biases of interpretation – while acknowledging the subjective, emotional or social influences that might derive from the researchers' experiences during the work. Yet academic discourses are like any other – ways of organising meaning, within membership groups. Each such group's discursive practice 'delimits fields of relevance and definitions of legitimate perspectives and fixes norms for concept elaboration and the expression of experience'.[19] In other words, the production of academic knowledge involves members (researchers, theorists) in constructing particular ways of giving meaning to the world at the same time actively suppressing alternative interpretations.[20]

The work of Foucauldian sociologists of the Regulation School (see p. 70 and p. 313) has aimed at making visible the means by which officially sanctioned discourses (like those of state agencies, professional groups and academic experts) become part of the 'means of ruling' through which power relations are organised and structured.[21] These dominant discourses become part of the taken-for-granted systems of thinking, believing and speaking which shape daily experience, and which exclude other groups' perceptions and voices, making aspects of their being and feeling inaccessible. Becoming a researcher is one of the ways in which people are trained and socialised into membership of a dominant discursive practice; thus 'rational deliberation, reflection, and consideration of all viewpoints ... become a vehicle for regulating conflict and the power to speak, for transforming conflict into rational argument by means of universalised capacities for language and reason'.[22]

Women have been the group most clearly to identify the processes of exclusion achieved by these structures. The texts – words, numbers, images – of the academic world are the medium of 'relations of ruling', ideologically structured ways of organising and doing things, which largely exclude women, and give power and authority to particular men, while furthering the interests of men in general.[23] They reflect not merely a division of labour in which men do most paid and women most unpaid work, but also a social structure in which men's public world of administration and knowledge is constructed as universal, and women's private world of domesticity as particular. 'The means women have had available to them to think, image, and make actionable their experience have been made for us and not by us'.[24] Hence the project of feminist sociology – to construct a women's critique of 'scientific, objective' male sociology as partial and covertly partisan, and an alternative sociology which allows women's experiences to be acknowledged, validated and understood. These should include 'unspoken problems and guilty secrets', such as the stress experienced by the researchers, and power issues in interviews and within teams.[25]

We have already alluded to some of the stresses and pressures experienced by the research interviewer, and to the issues these raised within the research team. Helen Kay felt strongly that some of the nuances and emotional currents of the interviews – which were important elements in the relations she was trying to understand – were difficult to communicate with her male colleagues. Bill Jordan felt uncomfortable and frustrated about this apparent 'gap', yet unable to spend more time on interviewing, and it seemed preferable, in the interests of consistency, to stick to a single interviewer. While these problems were never fully resolved, we recognised their relevance for the study itself, since they reflected the very divisions of power, role and labour we were studying in households.

There were other problems in communication, over the language used by the interviewer in talking to respondents, by the interviewees in their accounts, and within the typed transcripts. During the interviews, there were sometimes difficulties in communication over apparently simple concepts. To Helen Kay, a question about a 'job' was relatively unproblematic; employment was something that was packaged in an advertisement (in the newspaper or Job Centre), giving details of wage, hours and other conditions. Yet this did not tally with some of our respondents' experiences. For them, paid opportunities were more likely to present themselves in the form of a knock on the door, and an offer of immediate – though sometimes very temporary – work. For instance:

Q: What made you decide to go back to work then, or look for a job then?

Mrs Ribble: Um ... you didn't look for a job.

Mr Ribble: Well, no, I didn't, did I. It just came to me.

Mrs Ribble: Yeah. Jim came up and said he had a big job on and he needed Steve to give him a hand [indistinct] ...

Mr Ribble: Yeah, no it was just ... it, work come available like, so I took it. But um ... if it ... well, if it come available earlier I would have took it, wouldn' I?

                                            (Mr and Mrs Ribble, 64)

Or again,

Q: How do you choose your job?

Mr Parrett: I don't choose my job.

Q: Don't you?

Mr Parrett: Just [indistinct] pretty versatile.

Q: Have you got a job a the moment?

Mr Parrett: Well, sort of. It is part-time, here and there, jumping around. When they want my services I just go in and do the odd day like. But, um, unemployed is my ... status at the moment. But, ah, I'm not a lot really. I've done a bit for my father, bit of roofing, always worked since I left school, did the odd job.

                                            (Mr Parrett, 18)

As we became aware of these issues, our aim was to include as much as possible of this material in our account of the research – to tell of these confusing, stressful and conflictive experiences, rather than presenting a tidied-up version in which they were all rationalised away or 'resolved'. In this way, we aimed to make our story convincing not by the bland and sanitised way in which such 'extraneous' material has been expunged, in favour of what is objective and relevant in terms of the dominant academic discourse, but by making it recognisable to fellow researchers, and particularly to those who grapple with everyday issues of gender and class. Above all, we wanted to relate our story, and our interviewees' accounts, to the new and occasionally subversive traditions which are emerging in modern sociology, which allow previously excluded groups' voices to be heard in academic and official circles, raising uncomfortable questions about the processes of rule.

Of course, this did not make for an easy relationship with our academic colleagues in the University, as we discovered when we started to give seminars about our work. One of the most disconcerting aspects of this process seemed to be the differences *and* similarities between the estate and the University's academic environment. On the one hand, merely to visit the estate is an uncomfortable reminder of the gap in living standards between those with secure employment and those on the margins of the labour market. (Helen Kay found this transition particularly uncomfortable in entering households like the Darts'.) Yet of course some domestic staff, and some postgraduate students with families, do live on the estate. Like Exeter itself, the University's pleasant environment masks poverty and inequality, and puts on a leafy cloak of monocultural pleasantness.

Critical – sometimes hostile – comments from colleagues reflected back into the team, and fed our disputes and discomforts over the interpretation of the data. Some passages are, indeed, extremely cryptic and ambiguous – often intentionally. Ms Otter and her friend Ms Clyst, both single parents, are talking about a period when Ms Otter worked at a bus station in a town in Hampshire: her partner, Mr Thames, intervenes.

Ms Otter:	But that was working as a ... kitchen assistant for the bus service ... I used to cook the meals there ... breakfast or ... tea or ... evening meals ... mainly ... It was ah ... they wanted a ...
Mr Thames:	Think they're very short of bus drivers.
Ms Otter:	They didn't have that ... I can assure you. [laughs] No they ...
Mr Thames:	[indistinct] ... good filling meals.

(Ms Otter, 20)

Helen Kay felt that this was a sexual innuendo by Mr Thames, and these were present in a number of the interviews. They were intentionally exclusive of her, or aimed at making her feel uncomfortable, and were therefore a significant part of what was being communicated by interviewees – either about the respondents' joint attitude to her as an outsider, or about potentially important sexual motives in employment decisions.[26]

(It is still difficult, in trying to reconstruct our team discussions, to decipher whether disagreements arose from our different roles in the research, from our different theoretical training, or from the inevitable tensions of trying to produce a joint piece of work. The most difficult part of the book to write has been this section on our disagreements – laboriously negotiated from a series of drafts by each of the team members, and a number of long discussions, which have included arguments about whether it should be included at all.)

Meanwhile, Helen Kay was trying to devise a method of coding and analysis of the interviews. Initially Spradley's method of coding and developing cultural domains was tried: it helped us re-assess the data but it did not seem a good 'fit'. For example, the outcome of one event might become the cause of another event for one household, but the same outcome might have no apparent consequences for another household. Hence comparisons were difficult, and we were confused whether we were trying to understand different processes or different ways of telling stories. Above all, we struggled with trying to analyse a sequence of decisions from an account given at one particular point in time.

Helen Kay drew images of the interview transcripts, highlighting the apparent decision trees. She stuck them up on the walls round her room. They did draw attention to some areas and lead to some useful team discussions, but our data seemed too complex to be susceptible to such methods – we too easily fell into linking statements without checking back to the transcript or tape to confirm the interviewee's meaning, but then later disagreed with each other about these interpretations.

She returned to pen, cards and a card-index system of coding, reading and rereading to note the significant concepts in the interviews, and finding new ones with each process. A large set of indexed cards was produced ready for reference in further analysis, and passages of transcript dealing with specific topics (housing, tax, benefits, self-employment, budgeting) were collected together for comparison between households.

THE FINAL STAGE OF ANALYSIS

At this point, Helen Kay's contract ended, and she moved on to a job in Scotland. Marcus Redley, a sociologist with a background in qualitative methods, was appointed to the project on higher-income households, which involved making comparison with the low-income group. When the stage at which the process of analysis in the low-income project stood was explained, he expressed a preference for working through all the interviews again, using a fresh pair of eyes to review the data without discarding all the work that had already been completed. So the final stage of the analysis was done by a new team comprised of Simon James, Bill Jordan and Marcus Redley, trying to make as coherent as possible an explanatory theory which took account of all the difficulties raised so far; drafts of our work were then sent to Helen Kay, who sent back her comments, and attended a final two-day discussion.

Our methodological problem at this stage can best be summarised as follows: how could we best interpret these interviews, bearing in mind our avowed aim to take seriously the respondents' accounts of their lived experience, but also give due attention to relevant theoretical issues? Marcus Redley looked on the interviews as poor people accounting to a sociologist for their employment decisions, in the context of their family membership – they knew that their partners were to be interviewed, and that the research plan included a joint interview. As Wright Mills argued, 'motive talk' should not be treated as referring to a state of the speaker's mind, but as doing work for the speaker in a particular context.[27] This line of thinking has been developed in relation to all descriptive activity, in the work of Cicourel on survey research,[28] Gilbert and Mulkay on scientific discourse,[29] and Gubrium and Lynott on 'family'.[30] Description is thus to be seen as a social practice, in which the object world is constructed in this particular interactive context.

Unlike a natural scientist, justifying experimental results, a lay person giving a version of his or her life is aware that the criteria applicable to this account are public and moral, not exclusive and expert ones. Interviewees construct themselves as people who reveal their identities as moral beings – their biases, commitments and omissions – making themselves susceptible to judgements. Hence, according to Cuff, they routinely 'produce and manage' their descriptions to make them as morally adequate as possible, displaying their accounts as proper and reliable, and themselves as competent and appropriately impartial.[31]

Accounts are thus intelligible within, and framed in terms of, roles and norms which are treated as part of a shared public understanding of the social world. But clearly we were not doing the kind of survey which seeks 'true' descriptions of the world by trying to control the potentially 'distorting' social nature of descriptive activity – for instance by asking carefully standardised closed questions that minimised the possibility of different interpretations.[32] As we have already seen (p. 15) respondents interpreted the same words quite differently: Mrs Ribble saw her role in the household as a 'paid' job, whereas Mrs Hodder, who did some part-time work in the early mornings when her children were younger, did not see her paid role as a 'real' job: 'it was just a little bit of pocket money like, really'. Some male interviewees described 'jobs' quite differently from the sense originally intended by the interviewer (p. 71). Far from seeing this as an obstacle to 'objective' (and therefore valid) research, we regarded this phenomenon of different interpretations within a shared, public discourse as what we were trying to understand.

Our method was interactionist[33] in the sense that we had gained access to our respondents' view of the world and the meaning they gave to their experiences; and in that we recognised our interviews as particular interactional encounters between researcher and respondent which generated descriptions specific to that context. Mrs Torridge shows in her interview that she is well aware of this.

'What made you actually, what, decide ... to ... interview people [indistinct]? Why did you, you know, the people who are with you decide to actually interview people about things like this?'

(Mrs Torridge, 24)

And Mr Nene asks

'Where's it all going eventually then?'

(Mr Nene, 14)

Interviewees were therefore constructing their accounts selectively and for a specific purpose, and sometimes contradicted themselves or each other. Should we be trying to distinguish the rhetorical from the factual – for instance, by using observations by the researcher, or trying to check information about their wage rates? And could the joint interview of each couple be seen as an opportunity to compare accounts and allow us to reach a reliable judgement about which parts of their stories were 'true'? Sociologists such as Denzin[34] have tried to resolve the problems of subjectivity and bias in interview data by such 'data triangulation'; assuming that consistencies and similarities between these sources are of greater value than discrepancies, and that the researcher can finally reach a single objective version of reality by this method. However, from the start we had rejected this option, recognising the inevitability of differences between accounts, and valuing inconsistencies and contradictions as sources of understanding. The joint interviews were therefore both conducted and interpreted as ways of investigating and clarifying different versions of decision-making, not eliminating bias or seeking one 'true' version of events.

What we needed to make explicit at this stage was our position in relation to the ethnomethodological critique of 'positivism' in social research.[35] Ethnomethodologists insist that for any one description of an object or event it is possible to construct an alternative description: hence description is never complete and further clarification can always be demanded. In ethnomethodology the relationship between description and what it claims to describe is said to be reflexive: the object is not independent of its description. Researchers, like lay people, are offered no way out of the 'accounting circle', in which they can endlessly be required to reconstruct their versions of their data. The best that they (and thus we) might do is to produce an 'acceptable' account for the specific context (a conference or a book).

Ethnomethodologists therefore focus on the methods by which social actors (including researchers) handle these very issues – how they use descriptions to make their worlds manageable and intelligible. They look at how the social order is constructed, rather than trying to look 'through' these constructions in an attempt to discover a 'reality' beyond. The taken-for-granted knowledge of lay people and professionals in situations like interviews (for a job,[36] or in a clinic) is a topic for investigation; there can be no specially privileged method (not even ethnomethodology itself) which escapes the requirement to perform its own specific contextual negotiation of its account of the world.[37]

But this approach would not go far towards answering our original research questions, or prove very satisfactory for our funding body. It would tend to drive us back into an analysis of how interviewer and respondent 'do' research interviews, by focusing, for instance, on the sequencing of questions and answers. Just as 'positivist' methods are unsatisfactory because they seek an external perspective at the expense of what is internal to accounts, so ethnomethodological ones are unsatisfactory because their target is the internal features of constructing an account.

Mrs Nene was asked about the consequences of her husband's preferences for badly paid work as a motor-cycle mechanic.

> 'Well that's why I had to go back to work because the motorbikes don't pay ... So I went back to work and that ... sorted that out [...] It just seemed natural that, you know ...'
>
> (Mrs Nene, 36)

Here she is saying something about the household division of labour, men and women in the labour market, and what is 'natural' for women (their taken-for-granted roles). What she means is as important as how she produces this meaning.

What we needed was a method that could handle both the 'internal' and 'external' features of descriptions. It was easy to see that our interviewees' accounts were producing and reproducing the social context in which they occurred: but these accounts were themselves a product of the context in which they arose. We found a way of analysing both these elements in our data in the 'realist' method,[38] which understands interview accounts as organised by the artful practices of the respondent in that specific context, but simultaneously displaying cultural norms and roles.

This helps to bridge the otherwise alarming gulf between the 'externalist' understanding of accounts as reports on external realities, and the 'internalist' understanding of the same data as conversational practices through which interviewer and interviewee do various talking activities. Concepts such as 'man' and 'husband', or 'woman' and 'wife' in our respondents' accounts are *both* linguistic devices to indicate membership categories, *and* appeals to cultural roles and norms which display the structure of social relations on the estate, and the speaker's skills and judgement in deploying public standards to justify his or her actions.

Our interviewees show evidence of awareness that they are judged according to the accounts they give of the world, and they speak accordingly; they produce and manage their descriptions with a view to achieving moral adequacy.[39] This is not the same as objectivity. It is a description that is defensible, in the sense that it takes account of other possible points of view and recognises that the speaker is implicated in the situation described. Mr Tamar acknowledges that his attitude may be different from other men's when he talks about what he thinks a man should and should not do in relation to his own and his wife's employment (he himself has an unpleasant, insecure job, and was recently off sick with a heart complaint). He continues:

'No. No. No my place is out to earn a decent wage for my f, my wife and family ... and the home [pause] ... Like I said if I could earn the money and the wife could save her money then ... we'd be living in clover, you know ... and we, we wouldn' have, wouldn' have no worries if one of us was ill or anything like that [...] Umm, the only fear I've got is if, like I said, if the hospital turn round and says I've gotta give up work or ... touch wood I ... that that don't happen for a while yet.'

(Mr and Mrs Tamar, 44)

Hence these accounts of labour-market decision-making are to be seen as individual and unique to the speaker, but as occurring within a wider system of social relations of which the speaker and researcher are members, and displaying the cultural features of the speaker's membership group (family, community) and his or her knowledge of how to operate within that system.

The interviewee speaks as a member of the relevant social unit, with acknowledged responsibilities and commitments to other members, and thus as morally implicated in any 'troubles' that unit may experience, and open to blame or criticism for what happens. In particular (and especially when other members of the unit are to be interviewed), the speaker is aware that other descriptions of the same events (decisions) may be given, though there are a limited number of properly authorised alternative versions (i.e., accounts by other members, which Cuff calls 'determinate alternative possible accounts').

However, unlike Cuff, we would see the criteria for achieving moral adequacy as context-dependent – for example, Mr Tamar might give a different version if he was speaking to a group of his friends in the pub, or even to a male interviewer. But in any of these situations, Mr Tamar would be displaying what Silverman calls 'cultural particulars' – the external norms and roles which are culturally available to him, and the artful use of rhetorical devices for interpreting these in a particular context.[40]

In relating a particular utterance like Mr Tamar's to the wider social relations of the estate, the realist method allows us to address the theoretical issues discussed in the first chapter. The hypotheses we develop from the data can account for Mr Tamar's particular interpretation of how a sick man in his late 40s should behave, and this particular rhetorical justification of his possible future exit from his present job. We do this by showing how all the men construct their accounts in terms of a role of 'breadwinner' – provider of family income and worker – and legitimate their actions (including unemployment) in these terms. We also show that, as an irregular worker, Mr Tamar constructs benefits (in his case sickness benefit) as part of the income he provides. Finally, we demonstrate that all the households in the study but one (Mr and Mrs Kennet) have a strategy about expenditure, not employment; the idea of one partner 'earning the money' and the other 'saving her money' refers to different items of family expenditure (basic and 'extras' such as holidays). Mr Tamar is rhetorically acknowledging that their pattern (she has a regular job, he an irregular one) is an unusual way of meeting their expenditure needs, and justifying it in terms of his health.

Our analysis therefore allows us to link together the specifics of our interview data (our respondents' versions, their use of cultural particulars) with the economic and social structure of the estate. It allows us to see how their economic reasoning about their decisions relates to their moral and social reasoning, and how these in turn relate to changing patterns of employment, wage rates, benefits rules and income tax regulations.

This understanding of interview data is in line with the recent analysis by Janet Finch of qualitative research evidence on family obligations to adult kin in modern Britain.[41] Using the studies by Firth, Hubert and Forge[42] and Lewis and Meredith,[43] she argues that moral standards are treated as 'normative guidelines' by interviewees; intrinsically problematic family situations require judgement, interpretation and sometimes negotiation, and family members justify decisions in terms of the context and the current needs of others. Thus their accounts convey cultural norms about the criteria used to assess what kind of assistance is owed, to whom, for how long, etc., but also give speakers room for moral manoeuvre, within a system of public understandings of what is 'the right thing to do', sustained by conversations and disputes, among unit members and others, giving rise to reputation, honour or shame.

Realism assumes that there is a world that is independent of the descriptive practices that members use to describe it, but that it is not a world composed of objects (called 'decisions' or 'families'), but one composed of social relations.[44] Roles and norms are real in the sense that they are largely independent of the individual speaker, but they reconstructed and modified through individual speech acts.[45] Society can be seen as an ensemble of structures, practices and conventions which individuals reproduce or transform and which would not exist unless they did so: it is neither independent of current human activity, nor entirely the product of it. The task of the researcher is one of reconstructing social relations from their articulation within individual accounts.

Our method of analysis, therefore, focuses on the 'cultural particulars' of the interviewees' accounts – the factual, objective structures of their cultural world that they reveal in their versions of decision-making, and the contingent, particular legitimations they provide within these structures. To provide an explanation of decisions involves an appeal to commonsense knowledge of social relations which is shared by interviewer and interviewee, through membership of the same society; but the analysis displays moral and cultural forms specific to the membership groups (social units) to which interviewees belong. The data therefore provide access to the moral reality of life in poor households – how poor people account for their misfortune or good fortune in the world of employment. Social structures are reflected in and expressed through the speech of the interviewees – in this sense the data reproduce the social relations of the estate.

CONCLUSIONS

In this chapter we have somewhat painstakingly reconstructed the process by which we chose our field of study, planned and carried out our interviews, and interpreted our data. We have been as concerned to identify the limitations as the scope of our research. We do not claim that this was the best or only way to study labour-market decisions in low-income households, or the impact of the unemployment and poverty traps. Nor do we claim our findings to be generalisable to other areas, or even to other council estates with high rates of social deprivation, or to poor people dispersed over a wider area.

We have argued that quantitative survey methods and qualitative case studies have different and largely complementary parts to play in the analysis of social phenomena. Our study was inspired by theoretical puzzles and disputes, and chosen to target a small area which enabled a particular theoretical focus. It aims to make universal statements about particular phenomena, specifying the necessary conditions for these phenomena to occur within theoretically significant elements.

In our study, the starting point is a small community with high rates of unemployment and welfare benefit claims among families with children. Our hypothetical explanation of the labour-market decisions in the households we studied is derived from an analysis of the respondents' accounts in which their roles and norms are reconstructed in such a way as to provide an understanding of social relations on the estate, and hence of the structure and practices in which decisions are made. This analysis is then refined and tested by subjecting it to repeated testing against the accounts themselves, yielding a more precise reformulation of the original hypothesis.

Each chapter follows this same method: Chapter 4 with the men's accounts, Chapter 5 with the women's and Chapter 6 with the joint interviews. In the conclusion we return to the theoretical disputes rehearsed in the first chapter, and try to identify the relevance of our study to the major social science disciplines, and the ways in which our hypotheses might be tested out in future research.

In each chapter we look at the way in which our respondents construct their decisions in terms of the multiple elements of their roles as men and women, and how this involves them in the use of economic and moral reasoning. Their rhetorical practices display the skills of reconciling economic and moral aspects of these roles, but also reconstruct and reflect the social relations of their culture. We address the issue of the individual's commitment to these roles, and the relationship between the autonomy claimed by the speaker, and the power structures implicit in the roles. In the final chapter we return to the question of how the roles themselves can be understood in terms of economic and social theory.

REFERENCES

1 See for example Richard Berthoud, *The Examination of Social Society*, Policy Studies Institute, 1985; David Collard, 'Social Security and Work After Fowler', *Political Quarterly*, Vol. 56, No. 4, 1985; Hermione Parker,

'Fowler's Ladle', *Basic Income Research Group Bulletin*, Autumn 1985, pp. 1–2.; A. Dilnot and G. Stark, 'The Poverty Trap, Tax Cuts and the Reform of Social Security', *Fiscal Studies*, Vol. 7, No. 1, 1986, pp. 1–10.

2 For studies which focus on decisions by claimants see Eithne McLaughlin, Jane Millar and Kenneth Cooke, *Work and Welfare Benefits*, Gower, 1989; and Jonathan Bradshaw and Hilary Holmes, *Living on the Edge: A Study of the Living Standards of Families on Benefit in Tyne and Wear*, Tyneside CPAG, 1989.

3 B. Jarman, 'Underprivileged Areas: Validation and Distribution of Scores', *British Medical Journal*, Vol. 289, 1984, pp. 17705–9. See also Bob Deacon, *Poverty and Deprivation in the South West: A Preliminary Survey*, CPAG, 1987.

4 J. P. Spradley, *Participant Observation*, Holt, Rinehart & Winston, 1980.

5 S. Jones, 'The Analysis of In-Depth Interviews', in R. Walker (ed.) *Applied Qualitative Research*, Gower, 1985.

6 For a fuller account, see Simon James, Bill Jordan and Helen Kay, 'Poor People, Council Housing and the Right to Buy', *Journal of Social Policy*, Vol. 20, No. 1, 1991, pp. 27–40.

7 Helen Kay, 'Can Respondents Give Informed Consent in Qualitative Research?', Paper given to Social Research Association Conference on Ethics, Policy Studies Institute, London, 10 October 1989. See also J. A. Barnes, *Who Should Know What? Social Science, Privacy and Ethics*, Cambridge University Press, 1979; H. K. Beecher, 'Some Fallacies and Errors in the Application of the Principle of Consent in Human Experimentation', *Clinical Pharmacology and Therapeutics*, 1962, Vol. 3, pp. 141–5; J. Finch, '"It's Great to Have Someone to Talk to": The Ethics and Politics of Interviewing Women', in C. Bell and H. Roberts, *Social Researching: Politics, Problems and Practice*, Routledge & Kegan Paul, 1984.

8 See for example A. Bryman, *Quantity and Quality in Social Research*, Unwin Hyman, 1988; David Silverman, 'Telling Convincing Stories: A Plea for Cautious Positivism in Case-Studies', in Barry Glassner and Jonathan D. Moreno (eds), *The Qualitative–Quantitative Distinction in the Social Sciences*, Kluwer, 1989, pp. 57–77; Julia Brannen, 'Dual-Earner Households in Early Parenthood: Some Methodological Considerations in the Interpretation of Data', Paper for the British Sociological Association Conference, Surrey University, 2–5 April, 1990.

9 J. C. Mitchell, 'Case and Situational Analysis', *Sociological Review*, Vol. 31, No. 2, 1983, pp. 187–211.

10 A. V. Cicourel, *Method and Measurement in Sociology*, Free Press, 1964.

11 N. Denzin, *The Research Act in Sociology*, Butterworth, 1970.

12 E. Goffman, *Asylums*, Penguin, 1968.

13 David Silverman, *Qualitative Methodology and Sociology*, Gower, 1985; Silverman, 'Telling Convincing Stories'.

14 Mitchell, 'Case and Situational Analysis'.

15 R. Dingwall, 'The Ethnomethodological Movement', in G. Payne, R. Dingwall, J. Payne and M. Carter (eds), *Sociology and Social Research*, Croom Helm, 1981.

16 H. Garfinkel and H. Sacks, 'On Formal Structures of Practical Actions', in J. C. McKinney and E. A. Tinyakin (eds), *Theoretical Sociology: Perspectives and Development*, Century-Crofts, 1967.

17 H. Sacks, 'On the Analysability of Children's Stories', in R. Turner (ed.), *Ethnomethodology*, Penguin, 1974.

18 Helen Kay, 'Research Note: Constructing the Epistemological Gap: Gender Divisions in Social Research', *Sociological Review*, Vol. 38, No. 2, 1990, pp. 344–51.

19 Magda Lewis and Roger Simon, 'A Discourse Not Intended for Her: Learning and Teaching within Patriarchy', *Harvard Educational Review*, Vol. 56, No. 4, 1986.

20 Philip Corrigan, 'In/Forming Schooling', in D. Livingston (ed.), *Critical Pedagogy and Cultural Power*, Bergin and Garvey, 1987; Chris Weedon, *Feminist Practice and Poststructuralist Theory*, Blackwell, 1987.

21 Philip Corrigan and Derek Sayer, *The Great Arch: English State Formation and Cultural Revolution*, Blackwell, 1985; Philip Corrigan, 'On Moral Regulation: Some Preliminary Remarks', *Sociological Review*, Vol. 29, No. 2, 1981; Michel Foucault, 'The Subject and Power', *Critical Inquiry*, Vol. 8, 1982; Derek Sayer, *The Violence of Abstraction*, Blackwell, 1987.

22 Elizabeth Ellsworth, 'Why Doesn't this Feel Empowering?: Working Through the Repressive Myths of Critical Pedagogy', *Harvard Educational Review*, Vol. 59, No. 3, 1989, p. 301.

23 Dorothy Smith, *The Everyday World as Problematic, A Feminist Sociology*, Open University Press, 1988, pp. 17–18.

24 ibid., p. 19.

25 Caroline Ramazanoglu, 'Improving Sociology: The Problems of Taking a Feminist Standpoint', *Sociology*, Vol. 23, No. 3, 1989, pp. 427–42; Caroline Ramazanoglu, *Feminism and the Contradictions of Oppression*, Routledge, 1989; Valerie Walkerdine and Helen Lucey, *The Politics of the Kitchen*, Virago, 1989.

26 Ramazanoglu, 'Improving Sociology'; Ramazanoglu, *Feminism and the Contradictions of Oppression*; Smith, *The Everyday World as Problematic*.

27 C. Wright Mills, 'Situated Actions and Vocabularies of Motive', *American Sociological Review*, Vol. 5, No. 4, 1940, pp. 904–13.

28 A. V. Cicourel, *Cognitive Sociology*, Penguin, 1973.

29 G. N. Gilbert and M. Mulkay, 'In Search of the Action', in P. Abell and N. Gilbert (eds), *Accounts and Action*, Gower, 1983.

30 J. Gubrium and R. Lynott, 'Family Rhetoric as Social Order', *Journal of Family Issues*, Vol. 6, No. 1, 1985, pp. 129–52.

31 E. C. Cuff, 'Some Issues in Studying the Problem of Versions in Everyday Situations', Department of Sociology, Manchester University, Occasional Paper No. 3, 1980, pp. 34–5. See also G. Baruch, 'Moral Tales: Parents' Stories of Encounters with Health Professionals', *Sociology of Health and Illness*, Vol. 3, No. 3, 1981, pp. 275–96.

32 See for instance C. Selltiz, *Research Methods and Social Relations*, Holt, Rinehart & Wilson, 1964, for the search for methods which eliminate bias and subjectivity and hence eliminate the social nature of descriptive activity in research, in order to provide an accurate version of a 'reality' beyond the interview.

33 In this sense we reject the idea of a fixed and stable reality available to the sociologist via the rigorous application of methods such as Selltiz's.

34 N. Denzin, *The Research Act in Sociology*, Butterworth, 1970.

35 See for instance H. Garfinkel, *Studies in Ethnomethodology*, Prentice Hall, 1967; R. Turner (ed.), *Ethnomethodology*, Penguin, 1974.
36 D. Silverman, 'Interview Talk: Bringing off a Research Instrument', *Sociology*, Vol. 7, No. 1, 1973, pp. 32–48.
37 Cicourel, *Method and Measurement in Sociology*. In ethnomethodological research studies, the sociologist either reflects on his or her own methods, or writes as a Kuhnian scientist undertaking research as a group activity with a community standard of validity.
38 Silverman, *Qualitative Methodology and Sociology*.
39 Cuff, 'Some Issues in Studying the Problem of Versions in Everyday Situations'. Cuff uses the example of wives' accounts of marital break-up, collected by a student sociologist. In his paper, the 'determinate alternative accounts' are those of the husbands.
40 Silverman, *Qualitative Methodology*.
41 Janet Finch, *Family Obligations and Social Change*, Polity, 1989, Ch. 6.
42 R. Firth, J. Hubert and A. Forge, *Families and their Relatives*, Routledge & Kegan Paul, 1970.
43 J. Lewis and B. Meredith, *Daughters Who Care*, Routledge, 1988.
44 See for example M. Voysey, *A Constant Burden*, Routledge & Kegan Paul, 1975, and Baruch, 'Moral Tales: Parents' Stories of Encounters with Health Professionals'. Voysey interviewed parents of disabled children: they presented their experiences as those of a 'normal family', despite the severe disruption of having a disabled child. This enabled them to pass as competent members of society. The public conception of family life was so constraining that to fail to conform to these norms might involve public sanction. The parents' accounts therefore use artful practices which display 'normal family life' (its norms and roles). Baruch's interview data were from parents of sick children making their first visit to a specialist clinic; he called their accounts 'atrocity stories'. They described doctors using technical jargon, asking probing questions and having no regard for parents' emotional state or child-care skills, but being themselves calm and rational. They showed themselves as morally competent by indicating their awareness of the doctors' professional norms, while describing their own distress and pain, thus indicating familiarity with medical practice.
45 Silverman, *Qualitative Methodology*, p. 176: See also R. L. Bhaskar, *A Realist Theory of Science*, Leeds Press, 1975

4 The 'breadwinners'

In this chapter, we look at the male interviewees' accounts of their employment decisions – how they describe these decisions and justify them to the interviewer. We trace the features of their roles as men that are common to all these accounts, and look for what differentiates them. In the end, we show that the only important differentiating feature is whether or not the man had a regular, full-time job. There are only twelve such interviewees; the rest are all 'irregular' workers, recently employed, self-employed or unemployed.

We then investigate how the structure and administration of benefits is constructed as influencing their decisions, and show how this casts new light on the poverty and unemployment traps. These men do not describe themselves as responding directly to the incentives and disincentives of wages, taxes and benefits, or the interaction between them. Rather they give versions of decision-making within a normative framework of how men should work and provide for their families, and how the labour market and the tax and benefits systems shape and constrain their efforts to fulfil their roles.

The common feature of the interviewees' accounts of labour-market decisions is that they are constructed by appealing to expected roles of men and women (as husbands and wives), and the norms that are attached to these roles. This is at the core of their retrospective reconstructions of their choices; other considerations, such as the incentive and disincentive effects of wages, benefits and taxation, in whatever combinations, are framed in relation to these primary aspects. In their descriptions of themselves as social actors, men and women justify their decisions (for example, to take or leave specific employments, or become self-employed, or remain unemployed) in terms of the roles we referred to in our initial analysis as 'breadwinners' and 'caregivers' respectively. These were our terms, not theirs; indeed, so taken for granted are these roles in the social relations displayed by these accounts that these respondents simply use the words 'men' and 'women' to connote their characteristics.

Our choice of terms referred to the sociological literature on the household division of labour.[1] However, we do not wish to imply that in our study these roles were static or monolithic, still less that they were complementary. Rather, both contained a number of elements which the interviewees tried to balance, using both economic and moral rhetoric to legitimate their actions and to display their adequacy in fulfilling the multiple demands of their roles. Hence what was meant by 'a man' and 'a woman' was complex, flexible and dynamic, and the particulars of their role performances had to be negotiated between partners. We have already given the example of Mr and Mrs Tamar to illustrate this. Mr Tamar – an irregular worker who is often sick, and who does much of the housework – still constructs himself as a 'breadwinner', and Mrs Tamar – a regular full-time worker for many years – still constructs herself as a 'caregiver'. We have found no better word to replace 'breadwinner', so we indicate a warning about its interpretation by putting it in inverted commas in the title of this chapter.

In focusing on the explanatory power of these concepts, our analysis takes a different theoretical stance from those of other studies of poor people's decision-making, which treat such roles as unproblematic. For example, Bradshaw and Holmes, in their study of living standards of families on benefits, deal in expenditures by 'families', and treat the household income, from whatever source, as a single fund. One example is given in the section on expenditure on alcohol.

One family spent £15.67 on alcohol to be consumed at home and £4 a week at the pub – representing 25 per cent of their total weekly expenditure. All the spending on alcohol was by the man who bought between six and eight cans of beer a night to be drunk at home and had three or four pints in the pub twice a week. This family were living within their income but only spent £14.35 a week on food and did not have a freezer. When this family were first approached about the project the woman was doubtful whether her husband would participate because of the amount he spent on drink. He often left her with only £15.20 for food and debts, but she was adamant that although he could be difficult 'he doesn't knock us about' and in that respect he was better than his friends. In fact, he was very co-operative and pleasant. They both said that she made all the financial decisions in the family, but as he borrowed the money to buy drink each day from his mother, and she had to be paid back on a Saturday, the woman wasn't left with too many choices.... They both freely admitted to his ability to earn £20 a day as a builder or to repair washing machines at £18 profit each, some of this he declared. ... He said his wife was 'managing marvellously' with the family finances ...²

The tone of this insert in a text, the whole thrust of which is to convey the deprivation and exclusion endured by families on benefits, is one of slight embarrassment and primness, conveyed in phrases like 'in fact he was very pleasant' and 'they both freely admitted'. No attempt is made to explain the apparent 'anomalies' in this example, or its relationship with the rest of the data. In our study, by contrast, the aim is to develop an analysis which will show how just such data can be explained, in terms of the roles of 'man' and 'woman'.

In this chapter, we consider the men's accounts of their labour-market decisions. All but two of our male interviewees (Mr Rother and Mr Plym) had experienced a number of job changes, and had experienced periods of unemployment, and eleven were currently unemployed (see Table 3.1, p. 66). In their reconstructions of these experiences, they reveal the criteria they bring to bear on such choices, by mobilising various aspects of what we call the breadwinner role. The role contains the dual notion of work and providing income for their families; their success in it is achieved through ability to earn and provide, which requires 'good' labour-market decisions.

The dual aspect of this role – working and providing – contains a potential conflict of values and standards. Being a worker involves the development of certain work and social skills in a men's world of reputation and competition; it can also be instrinsically enjoyable or at least satisfying in retrospect. Being a provider involves delivering income to a family; a man's earnings are seen in terms of a 'family wage', even though actual rates of pay and conditions of employment do not easily correspond with the notion of an income sufficient to meet weekly household needs. Men's constructions of themselves as both workers and providers can be deployed in a number of ways: to legitimate the avoidance of certain kinds of available employment (as too badly paid); the practice of taking 'cash jobs' while claiming social security benefits; walking out of a job; or continuing with a monotonous, low-paid regular job.

The male interviewees account for the labour-market decisions in terms of an economy of which they claim some knowledge. Sometimes this is couched in terms of global or national economic forces, at other times it is a more detailed description of local employment conditions, but in every case this knowledge (or recognised lack of knowledge) is of crucial importance in the legitimation of a decision. Without reference to the social and economic context, the decision would be indistinguishable from a pot-luck gamble; yet interviewees describe themselves as making choices which are legitimated by reference to one part of the breadwinner role (either worker or provider) in an attempt to achieve 'moral adequacy'.[3] The success or failure of their decisions is then constructed in terms of knowledge available through subsequent events.

In other words, the men see themselves as active in the making of their fortunes or misfortunes in employment, though within very strong constraints. For example, most of them had experienced being sacked or made redundant; they reconstruct such events in some detail, showing the forces (economic or arbitrary personal injustice) at work against them. These factors allow men to mitigate their moral responsibility for 'bad' decisions, which lead to periods when they are out of work, or the family gets into debt. The detailed accounts of sackings as arbitrary or unjust, and redundancies as the consequences of impersonal economic forces, therefore serve an important function in their representation of themselves as morally adequate breadwinners, sustaining the standards expected of that role.[4]

This contradicts Millar, Cooke and McLaughlin's analysis of poor people's decisions in terms of an 'employment lottery'.[5] The economic environment in which these men were making their decisions was indeed risky and uncertain, and the benefits system tended to reinforce rather than offset these features, as they point out, and as these interviewees elaborated in detail. However, even though to outside observers this gave decisions an element of gambling, the men themselves did not characterise them in these terms. Instead, they insisted that it was part of their role, as men, to make decisions based on the knowledge available to them, taking account of these constraints and uncertainties. To call the arena of these choices a lottery would – in their eyes – discredit the skills and responsibilities that they are displaying as breadwinners.

This chapter sets out our analysis of men's accounts of their decisions in terms of this role, and shows how tax and benefit considerations were brought into play in their descriptions of how they made their decisions. These factors were important at certain points in the accounts, particularly where men in very irregular employment, or who were unemployed, explained their reasons for doing cash work while claiming, or refusing to take low-paid work (benefits system factors); and where men who were not receiving means-tested benefits and were paying income tax contrasted their situation with others who qualified for family credit (tax and benefits factors). The advantage of our method here is that it allows these elements to be understood in the context of the wider structure of social relations that is displayed in the accounts, and enables decisions by unemployed claimants to be explained in terms of a theory that also applies to the decision-making of employed men.

It is important to emphasise at this point that the analysis of the men's accounts is at this stage treated separately from the analysis of the joint accounts, to be set out in Chapter 6. Men defined themselves as workers and providers, and justified their decisions in such a way as to present themselves as living up to the moral requirements of that role. Both men and women appealed to commonsense understandings of these roles and the norms attaching to them in their separate accounts, deploying them in ways which implied that they were not essentially contestable concepts. Yet in the joint interviews it was clear that the interpretation of the two roles, and how they meshed together, was indeed contentious, and could lead to conflict – though this was often played down, or treated with humour. For example, Mr and Mrs Ribble are talking about a time when they were living with her sister and brother-in-law and their two children. Mrs Ribble was pregnant and Mr Ribble was unemployed; he talks about the possibility of her taking employment.

Mrs Ribble:	[indistinct] I was pregnant.
Mr Ribble:	... but now ... I wouldn't have it anyway if ... if um ... the chance come up, I was on the dole and Sheila had the chance of getting a job I wouldn' let her do it.
Q:	Wouldn't you?
Mr Ribble:	No. I could go ah ... I couldn't be kept like. [laughs] I couldn't be kept by her, you know. I um ...
Q:	Is that what it would have felt like?
Mr Ribble:	Yeah. I would ... Yeah it would have. To me, 'cause I wouldn' have it. No way.

They go on immediately to recall what happened when she suggested taking a job.

Mrs Ribble:	We did have a row about that once, didn' we?
Mr Ribble:	Yeah, yeah, that's it.
Mrs Ribble:	We had a row about that once. Gotta think about our rows 'cause we very rarely row. [laughs] Yeah. When we do we go, don't us boy? [laughs]
Mr Ribble:	Yeah, they do, don't they?

They then reconstruct the argument:

| Mrs Ribble: | Yeah. I said that I should [take a job]. And he was saying, no you, you shouldn't, you know. We just ... And the fact that he was saying that, you know, 'What happens if you take the job and you, say, fall down the stairs or something?' you know. I thought, fair enough, I mean he was more worried about me and the baby, more than how |

much money we were gonna have at the end of the week ...

Mr Ribble: No, it wa'n' that at all. I, I just didn' wanna take, I wouldn' have um ...

Mrs Ribble: Yeah, it's not ... I mean, come off it, you were concerned about ...

Mr Ribble: Ah ... Um ... How to ...? I would have felt inadequate by not bringing in the money ... I was ... just about ...

Mrs Ribble: [indistinct] so stupid.

Mr Ribble: Yeah, well ... it's ah ... to me the ah ... if you're living together the man should bring in the money. I mean, fair enough, if you've nothing else like um ... if you're pregnant and you're already working when you meet, then obviously carry on. But um ... otherwise ... a man should be the money bringer, you know.

(Mr and Mrs Ribble, 39–40)

This is about the nearest any of our respondents came to a discussion of the roles which are implicit in all their accounts, and it reveals much that is fundamental but hidden in all of them. Mr Ribble strongly disclaims the idea, put forward by his wife, that his opposition to her taking employment was to do with concern for her and the baby: it was to do with his performance of his role as 'money bringer'. Later he defines more precisely the circumstances in which her employment would not violate his sense of moral adequacy as a man (when the youngest child is at school, during school hours) and the purposes for which her earnings can legitimately be used (for holidays, but not for housekeeping). Any other circumstances in which she took paid work would be an affront to his regard for himself as a man.

In what follows, we set out our analysis of men's decision-making by showing how their knowledge of constraints in the labour market is mobilised to construct a set of criteria (normative guidelines) consistent with the breadwinner role, and hence a range of employments from which choices are made. We then show how the outcomes of particular decisions are reconstructed, allowing knowledge to be modified and decisions reviewed. Hence what emerges is a 'provisional legitimation' of their current situations, and a qualified justification of past decisions in terms of their role; but change – chosen or unchosen – is always a possibility because of the structure of their sector of the labour market. Benefit and tax considerations play an important part in the construction of the options which are available within normative guidelines, and those which are ruled out by the interviewee but attributed to 'others', who are less scrupulous in fulfilling their roles.

Our analysis is required to explain the wide range of circumstances in which these men found themselves at the time of the interviews, from long-term unemployed to relatively securely employed, or fairly success-fully self-employed. However, we will show that grouping these men according to their current employment status is largely arbitrary and un-enlightening; the largest single group had recently started a new employ-ment, after experiencing many of the situations described by men in the unemployed and self-employed groups. Hence our analysis is primarily concerned with explaining moves between employments and statuses, and the theory we develop must then go on to explain why a minority of men come to be either long-term employed or long-term unemployed.

THE LABOUR MARKET

The men's accounts – sometimes quite lengthy and detailed – are historical: they tell a story about how they reached their current employment situation. Many of them locate themselves in a broad context – the national or global economy – and explain their employment changes by reference to large-scale economic forces, government policy and the restructuring of the labour market in their sector. Hence they display their knowledge of the demand for labour, and how patterns of employment have changed during their working lives.

'Before that I was working on the buildings for 8 and a half years. Before that I was on the dole for 2 months. Then I was on a government scheme for 12 months – the money was rubbish, Maggie's fault.'
(Mr Bure, 14)

'Well everything, everything altered so dramatically [...] you know, her policies was so ... totally different from what we'd been, everybody'd been used to; your stamp suddenly shot up; your income tax suddenly went wallop up; and 'twas, 'twas sort of kicking the working man out, the little man, the private businessman ...'
(Mr Dovey, 20)

'Most of the firms now are just taking on self-employed labourers [...] saves on redundancy and all that sort of thing [...] That's what I've found with the building trade over the last ... well, 5 years. All self-employed now.'
(Mr Parrett, 19)

'Some little toe-rag started up [...] he undercut us [...] we were spending ... sometimes 3 hours a day travelling to work ... miles and miles and miles away because this little toe-rag had undercut everybody in Exeter anyway. Us couldn't get ... us couldn't get work in Exeter anyway.'

(Mr Humber, 26–7)

One of the older men, Mr Tamar (aged 45) provides a historical account which charts his changes from a regular job with the railways (a major employer in Exeter in the 1950s and 1960s) to his present casual employment, doing night-work on microelectronic components. The account weaves together a description of changes in the labour market, and in his own fortunes (he suffered a heart attack in 1985).

'I decided on the railway. And I enjoyed that. That was one of ... it was *the* best job I ever had. On the railway. And um ... was an engine cleaner at first but ... then I become a fireman. And I was one of the youngest drivers in the south west. I was 17 and a half when I started driving engines [indistinct] my best mate beat me by 3 months [...] That was a rewarding job as well [...] I started in the railway in 1961 ... no 1959, just after I left school [...] and ... I was still on there in 1970. Until they started making a lot of redundancies and ...'

(Mr Tamar, 10)

He explains that his wife (now ex-wife) didn't want to leave Exeter, so he was forced to take redundancy rather than accept the offer of a transfer.

After this he went into the building trade, as a roofer until he fell 45 feet off the roof of a castle. He survived, but decided to take a more secure job at a roadside restaurant – 'I could take that for one of me second best [jobs]'. He was promoted to a section leader after 6 months, and went on a 3-day training course for supervisors after 12 months. But he was willing to muck in alongside his workforce.

'I was a working supervisor; if people needed to be served with food or cook, cooking food, then I used to do it [...] I wouldn' stand back and see 'em struggle. Especially when you get 30 or 40 coaches in – in a night. And you get 3 young ladies and 3 young women on a hot counter ... serving food and cooking ... and the queue's from ... there, right outside; you've gotta help. You've just got to ...'

(Mr Tamar, 13)

However, although he enjoyed this, and especially the team spirit it promoted, he left there shortly after suffering his first heart attack.

Q: What made you leave [service station's name] then?

Mr Tamar: Oh, my ex-wife left me ... um ... after 25 years. And she left me with 2 ... well young boy of 15 and um ... [indistinct] ... I just couldn't leave him on his own – specially night-times. And then that happened – I had a heart attack, mild one – and I had to give it up anyway; they couldn't let me back.

(Mr Tamar, 3)

After this he worked for a heavy engineering company, collapsed at work, and fell into a machine. He developed angina and was home for 23 weeks, and was advised to give up this kind of work. He then became self-employed and worked with his nephew on building sites, doing renovations of shops and flats, until his nephew went abroad. After a brief spell of unemployment, he started in his present employment, working nights; in 7 months there he had had 4 months off with illness, and is expecting to be sacked very soon on account of this. The employer, a man of less than 30, saw him as a liability: 'I mean he, he just don't care. He can get plenty of blokes, local blokes ... who'll work for him so, ...' Mr Tamar emphasises the casual, unprotected nature of his employment:

'... it's ... a type of firm that ... they got no i, no pension scheme, no unions ... um ... they got no ... ways and means of looking after ... their workforce. If you go, well you go. If you stay, you stay. If you work, you work. Simple as that. They're not interested, all they're interested in is getting the work out ... each month [...] The ... turnover, workforce out there, is ... well ... you can turn the workforce over about 3 times a year ... I mean there's 40 odd [indistinct] who work on nights [...] Yeah, on, on one side there's 30 odd people and ... and I, in 16 weeks I've been home ... there's 11 people's left; 11 people's come, and out of that 11 people that started 3 months ago there's only 2 left and another 9 started [...] It's a boring, mundane job – night after night ...'

(Mr Tamar, 4–5)

In his whole account, Mr Tamar constructs an explanation of how he has come to be doing 'inconvenient', insecure night work, 'just ... filing down a piece of ... metal about 9 inches long', where he is expecting to be sacked any day. He attributes the loss of his two 'good' jobs to decisions by his ex-wife; his other reasonably well paid employments ended because of illness or accident; now he is consigned to casual work because of his health and his age:

'Because ... I find now, after the age of 35 you're ... on the scrap-heap. I'm 45. And that makes [indistinct] makes a lot of difference, you know. Most of the jobs I've been for is mainly between the ages of ... 18 and 35 ... you know, they're a bit more dubious on taking somebody older ... I don' know why; I think we're more responsible ...'

(Mr Tamar, 4)

Other older men (such as Mr Dovey) tell a story of employment being restructured, replacing permanent jobs with irregular, unprotected ones or self-employment, and mature, responsible workers by young, uncommitted ones.

CHANGE AND THE LIFE CYCLE

Intertwined with accounts of the impact of wider economic forces is a more personal one, in which job changes reflect preferences for a particular type of work, or working conditions, or simply the need for change. These preferences alter over time, with some employment seen as suitable for young people, but not for older men.

In the dual role of being a breadwinner, the requirements of the worker for a stimulating environment, with variety, challenge and appreciation of skills, are not always compatible with those of the family provider. These men established themselves as workers while still single, but describe a process of ageing and taking on family responsibilities altering their choices.

> 'At the time I did not want to work inside. I liked being out in all weather, the cold, the wind and rain. In the summer we had our shirts off, walking around in shorts, like but now where I work I breathe in all these fumes and it is very noisy – we have no protection and I do worry about the effect on me but ... I am getting old. I don't think I want to be out in all weather. There is no security on the buildings.'
>
> (Mr Bure, 16)

> 'Working in a night club [...] On the door. I liked it. It was just too much aggro [...] You had all day to yourself and night times you [...] only 4 nights a week and it was really good, so I liked that. I wouldn' do it again; I'm too old now, but [...] Well, it's a single man's job, ha, really. Not if you're married it i'n [...] Well I used to come home with cuts and bruises and everything and ... it's just not a ... married man's life really. I don't think so.'
>
> (Mr Torridge, 3)

Mr Ribble:	At the time, yeah, I was thinking of applying, working abroad [...] water irrigation and working in the oil rigs; anything involving travel [indistinct] I think. I just wanted to get away at that time. But ... that was that. Um ...
Q:	What put you off doing those?
Mr Ribble:	Um ... I think it was the girlfriend done that actually; I just settled down again, sort of thing. I wasn't, for a while

> I just wanted to get out of Exeter and ... ah .. just travel a
> bit I think. That was all. And then ... as I say, I met this
> girl and I did settle down, but I just ... it just calmed me
> down from when I'm doing that so ...
>
> (Mr Ribble, 20)

Like many of these men, Mr Ribble had one experience of working away
from Exeter; the cavity wall insulation company that was employing him
moved to Wimborne, Dorset.

> 'So um ... they asked me, they give me a job up in Wimborne if I wanted
> it, which I took for something like, I think it was about 4 or 5 months
> living away, travelling home weekends, and um ... just got too much in
> the end. So I gave up the job. And that's when I became unemployed for
> ... um 8 months.'
>
> (Mr Ribble, 21)

Mr Ouse's father worked for a signmaking firm in Exeter, and he himself
worked for three such firms briefly on leaving school; when one of them
went bankrupt he decided to try something quite different.

> 'I went farming for a little while [...] First of all it was ah ... a mixed
> farm, you know, they done everything, um ... cattle and ... crops and that.
> Then I went [...] I couldn't handle the times; I mean I was like 18; I mean
> I wanted to get out, out and about like at night. And ... farm like, it was
> sort of up at 7, or start work at 7, un, until about 9 o'clock at night when
> the sun went in like. I couldn't, I couldn't do that. So I went to um ... a
> relief agency for farms and they got me a job in Tring in Hertfordshire,
> I was there for about 9 months on a pig farm, working 8 till 5 ... um ... I
> got bit fed up of that. So ... that's when I come back to [signmaking
> firm's name].'
>
> (Mr Ouse, 22-3)

Ever since, Mr Ouse has remained in Exeter, in sign firms. Our analysis is
required to provide a theory of how some men (Mr Rother, Mr Taw and Mr
Avon) stay in their jobs for many years, as well as how most have had many
changes. For this, see pp. 109–14 and pp. 204–19.

RESPECT AS WORKERS

A prominent feature of the accounts is the description of rows with
employers or supervisors at work, often ending in dismissal or walking off
the job. These descriptions serve an important purpose in depicting the
interviewee as a worker but with attendant demands for respect, not pre-

pared to put up with an unfair degree of exploitation, or undignified and insulting treatment. Part of being a worker (a man) is to refuse to accept what a self-respecting worker should not accept. That the interviewee is such a man is displayed in sometimes very lengthy and detailed stories of how disrespect was not tolerated.

Mr Ouse makes a contrast between his present (good) employer, and his previous (bad) one.

'It's the way ... I mean ... it's the way he asks you, I mean he, he don't say ... he don't push you into it; he asks you straight and he's a very sort of straight bloke, the boss, and ah ... you can't really refuse, you know. I mean he's been, he's good to everybody, I mean ... it's hard to explain, it's just sort of, the right boss, you can't say no to; that's all there is to it like. Um ... he's, he's sorted out with um ... pension plan for all the work staff like um ... because some of 'em, like my father works there as well, ah ... some of them are too old for this pension plan ... he's made another one for them [...] In the old place you'd go to work, you used to see your boss first thing in the morning like, he'd just walk straight past you. This place, he'll come up and say: "How's you getting on, how was the weekend? All right?" and have a real good chat with you like.'

(Mr Ouse, 19)

He describes his previous job as 'the same thing, day in, day out', and that a laugh would make everyone look as if they'd 'never, never heard that noise before'; but the final straw was

'a month before I left ... he started putting buzzers in, bells for when ... like, they wanted you to clock in at 5 to 8, you got clocking in machines and you gotta sign your name and all this sort of stuff like. Clock in at 5 to 8, stand by your bench with your overalls on, for when the buzzer goes, then start work, keep working – no smoking – keep working at ... until the buzzer goes again; then you can stop, have a, have a cup of coffee, a cup of tea; wait till the buzzer goes, start again. This sort of stuff ... carries on and on all day like. Just couldn't ... I couldn't hack that, couldn't do it. So I just had to get out.'

(Mr Ouse, 21)

Mr Wye, unemployed for 3 years, describes the treatment that led to him leaving his last job.

Mr Wye: Um ... I didn't like the attitude of ... in the last job – which was the um head cook – his attitude was you did it and I want you to do it, in catering, you know, and he actually looked down to his staff and said, 'well I want it done'.

You know, you get certain instances where you have a porter there and he was asking me to clean their boot off, you know, he might have had flour on his boot or something like that [indistinct] lean on the table and saying, 'Jim'll do this'. I actually don't like that attitude, you know. That was it. [indistinct]

Q: What do they (employers) do that makes you feel like that?

Mr Wye: Well they just talk you down, you know, they ... they don't actually treat you with respect ... like you would with they [...] One night [...] I went out 'cause my brother had his ... boy, and we went out and had a drink ... and I didn't go in the following morning and when I went back he more or less accused me of skiving of which it wasn' the case; just had a hangover and I didn' fancy going in.

(Mr Wye, 1–2)

Mr Derwent used to be a managing supervisor in a factory.

Mr Derwent: ... I had a lot of hassle from ...
Q: Really?
Mr Derwent: Yeah. I ... I was dismissed – well unfairly dismissed, I took 'em to court [...]
Q: Really?
Mr Derwent: Yeah. I wouldn't want that kind of bloody thing. Too much ha, hassle for the money what they give you. The ah workers there are earning twice as much as what you earn. You're in charge and you get all the responsibility and you don' get the money come the end of it so ...

(Mr Derwent, 13–14)

He makes it clear that he was doing well in the job for years.

'And then a new managing director came and I don't think he liked my face. Soon as he got there he starting moaning [laughs] ... Yeah. It changed overnight. Everything I was doing was all right until he got there so ... different regime I s'pose.'

(Mr Derwent, 14)

Mr Cam has just started work as a roadsweeper driver. He reconstructs almost verbatim rows he had with employers and others that led to him leaving jobs he had when he was younger and 'a little bit hairbrained'.

'If I thought I was getting a rough deal I'd tell 'em and leave you know, I wouldn't sit down, I wouldn't [child interrupts] I wouldn't let people walk over me you know. If I got a rollicking I gave one back, you know. If something went wrong and it wasn't my fault then I would tell 'em. I wouldn't ... I'm not a guy to sit back and take a rollicking which is not my fault ...'

(Mr Cam, 21)

He represents himself as someone who is willing to take any work 'so long as the money's there', but as insisting on fair treatment; this explains the many changes of employment that have taken place right up to the present.

'Well, let's put it this way, it's better to have a job, you know. I don't care what it is, you know. That's what got me about the dole when I went and signed on. He says um: "you can't put this down here". I says, what's that mate, you know. 'Cause I couldn't see what he, he was pointing at, you know. "You can't put that down there." I says, what do you mean? He says "anything". 'Cause it said on the top "What job would you like to do?" you know. I said I will do anything. Which is fair enough i'n'it? He says, he said "you can't put that down there". He got stroppy then, he got really stroppy. I said I'll do anything mate, I said have you got a toilet here? He said "yeah". I said I'll clean that one mate. You pay me I'll clean it. You know, that's you know. I'm just happy to have a job. That's all I want. I don't ask for a lot. All I want is a job and if I got a job I'm happy. You know. That's me.'

(Mr Cam, 28)

Mr Humber had just been sacked by his boss for having been 'on a bit of a bender – drink ... well, drink-wise, just after Christmas'. But this was part of a long-running story of disagreements: Mr Humber represents his ex-employer as self-important and overbearing.

'He's got a plaque – a solid [indistinct] granite plaque – all polished up, you know ... "Designed and built by [employer's name]" – yet he didn' do nothing, you know. He was, he was there just shoutin' the odds. Do this, do that, do it this way, do it that way.'

(Mr Humber, 18)

He had already left once, but had been persuaded – a wrong decision in retrospect – to return. He was planning to leave anyway. Mr Humber represents the job as badly organised and frustrating.

'It's no good me having a job where – well, like I was, up there – I was hiding away most of the time, 'cause there was nothing to do. And you

... you couldn' use your initiative to, to pick up a job and do it 'cause he'd come out and he'd ... huh ... he'd tell you you was doing it wrong; he don't want it done so ...'

(Mr Humber, 16)

The American sociologist Richard Sennett analyses such utterances by respondents in his research (on blue-collar workers who have 'risen' to white-collar jobs) in terms of class. He points out that class is a system for limiting freedom and that – while it limits the freedom of bosses in some spheres – it more obviously constrains those who must obey orders.[6] Sennett contrasts workers in Britain and Europe, who can feel self-respect even while recognising that they have less material freedom, work opportunities and educational choices than those of 'higher' class, with his interviewees, who constantly feel that 'their dignity is on the line'.[7] He argues that American workers' struggle for self-respect erodes their self-confidence, even when they are superficially successful, because the culture is so structured as to make them vulnerable. It puts a high value on knowledge as providing the means of freedom, but education remains a source of indignity because their working-class origins mark them out as culturally inferior in understanding and sensitivity.[8]

In our study it was irregular unskilled workers, not those who sought promotion, who spoke most in terms of self-respect (though some of the issues raised by Sennett will be discussed in the section on promotion and training – p. 114). Men like Mr Cam, Mr Wye and Mr Humber reconstructed rows with employers to define the limits of their willingness to comply with arbitrary, arrogant or pointless exercises of authority over them. Class was certainly at stake here, but these men were not striving for recognition in terms of the cultural standards of their employers: they wanted the dignity they saw as due to manual workers, and which was found partly in politeness and consideration by bosses, and partly in satisfaction with their own performance of their work. In this sense they took for granted a class system in employment, and defined their freedom and dignity in terms of the power relations in such a system.[9] But if an employer did not give them their due in dignity, they left the job; and if employers in general would not grant them respect they left the world of employment.

This resulted in them becoming unemployed or self-employed; usually it meant some of each. Men who were currently self-employed, rather than contrasting good and bad bosses, instead contrasted self-employment with employee jobs. They described self-employment as allowing a better balance between necessity and personal autonomy, and a greater degree of respect: hence, after a history of rows with employers, they displayed the advantages for the worker of this independent status.

'Self-employment it's um ... yeah, it's a challenge in a way, [indistinct] you go out and find your own work; if you haven't got work you just don't [...] Well I think the thing about [an employee job] was one, having to answer to someone, and two, was never being able to ah, voice your own opinion, you know what I mean? [...] When you're self-employed if, um ... I'm doing a job, people'll come up to me and say, "Well, what way are you gonna do that?" or, um, "How you gonna do this?" Whereas working for an employer you're supposed to do it in a certain way and you've got no, no option but to do it then.'

(Mr Ribble, 68)

'Well, 'cause you'm yourself, you know, I mean ... You haven't got nobody else telling you what to do; you can get on and do your work. Whereas you're on the building site you got people telling 'ee what to do all day long. I don't like people stood behind me. I like to be on me own.'

(Mr Hodder, 6)

WORK ORIENTATION

The men described themselves as active, needing to work to fulfil their personal needs as well as their roles as providers for their households. Idleness is characterised as boring and destructive of identity and self-respect. Yet all but two had experienced unemployment, and for some this had lasted for years. Hence they distinguished between being idle and being unemployed in various ways.

Several men construct the early weeks of unemployment as 'a rest' – time to be with the family.

Mr Derwent:	... myself I looked on it: oh I'll have a rest. But, you know, I been working for 'em nearly 10 years. I thought to meself: oh, I'll have a bit of a rest. 'Cause it was coming up to summer, wa'n't it?
Mrs Derwent:	Yeah. Yeah. We enjoyed it.
Mr Derwent:	Course then my rest turned into a long ... well early retirement wa'n'it? [laughs]. But then come the end – just after Christmas wa'n't it? – I thought well, I'll try and get a job and I got a job just like that, see. Just goes to prove there is jobs around if you want them. [child talking]
Q:	Was there anything in particular that made you decide to go out then?
Mr Derwent:	Not really. Just really the money got a bit tight wa'n'it?, just after Christmas. We spent a lot di'n' we? [child talking] I just went out.

(Mr Derwent, 18)

'Well, first I must admit, the first month I found, you know, relaxing, and having time to myself and time to do what I wanted to do and um ... Well basically after the first month the money ran out and then ah ... all I had to look forward to was weekly sign on day and that was it. No money. No going out in the evenings. Totally restricted. Cuts your life out completely.'

(Mr Ribble, 21)

Once a pattern of inactivity sets in, this is seen as destructive:

'It's just so boring, so totally boring. There's no meaning to life. You haven't got to get up in the morning for anything, have you? You just can't lay in bed till ... I started ... when I first was on it I was up ... laying in bed till about 12 o'clock and then going down the pub or something with two pound in me pocket [...] But um ... you get in a rut because there's no way out or you couldn't afford this, you'd have to get it from the club book or whatever.'

(Mr Parrett, 21)

Furthermore, what is initially a chance to strengthen relationships by being together more turns into a negative experience:

Mr Colne: It was more money than I was getting at [garage's name], but it was also ... being home here for 8 months it was ...
Mrs Colne: ... getting on each other's nerves ...
Mr Colne: ... mainly getting, it was mainly getting out and getting a job. So it was really in that case, after that time it was really take whatever come along, and it did happen that this come along, so, took it.

(Mr Colne, 8)

However, another way of being active while unemployed is to make major improvements to their houses – often involving structural work, and the labour of relatives or former workmates. Here the men's accounts contradict Pahl's findings, and especially his suggestion that informal work such as do-it-yourself building projects is uncommon among people who are unemployed.[10] In these accounts, such activities are well suited to periods of unemployment, which may even be taken to allow them.

Mrs Humber: You lost your [job], packed it in just after, didn't you? 'Cause then you started working on here [the home] [...]
Mr Humber: Yeah. Knocked it all down.
Mrs Humber: Yeah. Done it all himself.

(Mr Humber, 39)

'That's what I done, built all them, when I was on the dole, didn't I?'

(Mr and Mrs Ryton, 43)

Other kinds of informal work can also provide activity and income during periods of unemployment. Breeding animals, birds or fish is an absorbing interest and can be lucrative; so could hunting.

'That was, that [his birds] kept us above breadline really when I [...] was unemployed 'cause ... it was all for profit anyway, you know [...] I started, you know, with a few; same as me fish, you know, started with a handful so just ... let it grow from there [...] It was a challenge to have to try and breed 'em but [...] it just comes naturally to me ...

(Mr Humber, 30–1)

'I got 4 ... well 4 dogs, they're all curled up see. I go out hunting with 'em. That's the only, that's me, you know, that's the enjoyment I get [indistinct] that's the only enjoyment I get really ... going out with 'em [...] Night times [...] Yeah, rabbits, hares, foxes, deer or you know that's [...] ain't s'posed to some of the things but ... most of it I, I get it all. Like the dogs, I breed dogs, I used to have ... I breed 'em and sell 'em off see.'

(Mr Bow, 15)

This need to remain active, alongside the requirement to provide an adequate income for the household, is used to legitimate work for cash while claiming benefits on grounds of unemployment. Some deny that this kind of work is available, or say it is too risky (see p. 124), and others speak about their undeclared work while claiming only when the tape recorder at the interview is switched off. Altogether, 18 irregular and 5 regular workers among the male respondents tell the interviewer of doing undeclared cash work. Several describe ways in which they have earned money which was not declared to the benefit authorities.

'You know, boy down the road ... might say, like, oh my mate wants his house decorating and ... he'll say to someone else, oh his mate wants his house decorating and he'll say, oh I know somebody, and just gets passed around, you know, and it ... sometimes it comes to you, sometimes they go to somebody else [...] I can guarantee there's loads of people doing it, you know, there's hundreds of people doing these jobs on the side and all that.'

(Mr Itchen, 6–7)

Mr Derwent explains that he was able to get cash work to improve his position when unemployed.

Mr Derwent: ... the difference between me working at the time and me being on the dole was about 5 pound a week ... because I wa'n' getting paid a big wage when I was at work [...] there was a difference of around 5 pound and that ... that was swallowed up by going to work and back with the transport. So really the money side of it we di'n' really have as much problems as what other people did because p'raps they were used to earning more. We ... we weren't anyhow ... I picked up a few jobs on the side [indistinct, possibly 'like everyone else' ...].

Q: What sort of thing?

Mr Derwent: [indistinct] Did a bit of building work, di'n' I? Me friend's house, well he paid me some money for [indistinct].

(Mr Derwent, 17)

'SELF-EMPLOYMENT'

Doing undeclared cash work while claiming was common partly because of the large amount of unstructured, irregular work going on, to which this group of men had access. Demand for labour in this sector of the labour market did not take the form of employment on a regular basis; it was occasional, short-term, seasonal or contract work, or irregular 'agency' work. Men working in this way did not fit easily into the administrative categories used by the tax and benefits authorities. They also had some difficulty in explaining their status in the research interview (see p. 71), and when they called themselves 'self-employed', this referred to a number of different situations.

Most of the men in the study construct casual and unprotected work as giving them independence and autonomy;[11] a minority describe their fears of the insecurity and unreliability of this status. It is those in regular, secure employment who take the latter view; this is what distinguishes them from the others. Their fear of casualisation or redundancy causes them to hold on to their jobs, even when they are not very satisfied with them (see p. 109).

(i) Working for oneself

The first category of 'self-employed' workers are those who find their own work, and pay their own tax and National Insurance Contributions (if any). Mr Parrett's work is very irregular at present:

Q: Have you got a job at the moment?

Mr Parrett: Well sort of. It is part-time, here and there, jumping around. When they want my services I just go in and do the odd day like. But, um, unemployed is my ... status at the moment. But, ah, I'm not a lot really. I've done a bit for my father, bit of roofing, always worked since I left school, did the odd job.

(Mr Parrett, 18)

He goes on to explain that he worked as an employee for a time, but was made redundant.

'Well that's when I started, um, jumping around then, which is um, literally lots of people don't want to pay a bui[lder] ... well, I'll go in and do a brick wall whatever and that's how I've been really now for the past 2 years, something like that.'

(Mr Parrett, 19)

However things are difficult just now:

Q: So at the moment you're what, classed as unemployed, or ...?

Mr Parrett: No. Not at the moment, I don't think. No, at the moment I am, what you call? Self-employed for a while, but I don't find it very good.

Q: Really?

Mr Parrett: You can't ... you don't see the [indistinct] of it. So say if they got nothing for you, they say "sorry" so you're broke for a week or whatever. Then they call you in again. But like, I mean I keep myself busy. Me mother keeps me busy quite often – running errands for her.

(Mr Parrett, 21–2)

Only one of the men who call themselves self-employed describes himself as doing regular work on his own account. Mr Kennet has been a self-employed painter and decorator for the past 13 years.

'You go for a job when you're gone 40 – you're over the hill to some of these places. They want the young chaps. Um ... and I just couldn't get a, get a job anywhere else, so I, I thought well that's the only thing I can do. Start up on me own. And that, that's what, that's what I did. Um ... Like I say, I been, been going over 10 years – well nearly 13 years now.'

(Mr Kennet, 23)

He explains that, although he is able to get steady, regular supplies of work, it is not well paid.

> 'I haven' been earning a great wage because haven' got the trade although I been doing it a number of years, I didn', I didn' go in, have a, qualifications. I'm just self-taught. So I ... my prices are ah ... a lot cheaper than ... a professional.'
>
> (Mr Kennet, 24)

Mr Hodder has just started work again as a decorator after 2 years off because of a sports injury. He sees periods of being without work as part of being 'self-employed'.

> 'Nah, never worried me, no, I was out some, I'd be out and then I'd be starting again somewhere else. I was always looking around for work.'
>
> (Mr Hodder, 5)

Mr Dovey is now unemployed, but he was a self-employed cleaner for 11 years before he went out of business.

> 'before I was unemployed, contract cleaning, self-employed. I lost me main contract which was [name of firm] – which was 75 per cent of me work, so I packed it in. I had, you know, I had 2 choices; I could keep going and go bankrupt or ... clear off me books, pay up me bills for me cleaning material and finish the business, which is what I did. Yeah. Um ... and that's it since then ... nothing at all.
>
> I was hoping then to start again in the future, but of course it never materialised; that was the reason of going out with me head held high, paying up all me bills ... giving 'em all, you know, the odd stuff I had left, month's notices so that in some future time I would be able start up again. But of course it never materialised. And ah ... I'm 50 years old. Wrong age to get a job. First time I ever been on the dole in me life. Never been on the dole before. Yeah. Basically that's about it.'
>
> (Mr Dovey, 8)

He, his son, and occasionally his wife, used to work hard:

> 'Which meant to say we had to work late night times and early mornings which we were quite happy to do. We would be up 3 o'clock every morning, didn't bother us – we were our own bosses and earning good wages, but of course without [firm's name] it wasn't, it didn't pay us to keep going ...'
>
> (Mr Dovey, 17)

(ii) Agency work

Another category of irregular workers who call themselves 'self-employed' are those who get work through an agency. This means that they put together various bits and pieces in patterns that vary from one week to the next. Mr Torridge describes himself as 'everything – sort of ... general handyman, that sort of ... done warehousing mostly'. He works

'for an employment bureau and the work's thick and fast – sometimes you got it, you know and you're never out of work, and the next minute you got weeks without anything, so ...'

(Mr Torridge, 4)

Q: How do you manage about money? Presumably you don't know what, how much you're going to earn?

Mr Torridge: Um ... all depends on the hours I do really. I mean ... sometimes I can bring home ... ah, 120, and sometimes I bring home 70. Just all depends on the hours what I do. I get paid 2 pound 65 an hour, plus bonus, which brings it up a bit more so ... I always know roughly what I'm gonna get at the end of the week and if it i'n' a lot like, the dole office make it up anyway ...'

(Mr Torridge, 6)

He describes the administrative complications of this arrangement.

'it's just a case of having to sign off, sign on, sign off, sign on all the time, you know, so – I'm not actually unem..., they don't actually class me as unemployed, they class you know they c, call me part-time – that's what they call me anyway, so – I enjoy that. It's good.'

(Mr Torridge, 4)

From Mr Torridge's account, it becomes clear that undeclared cash jobs are fitted into his agency work. When asked about these he replies:

Mr Torridge: Um ... Well when I h, when I look for 'em I can get 'em, but I mean this week I've just took it easy, I haven't looked for anything, but ... I mean if I wanted to do ... cash in hand, painting and decorating, I could do it to-morrow ... you know, so ... just doing the basics, working with somebody, I could do it tomorrow so ... the, the money's there if I want it.

Q: Right. How do you find about that?

Mr Torridge: Just through friends ... you know, I got ...

Q: Do people come and ask you or do you ...

Mr Torridge: Well you ... well ... just say to 'em, 'Is there any work going?' 'Oh yeah, we'll see you later like, mate, mate', you know, 'Couple of jobs coming up, are you interested?' 'Well, yeah, all right'. So ... it comes. It's slow in coming but it comes.

Q: Right. Does it fit in with your warehousing job or does it sometimes clash?

Mr Torridge: They sometimes clash. I mean ... that, that kind of thing you, I just say to 'em, well look I got a job on at the moment, come and see me in a few weeks. If it's there still then I'll do it; if it's not then I won't [...] You know, I'd rather do the job I got at the moment, which is ware-housing, and just fit it in when I can and if it's ... well if it's not there, it's not there. So that's, that bring you back to signing on again, you know, so ...'

(Mr Torridge, 5–6)

Other men had past experience of doing agency work. Mr Cam describes a recent period when his irregular working pattern led to serious problems with the benefit authorities, and got him into debt.

Mr Cam: Some weeks I had, some weeks I'd pick up about 40 pound um which meant I couldn't pay me rent, I was having difficulty with the rent uh I think I owe the Coun-cil about 300 pound in back rent.

Q: What's that since ...

Mr Cam: Since I've been on this agency and the dole I haven't been paying. Which, which do you do [indistinct], do you pay your rent and not have any food for your children or do you not pay the rent and that is, all you've got to do it is leave it 5 or 6 weeks when you're not getting any money and you, 25 pound a time, see it takes you into the state where you'm into debt with everybody, you know. My overdraft with the bank, uh which is, I think it's going up and up every time I go in which is not very good and I think I got debts outstanding of about 600 pound which isn't, which is not very good.

Mm. It does worry me, it uh, I think it worries the wife more than it worries me, but uh, but I've been in this situation before. When I was first married I had 900 [indistinct] uh 7 year ago. Uh which we did get into debt then uh. It takes a long time to get out it that's the trouble.

It's easy to get into debt, but it, it's harder to get out, you know. You still got to live, you still got pay the rent and then you still got to live and you still got to try to pay your bills off. Uh you know it, it's hard to know what to do, you know, but it should, 600 pound should be paid off by Christmas with a bit of luck. If I, this job pays good money and I work seven days a week 14 hours a day then I can earn a total of about take home 200 pound a week which I can pay my debts off in 6 to 8 weeks with a bit of luck. Next time I will not go agency driving again. I'll just claim the dole.

Q: Why was that?

Mr Cam: Because it's, it's a lot of hassle because if I went back to agency again I'd be in the same position I'm in now, which is no good to me, putting myself back into debt. Um but, well I've, I never knew I could apply for family credit because nobody tells you you see, and when I finished with the rent rebate they automatically thought I was getting 22 pound and 4 pence from family credit, which I've had a argument about this because on the, when you fill out your housing application form they say down the bottom I have dec, through the form it goes do you get family credit, supplementary benefit which is the old, you know, one's family credit I can't remember what the other one is – income support. I says no, I told them I got family allowance and when they adjudicated the, me rent, they added 22 pound 4 pence each week on to me money which I wasn't getting. So I said to the girl in the office, I said really you'm calling people liars, you know. I signed that form on the bottom where it said if um the information you have given is not true and uh you can be prosecuted. But I put that, and they had, I put everything down, and they had adjudicated that I was getting 22 pound 6 pence or zero which I wasn't getting. So they've made me look as though I was a liar. My, I said no, I said you must be, because on the bottom of the form you sign that you've declared everything and you've not like you still adjudicated me having 22 pound 4 pence or 6 pence which I didn't have.

(Mr Cam, 13–14)

(iii) Subcontract work and unprotected employment

The third category of workers who describe themselves as 'self-employed' are those – mainly in the building trade – who subcontract with an individual (or firm), who deducts tax from their earnings, but leaves them responsible for paying their own National Insurance Contributions. However, they are not eligible for sick pay, holiday pay, redundancy payments and have to make their own pension arrangements, and when the work is done they have to find other work. In other words, neither the subcontractor nor the state (through unemployment benefits) protects them from periods of being out of work, though they are entitled to income support if they fall within the savings limits; it is less a system of 'self-employment' than one of unprotected employment. None the less, the men who are or have been in this category describe it as preferable to work as an employee with a firm.

> 'Yeah. I had a row with the boss in the end. I got the sack, but um ... I didn' like his methods and he didn' like mine I don't think. So ... and ... after that it's um ... I went back into building again. And ..., there I've stayed [...]
>
> As, you know, self-employed again. I mean I'm still self-employed now, but ... um ... it's, I work for a company but they um ... they can lay you off any time sort of thing, you know; just say, right the work's finished. All it is is subcontracting for big company and ah ... I enjoy the work. What they do is um renovations ... And we do all, do up houses and flats, convert barns. It's a bit of everything actually: plastering, painting and decorating, gardening, the lot. So ... it's something I enjoy doing; something different every single day [...] that's ... half of the reason why I went into self-employment as well. Um ... I don't like taking orders ... ah ... just wanna be independent sort of thing. And um ... I don't like being taken, spoken to like that anyway and I just told him what to do and where to get off and ... nearly every threat under the sun I think. [laughs]'
>
> (Mr Ribble, 23, 33)

Having experienced this situation, Mr Ribble says that he is moving towards working for himself, rather than going back into employment.

> 'If ... I change in any way I think it'll be um ... to become more ... um independent rather to employ ... um ... rely on an employer sort of thing. Um ... basically meaning ... um ... well I'd just like to go and do it on me own sort of thing, the building.
>
> (Mr Ribble, 32)

Mr Tamar contrasts his period doing subcontract building work with his nephew with his 'mundane, boring' employment in a factory.

'Last year I was self-employed for a while ... and ... done a lot of carpentry work on building sites [...] I was working with me [nephew], he had transport and we both had the means of doing it like [...] so ah ... travelled round the West Country doing work on building sites [...] ... um shops, flats, you know, ripping flats out and modernising them [...] Um ... that was another rewarding job, especially ... people still living in the house and they got you to do some work [...] you can see the finish [indistinct] you know.'

(Mr Tamar, 6–7)

SECURITY

The group of men who call themselves 'self-employed' emphasise variety and change as the sources of satisfaction in work; they minimise the problems connected with irregularity of work, treating it as an inconvenience associated with this status, rather than an overwhelming drawback.

'I mean winter time now if I'm outside doing something – don't know – you'd have to get more than two days a week. But I mean luckily I mean – you always scratch around and find – just something to do.'

(Mr Parrett, 23)

'Well, it's like I say, didn', don' make a living wage and – it – I'd, it's just that – you, you get that many changes from the jobs that you don't get tired of doing it.'

(Mr Kennet, 21)

In contrast with this group, another emphasises security and regularity of employment, and treats the risk of periods without work as a major threat. Hence both groups construct 'self-employment' as involving irregularity of work and income, but those in regular employment have a negative attitude towards this aspect of it. Unlike the 'self-employed' group, who see this as part of being a worker which is consistent with a worker's status, the regularly employed group place a higher value on security of income provision.

Mr Calder's story is that he left the air force, worked for a time as an agency driver, and for the past 7 years has been an employed driver for a firm. He regrets leaving the RAF, reconstructing his decision to do so with hindsight as a mistake:

Mr Calder:	Yeah. It was the biggest mistake I've ever made – coming out of the air force [...]
Q:	What's been the worst thing about coming out?
Mr Calder:	Security. Without a doubt, lack of security.

(Mr Calder, 22–3)

He describes working for a time for an agency, and then changing to his present regular job.

> 'the telephone rang [...] and it was a chap offering me work on an agency basis and ah ... that's how I started off as self-employed – agency I worked. I got the work off him and then I moved to another chap ... who was paying better money and ah ... I was there for 2 years and then ah I got in, that's how I got in with [firm's name], I did a lot of work for [firm] as an agency driver.'
>
> (Mr Calder, 24)

When asked what he did not like about being self-employed, he attributes to his wife the anxiety about irregularity of income.

> 'Well I, I didn't mind, my wife didn't like it, 'cause she, my wife, likes to know the money's going to be there every, every month, and I suppose she has to pay the bills [...] She sees to *everything* financialwise in this house, and I s'pose that's why she was worried 'cause some weeks I was plenty of work and other weeks, you know, you might get one day, two days, and of course the bills were still coming in ...'
>
> (Mr Calder, 24)

Seven years ago he was offered a regular driver's job.

> 'See I'd done a lot of work for them see [...] as a relief driver, self-employed ... and then this job come available and ah ... [indistinct] because as a, as a relief driver, agency, you know, you were doing all different things, you know ... driving milk tankers or refrigerated vehicles or ah ... but due to the money being there every week I thought well, yes so I took it.'
>
> (Mr Calder, 25)

He has mixed feelings about his present job. He has to get up at 3 a.m. each morning to start work at 4 a.m.; he gets no satisfaction from the job, because he has to drive the same routes every day; but he is worried about rumours of redundancies.

> 'they say the drivers are safe, but [...] there's going to be quite a few warehousemen ... finished in about 4 weeks' time [...] we still don't see how there's enough work to keep all the drivers [...] I must admit a few months ago, mind, I wish they had paid me off, but ah ... the way I felt, but there again, looking around jobs aren't that easy to get, ... so ...'
>
> (Mr Calder, 26–7)

Asked about what he would like to do, Mr Calder says he would want to move into management, and has taken a course to train for this (though he failed part of it). He then continues:

'But I'd like to work for myself, I'd like ... a little van and do sort of express parcels, things like that, you know [indistinct – whispering] she's dead against it, self-employed, she's not keen on that at all, so ...'

(Mr Calder, 29)

Again, Mr Calder claims that it is his wife's wish for security that keeps him in his monotonous and inconvenient job – but elsewhere in his own account he emphasises the importance to him of security, and his fear of not being able to find another job if he was made redundant.

Mr Cherwell is a supervisor at a roadside restaurant; he has been there for over 10 years. When asked whether he expects to stay there, he replies:

'Well ... I dunno really, but I ... I [indistinct – baby squeals] it's not too bad and that, you know ... the money's pretty good. But ... if somebody come up to me and offered me another job with ... more money then of course obviously ... or whether I'd like to be there say 6 months and ... they said, oh right, that's it we don't need you no more so and ... like it ... with this job here ... at least I have got a secure job ... and that, so ... if, if for instance, if I've done something really [indistinct] like pinching or something like that, then that's the only time they'll get rid of me. But at the moment I'm ... well secured, you know.

Unless ... not unless, if they went bankrupt, you know, that, that would be the ... other choice as well if they got rid of us, but otherwise at the moment the way it's going on ... they're building up um ... more buildings and cafés, restaurants and ... that [indistinct – baby shouting] ...'

(Mr Cherwell, 2)

later he adds,

'thing is [stutters] if I do leave this job and go to another job, I could be there, say 4 months and out of work again, so ... you know ...'

(Mr Cherwell, 7)

Recently he has been offered the chance of becoming a self-employed scaffolder; he doesn't like the idea of being self-employed.

'... well not unless if, if I could get, could get um a contract ... with a firm so ... full, full employment so that'd be all right. But ... going self-employed no, 'cause you got, you gotta pay ... your own stamp – National Insurance an' that – an' that, em holidays, well you, you'd be lucky to get a holiday [indistinct] 'cause you could be working 50, 60 hours a, a week here ...'

(Mr Cherwell, 11)

Mr Plym is a clerical grade civil servant, who has worked in several different posts; he, too, has had this job for 10 years. He had hoped to go from college to higher education.

Mr Plym:	... I'd hoped to go into teacher training originally. [...] That wasn't to be.
Q:	Do you still regret that?
Mr Plym:	Ah, I regret it a little bit but um ... I've seen so many of my friends who've gone on and done that and now they're unemployed. They're not doing anything, they're ... I've got 2 or 3 friends who've done that ... all great ideas of being ... journalists or whatever and they haven't fulfilled them at all. So I don't feel that disappointed. At least I've got a job and ... a job I enjoy doing, enjoy meeting people and ...'

(Mr Plym, 2)

Later he is asked if he ever sees himself going self-employed.

'Not at this stage, No. Fairly settled, I think. I ... I always been lucky so far, I've never been unemployed, but um ... can't see any future change in there. Unless they decide the [department's] offices ought to go. Then I can't see that happening; they talk about privatising ... every time you open a paper you see they're gonna privatise [department] ... an' nobody'd want them. I mean, who'd want them? There's no money about ... in them at all.

(Mr Plym, 11)

He likes variety and change, but within a structure of security.

Mr Plym:	I feel I've been very lucky, as I said, to um ... to be able to go from one job to another within one organisation so ... I've been very lucky. I mean other people have been terribly unlucky [indistinct] in one job, do it for a couple of months [indistinct] all of a sudden everything falls through and they're left high and dry. It's happened so many times to friends of mine ... It's ... one of those things really, isn't it?
Q:	[indistinct] your job's quite secure ...
Mr Plym:	Well secure as anything can be at the moment.

(Mr Plym, 12)

Mr Avon is a fork-lift driver, doing shift work; he has been with the firm for 15 years. He does shift work not by preference, but because the money is better and 'you gotta take the rough with the smooth'. Recently there has been a threat of redundancies at the firm.

> 'When I first went out there 15 year ago we had 96 working out there ... on 3 shifts. Now there's 2 shifts with 10 blokes [...] It, well yeah, worries me. It ... I isn' worried for meself, personally, but ... when you got a wife and 3 kids to look after and to support, you know, like I say, your dole money isn' a lot. Even if it was ... [indistinct] say I left tomorrow, of me own accord, well I wouldn' get nothing for 6 weeks for starters ... right ... So therefore we gotta scrip and scrave [sic] for 6 weeks right ...'
>
> (Mr Avon, 20)

He goes on to tell a story of how once, many years ago, he and his wife were sick, and were only able to get enough money for their rent, and nothing for food or other needs, from the benefit authorities (he quotes the exact figures paid). Mr Avon returns to the topic of redundancy at the end of his account, telling stories about how his and other firms have got rid of all their workers at a certain unit.

> 'I've learnt to be a sceptic where my firm's concerned [...] they can get rid of us any time they like.'
>
> (Mr Avon, 43–4)

In all the accounts by men in secure jobs, there is some reference to irregular work patterns as threatening, and a fear of redundancy and unemployment – linked to a loss of household income, and undermining the role of provider. In the case of the two men employed by local authorities, this threat is linked with the move towards competitive tendering and privatisation. Mr Rother is a foreman who has worked for a local authority for 24 years; the week before he was interviewed, he turned down the offer of a job with a private firm, because he decided to stay with the council; 'my little unit is like a little family, do you know what I mean? Can you get my drift? [...] workmates, they turn out as friends don't they? They're bound to after so many years.' But he does not feel secure.

> Mr Rother: we could be right knocked for six ... by the end of the year if I lose my job. All right.
>
> Q: Is that possible?
>
> Mr Rother: Possible? Privatisation. I could be out of work. It is like that. Redundant. Out of work. That is ... I mean, it's no good saying ... um that it can't happen because it can happen; it can really, it's really staring me in the face. It's there and it can happen.'
>
> (Mr Rother, 24)

Mr Severn is a gardener with a local authority; he has worked there for 20 years, but he is anxious that he may be made to do tasks which are inconsistent with his eyesight problem as a result of the new competitive tendering arrangements at work. He thinks that his job may be in jeopardy:

> 'if they make me mobile then that's it. Finished. And I'll, I'll go from there. 'Cause I'm sure I, I won't be out of work for, for very long.'
>
> (Mr Severn, 21)

Overall then, fear of losing their jobs haunts those in regular employment. They make a trade-off between the disadvantages of those jobs – sameness, inconvenient hours or lower pay – and the risk of unemployment. As Mr Nene, a foreman motorcycle mechanic for 13 years, puts it:

> 'It'd be nice to go labouring on a building site for 400 pound a week, but how long would it last? So ... stick with what I got really.'
>
> (Mr Nene, 19)

All these accounts therefore construct income from 'self-employment' as irregular and unreliable; the work is stimulating by virtue of change and challenge, yet the status is risky in terms of provision of earnings for the family. The small group (12 out of the 36 men in the sample) with regular jobs construct themselves as steady and responsible, but they do not describe the 'irregulars' in critical terms. Rather they show a certain ambivalence, and some wistfulness, about their own situation.

Thus the men's accounts reveal differences between the ways in which 'regulars' and 'irregulars' construct self-employment and unemployment. But they only provide hints and clues as to the origins of these differences in their household and wider social relations. Our theory of these normative and structural features of the distinction between regular and irregular workers' accounts will be set out in Chapter 6, pp. 204–5.

TRAINING AND PROMOTION

The men who had regular jobs were more likely to be positive about training and promotion than those with irregular employment. Mr Rother, Mr Nene and Mr Cherwell were all foremen or supervisors, Mr Calder was taking a management course, and Mr Wear had just been transferred (as a result of passing his driving test) to a new post. Mr Severn got his gardening job as a result of a training course. By contrast, such irregular workers as Mr Tamar and Mr Derwent had given up supervisory posts, and were currently doing unskilled jobs.

Mr Calder is ambivalent about his present position as a lorry driver on a regular route, and talks mainly about the alternative of self-employment.

However, his long-term plans may head in other directions.

Mr Calder:	Mind you I don't want to drive lorries all my life. I've got no intention of driving lorries till 65, none at all. But I think I'll still be there in the next 6 months.
Q:	What would you like to do instead?
Mr Calder:	Oh ... I wouldn't mind getting into management. I've took a, took a course for transport management ... and actually I passed the hard part and failed the damned easy part, and I couldn't understand that [...] so I've taken the [exam] again so ... I wouldn't mind management.

(Mr Calder, 29)

He spent £27 to attend night classes for this course, 2 hours a week; he has also found out about correspondence courses and residential courses which are much more expensive; he bought a book for £11.50, so he can resit the exam in a few weeks' time. Among the interviewees, Mr Calder's account is the only one with echoes of Richard Sennett's work on American blue-collar workers who have moved into white-collar posts. Like Sennett's respondents,[12] Mr Calder has to take orders from someone else (a transport manager) whom he blames for making his present job boring.

'I mean you try to explain something to our transport manager ... and, considering he's an ex-driver, you'd expect him to ... realise what you're on about ... but quite honestly there's times that you, you feel like [...] hitting your head against a brick wall. And ah ... that's the sort of ... transport manager you've gotta put up with, well it makes you think well, what's the point?'

(Mr Calder, 26)

However, Mr Calder believes it is his responsibility to 'make something of himself' – to rise above his situation as an ordinary worker, by becoming a manager. As Sennett points out, the belief in a personal responsibility for his own alienation at work, and for achieving independence by rising above his fellow workers through his ability, involves internalising class conflict[13] and isolating himself from his fellow workers, through an educational process.

Mr Calder comes from outside the area and has few friends on the estate: he and his wife would like to buy a house, but would prefer not to buy their present council house. In this they are almost unique in our sample (see Chapter 7, pp. 254–68). Mr Rother is also doing a course to take on extra responsibilities for safety at work. He is already a foreman with the local authority where he has worked for almost 25 years. But his progress has surprised him; suddenly in 2 years he has developed a career.

'Not through planning, not through planning. And not through looking for it. And it's, it's snowballed and [...] I was looking to get on myself once I knew what my capabilit ... it's, it's boiling down to really, I didn't know I had it in me. Do you follow me? [...] I'm 38 [...] And ah, I thought to meself well I know I got these capabilities in me so I, I was saying [...] sort of my direct bosses ... um [...] improving my job situation [...] I said I was interested and I'm going to night school, said I'm gonna pay for the course and go on it. And then I, get um a thing come down, saying we'll back you ...'

(Mr Rother, 16)

He says that he has not told his workmates because 'I would be a laughing stock' and that the others in the class at the college are all under 25. And he does not want to distance himself from his fellow workers.

'I enjoy their company as well. I've been with them ... I mean a lot of them are longstanding people like meself, you know, and perhaps some have got 20, 15, 10 years in, so they've known me when I was on the shopwork floor.'

(Mr Rother, 17)

Unlike Mr Calder, Mr Rother is very committed to living on the estate: he and his wife have been buying their house for the past 12 years.

'We got a lot going for us here ... all right. If promotion comes tomorrow and I go about ten places up the league, you know ... I still wanna live here; I still wanna have me mates; I don' want it to change me.'

(Mr and Mrs Rother, 72)

He makes it clear that – unlike Mr Calder and Sennett's interviews – he does not see dignity and self-respect as coming through rising as an individual above the mass through education, or through socialisation into the culture of a different class: 'I don't wanna go up and live on Nob Hill'. He adds that it would not be financially attractive to try to buy a house outside the area. If they bought elsewhere

'all right we're going up ... maybe socially, 'cause we've got a better property and all this and that, but we're going backwards as regards living and what goes on the table. Because there's the increase in mortgage that you got to pay [...] from our friends and all that, point of view, we got too much to lose by leaving here, and too much to lose out our pocket as well, haven't we?'

(Mr and Mrs Rother, 73)

Thus Mr Rother refers indirectly to class and social mobility through housing, and makes clear his firm identification with his fellow workers and with his community. Some of the same issues arise for Mr Plym, the civil servant, who is rather more wistful about alternative possibilities (see p. 112), having left college with one 'A' level, after originally planning to be a teacher. Asked if he would ever move from the area he replies

'Only if I get promotion I suppose. It's not a thing we're averse to – my wife and I have both talked about it. If we had to move away we would, but we've [laughs] ... we do like it here. I lived here all my life. Um ... got family around. We would prefer to stay here if we can but ... you know if, if you have to move away you have to move away, especially if you can get moved up north or somewhere where your house prices are cheaper [laughs] ... might be able to afford somewhere new.'

(Mr Plym, 9)

Mr Derwent is about to take his HGV driving test: he took the training in his own time, and paid for it himself. However, he would not want any other kind of promotion. He used to be a managing supervisor in a factory.

'Yeah, I wouldn't want that kind of bloody thing. Too much ha, hassle for the money what they give you. The ah workers there are earning twice as much as what you earn. You're in charge and you get all the responsibility and you don' get the money come the end of it so ...'

(Mr Derwent, 14)

When he was first a supervisor the job had the advantage of regular earnings, but then the workers got a pay rise and he did not. He now has no wish for a supervisory role, and in this he is like the other irregular workers, who prefer the autonomy of being able to earn higher – if more variable – wages through a diversity of activities. Yet both those who seek promotion (like Mr Rother) and those who avoid it (like Mr Derwent) define the disciplinary constraints and the opportunities for freedom at work in terms of the practices of power relations in the workplace.[14] While they are not drawn into isolated, individualised competition for recognition and respect (like Mr Calder), they construct their identities as competent workers and men in terms which reproduce the social relations of the factory or workshop – whether they pursue self-development through responsibility or through autonomy.

ACCEPTABLE AND UNACCEPTABLE EMPLOYMENT

Apart from this small group of 'regulars', the rest had all experienced frequent changes of employment and some periods of unemployment in the

1980s. They therefore constructed an account of these changes, including their time out of work, in terms of decisions within constraints; but the language of *choice* did not always seem appropriate.

Q:	How do you choose your jobs?
Mr Parrett:	I don't choose my job.
Q:	Don't you?
Mr Parrett:	Just [indistinct] pretty versatile.

(Mr Parrett, 18)

Q:	What made you decide to go back to work then, or look for a job then?
Mrs Ribble:	Um ... you didn't look for a job.
Mr Ribble:	Well, no, I didn't did I. It just came to me.
Mrs Ribble:	Yeah. Jim came up and said he had a big job on and he needed Steve to give him a hand [indistinct].
Mr Ribble:	Yeah, no it was just ... it, work come available like, so I took it. But um ... if it ... well if it come available earlier I would have took it, wouldn't I?

(Mr and Mrs Ribble, 64)

Within the accounts of changes, voluntary and involuntary, are stories about government employment and training schemes, and a variety of badly paid, difficult or dangerous activities. The men give their versions of the options open to them at various times, and reconstruct the outcomes of their decisions, modifying their judgements, based on the knowledge available to them at the time, with hindsight.

Mr Derwent took a job some 20 miles away, and borrowed his father's car to get there, soon after getting the sack from his factory job.

'after the first day I worked out how much it cost to get to work and back and well ... then we'd end up with, what? 40 pound a week [...] So [dog howls, indistinct] too much of that – 'specially after I worked out how much money I was getting [dog howls]. So then ah I gave that up as a bad idea [laughs].'

(Mr Derwent, 19)

Mr Itchen's employment ended 4 months before the interview.

'I walked out of me last job because ah on a gross of 70 pound a week he asked me if I wanted to go to college and take a City and Guilds and I said, yes. But come round to the week I was supposed to start and he decided to tell me I had to take a 15 pound a week wage cut and ... you know, so it meant I was bringing home 45, 50 pound a week – if I was lucky. So I says, I don't want to know. And I walk out and the result of that is they suspended me money [income support] ... it's only 20 ... 25 pound a week we get now.'

(Mr Itchen, 1–2)

In many instances, these 'irregulars' had little way of knowing how their decisions would turn out, and they represent themselves as willing to try most things – to 'have a go' – and learn from the experience. This is part of sustaining their role as breadwinners.

'I work with cyanide acid which everybody knows is dangerous [...] I work long hours; I can work anything from 7 o'clock in the morning till 8 at night, 7 days a week – which I have just finished [...] conditions are terrible. Still breathing in the fumes, the chemicals – you name it, I used it [...] When I took this job at 85 pound a week that was less than I was getting on the dole, but I took it because I didn't like being under my missus' feet all day. It was so boring, day after day, always the same. Never again, never ever again.'

(Mr Bure, 17)

Mr Ryton describes himself as a stonemason, but he has only recently become one:

'since last Monday. I started it last Monday [...] I'm enjoying it [...] Yeah. Working up [National Trust Property] at the moment ... that's about, just out, well just outside Minehead it is. Travel up there every day and back again, huh [...] it's about 60 miles I think, out of Exeter.'

(Mr Ryton, 20)

For some men, the claiming of family credit (formerly family income supplement – FIS) to make up low wages made a range of employments viable which would otherwise not have been compatible with their role as providers for their household.

'I was on [...] Manpower Services with the Exeter City Council [...] I was there for exactly 12 months [...] Yeah, that was good, it was good that was. We had fun that one [laughs] [...] They spent thousands on it and they went and knocked it down [...] You could claim FIS on that because you was cl... earning less than 125 pound so you had your wages made up to, say, 100 and, 130 anyway, you know, through FIS, and your rent ... half of your rent was paid, wa'n'it?'

(Mr Humber, 22–3)

Others describe family credit as a neglible sum, and insist on higher wages.

'We could get ... family credit ... [indistinct – laughing] was enough to give her her bus fare for 3 days [laughing] to work and home again, for

3 days [...] Job satisfaction, decent wage. And a bit of promotion. That'll satisfy me.'

(Mr Tamar, 9)

Mr Torridge constructs himself as willing to have a go at anything, especially when he was young and single. He did a Youth Training Scheme course 'helping the elderly' which in retrospect he perceives as 'waste of time. For the money, it was slave labour'. He then worked part-time in a cider factory, before being a night club bouncer, which he enjoyed, but felt was too violent for a married man, as he then became. After a period of unemployment he did painting and decorating on a Community Programme scheme 'which again I think was slave labour because you didn't actually learn how to do it'. Now he does agency work as a warehouseman, claiming for days when he is not employed. But he is quite specific about what would not be acceptable in the way of employment.

'I wouldn't work for under 80 pound. Well I can't; I got a wife and 2 kids so I can't. So ... 80 pound ... plus, is what I would do it for. Nothing less. I mean it might seem greedy but I gotta ... you know, s, keep the family supplied with food so ... there's no way I'd work for any less. I can't afford to.'

(Mr Torridge, 8)

This notion of a wage sufficient to feed and clothe the family is mobilised by men who were unemployed at the time of the interview, to legitimate their current status. In this way, the provider aspect of the breadwinner role is only adequately fulfilled by refusing unsuitable employment, or leaving a badly paid job. Mr Itchen, whose wage rate was cut to £45 a week when he started his college course, is a man who was willing to take a low-paid (£70 a week) job and claim family income supplement, but this experience has made him review his decision.

'Yeah. Financially better off unemployed. 'Cause the 36 pound a fortnight rent was paid and I get me 52 pound a fortnight supplementary plus the 25 FIS, you know, so [...] Really to go to work now I've got to be earning at ... well bring home at least 90 to 100 pound a week ... '

(Mr Itchen, 5)

Those who are longer-term unemployed construct a more general account of their situation in relation to the labour market. Mr Bow has been out of work for 7 months.

'I goes down the Job Centre quite often but there's not many kind of jobs what I wanna do, see. I want to ... wages about 150, something like that [...] they asked me whether I wanna do these government schemes, you know, it's ... it's not the same, you know, it's ... it's, well I've tried 'em before and there I was working 3 days, 3 days a week I think it was and 50 odd pound, something like that. And it was just so silly. I thinks it's disgrading [sic] a man, you know, to work for that wage – would you?'

(Mr Bow, 6)

Mr Exe has been unemployed for 4¹/₂ years. He was made redundant by the railways from a job earning £175 a week. He describes himself as willing to do any work: 'I'm not worried if it's down in any sewers or anything, just so long as the wages ... are there'. However

'the ones I did look for ... it was under 80 pound a week. And after you've took your ... national insurance stamp and everything else out of it, there's nothing left, is there?'

(Mr Exe, 3)

Mr Dovey thinks that his age (50) is against him getting another decently paid job, and hence that it was not worth him applying for jobs:

'to me things is getting worse. They say the job ... that the unemploy-ment figure's coming down – yeah ... ah ... maybe it is coming down but ... not like they tell 'ee it is. Not for one minute.'

(Mr Dovey, 13)

Hence unwillingness to accept low-paid work is justified in terms of the provider's role, by mobilising arguments which are also used by those in employment over what constitutes an acceptable 'family wage'.

'Well, I didn't exactly choose [...] to be out of work, it was that the job I had, you see, is ... I was only getting 65 pound a week and with 3 children it's a ... plus we had to pay, what?, 35 pound maximum rent, so that left us 30 pound a week to live on. And how can you live on that with children, see?'

(Mr Bow, 1)

'At the moment we get [indistinct] about 75 a week in benefits [...] If I go back work for less than that ... we are going to be worse off [...] So, unless I can get ... say about 100, 150 a week [...] it's gonna be ... a waste of time, i'n'it?'

(Mr Exe, 1)

These men do not mention family credit at these points in their accounts. However, as we shall show in the women's accounts, the crucial point about low-paid employment and household budgeting is the time it takes to claim this benefit. Although these men would in theory be better off in employment and sometimes regretted leaving a previous job, they described the situation immediately after taking low-paid work as inconsistent with their obligations of providing for the household expenses. These men go on to legitimate themselves as *workers* by describing undeclared cash jobs, which also provide income for 'extras' for the household.[15]

'VICIOUS CIRCLE': BENEFITS AND LOW PAY

The disincentive effects of benefits are widely discussed in the economic and social policy literature, but always in terms of the calculative, economic construction of decision-making. Yet our interviewees did not describe their decisions in this way: the irregular workers account for themselves as workers and providers with a responsibility to meet household expenses. These men and others give an account of what they describe as a 'vicious circle' between the labour market and the benefits system. The labour market will not sustain their requirement for a 'proper' full-time job with adequate wages, and the social security system is cutting back its provision, or making benefits more conditional, in order to drive them into low paid, insecure work.

'Like I said ... there's not many ... firms in Exeter ... that will pay over a hundred odd pounds a week, is there? [...] which we need ... to, to do everything [...] Well, I don't mind ... what work it is; I'm not fussed if it's down the sewers or anything like that. The main thing is ... um the money thing [...] 'cause if it's not, we will be up to our eyes in bills which we can't pay [...] Vicious circle, i'n'it? [...] Things which you are entitled to ... you don't ... government and DHSS have scrapped anyhow. So you know you ... you just ... lost out that way ... that way as well.'

(Mr Exe, 9–10)

'And for no reason they [DSS] stops your money half the time, don' 'em [...] I'm what, 30 pound, 30 pound short on my money this morning. I rang up this morning; they said, it'll be next couple of days so [...] And you can't, can't go and argue about it 'cause the're always right.'

(Mr Bow, 5–6)

Mr Itchen had been on a Youth Opportunities Scheme, followed by 12 months of unemployment; then another government scheme, and another 12 months out of work; then more short-term employment, before starting at a garage under the Restart Scheme. It was there that his wages were cut for going to college; he left, and then had a penalty cut in his benefits.

'you know, it's the same everywhere ... two evils i'n'it? Choice of two evils. Can't win with them [...] I've gone in and asked for a loan; they just say, no you can't 'cause ... you know, you got to be unemployed for 6 months and that's it, they just sort of send you away. It took me nearly 2 months to get milk tokens out of them for 2 kids ... but ah ...'

(Mr Itchen, 2)

For Mr Dovey, Mr Wye, Mr Exe and Mr Bow, the labour market was the primary cause of their situation – they had had better-paid jobs at an earlier stage, and insisted that the economy had moved against them. The DSS was a secondary cause, because of pressure and the inadequacy of benefits. They constructed their identities as frustrated workers, rather than as satisfied beneficiaries – as victims of an unemployment trap, not as voluntarily unemployed.

Because others were able to survive on low-paid work plus means-tested benefits, these men's accounts might be used by 'culture of dependency' theorists like Murray and Mead as evidence of the negative effects of generous or unconditional benefits. However, it should be noted that several of the other men spoke in similar terms, both of exploitative employment and of inefficient or pressurising DSS officials. Mr Ryton has just started work as a stonemason, but recently

'[I left my job] 'cause [the employer] wasn't paying my wages [...] when I just went down there [unemployment benefit office] to sign on after finishing with [employer's name], they asked for the reason for leaving that, and I told them I left voluntarily. They said, you'd be on the suspended claim and um ... I had to go down [DSS office] and fill in a load of forms down there [...] and I had to keep going down to [DSS office] and getting um ... these emergency crisis loans because I didn't have enough money to live on and then ah ... dole people didn't [indistinct] ... So it was like a vicious circle really. Huh.'

(Mr Ryton, 26–7)

Mr Colne, currently a car valeter, says he is willing to 'have a go' at any work, but that he was under pressure to take unsuitable jobs.

Mr Colne:	They were always pushing me into take ... I mean they were sending me things here for anything [...] Could have been anything, I mean dishwasher or anything they were sending me to go and ...
Q:	What, even part-time work?
Mr Colne:	Yeah, they were, yeah.
Mrs Colne:	That's right, yeah. Yeah, which is silly really because um ... if he went on, if he done part-time ... anybody who's unemployed and they do part-time work, you're only allowed to work so many hours before they start deduct-

ing the money out of your social money and that leaves
you only about, like, 10 pound from the social a week and
plus his wages which is only say, 30, 40 pound to live on
for a week.

(Mr Colne, 7)

By mobilising these arguments, the men construct a legitimation of doing
undeclared cash work while claiming benefits, as the only possible way of
breaking out of the 'vicious circle', until acceptable work 'comes available'. Mr Bow does frequent short periods of work for cash.

'I just takes a chance of finding a bit of work [...] 'Cause the moneywise
here – the money on social security it's not great, you can't, you know I,
my wife can't live on it, she's always arguing all the time 'cause she
haven't got the money, she ha'n', can't go to the shop and get this and
get that. And it's ... not very nice to sit around and see a woman, see,
she'll go in the shop and she can't buy a dress, and that's not very nice.
But that's the only way; it's either that or go out, go out pinching. Now
if I go out pinching I'm in prison.'

(Mr Bow, 9–10)

Mr Itchen can relieve his situation in the same way.

'Yeah. I can, I can probably get ah ... few decorating jobs or building
jobs like, you know ... As I, as I say I've done it all [...] Well, it's not
easy; it's all word of mouth ...'

(Mr Itchen, 6)

Mr Exe says that this kind of activity is getting more difficult:

'Well you see ... you ... it's, it's awkward now ... 'cause now they've got
these ... detectives going round, you know, you can't do nothing, you
know ... you just gotta stay where you are ...'

(Mr Exe, 6)

It is not only those currently unemployed who describe doing undeclared
cash work; in all, 23 interviewees say that they have done undeclared cash
work, of whom 12 did such work while they were claiming benefits, and the
other 11 did work which was not declared for income tax when they were
in employment or 'self-employment'. Among those currently unemployed,
one denies doing such work, and two do not mention doing any.

Another way in which undeclared cash work is legitimated is by arguing that the administrative arrangements around benefits penalise those doing irregular, short-term or contract work, by getting them to sign on and sign off, and reprocessing their claims each time.

''Cause you gotta sign on, then you go down to the social security and ... that goes on for ages and when you re-sign on ... you're like 2 weeks in arrears, and you can't have any money for 2 weeks, 'cause it's all changed, I dunno, it's all changed how, it's ... ah ... So I don't bother, I just goes and gets the work and takes a chance.'

(Mr Bow, 9)

'... pain in the neck, 'cause you've gotta go in every time and start a new claim and ... if you do it right they get it through to you a few days later, if you don't do it right – like the first time I didn't do it right and it took them weeks, you know.'

(Mr Torridge, 5)

'See, a lot of the labouring jobs, see, you get, you get 6 months' contract and then you're off; you're finished again, which makes it awkward when you gotta go and sign on, 'cause you got 3 or 4 weeks where it takes to sort it out and you got your family to look after. Really that's a nuisance, that is, that you have to go back and sign on again, wait 3 weeks before you get your money; I mean, then they don't worry what you're gonna do in between ...'

(Mr Wye, 7)

From the accounts of other irregular workers, not currently claiming, it is clear that this practice is commonplace, and that men who describe themselves as 'self-employed' have done undeclared work for cash both while claiming, and while working for themselves (i.e. not declaring it to the tax authorities). In this fragmented, casualised labour market, undeclared cash work is constructed as a legitimate way of getting out of administrative traps which frustrate the active worker who wants to be a successful breadwinner.

One of the men, Mr Frome, constructs himself as 'outside the system' because he is explicitly avoiding any form of regular employment. Middle class in background, with quite wealthy parents and parents-in-law, his account is framed in different language from the others – yet it has many features in common with those of the other 'irregulars' in its description of the 'vicious circle' in which there is pressure from the benefit authorities to take work, yet a shortage of regular, decently paid jobs. Like them, he is content to do occasional cash work, trading off autonomy and variety with insecurity – but he has a wider range of options, because of his family's resources. He explains that he is now doing a 'training course', and will then apply for an Enterprise Allowance (he was the only interviewee to do this, mainly because he could produce the £1,000 needed to qualify).

Mr Frome: Because um ... well, you see, since they, the government changed their situation where, you know, you have to now ... I mean they've, they've even changed the forms and things at social security or the, at the dole office, where now they can pretty well stop your money if you can't prove that you've been looking for work ... and um they call you in every sort of few weeks and you have to sort of go to one office and then another office and have a couple of interviews and they sort of want to know what, what jobs you've applied for. And as I've ... never really wanted to apply for any it made my life a bit tricky, so I just sort of went through the sort of standard thing of telling them that um ... I'd looked in the job centres and I'd looked in the local papers and I'd been talking to people, asking them for work. I mean none of which I'd done, 'cause I didn't want any, but the [laughs], but I mean for some reason they expect you to say this and once you've said it all they sort of, then try to put you on to a course of some kind, you know ... And so I went on to one course – I don't know – a year or so ago which was absolutely ... hopeless, and in fact I walked out because um ... I was, actually I was losing money because I was just doing a, a couple of days a week for ... as a building labourer for somebody, just a sort of one man band, who just needed somebody to hold things, and um ... so I left, I left that course before um ... so that I could still go into him on a Thursday and Friday, which seemed like a good idea, but then ... since then I've been thinking that as they're going to be hassling me so much I might as well ... sort of do something to keep them off my backs ... off my back, so um ... this last time they tried to put me on to a sort of ... incentive type course, you know, where they hype you and use lots of buzz words to get you motivated ...

Q: Really?

Mr Frome: Um so I thought, oh well I'm getting sick of this, so I, I'll just, I'll do it properly this time so I, I told them I wanted to be um ... a b, restorer of pottery and porcelain, which is something I've had an interest – I mean I've been doing it myself for a couple of years anyway – again sort of ... ah, you know, just sort of on the side ... doing a little bit here and a bit there and going round to jumble sales and sort of, basically getting my beer money out of it so that ... 'cause I mean my beer money can't come from social security 'cause there just isn't any extra there. So um ... I've been doing this for a couple of years, and so I sort of says to them, well ... you know, is there any way that you can train me? And, and I mean, they, they said, no. Um ... Because they hadn't got it on their books and it, if it wasn't on the books then it can't exist and so they can't pay for training for it and um ... So I said, fine, well if I can find somebody to train me will you pay them? They, they eventually sort of ah, reluctantly agreed to that. Um ... I think the, the main thing was that they wanted a certificate at the end of it; a piece of paper to say ... you have ... you know, been on so and so and now you can do so and so, because I mean, restorers are just, they're sort of nearly always one man bands ... and they don't have sort of ... you know [laughs] courses that they run that they can give you a diploma at the end. All they've got is what, the techniques they've worked out themselves ... But I found, I found a very good restorer out at [place name] and um [...] ... so I, I've finished training with him now and really I'm just, now I'm at home again ... well I never really left, 'cause I, I didn't want to do any of their training where you're away and things, because we are happy at home ... so I'm, I'm building this little workshop on the back and um ... practising away at home, you know, until I'm good enough at it. Then I intend to sort of ... I suppose, do all the things they want, you know, sort of ... come off of training and go on to the sort of 40 pound a week scheme and ... um ... go onto FIS [laughs] and basically get pretty well the same money off the government as I am now except through different channels and then they won't keep hassling me every few weeks to get a job. Yeah. And that's it.

Q: When you say the 40 pound a week, is that the Enterprise Allowance?

Mr Frome: Yes. Yes. I've ... c, I'll just, I'll borrow a thousand

> pounds off somebody; you only have to have it for 3 days.
> You just have to prove you've got a thousand pound in
> your bank, then they'll give you the 40 pound a week and
> then you give the thousand pound back to whoever lent it
> to you. [laughs]
>
> (Mr Frome, 29)

Hence the apparently 'deviant case' of Mr Frome – a self-proclaimed
avoider of employment – reveals the same structure of social relations as
the accounts of other 'irregulars'. Although he constructs himself
somewhat differently, his account reveals that his 'breadwinning' consists
of occasional short-term work for cash with the receipt of regular income
from the state. Rather like an agency worker, such as Mr Torridge, he has
now made an official arrangement under which claiming is combined with
earning, though he is able to take advantage of the Enterprise Allowance to
achieve this.

INCOME TAX AND THE POVERTY TRAP

Our interviews give a very different picture of the interaction between
taxation and benefits from the ones in the standard economic and social
policy literature. They add to knowledge of this phenomenon, by showing
how low-paid regular and irregular workers construct their decisions about
taking on or refusing extra hours of employment, or changing employments
or roles within a firm. They therefore provide new theory about the poverty
trap. Interviewees in employment earned low basic wages, yet were keen to
maximise their earnings. Hence they were eager to do any overtime that
was available. In fact, if offered a choice between employment with a
higher basic wage but no overtime, or one with a low basic rate and high
overtime, most chose the latter.

> 'But at the moment I, I don' want it [promotion]. 'Cause [...] what the
> management gets is [...] poor to what I get.'
>
> (Mr Cherwell, 5–6)

> The other place I used to work a lot of overtime, I used to do about 70–80
> hours a week over there. Course over here you can only do about 45–50
> – a drop in money see. So basic's not very high but you used to make it
> up on overtime.'
>
> (Mr Derwent, 13)

Most of these men who worked a lot of overtime acknowledged that they
paid a substantial amount of income tax on their extra earnings, but said it
was still worth while.

Even working the hours I do – if I was to work 70 hours I'd still only take home about 150 pound. It isn't a lot really [...] I only take home about 150 [at present], that's after paying tax and that [...] You still end up with a little bit more.'

(Mr Derwent, 23)

However, this man acknowledged that he was hardly any better off than if he worked a 40 hour week and claimed family credit – for which he was currently not eligible.

'No. 'Cause I do the overtime. See that's the trap I fall into, you see. On my basic I would do, but I do the overtime so I got the extra money, so that's another area where it's wrong [indistinct], I mean I could perhaps work flat weeks for, say, 2 months, and claim everything, then go back to working overtime – right – and that's something what could be looked into there [...] Whereas, say, the bloke next door could be earning a lot less than me, or earning the same money as me on basic, but perhaps he won't do overtime he makes all the claims and ends up with the same amount of money as what I do.'

(Mr Derwent, 24)

This was a typical way in which our respondents recognised the poverty trap – as caused by a combination of income tax on higher earnings, and overtime which took them just outside the limit for family credit. They experienced this as unfair, in comparison with others who worked less, or not at all.

'I can't [...] apply for family credit [...] They brought advert out, advertising the fact that people would apply for it. And in the advert this chap was earning 170 pound a week and he got it [...] Well I'm not earning ... I'm not ... you know, his take home pay was 170 pound a week. My take home pay is a darn sight less than 170 pound a week, but he, you know, he was s'posed to have got it [...] Well, 'cause in their opinion I'm earning too much money. The money I'm earning I should be well off. Yet I can, I can give you ah ... a list of 9 or 10 people in this ... [estate's name] – right – who go abroad every year for a holiday; who drive a nice car; and they've never worked a day in their, never worked a day in their life.'

(Mr Avon, 22–3)

For these men the poverty trap was not a matter of fine calculations of marginal tax rates, leading to adjustment of hours worked. It was a way in which official policy defeated their income-maximisation behaviour, and baulked their attempts to behave as good economic providers. It was those who were not influenced by the unemployment trap at the time of being interviewed who recognised the poverty trap, and considered it unfair on those who tried to work their way out of poverty. Because men construct themselves as workers, most perceive and resent the 'vicious circle' of the unemployment trap, but are willing to 'have a go' at working their way out of it by various means, including spells of working for cash while claiming. Several also recognised the poverty trap, and commented on its injustice, but when offered the chance of overtime chose to ignore it. Hence it is their construction of their identities as workers and providers which causes men to be relatively impervious to these disincentive effects on taking employment or increasing earnings.

CONCLUSIONS

In analysing our data on men's decision-making, we spent a good deal of time trying to produce categories of respondents that explained the variations in their accounts. The obvious method was to put them in categories according to their current employment status, and then try to explain this outcome from their accounts. This of course fitted the structure of their stories, which were essentially historical explanations of how they reached their current employment status.

However, it eventually became clear that this approach was of little value. To understand the hidden structure of social relations revealed by the men's accounts, their current status was of limited significance. All had one common feature – the 'breadwinner' role as normative for a man – but beyond this, employed, self-employed and unemployed men constructed similar accounts of the wider economy, described similar experiences of government schemes, casual or short-term work and unemployment, and made similar criticisms of the tax and benefits system.

The more we looked at these accounts, the more it became clear that there are only two relevant categories – 'regulars' and 'irregulars'. The twelve men with regular, long-term employment describe social relations of employment, earnings and consumption (such features as training, promotion, occupational pensions, holiday pay and redundancy entitlements) which distinguish them from the rest.[16] They also are palpably aware that they are holders of a scarce and dwindling asset which, for all its disadvantages, confers security and regularity of earnings.[17]

All the rest share experiences of being without earnings, and often without any income, for short or long periods. Some (such as Mr Tamar and Mr Exe) have had regular jobs in the past, but they do not expect ever to have them again. These experiences have given them more in common with each other than with the 'regulars'. There are no essential differences in the social relations constructed by the employed, the 'self-employed' and the unemployed, and most have moved between these statuses fairly frequently in the 1980s, including periods when they were doing undeclared cash work while claiming, or while 'self-employed'.

However, there is also a paradox about rejecting the use of administrative categories – derived from government departments – in the understanding of these accounts. On the one hand, as we have emphasised throughout this chapter, the irregular workers who form the great majority (two-thirds) of our sample do not easily fit into the classifications devised by the employment, benefits and income tax authorities. Yet on the other hand their descriptions of their decisions are largely framed in terms of the rules of those departments, using their terminology and regulations to explain their actions. One of the rhetorical skills the interviewees display, as part of their accounts of themselves as morally adequate men who are workers and providers, is their knowledge of the government's employment and training schemes, the income tax and the benefits systems. Indeed for all irregular workers (with the exception of Mr Kennet – see Chapter 6) this knowledge, and the ability to make calculative choices based on a detailed application of it, is central to their legitimations of their decisions, and to their constructions of themselves as morally adequate 'breadwinners'.

The paradox provides a powerful instance of Michel Foucault's insights on the relationship between state power and knowledge in modern societies.[18] In defining categories of eligibility, need, obligation, contribution and so on, government agencies also define the terms in which these men's struggle for identity and autonomy can be carried out. The state's power to organise and discipline claimants through its officials' knowledge of the nature and causes of poverty and unemployment provides the framework in which our interviewees construct themselves and give meaning to their decisions.[19] Their freedom – whether expressed by doing undeclared cash work or by becoming 'self-employed' – reproduces the power relations between themselves and the state's agents, even as they struggle to improve their material situation. But in our study (unlike Sennett's, for example) this does not have the effect of individualising them, or forcing them back on their own isolated resources. As we shall see in Chapter 7, these men still co-operate and feel solidarity with each other in many of the identities they share, as irregular workers, claimants and residents of the estate.

However, this analysis of the men's accounts does not exhaust the possible explanations of variation within them, since it may be that putting these together with the women's accounts and the joint interviews, an alternative or enhanced theory of decision-making will emerge. It is to the women's accounts that we turn in the next chapter.

REFERENCES

1 The terms vary, however: see for example, W. L. Slocum and F. I. Nye, 'Provider and Housekeeper Roles', in F. I. Nye (ed.), *Role Structure and the Analysis of the Family*, Sage, 1976.

2 Jonathan Bradshaw and Hilary Holmes, *Living on the Edge: A Study of the Living Standards of Families on Benefit in Tyne and Wear*, Tyneside Child Poverty Action Group, 1989, p. 84.

3 E. C. Cuff, 'Some Issues in Studying the Problem of Versions in Everyday Situations', Manchester University, Department of Sociology, Occasional Paper, No. 3, 1980.

4 The practice of constructing themselves as providers, even when they have manifestly been unable to earn a regular wage to support their families, can be compared with Voysey's finding that parents of handicapped children construct their family life experiences according to the paradigm of a 'normal' family, as a way of avoiding stigma. See M. Voysey, *A Constant Burden*, Routledge & Kegan Paul 1975.

5 Jane Millar, Kenneth Cooke and Eithne McLaughlin, 'The Employment Lottery: Risk and Social Security Benefits', *Policy and Politics*, Vol. 17, No. 1, 1989, pp. 75–81.

6 Richard Sennett and Jonathan Cobb, *The Hidden Injuries of Class*, Cambridge University Press, 1977, p. 25.

7 ibid., p. 29.

8 ibid., p. 60.

9 David Knights and Hugh Willmott, 'Power and Subjectivity at Work: From Degradation to Subjugation in Social Relations', *Sociology*, Vol. 23, No. 4, 1989, pp. 535–58.

10 R.E. Pahl, Divisions of Labour, Blackwell, 1984, pp. 250–1.

11 See for example J. Friedmann and S. Ehrhart, 'The Household Economy: Beyond Consumption and Redemption', paper delivered to the World Sociological Congress, Mexico City, 1982; N. Redclift and E. Mingione, *Beyond Employment: Household, Gender and Subsistence*, Blackwell, 1985.

12 Sennett and Cobb, *The Hidden Injuries of Class*, pp. 94–5.

13 ibid., p. 98.

14 M. Buroway, *Manufacturing Consent*, University of Chicago Press, 1979.

15 See also Robert Turner, Anne-Marie Bostyn and Daniel Wright, 'The Work Ethic in a Scottish Town with Declining Employment', in B. Roberts, R. Finnegan and D. Gallie (eds), *New Approaches to Economic Life: Economic Restructuring, Unemployment and the Social Division of Labour*, Manchester University Press, 1985, Ch. 26.

16 Bill Jordan, *The Common Good: Citizenship, Morality and Self-Interest*, Blackwell, 1989, Ch. 6.

17 Philippe Van Parijs, 'A Revolution in Class Theory', *Politics and Society*, Vol. 15, No. 5, 1987, pp. 453–82.

18 M. Foucault, M. Morris and P. Patten (eds), *Power, Truth, Strategy*, Feral Publications, 1979; M. Foucault, *Discipline and Punish*, Penguin, 1979; M. Foucault, 'The Subject and Power', in L. Dreyfus and P. Rabinow (eds), *Michel Foucault*, Harvester, 1982.

19 Knights and Willmott, 'Power and Subjectivity at Work'.

5   'Fitting it all in'

The women's accounts of their employment decisions are constructed within a rhetoric of obligations to other family members, as wives and mothers, responsible for child care and unpaid domestic work. Hence paid work has to 'fit in' with their primary role as caregivers. It was therefore tempting for us to analyse the women's accounts as the counterpart of the men's – as accounts in terms of a 'caregiver' role which neatly complemented the 'breadwinner' role in which the men's versions are constructed.[1] However this does no justice to the complexity of the different aspects of being a woman in this community, or the rhetorical skills with which the women interviewees describe how these 'fit' together. The role of women can better be seen as fitting in all these different elements, under an overall requirement that children's needs come first, and that women have primary responsibility for child care.

Just as the men's accounts contain internal tensions between aspects of their role – worker and provider – so the women's display complexity, conflict and some dilemmas, which are handled by means of a debate – with themselves, with kin or with the interviewer – in which the claims of their responsibilities, opportunities and needs are rehearsed and negotiated. Women describe daily or weekly routines which require them to fit in child care, domestic work and paid work, and to make the arrangements necessary for their primary (unpaid) duties to be reconciled with their paid working hours.[2] Their accounts describe formidable feats of organisation and energy[3]: they display subtle skills in the rhetorical management of these aspects of their role.

The main elements in the women's accounts are responsibility for child care, contribution to household income and personal fulfilment or development: the first is primary, and the third, which comes far behind the second, is absent from some interviews. The women speak as members of households: they construct morally adequate accounts of their contributions to household needs. Their obligation to put children's needs first is binding, and it is in tension with the other two. In these households, the woman's paid work is often the only way to lift the household income above a poverty level, up to one where children can take part in social and educational activities, holidays can be taken, or their council house can be purchased. Hence, although all the women construct themselves primarily as caregivers, many of them go on to describe a contribution to the household income which is essential for the standards of living to which the family aspire.[4]

The rhetoric of 'fitting in' which is so extensively used in women's versions can give the impression that women's labour-market decisions are secondary to men's, and that the woman's role as caregiver and secondary earner fits the man's as breadwinner as a glove fits a hand. This is not the case.[5] Women have to make their own decisions, and their own arrangements, balancing the different requirements of their role. The rhetoric of 'fitting in' describes this activity of deciding, arranging, negotiating and managing, rather than the outcome. Women give accounts in which they are proactive, not reactive, and make choices in line with priorities which are theirs: they describe themselves as exercising judgement and skill in these decisions. Their moral adequacy is displayed in fitting together all these elements in a woman's role, rather than in complementing or supplementing the role of their partners.

The women interviewees' labour-market histories are different from men's. Before having children, many had a succession of low-paid and irregular employments,[6] though some had secure full-time work, and stated that they were earning more than their husbands. All gave up full-time work on having their first child, or within a year afterwards, and only three went back to any form of paid employment after the birth of their second child. At the time of interview, only one of the women with a child under 5 was working full time. Hence the birth of children, and especially second children, was a major turning point for women's employment.[7]

A second feature which emerges from the women's accounts is that the market for their labour, though poorly paid and often involving very difficult hours, is more *regular* in its demand than that for men (both in the sense that it fluctuates less, and that the demand is for regular employees). Women with children tended to work part time (15 in our sample, compared with only 4 in full-time work), but their hours did not vary much from week to week, and none were on short-term contracts (though 3 helped their 'self-employed' husbands on a part-time basis). It also becomes clear from the women's accounts that, although they give up their employment when their partners become unemployed (because of the rule under which any earnings above £5 are deducted from income support benefits) their return to work makes an important impact on the employment status of their partners, especially when the latter are 'irregulars'.

A third aspect of the women's accounts is that, although women always describe their work as 'fitting' their children's needs, where they have regular work their partners may 'fit' their employment round the woman's, rather than *vice versa*. This is a feature of Mrs Cherwell's account of the changes in her working hours since she (unexpectedly) had a baby by this marriage, her children by her previous marriage being 21, 16 and 14. When the baby was born, she was working at the same roadside restaurant as her second husband; she took 4 months off to have the baby before returning to full-time work.

> 'Yeah ... I didn't intend to go back to be quite honest, but then ... I thought I needed a break ... I needed to get away ... I wasn't really into having babies ... didn' really need it [laughs] did I? So I really thought ... that I needed to get back and to have those few hours break ...'
>
> (Mrs Cherwell, 24)

She explains how her present hours work in with those of her husband (at the same restaurant).

Q: How do you manage with her [baby] normally? Who looks after her when you're at work?

Mrs Cherwell: My ... Well my husband. 'Cause he comes home at 3 and I go in at 3. Well my mother comes up ... twice ... What happens? We're both off on Mondays; he's off on Tuesdays; I go in Tuesday afternoon; I'm off today. So my mother comes up Wednesdays and Fridays ... and.. sits with her and she ... it's only an hour and 20 minutes you see from when I leave to when he gets home so she sits for that time, with her. And Saturdays and Sundays ... then Mum comes, sometimes comes up Saturdays, but a friend haves her Sundays so ... it's not too bad. It's only a matter of ... she's only left for about an hour and 20 minutes, hour and a half ... about 3 days a week, that's all'.

(Mrs Cherwell, 25)

How this pattern became established is explained in an exchange which includes comments from Janet, her sister-in-law, who is holding the baby during the interview.

Q: Did your husband offer to help [indisinct]?
Mrs Cherwell: Oh yeah, yeah. He's ... yeah ...
Q: He's quite happy about it? ...
Mrs Cherwell: Yeah, he's better with her than what I am...
Q: Is he?
Mrs Cherwell: I'n' he?
Janet: Yeah.
Mrs Cherwell: You gotta admit that. [laughs]
Janet: Yeah, he is.
Mrs Cherwell: Yeah, he's got a lot more patience. [laughs]
Q: Did he encourage you to go back to work or did he stand back and let you [indistinct]?
Mrs Cherwell: [indistinct] Yeah, it was entirely up to me. Yeah. I ... you know ... you do what you wanna do, sort of thing. And he'll just fall in with it; I mean he falls in with anything anyway. [laughs]
Janet: 'Cause he's a [indistinct].
Mrs Cherwell: Yeah.
Q: Did he change his hours when you had the baby or ... was that [indistinct – baby screams] ...?
Mrs Cherwell: He changed his hours when I, we had the baby yeah. He used to do shift work, yeah. I mean we, we both worked together ... we both ... we both used to go to work together and come home together. Um ... We'd do so many days at 7 in the morning till 3 in the afternoon, then we'd do so many days – we'd have our rest days – then 3 to 11, and ... but we always work and come home together; we always worked together. All the time.
Janet: Couldn't get rid of him could 'ee?
Mrs Cherwell: Pardon?
Janet: Couldn' get rid of him ...
Mrs Cherwell: No, couldn' get rid of him. No. So um ... Yes, he had to change. Yeah.
Q: Is that something you've worked out gradually or ...?
Mrs Cherwell: Yeah, well, we thought about like ... him doing what, I mean we could have done it like alternate, alternately – him doing so many earlies and then I doing an early and ... him doing a late, but ... I find it easier to be working evenings; I ... but the evening ... I've had enough ... and I ... I can't handle her in the evening; he's got more patience. Whereas I can't have her running round at 9, 10

> o'clock at night; it gets on my nerves ... you know ...
> whereas he doesn't mind you see, so I decided that I
> would be out of it evenings and ... be home in the
> morning.

(Mrs Cherwell, 25–6)

However, Mrs Cherwell anticipates that she will not be in the job in 6
months' time.

Mrs Cherwell: No, I shouldn't think so, no. On account of this. I'm ...
I'm not gonna be able to rely on my mother for much
longer. I mean she's nearly 70 ... I'm not gonna be able to
rely on her; she's not gonna be able to handle her once
she's started ... running round everywhere. You know ...
So ... No, I can't ... I can't visualise me being there much
longer.

Q: What do you think you'll do?

Mrs Cherwell: Nothing. Won't be able to do anything. I don't think.
'Cause then he'll go back on shiftwork, you see, so it
makes it difficult then [indistinct] to get a job anywhere,
you know ...

Q: Why will he go back on shiftwork?

Mrs Cherwell: Well because he would ... I mean the, I mean he's only
doing that because I'm there. I mean it's for their benefit
as well isn't it? If he could ... if he could work what we
wanna do I wouldn' be able to work at all ... so rather than
lose me they fall in with ... what you .. what you .. what
they want you to do. But if I was to leave he would go ...
'cause he's con, he's contracted for shiftwork so he
would have to go back on the shiftwork, you see. They
only do it as a favour to us really ... you know ... I mean
a lot of people do work [indistinct] out there, but it's
because they need you, they don't want you to leave ...
you know ...

(Mrs Cherwell, 29)

It seems clear from this account that Mrs Cherwell chooses her hours
according to her preferences in relation to child care, and that Mr Cherwell
'fits in' with these, according to the household's income requirements. This
arrangement will only come to an end when Mrs Cherwell's mother is no
longer able to provide the 'bridge' between Mr and Mrs Cherwell's hours
of work.

What emerges from the women's accounts is that they are exercising judgement in handling the complex demands of their role, and the display of this judgement – demonstrating a proper ability to contribute to the household's welfare by managing the demands of caregiving, income generation and personal fulfilment – is the rhetorical task of the interviews. The women achieve a morally adequate version of their work decisions by such accounts, and rehearse with the interviewer their reasons for particular choices, in terms which appeal to taken-for-granted actions about what it is to be a woman. However, they recognise that the role is not static or set – that their decisions, while following certain general principles (which are themselves contestable) both require judgement, and are open to criticism and questioning from others. Furthermore, their decisions have to be negotiated with spouses, kin and friends, because they both reject and cannot afford childminders, and hence have to find substitutes to fulfil their primary responsibilities. They recognise real dilemmas in this process: Mrs Cherwell acknowledges

> '[pause] Um ... oh, I don't know; it's difficult. I don't really wanna leave work ... but ... then she's gotta come first, you know ... [indistinct, laughs]'

> (Mrs Cherwell, 31)

This has important implications for the analysis of work decisions in terms of 'household strategies'. R. E. Pahl acknowledges that partners may, under certain circumstances, pursue *independent* strategies, but considers these to be special cases.[8] By contrast, Finch argues that, even in ordinary two-parent families, the woman is often required 'to develop satisfactory coping strategies for fitting her life around her husband's work'.[9] This is recognised in other studies, such as Yeandle's, which shows how women negotiate with kin and friends 'to free themselves from certain of the childcare and household duties ... in order to take up paid employment',[10] and Porter's study of 'paradigm housewives', which suggests that those outside the labour market 'develop their own strategies for understanding and coping with other experience as it is mediated to them'.[11]

Hence our analysis of the women's accounts must explain both the overall framework (in terms of the role of woman) and the detailed outworkings of this role, in which the woman 'fits' the various elements in it together. At the end of the chapter we return to the notion of 'strategy', and discuss the extent to which women's individual and collective strategies emerge from these accounts.

CHILDREN'S NEEDS

The women construct their accounts of their decisions primarily in terms of the needs of their children. They justify the hours they work by explaining how they are able to make arrangements for the children's care which are consistent with their best interests. After saying what jobs they are doing, they go straight on to explain how this 'fits in' with their family responsibilities.

Mrs Avon has just started work as a cleaner at a sports centre, having changed from being a cleaner at a hospital.

> 'It works out just nice really, 'cause if my husband's on like what he is this week, on early shift, my friend up the road has them for me. I take them in about quarter to 8 and she has them until half past 8, till it's time for them to go to school, see. But it's then, like where my husband's on night work, he comes home about half past 6 and I leave the home about 10 to 8 so he's here to keep an eye on the children, see, so ... and get them off to school that way. So that works out better than the other job I had really.'
>
> (Mrs Avon, 1)

Mrs Avon gave up the hospital job mainly because the hours involved meant she wasn't meeting the children's needs.

> 'I used to start at 5 o'clock and finish at 8 and ... I never used to see them ... children hardly, and my husband was working late shifts ... you know, you'd have to chuck 'em here, chuck 'em there and ... I'd have to phone my dad to see if he would come over and look after 'em until I came home from work or ... they would have to go up with their nanny [granny]. I know she didn't mind doing it but ... I felt guilty in a way, you know, 'cause lumbering them on my husband's mother all the time, see, so I mean ...'
>
> (Mrs Avon, 1–2)

The present arrangement is a big improvement.

> 'I finish 10 o'clock ... then I've got the rest of the day to myself then to come home and do my housework, you know, and get their tea going; then I can spend the rest of the night with the children, when they come home from school, see. I like to spend as much time as I can with 'em but ... [indistinct] and getting up for school and that, but ... otherwise I could never see 'em, see, if I was still up there.'
>
> (Mrs Avon, 2)

Later in the interview she is asked whether she ever sees a time when she might want a full-time job.

> 'Oh yes. It ... When, when they're old enough ... to leave in the house on their own, I mean. Until then, then I won't do it. But I mean once they are of age then I would like to get a full-time job, yes I would [...] This one's only 8, so I mean I got a few years ... yet before I do get a full-time job.'
>
> (Mrs Avon, 10)

Mrs Calder works part time as a stock controller, filling shelves in a large store.

> 'Yes, I can't take on full time; I've got two children under school age, two in school and ... I wouldn't consider ... full-time work at all because it's um ... I like being at home during the day with the children, and I don't think it's viable to pay a child minder to have your children to go out full time when there's another way of doing it ... so part time suits me, the hours suit me and ... we're working it between us ... and its working out quite well.'
>
> (Mrs Calder, 1)

Mrs Calder wanted to 'fit in a job where it doesn't affect the children, my husband too much', she says:

> 'I enjoy being here with the children. I like being a mum ... I like being a, a housewife, to a certain extent ... um ... I don't feel a desperate need to go out full time to work [...] I'm not out of the house for ... for too long or away from them, 'cause they're in bed when I go out. And um ... they're quite happy for Dad to see to them ... but ah, he's always helped with them anyway so it's nothing unusual for Dad to give them their tea and put them to bed. And um ... they don't mind me going out, they just "bye" and ... they know I go to work now. And its, its just part of it, you know, they've accepted it very well.'
>
> (Mrs Calder, 2)

Mrs Derwent is a peripatetic care assistant, working for a voluntary agency; her children are aged 2, 4 and 6. Asked if there are any disadvantages in her job, she replies:

> 'No, the only disadvantage really is, I mean, my children I mean because, 'cause like 4 days a week I've got to get my children up at 6 o'clock in the morning and I've got to sort my ... well they go up my sister's at quarter past 7; that's a shame on them but then again, I mean,

we're taking over the house [buying from council] – we need the money.
I mean, so I mean it'll be better off for them as well [dog barks], you
know more than, you know I'm not doing it just for extra money for
myself [dog howling], we're doing it ... the things we wanted to do but
could never afford to do...'

(Mrs Derwent, 2)

The same theme appears in other women's accounts.

'It was just temporary during the summer you know. And I mean it's
good, it's good money and the hours suit me because the kids are in bed
when I go. They're still there when I get home.'

(Mrs Parett, 2)

Mrs Wear would be willing to do more hours in her cleaning job.

'Yes. As long as I could fit it in round the children. And I don't have to
get anyone to look after them.'

(Mrs Wear, 5)

'I sort of tried to figure out something easy ... Sort of taking with the
little one around as well.'

(Mrs Plym, 13)

Mrs Nene used to take her children to her mother's house before school,
and pick them up from there at the end of the day.

'She's only 5 minutes across the road like, so um ... that was just
convenient actually, you know, 'cause she was always home to look
after me father 'cause he was disabled, like, and um ... that's what we
used to do .. drop 'em off and pick 'em up in the evening like [...]. I still
dropped them over till ... ah ... must have been about 2 years ago. I
decided that um ... well you got to trust 'em at some point or other and
Emma is 16 this year ... so she was about 14 and Stephen's 3 years
younger than her, but um ... they always came home together like. So ...
trusted them. I think they're not too bad so ...'

(Mrs Nene, 8)

Mrs Cherwell is planning to leave her job at the roadside restaurant when
her mother can no longer 'bridge the gap' between her hours and her
husband's:

'I don't really wanna leave work ... but ... then she's gotta come first, you
know ... [laughs, indistinct].'

(Mrs Cherwell, 31)

There follows an exchange between Mrs Cherwell and her sister-in-law, Janet, in which they insist they always give priority to children's needs. This involves making sacrifices when children are very young, but they get more interesting as they grow older. Janet says she puts her children before her husband.

Children are constructed as needing their mothers, particularly in the years between their first and fifth birthdays; and needing family substitutes for their mothers to look after them until they can look after themselves.

CHILDMINDERS AND CHILD CARE

Because of this construction of children's needs, childminders are rejected as an unsuitable way of fitting in employment with family responsilbilities. In explaining why they do not use childminders, the women put this first in terms of children's needs, and secondly in terms of the cost.

Mrs Derwent: Oh no, if it wa'n't for the fact that my sister would do it I wouldn', I wouldn' work. I would never. I would never sort of put 'em in a, in like a childminder, no, never, I mean that's one thing I've always, I've always said. I would never, ever, if it come to the crunch for that ... I mean like if my sister ... couldn't have 'em for one day, well then my husband would get up, you know, although he'd be tired he could catch up the next day but we ... you know, if it come to the point where Teresa wouldn' have 'em I'd be ... I'd just have to give up work. I wouldn't sort of push 'em off onto other people – definite.

Q: Why is that?

Mrs Derwent: I don't believe in it. I mean I s'pose because I was a child's nanny and I saw what the children went through, although they loved me, it wasn' the same as having their mum and dad around, or their mum around more than anything [...], the people that I was looking after their children, they came back home from work – they were too tired to actually get ... back into it. All they wanted sort of was kids bathed and bed and there to have a quiet evening, you know, and I could never get like that. I would never ... I mean I've never ... I mean if I go out it's only my mum or sister or my next door neighbour an' that babysits. I would never sort of go out of my way to get a babysitter that I didn't know, you know I didn' I'm not the type and my husband wouldn't let me anyway; he's adamant there, like I say we need the money, but I mean, I wouldn' sort of put ... I'd always put the children first.

(Mrs Derwent, 8)

However, Mrs Derwent constructs nurseries as meeting children's needs; one of her pre-school children is already at a nursery, and the other would benefit from one.

'And my daughter, she's at full-time nursery down the end there. They got a full-time ... which is the same hours as school anyway. So she gets 5 days a week down there [...] Then there's the little [...] Then I got the 2 year old which is the ... he's the one that really needs play school [laughs] [...] Ooh he's a devil.'

(Mrs Derwent, 3)

Mrs Torridge had just given up her job as an assistant in a home for people with learning difficulties. She says she will have difficulty in finding another job with such suitable hours.

Mrs Torridge: There's not many that suit, with the hours of the children, where with that job I had it was easy enough to do, 'cause the children were just about to go to school when I left, or ... well about an hour after I left and I was always here when they came home.

Q: Is that important to you?

Mrs Torridge: It is with my two because they tend to ... squabble and fight a lot ... and ... run wild [laughs]. Just normal kids, you know. And ... if they can made a mess they'll make it if you're not here to look after them.

Q: Would you ever let, get a minder to look after them?

Mrs Torridge: [pause] No, because they fight too much and it wouldn't be fair on other people to ... look after them. I mean my dad – that's his wheelchair out there – he ... looks after them if I'm not around, but ...it's not fair on him all the time, so ...I couldn't ask anyone else to ...

(Mrs Torridge, 19)

Mrs Humber is thinking of returning to work after leaving some 2 years ago to have a baby. But

Mrs Humber: I want some, like, either a night job or ... where I could work all night, or otherwise, sort of like, 10 till 2 or something like that ...

Q: Because?

Mrs Humber: Of my children [...] I wanna be here when they go to school [...] and I wanna be home when they come home. I don't like to think that I've got to ... leave them with somebody else [...] or get someone to pick them up, that sort of thing [...] Well yeah, cause I, I don't really believe I can ... putting my children on to anybody else while I go out to work.

(Mrs Humber, 9–10)

Mrs Cam used to have a part-time job packing shelves. Her husband looked after the children in the evenings.

'He used to get home about half past 5ish and I didn't have to start till 6, so, I mean, if I'd had to get anyone in to look after them I wouldn't have bothered to do it, but as he was here the children didn't feel too bad about it, you know.'

(Mrs Cam, 4)

Mrs Cherwell is asked whether she would ever use a childminder.

Mrs Cherwell: No, I wouldn' do it.
Q: Why not?
Mrs Cherwell: I just wouldn't. I don't ... No, I don't think, I don't think it's right; it's like if my, if my mother ... I mean Janet says that you know ... that she would look after her ... I mean I've got a lot of people that would look after her but I don't believe in Tom, Dick and Harry looking after them, you know I ... I think they need to be looked after by, you know, just a certain person. No I ... I wouldn'. No. No I wouldn' like that.

(Mrs Cherwell, 30)

Clearly willingness to use a childminder is not considered to be consistent with a morally adequate account of themselves as mothers. It is of prime importance that they construct themselves as putting their children's interests before their own. However, a secondary reason for not using a childminder is the cost.

'I didn't have to get a babysitter 'cause my husband was there. Which made things a lot easier for us. I mean it was less hours, less pay; but you know, didn't have to pay a babysitter which has ... saved in the long run anyway.'

(Mrs Wear, 2)

'You know, you go out to work and you've got to pay for a babysitter to have your kids ... so I think well that's just a waste of time, you're working to pay the babysitter.'

(Mrs Humber, 10)

'I did consider full time but ... I'd had a childminder full time before and its ... just couldn't afford it. It was too expensive.'

(Mrs Plym, 14)

Mrs Ryton says that she will not return to work till her daughter is older.

'I'd like to work again, but not while she's this age, you see ... you wouldn't let Mummy go, would you? She's a proper Mummy's girl.'

(Mrs Ryton, 1)

However, later she explains the economics of her decision.

'I mean, I would have to pay quite a bit for a childminder and that ... by the time it all, you worked it all out, it wouldn't have been worth going to work for it, would it really? [...] but if I see something come up again like that I'll probably apply for it ... 'cause I'll know they're safe, in safe hands with their dad and I won't have to pay him so it'll be ideal for me; it'll be a bit extra money to put towards the bills that we're in debt with at the moment.'

(Mrs Ryton, 12)

WOMEN'S OWN NEEDS

Although there is unanimity among the women that children come first, and they all subordinate their own needs to those of the children in their accounts of employment decisions, this does not imply that they all find the role of being a home-based mother a satisfying one. Both among women in employment and among those outside the labour market, there are many who construct full-time child care as boring, frustrating or stressful, and who see paid work as providing a necessary break, and an opportunity for adult social contact. Hence employment is seen as a way of fulfilling women's own needs for a suitable way of life, and even to safeguard their mental health. After giving financial reasons for working, Mrs Derwent adds:

'Plus I couldn' stay at home. Not now. I tried it, like I was at home for a few months, drove me mad. It drove me mental [dog howls] so bored, you know. I was you, oh, completely bored with it, but oh, [bird screeching] worse place [indistinct] [laughs] [indistict] anywhere, but 'em I enjoy it.'

(Mrs Derwent, 3)

She remembers giving up her job when she had her first child.

'Well at the time I think, you know, all I could think of, "good no more work" [laughs]. Although I loved it, do you know what I mean? It seemed a nice break, you know, more than anything. But then I got a bit bored [...] I sort of done [name of home sales technique], so I could get back into meeting people ...'

(Mrs Derwent, 6)

Mrs Rother has two cleaning jobs, one in the early morning and the other in the evening.

'Yeah. I looks forward to going out ... you know ... gives me a break from ... the little one – 'cause he's a handful ... and that ...'

(Mrs Rother, 7)

Mrs Ryton looks forward to going back to work when her daughter is a bit older.

'like I was saying to you, when I've finished all my housework and that and ... you've got absolutely nothing else to do and she's asleep and John's playing, I think, you know I, I wish I was back at work again like I used to be. Where I'm always on the go. Because at work you can't, you don't get the time, do you? to sit around like this and ... you know. I used to like working because my mind's more occupied; 'cause I was always, always doing something.'

(Mrs Ryton, 4–5)

Mrs Itchen misses the full-time job that she gave up to have a baby.

'I don't really do a lot actually apart from get up in the mornings and look after the kids and the house [...] I'd like to do something else as well [...]. Break from the kids and the house. And Nigel [husband] as well [baby yells] I, I think that's the main thing and I, I dunno, I s'pose I got a bit of me own freedom, as well. Something I can do on my own.'

(Mrs Itchen, 12)

Mrs Cherwell intended to give up her job when she had her (late, unplanned) baby.

'I didn' intend to go back to be quite honest, but then ... I thought I needed the break ... I needed to get away ... I wasn't really into having babies ... didn' really need it. [laughs] Did I? So I really thought ... that I needed to get back and to have these few hours' break.'

(Mrs Cherwell, 24)

These women present the need for a break from the tasks of mothering as normally compatible with the role of a mother who puts her children first. They construct work as more fulfilling of women's own needs than child care, which is described as boring or stressful and they justify paid work as a way of preserving some equilibrium in their own daily lives. Mrs Plym sums up:

'I like going out and meeting other friends and ... the 4 hours that we go out it's a break from ... the kids. [laugh] [...] It feels like work, yeah, but it's not ... that hard work. I mean it's like a break away from the kids an' I've got that extra money to treat the kids with as well.'

(Mrs Plym, 20)

Mrs Hodder was bored at home and found little to do once she finished her housework, when her children were at school. She describes how she decided to take a job as a chambermaid.

'I thinks well at least there's a chance to get out and meet different people as well, 'cause you do meet some nice people and some strange people that sort of job [laughs]. There's some weird pop groups and that in there.'

(Mrs Hodder, 17)

Mrs Avon has just started a new job as a cleaner.

'I thought, well, just that little bit of independence: I've been home [indistinct], I've had a nice little rest. I've had a couple of months off work and ... this little job came up so I said, yeah, I'll take it, and I, you know, just grabbed the job. And ... it's ever so easy. It's a lovely little job. And all the girls down there, they're all young girls down there [...] they are a nice crowd to work with.'

(Mrs Avon, 4)

Mrs Calder explains that she took her part-time job as a shelf-filler for financial reasons, but has found unexpected benefits for herself.

'So ... I think I, I started out thinking I'll do it because it'll mean extra money for the family. But now I'm doing it ... I'm um ... I'm doing it more for my benefit, it gives me something else to think about than seeing to nappies and meals and cleaning the house and um ... I'm using my brain a little bit, which I wasn't before. You can ... you could run a house on auto-pilot, if you want to. And um ... I was leaving the grey matter sometimes, and having something else to think about is quite stimulating, and the money is a bonus. So ... I've changed my opinion from wanting a job to actually doing it [...] I think I've a pretty good deal here so ... I'm a bit like the cat with the cream at the minute, I'm quite pleased with myself.'

(Mrs Calder, 4)

WOMEN'S EMPLOYMENT HISTORIES

One group of women described having monotonous, badly-paid jobs after leaving school, with frequent changes interspersed with periods on government schemes or claiming benefits. Among the younger women there were 13 with early employment histories of this kind, 7 of whom said that they had fallen pregnant without planning and before marriage. None of these was eligible for maternity leave or maternity pay because they had not been in their job long enough. Only one of this group said she had made a *decision* to have a child:

'Then I got married and had my son [...] That was my decision to leave work then, to start a family.'

(Mrs Ouse, 6–7)

Several women expressed mixed feelings about leaving work to have their baby, but those who returned to work were sad about not being at home to witness developmental milestones. Hence the accounts of the role of full-time housewife as monotonous and unfulfilling, and of paid work as stimulating and satisfying, are qualified by the accounts of those women who talk about missing their children on returning to work, and the pleasure they get from being involved full time in their development, especially from the ages of 1 to 5. Mrs Humber was persuaded by her previous employer to go back to work as a shop assistant soon after her baby was born.

'I think my little girl was about 8, 9 weeks. They needed somebody, so they called on me, and I went back but ... I didn' enjoy it so much [...] 'cause I sort of missed [...] not having my little girl round me [...] But I decided no. I missed the things that my little girl started to say and do ... and [...] I thought I should be there so [...] I packed it in [laughs].'

(Mrs Humber, 4–5)

Mrs Frome went back to work when her son was 4 months old.

'It was okay up until I suppose ... he started becoming interesting, then I found I was missing out on rather a lot and [indistinct] sort of found it very difficult to reconcile the two, which was one of the reasons, another reason for giving up ... at the end of '81, 'cause I was ... felt that I was missing too much. I mean, as I was lucky enough to actually see him take his first steps 'cause it happened to be in an evening and I was here, but I could have missed that and, you know ...'

(Mrs Frome, 4)

Another group of six women were eligible for maternity pay because they had been in the same job for a sufficient period: five of these had also been married for some time before pregnancy, as had the four who were eligible for maternity leave. Some of these women also reconstruct their working lives before marriage as having provided opportunities which now elude them. Having children limits the range of labour-market options open to them, and rules out ideas they had when younger about the kind of work they would really like to do. Mrs Nene works as a charge-hand in a box factory, but she would prefer to work in an office.

> 'Yeah, I always wanted to work in an office. I did when I first left school you see. I can type and ... do all and ... telephonist and all that, you see. But then when ... back when I was looking for this job they, everybody was saying: "oh you'll never get a job", you know, "they're hard to come by", and all this ... and um ... when I actually first started looking – which must have been 11, 11 years ago when I went back to work – and I couldn't get a job. I went for umpteen jobs. I phoned up about 'em; went to interviews, and I couldn't get anything. And I took a job that was out Crediton that was working on a farm and that was grading eggs.'
>
> (Mrs Nene, 4–5)

Mrs Ribble described herself as 'a housewife and a mother', and says that she has not worked for 3 years.

> ''Cause I've, when I got pregnant then I gave up work ... Well, I didn't have to give up work, I gave up work beforehand ... 'cause I was gonna join the police force, you see [...]. But then I met Steve and ... we decided on having a family so ... I thought it was a waste of time [...] I've always wanted either to either join the army or join the police force ... you see. Ever since I was 12 years old [...] Because my parents said no to the army ... and they were adamant [...] so I said about the police force to 'em and I sort of got 'em round to it, you know. So ... they said yes [...] I'd love it. That'd be my life, it would .... That's my life's ambition, to join the army, but obviously I can't now because I've got Michael and Steve and ... so ... we're settled now into my own little routine.'
>
> (Mrs Ribble, 3–4)

Later, she explains that she was about to try to join the police force when she met her husband.

> 'So I went out [...] tried to um ... sort of join up [...] and I met Steve, my husband, and sort of ... I told him my plans and he said: "Well it's either the police force or me". And I thought, oh here we go again. [laughs] [...]

Then I was hopelessly in love, you know. [laughs] After 3 years I don't know how though. [Talks to child – child crying] Sorry about that.'

(Mrs Ribble, 5)

Mrs Cam left her job when she was expecting her first baby (now aged 6) and has only been employed briefly since. Before getting married she worked for a time as a hairdresser. When asked what led to her doing that, she replies:

'I don't know really. I was out of work and I just wanted a job and I fancied, 'cause I like painting and drawing and art, anything arty, so I thought I'd, you know, do something like that. [...] If I had the money to start I'd like to do, sort of paints and, you know, it's getting the money and all the equipment to do it, you know. I do oil painting as well and I, if I could have the money behind me I'd like to sort of start something like that – it's having the money.'

(Mrs Cam, 2)

Mrs Calder gave up her career in the forces when she had her first baby – she says she was pressured by her parents.

'... and um ... although I don't regret my son ... I do sometimes wish I'd carried on a bit longer ... and um ... but still, you know ... that's it.'

(Mrs Calder, 9)

Mrs Parrett has six children; she does shift work at a service station café, but she would like to change to something completely different. She is attending adult classes locally.

'I left school and I, I mean I had my family early. I had Helen when I was only 17 and I think the thing was I just didn't ... I left school and I went straight into shop which I just didn't want to do anyway and, but I wish now I'd sort of studied more at school, you know. It's now I'm regretting it. Because the only thing I can work at in the paper is cleaning, cooking and that and I don't want to do that. Now that the kids are all at school and everything I want to do office work or something. So this is why I'm back at taking my English and Maths and typing and everything. [laughs] But whether I'll get them or not, I don' know. Keep me fingers crossed. But ... it's so different now because I want to do it. You know ... When I was at school I didn't want to do it. [laughs] But now I want to do it and I'm enjoying it.'

(Mrs Parrett, 1)

Mrs Parrett did work briefly in an office, for a building supplies firm, which was 'lovely' – 'and then I went and got pregnant'. Since then she has done part-time work for the sake of the family income, but now she is considering her own needs for the first time.

'now if I went for something now it would be because I wanted to do it, not because of the money side of it. You know. I think the thing is you get into a situation where ... well I am myself now, that I'm thinking damn everybody else I want to do what I want to do. You know, I've always done everything else to fit in round my family and you know and the worm's turning [laughs]. You know, I got, I mean ... it sounds ever so selfish I think because I've always put ... well I've always put the little ones, always in front of me, I've always put me family first and thought no I'd better do this because, you know, they come first. Best do this, no because it won't fit in with their hours, you know. But now because they're out to school and I think oh at last nearly 15 years I've spent at home bringing children up and it's about time I wanted to do ... I ... it's about time I done something for myself, you know. And let everybody else try and fit in with me for once [laughs].'

(Mrs Parrett, 6)

Mrs Parrett deploys exactly the same rhetoric as the other women in displaying that she has adequately fulfilled the moral responsibilities of a mother, and then shows how meeting her own needs is now consistent with her children's current situation at school. She goes on to describe the extra room for manoeuvre she has gained, in terms of her plans for her future, through the children's support and encouragement.

'They, they're ever so pleased, especially me older girls like. They ... you know, they think, oh Mum you're ever so brave [laughs] especially as far as like the GCSE they were saying, because I mean I never had nothing when I left school, nothing whatsoever [...] yeah, they think I'm ever so brave. They say, oh Mum, it's school tomorrow i'n'it for you. Yes.'

(Mrs Parrett, 6)

Mrs Parrett demonstrates the considerable amount of rhetorical work that has to be done by a woman to justify following a course designed to get her a job in line with her original aspirations, rather than to meet the household's income needs. Although other women talk wistfully about their previous hopes of more pleasant or fulfilling employment, she is the only one with a plan to further such hopes.

CONTRIBUTION TO HOUSEHOLD INCOME

All the women in employment give income as their reason for working along with fulfilling their own needs – for a break, company, stimulation and a 'bit of a life' of their own – often the financial motive is the first to be mentioned. Women construct their reason for working as contributing to the household income, and especially to items for the children's needs, and not for their own needs. Mrs Hodder describes how she returned to work when her husband was off sick. She took a job as a chambermaid; at first she says this was for her own needs, and for income for herself:

'Well, it was my first job for 16 years, that's all; I went back out to work, just to get a little bit of independence. I mean, since I been there I keeps on saying I'm gonna chuck it in, but you, sort of like just stay there and plod along I s'pose.'

(Mrs Hodder, 12)

However, later, when asked if she keeps any money for herself, she replies:

'No. I always says, oh I'll go to work, go out to work and get a little bit for meself, but I never do. It always gets put right back into the house.'

(Mrs Hodder, 19)

Mr Hodder is a self-employed painter and decorator, whose work is irregular. Mrs Hodder explains the family finances.

'We don't really have sort of one ... sort of like at ... well he gives me some money sometimes and I pays all the bills with it. But I mean, savings ... never save nothing [laughs] ... Sort of like you always have, you saved up a little bit like ... I used to save up some money and then it's always the kids wanted new clothes for school, or new shoes or something, you know it was never spent on me or Tom, not very often [...] I mean I always have enough for me cigarettes ... but I mean that's all I really have, you know, I'm not really bothered about nothing else. [...] We sort of like, I mean when he isn' working, I mean ... it all comes out of my money, but when he's working he gives me a little bit extra ... and sort of like all gets paid out of that. I don't know how [indistinct – laughing] sometimes, but it does all ... manages to get paid.'

(Mrs Hodder, 20)

Mrs Rother does two part-time cleaning jobs.[12] She says 'I gets fed up with cleaning, but still ... you gotta do it'. She explains why she went back to work.

'Well, it'd just started on buying the house and that and ... decided to go out to work, to help ... and that .... 'Cause he wa'n't bringing home much, see, so ... I had to go to work.'

(Mrs Rother, 2)

The second job she took for the money for a holiday.

> 'I wanted to go abroad so I decided ... I had to take a morning job to pay for meself to go to Spain, you know ... this only lasts till, what .... again ... then it got to be renewed and see ... who gets it, you know ... the job again. If not, us is out of a job. It's only for .... go to Spain [...]. What I gets down [firm's name] pays for me to go to Spain. Pays well, he's getting the spending money; I'm saving for the holiday ... and that.'
>
> (Mrs Rother, 2)

This sounds like a holiday for her, but it emerges that all the family are going. Here again, what sounds initially like her own money for her needs turns out to be for the family budget.

Mrs Avon's husband, like Mrs Rother's, is a regular worker, but she too emphasises that he earns a low wage. When asked why she decided to take a part-time cleaning job, she replies:

> 'Um, I think really, the only thing really was the money. That's all. I mean, we were, we were struggling, weren't we? I mean [...] what my husband gives me; I mean he, he do help out if he can [indistinct] he's good like that.'
>
> (Mrs Avon, 4)

Mrs Wear is also married to a regular worker (her husband is a storeman with a local authority). They, too, are buying their own house, and she works part time as a cleaner at a school.

> 'We can pay the mortgage and things with my husband's pay but mine pays for ... It pays the phone bill and odd things and bits for the kids and the mortgage rate's gone up so much – do another job as well I think [laughs] keep things going.'
>
> (Mrs Wear, 2)

Mrs Nene's husband is a regular worker (a motor-cycle mechanic). She did not like her job in a box factory when she started, but she describes her thinking as follows:

> 'I didn't like it, but I, I still had to go like 'cause I thought well if, if we need the money then it's a job and I ... must go and do it.'
>
> (Mrs Nene, 8)

Since then she has become a full-time charge-hand at the factory, although she would prefer to do office work. They, too, are buying their own house.

Mrs Calder's husband has a regular job as a lorry driver. When asked why she became an evening shelf-filler she replies:

'Financial reaons ... as much as anything ... um ... bit of extra money.'

(Mrs Calder, 4)

She explains that she wants to make a contribution to the family's income.

'my money will go straight into the joint bank account ... for family funds, you know, for running the home and what the children need and um ... in a month or two ... you know ... perhaps ... a little bit will be sidetracked into a ... a holiday fund or something like that [...] Rather than say, oh no, that money's mine, I, I earned that, you ... you can't have that, that's not for the gas man, that's for me. I, I couldn't do that [...] He's [husband] worked all our married life and supported us, so now I'm working a little bit I don't see that's mine, goes into the fund as well. It's just my contribution. So ...'

(Mrs Calder, 5)

SIGNIFICANCE OF WOMEN'S EARNINGS

Because women define themselves primarily in terms of their caregiving role, they construct their wages as supplementary to their husbands' earnings and themselves only conditionally as earners. Yet they describe the social relations of the estate in terms which reveal that women's labour-market situation is potentially as strong as or stronger than men's.[13] Mrs Derwent and Mrs Plym both gave up jobs to have babies when they were earning more than their husbands were.

'Well at the time I think, you know, all I could think of "good, no more work" [laughs]. Although I loved it, do you know what I mean? It seemed like a nice break, you know, more than anything [...] And then, I must admit, I mean ... and the money went tight because at [children's hospital where she worked], I mean, it was very good pay, you know, I was on a lot ... well more money than what my husband was ... you know, to lose that, you know, to go to his wages we found it really, really tight.'

(Mrs Derwent, 6–7)

'Well at the time we thought we could manage [indistinct] with my husband's wages at the time, but now we sort of wish I did go back and [...] Well if I went back ... 'Cause at the time I was earning more money than my husband ... but now it's sort ... it's the other way round [laughs] ... but at the time I was earning good money an' ... sort of [sigh] ... we missed it for a while because we struggled for the first couple of years when we got married but ... apart from that it was all right.'

(Mrs Plym, 16–17)

When asked what led to her going back, Mrs Plym replies:

> 'Um ... for the extra money ... for a few more of the ... old luxuries [laughs].'
>
> (Mrs Plym, 17)

Both Mrs Derwent and Mrs Plym were found their jobs by their husbands when they eventually returned to work. When asked how she came to hear of the job at the voluntary agency where she works, Mrs Derwent replies:

> 'My husband did. He was looking for a job 'cause he was unemployed – well a while ago now – and he seen it in the Job Centre and he come home and told me about it. And he said: "Oh ring up". Because you're on your own and I haven't got ... you know I get a list given to me each week and then, sort of, you know I don't sort of come into contact then with the rest of it [...] And I didn't ring 'em and then he said about it again so I rang up. And I had to go for an interview and I got it.'
>
> (Mrs Derwent, 12)

> My husband. [...] he said what jobs were going 'cause he kept an eye open for me and this one came up.'
>
> (Mrs Plym, 17)

These elements in the women's accounts – their high earnings prior to having children, the struggle when they gave up work, and their spouses pointing them back into the labour market – were absent from the accounts given by Mr Derwent and Mr Plym. However, they are not prominent factors of the women's accounts; rather they emerge in response to questions, in descriptions which rely on the construction of their roles as mothers rather than wage earners.

Mrs Humber has been out of the labour market for a number of years, looking after her children. However for a time she did work in an old people's home.

> 'I s'pose we're a bit short of cash and ... I would, I would, like women always seem to get a job quicker than a man [laughs]. So that's why s... went out and got a job....'
>
> (Mrs Humber, 5)

At the time of the interview, Mr Humber has just lost his job and Mrs Humber is looking for night work in an old people's home.

> 'At the moment we're both looking at something [...] but it, at, it's easier for me [...] what we can see that to get a job [...] than it is for him.'
>
> (Mrs Humber, 8)

Mrs Humber is, like most of the women with two or more children in our sample, experiencing financial pressures or mounting debts. She is looking for a part-time job, which is the prefered option of almost all of this group of women interviewees (including those currently outside the labour market because their partners are unemployed and/or they cannot be relied on to help with child care – see pp. 173–4). Sixteen of the 23 women with children under 5 at the time of interview had taken some paid employment, usually because of financial need. In spite of their insistence on their children's needs, and their primary role in meeting them, a large proportion were working at hours when young children might want to see their mother – before school or at bedtime.[14] The women themselves were very conscious of this contradiction (see the quote from Mrs Derwent, p. 141). The following table indicates how patterns of demand for part-time female labour required them to accomplish this difficult balancing of 'fitting it all together'. Unskilled part-time cleaning, catering and retail employment is available in the evenings or early mornings, as firms adopt 'flexible' employment policies to reduce labour and on-wage costs.[15]

Table 5.1 Women in part-time employment – periods of the day worked

Age of children at time of work	Mother's hours of work				
	6–9 a.m.	9 a.m.–3.30 p.m.	4–6 p.m.	6–10 p.m.	10 p.m.–7 a.m.
All under 5	1	1	1		
Some under 5, others 5–15	3		1	2	1
All 5–10					
Some 5–10, others 10–15	1				1
All 10–15	1	1			

Three other women (Mrs Wye, Mrs Tamar and Mrs Nene) had established a pattern of regular full-time employment – all in factories or warehouses. Mrs Tamar and Mrs Nene are both long-term, full-time workers. Mrs Tamar earns £97 a week; she has been a machinist at the same firm for 13 years, and before that worked in the same job for another 9 years. In between she stayed at home to look after her son.

Mrs Tamar: ... because I didn't have anyone else to sort of look after him so ... I had to stay at home.

Q:	Would you have preferred to be at work?
Mrs Tamar:	I dunno. I'd, I think the break ... and being with him when he was growing up ... was ... a better idea, because you miss the interesting parts of it don't you, when they're growing up. Between 1 and 5 is their best time I think, when they're growing up.
Q:	What made you decide to go back to work?
Mrs Tamar:	Money.
Q:	You went back part time did you?
Mrs Tamar:	No, full time.
Q:	How did you organise child care?
Mrs Tamar:	Well, my ex-husband used to look after him. 'Cause he was on ah ... a taxi driver and he used to ... have him during the day when I was working, 'cause he used to work during the night. So it worked out all right [...] I mean it was a thing that had to be done. We needed two incomes. So...

(Mrs Tamar, 23)

Clearly Mrs Tamar was the regular worker in her previous marriage, and she is again the regular worker in her new marriage; Mr Tamar has had long periods of illness, and is expecting to get the sack from his night job. Mrs Tamar speaks of her job much as the men with regular jobs speak of theirs.

'I know everybody and everybody knows me [pause] never really thought about changing. Got used to everybody there [laughs] [...] Six years from now I expect I'll be in the same job [...] I think I'll stay there now till I retires I think [...] That's not very long to go. Twenty years, I should imagine I should still be there if the firm stays open.'

(Mrs Tamar, 21,24–5)

Mrs Nene is now a full-time charge-hand after 9 years of working at the box factory. She does overtime every Saturday, and her earnings are £114 per week, excluding overtime. Her wages are clearly important for the household finances.

'Well I s'pose generally, I mean, we ... we managed on what my husband earned, but ... you know ... it was ... it could ha' been better. I mean his wages had never been ha, a hundred per cent. He's a motor-cycle mechanic he is, but ... um ... it's not well paid at all. So ... I s'pose that was my main reason really. We needed the money so I decided to go back.'

(Mrs Nene, 5)

Although in terms of our analysis of the men's accounts Mr Nene is a regular worker, Mrs Nene sees him as able to pick and choose what work to do – unlike herself.

'he can't understand, you see, why people do jobs that they don't like because he's never had to. He's always done his motorbikes and ... all right he's been made redundant from a couple of places and what have you ... but he's always done jobs in between, but he's only done 'em for a short period of time; he's never had to, like, stick at it, 'cause he's always gone into the next motorbike job, so ... he can't understand, you know, if you don't like then you don't do it, as far as he can see [laughs], yeah. Yeah, he's never come across that there – or yet. I think that's him. [pause] John.'

(Mrs Nene, 9)

Even in these households, where the women provide the *more* regular as well as a substantial part of the income from their wages, their contribution is seen as allowing the family to enjoy 'that bit extra' – luxuries like holidays, sports clothing or outings for children, and the chance of buying their own house. It is also clear that a regular contribution from the woman partner is essential for any couple seeking to buy their council house.

'We would have to have both of us working to ... all the time, to be able to do it. Wouldn' be able to do it on one salary alone. It would have to have something like with us working ... both of us working full time .. to do it.'

(Mrs Tamar, 27)

'So we've bought this one now, so I mean I'll have to work for the rest of me life ....'

(Mrs Derwent, 31)

Hence it is clear that women's wages are vital for the household incomes of those couples who aspire to the 'extra', and especially to owner-occupation. But in the case of women with partners in irregular work, the significance of women's employment goes beyond this; on occasions it determines the man's employment status. Mrs Hodder describes how she returned to work when her husband was still receiving benefits. Mr Hodder had been home for over a year with a sports injury, having previously been a self-employed painter and decorator, and they were having difficulty living on benefits.

'Part of the reason ... that's why I did take a job because he was home all the time and I was home all the time and we used to be getting on each other's nerves and I used to think, well, he was moaning about money, I was moaning about money ... and so I thought oh I'd just as well go out and get a job, I s'pose that in part of a way that's why I took it, you know to get out of each other's way. You know I think we used to see too much of each other, you know being home here all the [...] Well he couldn't go very far obviously.'

(Mrs Hodder, 20)

Mrs Hodder is asked whether her earnings were deducted from their benefits.

'Oh no. No because we were able, able to claim FIS then, you know like he used to get his sick money ... and I was getting my money so that was, that wasn' all that much so we ... because you're ... one person's working you can claim the FIS then so we was better off and ... well we was only about 30 pound a week better off, but I mean 30 pound was 30 pound; it was extra money to pay the bills. So it was better in a way.'

(Mrs Hodder, 20)

Mrs Hodder is asked whether she knew she would be eligible for FIS.

Mrs Hodder: Yeah, because we, before I even took the job we went down and asked about it. And they said we'd be 50 pound a week better off. Well when it come to it we has only 30, so I mean that wasn' too good ... but there again it wasn' even 30 because by the time I'd paid me bus fare it worked out about 25 so we wasn' really much better off. But I mean at least it was a little bit of money what I could call me own, you know. Whereas before it was sort of like all Tom's money. You know, he was getting his sick money, plus his supplementary money and it was sort of like, oh if we had a row, it was all my money. So I thought, oh I'll go and get me own [laughs]. 'Cause we used to have a few rows, you know, like when he was home.

Q: Was he surprised when you took a job?
Mrs Hodder: Well I think he was in a way. I don't think he liked it first of all, you know, that I was out working and not him. You know, but he kept on saying ... he used to keep saying, well why don't you try and get a job. So I thought well in the end I did and I think I shocked him in a way, that I ... He ... Well I think even now he don't think he, he'd think I'd stick it so long. You know I keeps on saying oh I'm gonna chuck it in, I'm fed up with it. I still carries on ... But ...

(Mrs Hodder, 21)

In his account of his return to work after his injury, Mr Hodder is very vague about timing, but recalls that it was after his wife took the job in the hotel. In the joint interview, the question arises as to who will look after the children during the long summer holidays. Mr Hodder insists that he is far too busy to do so; however, when Mrs Hodder met the interviewer by chance shortly afterwards she remarked that he had signed on again in order to take care of them. Thus Mr Hodder's decison to return to work after his injury was timed to follow his wife's return to the labour market, and his withdrawal from his work, and reversion to claiming benefits, was timed to cover for the children's school holidays.

Mrs Parrett makes it clear during her interview that she is fed up with her job in the service station café, both with abuse from customers and with her supervisor's attitude towards the workers. By the time the joint interview occurs, Mrs Parrett describes giving up the job, and justifies the decision with a detailed description of the bad treatment she has received. Meanwhile in the joint interview Mr Parrett, the irregular self-employed building worker, describes himself as a 'foreman [...] in charge of ten blokes and I tell 'em what to do and, if it's not done then I come down on them like a ton of bricks'. Yet shortly after their joint interview, Mrs Parrett met the interviewer, again by chance, and said that he had decided to claim as unemployed again since she was no longer working. Mrs Parrett's regular income, like Mrs Hodder's seems to have had an important effect on her husband's motivation to be self-employed rather than unemployed. This will be further discussed in Chapter 6.

Thus although women construct their accounts of their labour-supply behaviour in terms of their roles as caregivers, the social relations revealed by their accounts are such that their contributions to household income take on a far greater significance than this version of their role would seem to imply. For wives of regular workers, their earnings make the difference between poverty and the slightly better quality of life enjoyed by those who can afford 'extras' for the children, and to buy their council houses. For wives of irregular workers, their employment status can make the difference between the husband signing as unemployed (and probably doing undeclared work for cash) and changing to 'self-employed' or taking a job.

WOMEN AND THE UNEMPLOYMENT TRAP

Yet despite this significance of women's employment status for men's, all but one of the wives of unemployed men in our sample were themselves unemployed. In line with the findings of Daniel,[16] Bell and McKee,[17] Morris,[18] and Millar, Cooke and McLaughlin,[19] they describe themselves as being in a situation where it is not worth working, because their earnings are deducted from their partner's benefits.

Mrs Dovey and her husband have both been unemployed since his cleaning business closed down 3 years ago. Asked whether she has thought about getting a job, she replies:

'Yeah, very often. But ah ... I don't know that it would be worth my while really because ... they would stop my money and then ... we'd still be left with nothing really [...] They're low pay aren't they? I keep saying I'll get a job but ... like, say, work in the hospital or something like that ... but time you've paid the rent, you would have to pay the rent, bit extra on the rent and ... um ... have to pay for, what else? Would have to pay for ... [pause] ah bus fares and things like that I suppose and ...'

(Mrs Dovey, 4–5)

Mrs Parrett describes how she came to leave the service station café after an earlier period working there.

'Then me husband lost his job so we had to go on social security and they would only let me earn 4 pound. They'd only let me keep 4 pound out of 20 pound that I earned [laughs]. So I soon jacked that in. I thought no I'd, it seemed a bit pointless me working 8 hours for 4 pound, you know.'

(Mrs Parrett, 2)

Mrs Itchen's husband has recently given up his job because of having his pay reduced for attending college. She has considered working.

'Well if I was gonna go out to work then I wouldn't go out part time. I'd go out full time. Because part time it's just a waste of money because ... it's just a waste of time because they're just gonna ... whatever I earn they'll take off, off of Nigel's dole money, see. So really it won't be worth it in the long run, but I think I can earn up to – I think it's 20 pound a week before it affects the money.'

(Mrs Itchen, 12)

Here Mrs Itchen constructs a rule over disregarded earnings which is more generous than the actual DSS maximum (£5), and which allows her to do more work for cash than the authorities would actually permit. Mrs Frome describes the rule a bit more accurately, but breaks it.

'I also get terribly irritated by the fact that ... you know, pensioners – well fair enough, they've done their bit – but they're allowed to earn 60 pounds a week before their pension's affected. We can earn 2 pounds or 4 pounds a week ... and then they stop your money.'

(Mrs Frome, 9)

She has been working as a helper at the primary school.

'The headmistress asked me if I'd do it [...] And, and I let her know I was on social security and she said, oh well ... that's up to you, sort of thing, so ... I did it anyway [...] And she wouldn't have, wasn't going to say anything – tell on me. Ah ... but she'd ... 'cause I was in the, the deputy head's class ... that Natasha in and I was doing reading with them every Tuesday afternoon ... and it was her who said, who suggested that I ... that she asked me if I'd like to do it.'

(Mrs Frome, 7)

Mrs Frome thinks the earnings disregard should be more generous.

'But I think there should be a system where ... yes you can earn, you know, 30 pounds or 40 pounds a week ... without it affecting your, your social security. I think they'd probably find then ... that a high, that a lot of the fiddling would stop because you know, people who are earning less than that, you know, aren't declaring it and then, it's asking the government that to take them to court and all the other hassles .. and watching them and everything else. Whereas if they were just to pay it out then ... a lot of it would stop.'

(Mrs Frome, 10)

Mrs Bow has done cleaning jobs part time since her children were born, but her husband is now out of work.

'... it's not worth doing it, 'cause they only takes it anyway ... social takes it [...] unless it's cash in the hand, without them knowing.'

(Mrs Bow, 18)

Thus it becomes clear that, although – like their husbands – these women describe a system which makes it not worth their while to do paid work, in practice they may take part-time employment without declaring it to the benefit authorities. They construct various ways of legitimating this -- some of them complex and ingenious. Mrs Humber recalls a period when she did night work in an old people's home when her husband was unemployed.

'I could only earn so much anyway [...] but I paid tax. If I didn't pay tax then I could only bring home so much 'cause [...] the DHSS would take the rest [...] because I paid tax and I was paying insurance I was classed as a single woman [...] I dunno why, but that's just the way they done it. I was all, I was classed as a single woman. So I was allowed to bring home 46 was the most wasn't it? Which I never earned anyway, because it was, sort of like, taxed ...'

(Mr and Mrs Humber, 40)

Later Mrs Humber says she will not take another night job, now that her husband is again unemployed.

'because it just won't be worth me working, 'cause you're only allowed to earn .. I think you're only allowed to bring home 12 pound and there's no way I'm working all night for 12 pound.'

(Mr and Mrs Humber, 42)

Mr and Mrs Derwent were both out of work for a time before they took their present jobs. Mrs Derwent is asked about starting work when her husband was still unemployed.

'Yeah but that was really ... oh well ... I don' know [indistinct] but that was when ... on the side ... I started ... and this one ... this, this wasn't like the old people. This was just in a pub. I done a couple nights and they paid me like cash in hand although I shouldn't say it but ... it wasn't much but it helped ... I mean unemployment was nothing – hardly – and ... we needed the money. But then as soon as he got a job I went [...] he started his job in February and I got a job in April, like, you know, once he was back in employed then I went and got one. A proper one.'

(Mrs Derwent, 10)

So for the wives of irregular workers, cash work is part of the way in which they contribute to household income during their partners' periods of unemployment. However, the women in this group construct in more detail the consequences of low and irregular pay, and are more critical of the administrative arrangements around benefits than their husbands – probably because it is their budgeting that is directly affected. Mrs Ryton describes how she experienced the situation when her husband's wages were very low, and then when they were not being paid in full by his previous employer.

'He was getting something like 56 pounds a week for doing the work but then they'd make up by the dole as well – I can't remember how much – it ha'n't very much dole money, worked out he was 10 pound better off than being in the dole altogether.'

(Mrs Ryton, 6)

He then went to work for a builder whose method of payment was unreliable.

'his boss used to pay something stupid like 30 pound cash and the rest of it made up in a cheque form, which bounced [indistinct], some weeks we were just getting 30 pound to live on which is ridiculous and my husband is now taking [employer] to court over it, 'cause he still owes him 350 pounds outstanding wages.'

(Mrs Ryton, 6)

Now he has started work as a stonemason, but they have to pay £25 a week in rent arrears to clear their debt.

'he's on a low wage so we ... applying for Family Income so we've got to wait now, to hear from them to see what sort of rent we got to pay now, 'cause we can't afford to pay 25 pound a week any more [...] I phoned up today actually and said, you know, I said we need some more money and they said, will you ... the earliest we can pay you is Friday [...] they made a mess up with the computer a couple of weeks ago and Ed signed on Tuesday; our giro was due Thursday so [...] we waited Thursday morning [...] and we waited and waited till the second post [...] and it didn't come [...] so I ... Ed got straight on to the phone and said, look where's my giro [...] and they said, oh sorry there's been a mix up you won't be able to get it till Monday – Saturday or Monday. And he goes, well look, you know, I've got a wife and two kids here and I've got bills to pay, rent to pay. What are we meant to do – 'cause this was Thursday – from now till Monday [...] I got no money at all for food. And they said, well you can always have an emergency loan form at [DSS office], a crisis loan it's called. And he went in there and he got something stupid like, he queued up for about 2, 3 hours, 'cause I went in there with him, [...] I waited for him at 3 o'clock and he actually turned up at 5 o'clock [...] and I said, well I hope it's worth it, you know, waiting all that time, and he, he said, right – here it is: 17 pound, you know [...] The money did turn up eventually and we thought, well this can't be right: 65 pound [...] He went in and he found out that 65 pound in fact had to last us for 2 weeks [...] he said, we can't survive on 32 pound a week, you know, it's stupid [...] and they said, I'm sorry Mr Ryton, until we sort out the reason why you left your last employer that we, we can't put your money up. And he said, I've told you once: I left him because he was messing me around. He was [...] paying me by cheque which bounced [...] He said that's the reason I left. And yet they don't accept that is a good enough excuse for leaving your employment.'

(Mrs Ryton, 14–16)

Comparing the women's accounts with the men's, it is clear that irregular work causes far more disruption, debt and destitution than the men describe. The men portray periods without work, or with very variable earnings, as something to be endured, and although they do criticise the benefits system for penalising them, it tends to be in general terms – as part of the 'vicious circle'. The women's accounts give vivid details of what it is like to be caught between unreliable employers and an overstretched benefits system, which is in any case not geared to irregular employment and pay. Hence it is understandable why so many couples prefer claiming and not declaring their occasional earnings to doing declared part-time work, or low-paid work with family credit.

Mrs Itchen is experiencing the same kinds of difficulties as Mrs Ryton. Mr Itchen claimed family credit when he was doing his low-paid garage work; now he is unemployed.

> 'Family credit, yeah. We get that now from when he was ... at the garage. But see then, with that now ... now they've changed it you don't ... you're not allowed a rent rebate, see, with that, family credit now. Whereas it was FIS you were allowed a rent rebate with it see. We can' now. Yeah, they changed it all haven't they? [...] 'Cause we got so far behind in our rent ... that we nearly got kicked out of here. [...] We're not entitled to it. Not since that ... they've changed it all [...]. We [indistinct] loads and loads of debts. I just forget about 'em. 'Cause there's no good worrying over 'em. They can't get blood out of a stone for starters 'cause if I haven't got the money they can't have it. [...] Our dole money and that doesn't last us – Mum, me mum keeps us [indistinct]. I don't have to pay her back. But if I want money then me mum's always there to give it to me. Because if it wa'n't for me mum we wouldn't survive on, on the money that Nigel gets. The dole money.'
>
> (Mrs Itchen, 12–13)

In the women's accounts, their moral adequacy is enhanced by their contributions through earnings, and their partners who are irregular workers are not constructed as the 'breadwinners' that their own accounts portray them to be. Mrs Torridge is even more forthright in her criticisms, not only of the benefit system, but also of her husband, from whom – by her account – she is now separated. She was earning a modest wage as a care assistant in an old people's home, until her employer cut her hours.

> 'I applied for family credit while I was earning 83 pound ... and then he decided to cut my hours and ... before he decided to cut my hours the forms came through for 83 pound ... and then, by what they told me it would take quite a few months to sort out ... so I thought, well, there's no way that I can afford to live on 46 pound until they decide to sort the family credit out. Because, before I gave my notice in I went down to Income Support and asked them if they could make my wages up until ... I received family credit, and they said there was no way that I could

do it [...]. There was no way that I could afford to stay on 46 pound until family credit come through.'

(Mrs Torridge, 15)

This led to her leaving the job.

'That was the only thing I could do really. I mean, I was getting more through being unemployed than what I was making. [...] I just couldn't wait for the [...] family credit to come through [...] I regret it in a way now, 'cause it's so boring, but ... it's the only thing I could do at the time.'

(Mrs Torridge, 16)

Mrs Torridge constructs her husband's irregular work rather differently from his account (p. 105).

'And then when I gave it up he ... found a job with the [agency's name] and they found him jobs when they've got them [...] Um ... the last three jobs he's had has been working in warehouses ... you know, or loading lorries and ... things like that. But it all depends on what the [agency's name] gives him [pause]. He hasn't got a proper job, he, he's one of these people that can't settle down to just one job; he's gotta have a variety every so often; he can stick a job for about a month and then he's gotta change to something different [...] Well, we're separated [...] so I mean I see him every day ... but that's about it, I couldn't ... stay with him all the time, not ... apart, until he sorts hisself out because he's so ... bad-tempered and irritable ... that I can't, can't handle it. [...] Well he's flitters from here to there at the moment; he hasn't got a permanent address 'cause he's not ... um ... with him on the agency books he can't really sign on because if he get a job he's gotta sign off and he might have a job for 2 weeks and then he's gotta re-sign on again and it's just going backwards and forwards, so he would rather not sign on and live the way he's living. And if there's a week when he do'n' get any work that's the week he do'n' get any money.'

(Mrs Torridge, 20)

In her account, she claims weekly as a separated woman with children; in his, he signs on and claims for his family when his work is unavailable – a major discrepancy in terms of his breadwinning capacities. She continues:

'he'll get fed up with it in the end and he'll realise he's gotta look after his own self. 'Cause he's really he's ... quite immature for his age, he's [...] coming up 23 but [...] he seems to think everybody owes him something [...] he hated me working anyway; he [...] wouldn't ... go and look for a job ... and I was bored so I made the effort and went and got

one and ... there used to be arguments all the time about me working ...
'cause he said I was never spending any time with him [...] I didn't really
take any notice of what he said because if [he] wasn't gonna make the
effort someone had to.'

(Mrs Torridge, 21)

Mrs Torridge sums up the plight of the woman married to an unemployed
or irregular worker in the present benefits system.

'there's nothing I can do about it unless I can get a full-time job [...] I
mean if you work 24 hours, you can claim ... family credit, but it takes
that amount of time to come through, so you've gotta get a 40 hour a
week to get some money in so that you can keep your house running.'

(Mrs Torridge, 23)

However,

'I looked in the paper last night for a job but ... there's not many that suit,
with the hours of the children.'

(Mrs Torridge, 19)

INCOME TAX

The preponderance of part-time work among our women respondents is
constructed by the women themselves as taking this form because of their
children's needs. However, there is an acknowledgement in some of their
accounts that employers design part-time hours to remain below the income
tax threshold and/or the then lower earnings limit for National Insurance
Contributions.[20]

'Well I was below the tax level 'cause ... mm... the boss ah, something
to do, it was below the tax and below the national insurance level,
something to do with, if he went above the national insurance level he
had to pay out nearly double, which wasn't gonna be worth it, so ... I was
below it there.'

(Mrs Wye, 20)

However, some women also acknowledge that they limit their hours of
work so as to stay below the level at which they would pay income tax and
National Insurance Contributions. Mrs Parrett has reduced her hours of
work at the café to avoid tax.

Mrs Parrett: Well I don't pay tax. No I don't earn enough to pay tax. I
think I've paid 2 pound national insurance but it doesn't
bother me. It used to bother me when I worked 5 nights,
[laughs] when they were taking tax I used to get so angry.

Q: 'Cause, you know, I would work 5 nights and probably get the pay of 4 nights so you were doing one night, sort of, for the taxman and that used to annoy me. [laughs]

Q: Did you ever reduce your hours because of it?

Mrs Parrett: Yeah [laughs]. Yes. We all worked it out. There was a lot of us together, we worked it out that um if you worked 2 nights or 4 nights it was just right. But if you did like the third night or the fifth night that was when you got allowed for, it was really ah, simple to work when we all sat and sort of looked at our hours and that. So we all decided to cut our nights [laughs] [...] obviously if I thought, you know, oh God so-and-so's got to have this for school or something I would do an extra night [...] you know, like, say well Hannah she's just been picked for the area finals for the netball so she had to have all the kit. But I thought well I'll just do an extra night and that's her business sorted out.'

(Mrs Parrett, 8–9)

Mrs Calder has just started work as a shelf-filler.

'working 20 hours at that pay scale, I think I just tip over the amount that I could earn without paying tax and National Insurance [...] If I do extra hours, it'll take me ... well over, and it'll affect how much I pay, so ... in um ... in the future ... I'll have to work it out, and see if it's worth my while ... doing extra hours. It might be more beneficial to one to say, no, I'm sorry I can't, and stay ... on my basic wage ... than do overtime and end up paying more tax and ... and insurance ...'

(Mrs Calder, 8)

None of the women construct a concept of the poverty trap similar to the one deployed by some of the men – though they implicitly recognise it in what they say about taxation. The most explicit critical comment, which puts her situation in an overall context of social relations in present-day Britain, comes again from Mrs Torridge.

'But I don't, I don't agree with the way that people who are earning a lot of money seem to pay ... pay ... you know, not much more tax than the people who are on low income ... because I think that's unfair, really. I mean they probably do less hours than the people on low income that's working and they seem to get a hell of a lot more money for it.'

(Mrs Torridge, 26)

This is the nearest to a political statement and to an explicit recognition of their class situation, in the women's accounts. Yet they do reveal very clearly how their household role interacts with their labour-market position to constrain their options. Income taxation is the final link in a structure of social relations which gives them very little room for manoeuvre.

None of the women are working in skilled occupations or have been given training. Mrs Nene, as a charge-hand in a box factory, is the highest paid; she gets just over £3 an hour – most get around £2.50. All but the three full-time factory workers (Mrs Nene, Mrs Tamar and Mrs Wye) are doing work that duplicates their unpaid domestic duties – cleaning, cooking, handling or serving food, looking after people. Several have abandoned or postponed indefinitely their youthful hopes of more pleasant or interesting jobs, in favour of unskilled, low-paid work to sustain household income.

Such scope for choice over employment as they are able to gain is achieved through the assistance with child care and household work that they are able to get from kin and friends and from their partners. The women who are in employment consider themselves fortunate – both in terms of household income and in terms of breaks, stimulation and company – in comparision with those who are at home. The latter, especially those with unemployed husbands, would prefer to do some paid work. Hence this issue of husbands' willingness to help with child care is a very important determinant of women's labour-supply decisions.

SHARING TASKS WITH HUSBANDS

Since women construct their role in terms of the needs of their children, the only way that they can justify doing paid work is by demonstrating that the arrangements for caring for them while they are at work meet their needs. Since they reject having them looked after by childminders, on the grounds that this does not meet their needs and is too expensive, they rely on friends, kin and spouses for child-care cover.[21] Essentially they construct themselves as finding a proxy for themselves in their absence at work – someone who can substitute for them as a reliable, familiar figure, giving the children security. The commonest arrangement is for their husbands to provide this care, often with assistance from female kin or friends.

Mrs Calder has just started night work as a shelf-filler. She describes her feelings about leaving the children with her husband, a lorry driver.

'We're all new ... and we're all finding our way a little bit, so um ... I think ... the only thing ... I do sometimes walk to the bus thinking, ch ... you know ... I'd like to have been there at bathtime and I'd like to have tucked them up ... and I wonder if Dad'll remember that she needs you know, her hair done before she goes to bed and ... and ... silly little things like that. But that's just ... because I've done it for so long ... it's um ... it's habit. Um ... I don't think I mind ... Dad taking over. I don't feel ... you know ... I'm their mum I should do it, that's not a thing. I'm quite happy for Dad to take over [...] And um ... he takes over very well so ... I got no problems where the, the family's concerned, so ... at the moment, it's, it's running ... very nicely ...'

(Mrs Calder, 3)

Mrs Wear has done a cleaning job in the evenings for some time. Her husband, who is a local authority storeman, looks after the children.

'Yeah. He doesn't mind. Only ... occasionally he'll sort of go off to skittles and then his mum and dad'll have the children. They'll come over here 'cause I mean they go up [indistinct] sit here until he comes home or until I come home or whoever ...'

(Mrs Wear, 5)

Mrs Cherwell's arrangements with her husband and mother have already been set out in detail. Mrs Rother, who has two cleaning jobs, relies on a neighbour to bridge the gap until her husband takes over care of the children.

'I gets me neighbour across the road. She has them mornings ... and that. And me husband haves them night-times when they comes in [...]. Works out lovely. Yeah. She don't mind doing that.'

(Mrs Rother, 6)

Mrs Nene started work at the factory 9 years ago; her husband is a motorcycle mechanic. She took the children to her mother's house before going to work – she lives close by. Her husband used to take her to work in the mornings.

'he used to drive me out and back every day, used to like drop me off at 10 to 8 which gave him time to get to work and then I'd have to wait after 5 for him to pick me up [...] when we went for the interview [herself and a friend] I had to catch 2 buses, so we'd worked it out, you know ... by plan that we were gonna catch 2 buses [...] we'd already taken the job on the Monday like, and came home and told him [laughs] at, so um he said, well it was alright and he would drop us off before work ... 'cause his hours is supposed to be 9 till 6, but he actually changed them to do 8 till 5 so that he could, that he would drop us off. But they didn't mind actually, 'cause it meant the garage was open, was open an hour earlier and it was still open till 6 at night. So I s'pose they gained, really, as well as what we did ...'

(Mrs Nene, 13)

Mr Nene also shares the domestic work.

Mrs Nene: ... we do it in ... jointly, like, I mean ... he does quite a bit
               [...] So um ... No, he comes home dinner times like and ...
               he'll hoover up and polish or put the washing out and
               what have you so um ... it's just ah, you know ... it's gotta
               be done joint, I mean you couldn't put it one or the other
               could you, it would be too much.
Q: Have you always shared?
Mrs Nene: No, before I went to work ... before I went back to work,
               like, you know, when I was home with the kids then I did
               it and ...
Q: Are there any jobs you wouldn't share?
Mrs Nene: No. No. He helps with the housework, I help with the
               decorating and things like that when it needs doing, so ...
                                                              (Mrs Nene, 12)

The women who get this kind of assistance with housework regard their
husbands as exceptional. Mrs Ribble describes her self-employed building
worker husband's efforts in the house.

'I had a doctor's appointment – and I hadn't touched the house. I
couldn't .... didn't have time. And I came home and the house was
spotless, dinner was on and he ah ... as he says he's done a 8 hours work
and he came home and he went through the house. Hoovered the bedrooms even [...]. If he has a day off, then he takes the kitchen and the
main bedroom and then I do all the rest [...]. And when he does those two
rooms, I must admit when he does the bedroom I do go behind him but
when he does the kitchen it's spotless [...]. He's been on his hands and
knees scrubbing the kitchen floor before [...]. Yeah, he's really good.
I've got one in a, I've got the one in a million [laughs] ... literally. I've
got the one – the one and only.'

                                                              (Mrs Ribble, 13)

Mrs Derwent works between 12 and 19 hours a week as a peripatetic care
assistant, but her husband helps with the cooking and housework.

''cause you've you know ... as soon as I come home from work I still got
the chidren; I've still got all the washing, the ironing, the cooking,
[laughs] you know, although Terry does help me. He is ever so good like
that, if he can, you know, it was ... he did. Cook the meals up to New
Year and my New Year's resolution was I'd cook [laughs] [...] I'm not a
very good cook and the children tend to go "yuk" if Mummy cooks it [...]
it's tends to be, "yuk, why i'n' Daddy cooking?" [...]. Really, I mean it's

the woman's job to cook i'n'it? [laughs] ... Well I think so, I mean, well whether it is in these times, but I mean my mum and dad think it's slightly disgusting to think that Terry's cooking the meals an' that. I mean he's ever so good, I mean, if I said "Oh Ter, the bedroom needs doing", he'd, he'd go and do the bedroom. It don't worry him if I, you know, although he don't like the ironing when he's on day off, ... but I was stood here with an ironing board he'd say: Well, you know, you do yours and Amy's and I'll do the boys' and mine. He's ever so good like that. You know, people used to take the mickey but it don't worry him. He's always said: Well look, Ter, Rachel works – although, you know, I'm only working part time he'd say, you know, I work so I need help. And he's very, very good like that.'

(Mrs Derwent, 9)

These accounts describe some kind of process of reciprocity over paid and unpaid work, which will be investigated further in the next chapter. However, there is another group of women who describe their husbands as unwilling to help with child care, and whose labour-market options are therefore severely restricted. Mrs Severn's husband is a local authority gardener; she has not worked outside the home since she had their younger child, now aged 2, though she has done some childminding for other people. She herself rejects the idea of 'dumping them on someone else', and would like to do some paid work if she 'could find something evenings which works in with my husband's working hours'. However, when asked whether he would be happy with this, she replies,

'[laughs] I'm not sure. [laughs] Let's say he's never changed a nappy and that sort of thing or put him to bed or ... so I don't know that it would work out [...] I think he'd prefer me to find something during the day but ... it still means leaving Patrick with somebody else which ... at the moment he, he's you know, he's talking and doing things and learning and I feel he needs me round, you know [...] Well yes really. It's a 24 hour job. But um I still feel I'm out of contact with other people and I don't have a lot of friends and ....I get fed up with me own company a lot and go out for walks and things like that but ah ... I still feel I don't want a job at the moment. [...] The money would be useful but I still think it's important those first 4 years to be with him. Can't bring back those first 4 years and I think you miss so much ...'

(Mrs Severn, 5)

Mrs Cam's husband is an irregular worker, who has just started as a roadsweeper driver after a period of agency driving work. She worked regularly as a nanny and a hairdresser before she was married, and has an interest in painting, but has only briefly done some part-time evening shelf-filling since having her children (now aged 6 and 4). She says she may wait to get another job until both children are at school full time, and then get daytime employment. Asked if she would get a job if her husband was unable to find one, she replies:

'The trouble is, you see he, he's, I can't always depend that he will be there to look after them you see, like he hates staying in the house. He'd rather go out and do sort of odd jobs or something, you know, but I suppose if we discussed it and he really couldn't get a job for some time, well yes, um, you know, now Christmas is coming I can always get a job somehow around, you know. As long as, as long as there was someone to look after the children and I didn't have the worry of who was going to pick them up I, I would go out to work full time. [indistinct] ... we can't because he doesn't want me to have to go out you know, he feels that I shouldn't have to go out and work, you know...?'

(Mrs Cam, 9)

Her only possible solution, at a time when they are in debt and serious rent arrears, was to consider taking work packing and addressing envelopes at home.

'I mean I can earn 30 pounds for a hundred envelopes, so you know it doesn't take a lot of [...] Yes that's something I can do sort of in between the housework and you know, or in the evening.'

(Mrs Cam, 10)

Mrs Spey has not worked since having her children, now aged 11, 8, 6 and 2. Her husband has been unemployed for 3½ years; when asked if she would like to get a job, she explains

'... you're usually sort of worse off moneywise anyway [...] Unless I could, you know ... but like I said it would be difficult at the moment 'cause I've got no one to watch the children you see.'

(Mrs Spey, 6)

The implication is that Mr Spey is not suitable or willing to take this role. Mrs Torridge is more explicit about how her husband's attitudes affect her choices. She says that these have contributed to her decision to separate from him.

'And that's when we split up because there was no way I could stay home with him being here 24 hours a day. It's too much [...] he ... just got no intentions of getting a full-time job. And I just don't see why I should have to work ... and then come home here and do the housework as well when he's just sat here doing nothing [...] I mean, he didn't do anything; he just used to sit home here or ... go out during the day or whatever, he, you know ... he never made no effort to help in the house at all [pause] I mean if he'd been one of these husbands that had to stay home and look after the kids ... and done the housework then I could have probably stuck it, but not doing ... all of it [pause]. And that's what ... most of the rows and arguments were about.'

(Mrs Torridge, 21)

Hence the husband's willingness to do some child care seems to be a crucial factor in the woman's labour-supply decisions. The importance of this is illustrated in our only example of a man and a woman 'swapping roles'.

'ROLE REVERSAL'

Only one of the couples in our sample has a man who is currently outside the labour market and a woman in full-time employment. This confirms Morris's finding[22] that many women leave their employments when their husbands become unemployed, and very few go back while they remain unemployed – though our evidence leads to a modification of this finding in the case of irregular workers, where the woman's return to work may lead to the man changing his status from claiming while doing cash jobs to self-employed (Hodder, Parrett). However, several women point out that full-time work is more feasible than part-time for them, so long as their husband is willing to do the child care (Itchen, Torridge, Spey). However, none of these men could be relied upon to give child care.

Our analysis shows that this is *not* a role reversal, in the sense that the man takes over the woman's role. Rather the woman satisfies herself that she can fulfil her responsibilities for her children's needs through the substitution of her husband for herself – an extension of the system adopted by women in part-time work. The woman still has the caregiving role, and the man the breadwinning role; each merely acts as a proxy for the other.

Mr Wye's account makes it clear that he still regards himself as a breadwinner, even though he has not been in employment for 3 years.

'Oh yeah, I mean I'd look for a job but it's gotta be what I want it to be, you know, I mean, catering or labouring ...'

(Mr Wye, 3)

He describes losing a number of jobs through rows with someone in authority; he regrets leaving one of them.

'That's the biggest regret I got: leaving there. I think I was bringing home 170, yeah, 'cause I was doing sort of 7 day a week then, but I didn' mind it 'cause the money was there. But that's my biggest mistake [indistinct] my life time; that job there [...] 'cause that's where I got on with everybody.'

(Mr Wye, 6–7)

He describes doing a number of short-term labouring jobs, and then having to sign on and wait 3 weeks for their benefit claim to be sorted out.

'that's actually where the tension sets in [...] 'cause you're going for 6 months, laid off, back up here, sign on, 3 weeks with no money. And then you have to go down, knock on the door to social every 5 minutes. And that's where the tension starts. I mean I think that's where a lot of people can actually split up with [...] the aggro of trying to sort it out.'

(Mr Wye, 8)

He says this led to his wife working full time.

'Well you just gotta rally round the family now, which really you shouldn' have to go that far I don't think; still ... this is why Linda went back to work again – at least your job is secure i'n'it.'

(Mr Wye, 8)

He looks forward to returning to work in due course:

'if I went back to work sort of a daytime then it would mean I'd have to bring home a standard wage what Linda's bringing home; I'd have to actually think about that because that's the money [indistinct]. So for me to go back work I would actually have to get the same sort of money [...] I look after the kids but ah ...will soon get rid of them soon 'cause she'll be in nursery soon so [laugh][...] Well I mean it would, it would have to be secure and it would have to be hospital work, I should think, or catering or something like that. It would have to be secure enough that I wouldn' have to worry about 6 months' time getting the sack.'

(Mr Wye, 10)

He talks about looking after the children.

Mr Wye:	... normally Linda will see to the kids when she comes home, the tea would be there and then I'd put they to bed; she, she don't put them to bed, I do [...] 'cause it's 8 hour day, i'n'it? Sometimes you're working till 9 i'n' you, on a Wednesday, so I have to put 'em up [...]
Q:	Do you do the housework?
Mr Wye:	Yes, very reluctantly but a ... [laughs]
Mrs Wye:	Swop places. I go out to work: he stays home.
Mr Wye:	Yeah, but ah I'm not into housework, not that much

[laughs]; I don't think blokes is never ... meant to be housework proud or anything.

(Mr Wye, 11)

Mr and Mrs Wye have 'swopped places' but not roles; he still portrays himself as the frustrated breadwinner who is temporarily looking after the children, as the family 'rally round'; she describes how she sees her role as follows:

'Yeah, I think you were out of work at the time, so I went back part time, 'cause I didn't know whether I would have liked to gone back work or whether I would have prefered to have stayed home with the children so I thought, well, I'll go back part time and see how it goes. And ... it seemed to be working out all right; David was managing all right home with the kids, so that was ... so we talked about it and said about me going full time since he was having no luck at finding a job at the time and ... I went full time. And it's been working out ever since ... seems to be working out. Kids seem happy enough; they're not wanting, they're not crying when I go off to work in the morning, say, oh don't want you to go this morning. If they started doing that then I would have said, right – enough's enough, you'll have to find a job and I'll stay home. But ... they'm quite happy with Dad home. I think he's a bit softer than Mum – lets 'em get away with more things than Mummy would – du'n' he?

(Mrs Wye, 16)

She says she missed the children at first, but the money situation made it necessary, because they were getting into debt on social security. She found full-time work tiring at first, especially overtime. She started with the firm 9 years ago, left when she had her first child, went back briefly but gave up to be with him, had a second child (now 3) and then returned part time when her husband lost his job again. Now she is warehouse manageress; she discussed the offer of promotion with her husband before accepting the extra responsibility.

Mrs Wye: 'Cause I wasn't sure whether I could handle ... giving out orders and ... if any flak came back it comes back to me but ah ... we talked about it and I said [...]

Mr Wye: [indistinct] reassuring really 'cause you wanted the job [indistinct].

Mrs Wye: Yeah. Yeah. I would have. I wanted to take it but I wasn't sure whether I was the right sort of person to be in charge. Whether I was too soft or anything ... but eh ... seems to be working out all right. Seem happy enough with me anyway so ... [...] bring home about 125 a week, so it's

not too bad. You know before I had the ... went up to
manageress, I was bringing home 95 so ... it's gone up
quite a bit now.

(Mr and Mrs Wye, 19)

In reconstructing the process later in the interview, Mrs Wye remembered
that before she returned to her present firm she worked part time at the
hospital.

Mrs Wye: I had Alice ... um ... and I think I went up there, I'd only
            been, I'd only had Alice about 5 weeks, wasn't it? Yeah,
            5 weeks I'd had, Alice been 5 weeks old and I went up the
            hospital part-time evenings. And I was up there for about
            18 months.
Q: And that was because you were short of money?
Mrs Wye: Yeah. Yeah. 'Cause David was ... were you working
            then? No, you was on the dole then weren't you? You
            were claiming dole money for you and the kids and so I
            went out and got ... I can't remember now. I think you
            might have been out of work and we was on dole money
            so I went for ...
Mr Wye: I was learning and word process, might have been on a
            course.
Mrs Wye: Yeah, that was it.

(Mr and Mrs Wye, 22)

It sounds as if Mrs Wye may originally have returned to the labour market
by way of an undeclared part-time job, while her husband was claiming,
though she later corrects this at his instigation. Her account is in line with
those of Mrs Derwent and Mrs Hodder – women whose husbands were
irregular workers or unemployed when they started work, and where the
opportunity arose because of their ability and willingness to take over the
child care during the women's working hours. Mrs Wye retains the role of
caregiver, and justifies here full-time employment in terms of the children's
needs before she describes her responsible role at work. Like the other
women with 'good' partners, her employment choice is derived from being
able to pass over her 'duties' as a carer to her spouse.

Three other households in which the man is an irregular worker may
have experimented with such an arrangement, and then abandoned it. The
accounts do not make this clear, and we failed to pick this up at the time
because they were embedded in descriptions which do not focus on this
aspect. Mrs Frome went back to a full-time job as a copy-taker on a local
newspaper some 4 weeks after her eldest child was born. Her husband, who

was unemployed at the time, looked after him for about a year, until she gave up the job. Since then neither has been in any form of paid employment except undeclared cash work, which both do. Asked how she found work after having the baby, Mrs Frome replies:

'It was all right at first. It was okay up until I suppose ... he started becoming interesting, then I found I was missing out on rather a lot of [indistinct] sort of found it very difficult to reconcile the two, which was one of the reasons, another reason for giving up ... at the end of '81, 'cause I was ... felt that I was missing too much, I mean, as I was lucky enough to actually see him take his first steps 'cause it happened to be an evening and I was here, but I could have missed that and, you know ...'

(Mrs Frome, 4)

The other reasons Mrs Frome gives are to do with changes at work – her boss was leaving. It is unclear whether this decision was seen as abandoning an experiment, or simply as an *ad hoc* one, made in response to current circumstances.

Mrs Itchen and Mrs Colne both took full-time jobs soon after having their first children, in spite of having very little labour-market experience previously. Mrs Itchen had been on a government training scheme and had one short-term employment; she was still in her teens when the baby was born. However, she took a full-time job, found by her sister, as a counter assistant in a fast-food outlet. Her reason was that her husband had lost his job, and was ineligible for benefit at the time. Soon afterwards, however, Mr Itchen took a job as a cook at the same place, and when he had to leave for medical reasons (an allergy) and she became pregnant again, she left. She subsequently miscarried, but did not return, having found the work very tiring. Her mother looked after her first child while she was working. As we have already seen, Mrs Itchen has since had another baby, but would like to return to work. She sees full-time employment as the only realistic option, because of benefit rules. In other words, she has not ruled out the idea of becoming the main, or more regular, worker in the household – but she cannot rely on her husband for child-care assistance.

Mrs Colne was pregnant with her first child before she left school, and had no subsequent employment, yet after her second child was born she took a full-time job as an auxiliary nurse for 3 or 4 months, with her mother looking after the children. In the end she decided to give it up when 'it wasn't working because I never saw 'em'. She was thinking of working again when the children were both at school, but then had a third child. No reference is made in her account to Mr Colne's employment status at the time of her full-time job, but he has been as much out of work as in it in recent years, and it seems probable that he was unemployed at the time. However, it is clear that he does little in the way of child care or domestic work. When asked about housework she replies:

> 'I do most of it, which I don't, I don't mind really; it's like getting up ... if she wakes up in the night, I'll always get up. I've always have done, with the kids, haven't I?'
>
> (Mrs Colne, 17)

Here again, it sounds as if Mrs Colne tried to become the main or regular worker, but abandoned the idea because of giving higher priority to her relationship with the children, and because her husband played little or no role in child care.

WOMEN'S DECISIONS AND WOMEN'S INTERESTS

Our analysis of the women's accounts shows how all make their labour-market decisions within the context of household constraints: on making these decisions they take into consideration their primary responsibility to make provision for child care and household work. However, the care-giving role – though important and to some extent rewarding when the children are in the stage between infancy and starting school – is described as boring, isolating and frustrating. Thus the opportunity to do part-time work is welcome as a break, for company and for mental stimulation.

The earnings of the part-time employed women (just under half our sample) go towards 'extras'. The income they can earn is an important factor in household finances. Women's accounts display their moral adequacy in terms of negotiating their household contribution, and balancing the elements in their role, while meeting some of their own personal needs. This allows their households to afford what would in more comfortably off families be seen as essentials – items like children's clothes, trips and holidays, and the taking up of the option to buy their council house. For households with a man in regular but low-paid employment, like the twelve in our sample, the woman's wage (full-time or part-time) makes these things possible. Of these twelve, the one in which the woman is outside the labour market (the Severns) is apparently the hardest pressed financially.

> 'We're finding it a struggle financially without another wage coming in but still [...] I'm quite happy to stay at home ... um ... like I say it is a struggle financially [laughs] ... if the time comes when I have to get something then I'll have to get something, you know.'
>
> (Mrs Severn, 4)

For those households with a man who is in irregular employment (the rest) the woman's employment status is clearly a key determinant of household income, and we have shown how it can actually determine the employment status of the man. Yet it in turn depends on the woman's ability to arrange child care, and this crucially involves the husband, who in every case of a working woman plays some part in the cover for her absence. Hence our analysis has got us so far to the point of recognising that the key to whether the woman becomes a full-time regular worker (like Mrs Wye, Mrs Tamar or Mrs Nene), or both spouses are unemployed for long periods of time (as in the cases of Mr and Mrs Spey, Mr and Mrs Bow, Mr and Mrs Dart and Mr and Mrs Exe) is whether they can negotiate arrangements which allow the woman to contribute to household income through her labour supply. Hence the decision-making process, revealed through the joint accounts, is the remaining piece of the jigsaw.

However, there is evidence in the women's accounts of *individual* strategic thinking about their role, and how the potential tensions and conflicts between its elements can be reconciled. These women do, as Finch suggests, develop strategies for fitting together their responsibilities and contributions in ways which are consistent with the regular or irregular work done by their partners.[23] Furthermore, the strategies by which they achieved these feats of 'fitting it all in' went far wider than the household.[24] As we have shown, they included kin and friends as proxy child-care providers, whereas men did so only in a few instances in relation to transport. Hence women can be seen to plan and negotiate their labour-market participation in a way which is particular to their role as women living with partners and children – its moral and social requirements – and as part of an individual, personal coping strategy.

Furthermore, there is also some evidence that women pursue collective strategies with other women which reflect a consciousness of what they have in common, and in an effort to further their interests as women.[25] This is not done by groups of neighbours or friends in any systematic way, but mainly by female kin, who assist each other's coping strategies. Ms Otter has been a single parent, and still claims as such, though she now has a relationship with an irregular worker, Mr Thames. She is planning to be a childminder now her mother's children are all grown up; in this she is following in her mother's footsteps (see p. 262). It seems that she will look after the children that her mother minds during the time when her mother does 'a little part-time job on the side', because her mother can no longer claim income support, but Ms Otter does. Mrs Colne is fostering a teenage boy who was previously fostered by her mother: she took over as foster parent at her mother's suggestion, and finds it financially quite rewarding, as well as allowing them 'to keep it (the fostering of the boy) in the family'.

As her husband is an irregular worker the regular income from fostering is valuable. Previously her mother looked after her children while Mrs Colne briefly worked full time (see p. 17).

Mrs Tavy now cares for her 27-year-old spastic daughter, the first of her seven children.[26] Her mother gave up her job as a fully qualified nurse to care for her from the age of 4 until a year before the interview. Mrs Tavy moved into her mother's flat, and took over care of her daughter when her mother died. Just before her mother died, Mrs Tavy came back to Exeter from London, and lived with another of her daughters, who is married and lives about 12 miles from Exeter, while she helped her mother, who needed medical treatment. The married daughter looked after Mrs Tavy's two youngest sons, aged 8 and 14, while she was in London. The rationale for this was that their schooling would not be disrupted; the move to London was mainly because of Mr Tavy's (irregular) employment. The married daughter still has them for most of the time, and they come to Mrs Tavy every other weekend. Another married daughter, Mrs Ouse, who is also one of our interviewees, lives nearby and works part time as a cleaning supervisor. Mrs Tavy cares for this daughter's children while she is working. Mrs Ouse describes the task of 'fitting in' her job in the mornings.

> 'It's got to fit in with mum and it's got to fit ... and I've got to come back in time for her to see to um her [spastic] daughter, you know, ah, see to me sister, like.'
>
> (Mrs Ouse, 4)

Later in the account, Mrs Ouse says that she has had to borrow from Mrs Tavy when she and her husband got into debt, in order to pay her bills. So Mrs Tavy (whose husband is out of work, and thinking of becoming a self-employed fisherman) is at the centre of a complex web of mutual assistance which has spanned three generations, and which focuses on her handicapped daughter, whose attendance allowance is an important element in her income. Mrs Tavy describes her coping strategy in terms which include help from her married daughter as an important factor in allowing her to care for her handicapped daughter, and Mrs Ouse describes her employment/child-care strategy in terms of her mother's availability to 'baby sit', with the handicapped daughter as an important time constraint on this.

These complex arrangements, which have had to be negotiated and renegotiated under changing circumstances (geographical moves, illness, death, children's developmental needs) reflect a shared understanding between three generations of women about women's roles, and how they can be supported by other women. In these accounts, Mr Tavy (who is Mrs Tavy's second husband) is a shadowy figure, who is scarcely mentioned.

The women in the family have devised a joint strategy for coping with the care needs of a handicapped adult and a large number of dependent children which makes little reference to income or unpaid work contributions from men.[27]

Most women in employment got some help with child care from female kin or friends. However, the other women married to irregular workers were more vulnerable to delays or cuts in benefits than Mrs Tavy, with her regular attendance allowance. They were as much or more the victims of the 'vicious circle' between male labour-market casualisation and fragmentation and the highly conditional, complex, overstretched benefits system as men. Quite apart from their difficulties over getting reliable child-care arrangements involving their husbands, Mrs Cam, Mrs Torridge and Mrs Itchen have experienced serious problems leading to delays and debts over claiming benefits to which they were entitled; and despite having 'good' husbands, Mrs Ryton and Mrs Parrett report very similar problems and consequences. Far from helping women re-enter the labour market when their husbands are not in regular work, according to their accounts, the system creates a whole series of extra problems, which require time and energy to resolve, and sometimes exacerbate difficulties in marital relationships.

CONCLUSIONS

The most striking thing about the women's accounts is their construction of a role which gives priority to their children's needs, and hence subordinates their contribution to household income through employment to secondary significance. Yet – because of the unfavourable labour-market situation of the men, and the relative strength of demand for female labour – it requires considerable rhetorical skill to reconcile the primacy of their responsibilities for child care with their actual employment decisions. Women make an important contribution to income in the great majority of households where the man is in work, and in six households (the four women in regular full-time work, plus Mrs Hodder and Mrs Parrett) their earnings are either greater than those of their partners, or sufficient to determine their partners' employment status.

Why then has the caregiver role persisted as such an overriding moral requirement for women, when the labour market in this sector has changed so much? Is this evidence of a time-lag: that the norms surrounding household roles are derived from the economic conditions of the previous generation? If so, how can decisions based on *roles* which have not been structured around current opportunities and constraints be seen as *rational choices* within these constraints? Are the roles themselve. , and the moral requirements that attach to them, not 'irrational' in some fundamental sense, and must this not infect the choices made within them?

These questions raise issues about the relationship between rational choice theory and social structure. Theories of decision-making derived from micro-economics start from a self-interested actor working out choices within a structure, which is itself being generated by the choices of other such individuals. Yet in practice, of course, pre-existing social structures give rise to the terms of exchange between individuals, and the pattern of social relations, particularly power relations: these shape the behaviour and attitudes of actors, fit their choices to the options, and determine their interests.[28] In this case, women's structural position, power disadvantage and range of choices have not been much altered by the recent changes in the labour market, which have mainly disadvantaged their partners rather than empowering themselves. Demand for married women's labour has increased – but mainly in part-time, low-paid, labour-intensive work, such as cleaning, catering and caring. There is scant evidence in our research that women are less discriminated against, in terms of regular, full-time jobs. Only Mrs Wye can be singled out as someone in a job which was traditionally held by a man. Hence – far from being ill-suited to the requirements of a restructured labour market – these women's construction of their role and its moral responsibilities is shaped and reinforced by the demand for their labour, as secondary, part-time workers.

The analysis of the joint interviews puts the focus of our study back onto household decision-making, and relations between couples. The women's accounts provide few clues about these processes; they construct their moral adequacy in terms of the tasks of mothering, homemaking, contributing to household income and attending to their own needs. Above all, what is absent from them is any direct reference to the power relations between men and women in households – to issues of who has the final say in decisions, especially when interests clash.[29] All this is implicit rather than explicit – in the yearnings for a part-time job of Mrs Severn, Mrs Cam, Mrs Bure and Mrs Itchen, for example. Only Mrs Torridge describes a conflict of interest with her partner, and her response is to withdraw – albeit partially and temporarily – from the relationship. Autonomy – such as that exercised by Mrs Tavy – is constructed within the taken-for-granted terms of men's easier access to the labour market, and the resources it supplies. How does this affect the way in which couples make decisions?

REFERENCES

1 See Jane C. Hood, 'The Provider Role: Its Meaning and Measurement', *Journal of Marriage and the Family*, Vol. 48, 1986, pp. 349–59, for a critique of this view.

2 J. Martin and C. Roberts, *Women and Employment: A Lifetime Perspective*, HMSO, 1984.

3 Michael R. Frone and Robert W. Rice, 'Work–Family Conflict: The Effect of Job and Family Involvement', *Journal of Occupational Behaviour*, Vol. 8, 1987, pp. 45–53.

4 Valerie Kincade Oppenheimer, 'The Sociology of Women's Economic Role in the Family', *American Sociological Review*, Vol. 42, No. 3, 1977, pp. 387–406. See also A. H. Amsden, *The Economics of Women and Work*, Penguin, 1980.

5 Hood, 'The Provider Role'.

6 This is consistent with other research studies, such as Diana M. Pearce, 'On the Edge: Marginal Women Workers and Employment Policy', in C. Bose and G. Spitz (eds), *Ingredients for Women's Employment Policy*, State University of New York, 1987, pp. 197–210.

7 Marie Agnès Barrère-Maurisson, Françoise Battagliola and Anne-Marie Daune-Richard, 'The Course of Women's Careers and Family Life', in B. Roberts, R. Finnegan and D. Gallie, *New Approaches to Economic Life*, Manchester University Press, 1985, pp. 431–58.

8 R. E. Pahl, *Divisions of Labour*, Blackwell, 1984, p. 329.

9 Janet Finch, *Married to the Job*, Allen & Unwin, 1983, p. 70.

10 S. Yeandle, *Women's Working Lives*, Tavistock, 1984, p. 140.

11 M. Porter, *Home, Work and Class Consciousness*, Manchester University Press, 1983, p. 51.

12 S. Cameron, 'Married Women in Jobs', *Social Policy and Administration*, Vol. 19, No. 2, 1985, pp. 112–20, examines evidence about women with two jobs from the General Household Survey, and finds evidence of 'life-cycle squeeze' – the impact of heavy family expenditure because of the cost of children. See also H. Wilensky, 'The Moonlighter as a Product of Relative Deprivation', *Industrial Relations* (California), Vol. 3, No. 4, 1963, pp. 105–24, and J. S. Alden, 'The Extent and Nature of Double Job-Holding in Great Britain', *Industrial Relations Journal*, Autumn 1978, pp. 14–33.

13 For the implications of career and role expectations on women's employment histories, see Cynthia Rexroat, 'Women's Work Expectations and Labour-Market Experience in Early and Middle Family Life Cycles', *Journal of Marriage and the Family*, February, 1985, pp. 131–42; Margaret Attwood and Frances Hatton, '"Getting On": Gender Differences in Career Development: A Case Study in the Hairdressing Industry', in E. Gamarnikow, D. Morgan, J. Purvis and D. Taylorson (eds), *Gender, Class and Work*, Gower, 1983, pp. 115–29.

14 Kathleen Geison, *Hard Choices: How Women Decide About Work, Career and Motherhood*, University of California Press, 1985; See also Anna Pollert, 'Women, Gender Relations and Wage Labour', in Gamarnikow, *et al.* (eds), *Gender, Class and Work*, pp. 96–114.

15 Phyllis J. Johnson and Francille M. Firebaugh, 'A Typology of Household Work Performance by Employment Demands', *Journal of Family Issues*, Vol. 6, No. 1, 1985, pp. 85–105; Joseph H. Pleck and Graham L. Staines, 'Work Schedules and Family Life in Two-Earner Couples', *Journal of Family Issues*, Vol. 6, No. 1, 1985, pp. 61–82; Joan Acker, 'Class, Gender and the Relations of Distribution', *Signs: Journal of Women, Culture and Society*, Vol. 13, No. 3, 1988, pp. 473–97.

16 W. Daniel, 'The Unemployed Flow Interim Report', Policy Studies Institute, 1981.

17 C. Bell and L. McKee, 'Marital and Family Relations in Times of Male Unemployment', in B. Roberts, R. Finnegan and D. Gallie (eds), *New Approaches to Economic Life*, Manchester University Press, 1985.

18 Lydia Morris, 'Renegotiation of the Domestic Division of Labour', in Roberts et al., *New Approaches*.

19 J. Millar, K. Cooke and E. McLaughlin, 'The Employment Lottery: Risk and Social Security Benefits', *Policy and Politics*, Vol. 17, No. 1, 1989, pp. 75–81.

20 Joseph A Pechman, 'Taxation', in R. C. Caves and L. B. Krause, *Britain's Economic Performance*, Brookings Institute, 1980, pp. 218–24; C. Lowell Harris, 'Taxation, Incentives and Disincentives and Human Motivation', *American Journal of Economics and Sociology*, Vol. 44, No. 2, 1985, pp. 129–36; Meredith Edwards, 'Social Effects of Taxation', in J. Wilkes (ed.), *Politics of Taxation*, Australian Institute of Political Science, 1981, pp. 142–61.

21 Lydia Morris, 'Employment, the Household and Social Networks', in D. Gallie (ed.), *Employment in Britain*, Blackwell, 1988, pp. 279–304.

22 Morris, 'Renegotiation of the Domestic Division of Labour'. See also M. Kell and J. Wright, 'Benefits and Labour Supply of Women Married to Unemployed Men', *Economic Journal*, 100, 1990, pp. 119–26.

23 Finch, *Married to the Job*.

24 Pahl, *Divisions of Labour*, p. 133.

25 Porter, *Home, Work and Class Consciousness*.

26 Yeandle, *Women's Working Lives*, p. 152.

27 For carers' strategies see H. Graham, *Women, Health and the Family*, Wheatsheaf, 1984, p. 170.

28 John Wilson, *Social Theory*, Prentice Hall, 1983, p. 97.

29 See for instance R. O. Blood and D. M. Wolfe, *Husbands and Wives: The Dynamics of Family Living*, Free Press, 1960; H. Dreitzel, *Family, Marriage and the Struggle of the Sexes*, Macmillan, 1972; Graham Little and Elsie Holmström, *Family Authority*, in A. F. Davies, S. Engel and M. J. Berry (eds) *Australian Society*, Longman, 1977; S. Edgell, *Middle Class Couples*, Heinemann, 1980, Ch. 5; R. L. Warner, G. R. Lee and J. Lee, 'Social Organisation, Spousal Resources and Marital Power: A Cross-Cultural Study', *Journal of Marriage and the Family*, Vol. 48, 1986, pp. 121–8.

6 Joint decision-making?

In this chapter we will analyse the decision-making processes in our study households, with particular reference to the idea that they reveal a 'strategy' by the partners. In the first part of the chapter, we address the question of how these interview accounts relate to an analysis in terms of 'strategy', and show how their moral framework of 'jointness' in decision-making is implemented in practice. In particular, we reject the notion of a household work strategy, finding evidence for this in only one family (the Kennets); instead, we show how labour-market decisions are related to systems for managing household finances.

The third stage of our study of each household's labour-supply decisions was to interview both partners together, trying to focus on what influence (if any) they had on each other's employment decisions, and how they reached decisions over issues such as child care, housework and budgeting. The aim was to get them to talk about how their employment choices 'fitted together', and what household processes led to the outcomes they had described in their individual accounts.

Was this a different exercise from the separate interviews with men and women? The individual accounts were retrospective reconstructions of the person's employment history, described to a researcher who was known to be interviewing their partner also, and later both of them together. We have shown that these accounts take the form of a rhetorical justification of decisions in terms of the primary roles of men and women as breadwinners and caregivers. They aim to show the interviewee as a morally adequate person, who anticipates the alternative version to be given by his or her spouse (the determinate alternative possible version).[1]

The joint interviews take the same form, in that the couples endeavour to give a morally adequate account of their decision-making processes. In this case, however, the norm that governs their account is one of 'jointness' or 'partnership': they strive to construct decisions as ones reached by processes which involve discussion and agreement. Having given their individual versions of employment choices, they then display rhetorical skills in demonstrating how they fit their roles together – rather as the individual accounts display skills in balancing the various elements in their roles. The partners support, modify or challenge each others' versions during the joint interview, whereas in individual interviews some tried to anticipate and sometimes even occasionally to counter each others' versions (for example Mr and Mrs Calder, p. 110).

Some of the pairs of individual accounts are so dissonant and non-congruent that it is not surprising that no joint interview took place. Where there was obvious tension and resistance, or one partner or both made excuses about a joint interview, Helen Kay did not push the issue when she felt that it might tip the relationship into instability or dangerous conflict, or expose one partner to humiliation or violence (see pp. 63–5). The clearest example of such disparities and tensions is that of Mr and Mrs Torridge: Mr Torridge gives a perky account of himself as a diligent but irregular worker, providing income for the household, while Mrs Torridge describes him as lazy, immature and unreliable, and says they are separated until he can 'sort his-self out'. In these circumstances, Helen Kay judged that evasion of a joint interview by the couple should not be challenged. In these couples it is as if the gap between the two accounts – the man's and the woman's attempts at providing a morally adequate version of their own decisions – is too wide to bridge in the joint interview situation. There were nine households in which no joint interview took place: unfortunately in two others (Medway and Itchen) the recording of the joint interview was inaudible.

Where a joint interview did take place, what emerges from the recording is a sequence of rather disparate speech forms which include:

(a) *Joint reconstructions*: In some parts of joint interviews the couple take turns in reconstructing a decision or situation, often in brief, in-complete sentences, as if they are trying to frame a single, internally coherent account of what has happened or is happening. Such passages occur at various points of most transcripts, but there is often one near the start of the interview. When Helen Kay returned to see Mr and Mrs Parrett together, she found that Mrs Parrett had acted on the discontents she was expressing about her job (at the roadside café) in her individual interview.

Q:	Can we chat about how you fit your two lots of work together, and how you make decisions about things?
Mrs Parrett:	But I'm not working no more now.
Q:	Aren't you?
Mrs Parrett:	No.

Mr Parrett:	She finished.
Mrs Parrett:	I finished it ... I chucked it in.
Q:	Oh.
Mrs Parrett:	Uhuh. What does that give us eh? [laughs]
Q:	What happened to make you decide that?
Mr Parrett:	Oh it was nothing to do with our working ...
Mrs Parrett:	No but ... no, no, no. It was just that ... well, I told you didn't I, I was unhappy.
Q:	Yeah.
Mrs Parrett:	And it just ... I think it's couple ... well how long is it now – 'bout 3 weeks, about 3 weeks ago I was meant to go in on the Friday night and me friend ...
Mr Parrett:	That was the last time you came.
Mrs Parrett:	... me friend came for me to go to work and I said 'tell her I'm not going back' and I just ... haven't been back since.
Mr Parrett:	Bit of animosity at work.
Mrs Parrett:	Yeah I've explained to ...
Mr Parrett:	Sort of animosity at work.
Mrs Parrett:	... I've explained to her the ... nastiness and ... um ...

(Mr and Mrs Parrett, 27)

Mr and Mrs Cam's situation had recently changed: he had just started work as a driver of a roadsweeper when the individual interviews took place. They start to talk about the situation since he took up this new employment, Mr Cam doing most of the talking. Helen Kay then asks Mrs Cam about how she is finding things at home with the children.

Q:	Do you find it hard having the kids all day on your own?
Mrs Cam:	Well no ... Well Emma's at school all day and Luke's at nursery half day um ... Well he's got to work and that's it. I mean you just put up with it. It was ... It's better now than when he was on shift work ...
Mr Cam:	Least I come home every night.
Mrs Cam:	... at least I know he's gonna be home between 6 and 9 o'clock [laughs] or round about.
Mr Cam:	Least um and um it's regular you know, pay.
Q:	What, you don't know what hours you'll be finished at?
Mr Cam:	No. No. 'Cause the ...
Mrs Cam:	We're hoping to get a telephone so he can ring up – oh I'm gonna be late tonight – then I know. But I know if he's not here by a certain time that he's still working.
Mr Cam:	We got 2 ... If anything happens I got 2-way radio in me lorry. I get in touch with my [indistinct] and he'll send

	somebody round, you know, which is fair enough. If anything happens.
Q:	Just ordinary overtime you just have to wait until he arrives?
Mr Cam:	Awh.
Mrs Cam:	Ah I didn't ... Yeah.
Mr Cam:	You know I come home ah Fridays is the worst day ah ... Every builder wants us on a Friday because it's weekend. Saturdays we get a lot of work because we can't cope with it Friday.
Mrs Cam:	That's the only time really on Saturday and ...
Mr Cam:	Saturday yeah – it, it's a short weekend.
Mrs Cam:	But um ...
Mr Cam:	No it's – it isn' too bad. You got to you know ...

(Mr and Mrs Cam, 33–4)

(b) *Individual reconstructions*:   Other sequences consist of one of the couple giving an account of a decision so as implicitly to claim to speak on behalf of the other – to be conveying to the interviewer a joint decision, or a mutual understanding of a situation (though in practice doing all the talking) while the other's response remains minimal and ambiguous. Mr and Mrs Rother are asked about decisions over his overtime as a local authority foreman, when this clashes with her cleaning work.

Q:	So did that mean that you couldn't do any overtime?
Mr Rother:	Well, unless, unless I sort of ... if it was overtime that was available on a sort of Saturday morning ... then I could do it easy, but if there was um ... 'cause for several years I came off the ... winter [...] rota; I came off of that, which is overtime, but I came off that because we couldn't work it, you know, we didn't have nobody that we ... thought. We had people offer, around here, but not people that we thought were ... um ... up to looking after our children. Perhaps that sounds a bit of [indistinct] ... you know, they were married people and that, but yet again ...
Mrs Rother:	Um.
Mr Rother:	... you know, um they didn't appear to be on the ball enough for us, so you know ... we wouldn't, you know, just couldn't do it. It was better to have ... a regular weekly wage coming in, of hers. Than sort of sporadic overtime.

Q:	Right. Was that a choice?
Mr Rother:	How do you mean?
Q:	You think you can actually ... You thought that was a definite choice – between your overtime or your wife's work?
Mr Rother:	Well the overtime could be, say, you know, an hour a week. The Saturdays were every other Saturday morning, at that time [indistinct]. But the ... sort of working on in the evenings and the winter [...] I mean, similar to this year, I mean I've been out twice so far, since the ... and that came in the 1st of October, winter, you know, the standby list. I've been out twice. See. And that was ... both occasions was 6 hours a session wa'n'it?
Mrs Rother:	Yeah.
Mr Rother:	But ... you know, it's better to have something regular so I dropped doing that for a few years. And then, well, we've got Maude and George opposite who are ... 57, 58 ...
Mrs Rother:	[indistinct] and they babysits.
Mr Rother:	And if I'm pushed – 'cause now, I, I am a bit pushed if somebody says, can't do it ... Then I've got to step in and cover it. D'you follow me?
Q:	Yes.
Mr Rother:	Right. And it's a, it's a must; I gotta do it. And ... and as I say, they've had their family and they're off their hands and ... my three children get on fine with them, 'cause they've been our neighbours for years, since we've been here like, you know. They're very, very good. They're people ... salt of the earth people, you know, ah you can sort of rely on 'em hundred per cent, d'you know what I mean, you know, you go away and ... like, I go back at ... 6, if there's a winter [job], you know – right. I know the wife will be in by 20 to 8 and I know for that hour and a half that I'm away that my kids are perfectly safe. And I know I'm not gonna come home to ... nothing, do you know what I mean?
Mrs Rother:	Um.
Mr Rother:	I feel very, very confident if they are ever with them.

(Mr and Mrs Rother, 32–3)

It is important to note that the joint interviews involve frequent switches between joint and individual reconstructions; for example, Mr and Mrs

Rother, shortly after this passage, reconstruct the possibility of her losing her job as follows:

Q:	You mentioned to me that you might be made redundant. Is that right?
Mrs Rother:	Yes. Yeah. Yeah. In ... August i'n'it? Up [local authority building].
Mr Rother:	Yeah. That's council [indistinct] tender.
Mrs Rother:	And that one is April.
Mr Rother:	[Name of superstore] might go in April.
Mrs Rother:	That's already contractors.
Mr Rother:	Yeah, that's already i'n'it?
Mrs Rother:	So they've had so many contractors down there, though.

(Mr and Mrs Rother, 47)

Although one partner tends to take over the process of individual reconstruction on behalf of both, this is by no means always the pattern: with many couples, different decisions are reconstructed by different partners.

(c) *Contested reconstructions*: Much less common than the above two sequences are contested reconstructions, in which the couple disagree about what happened, or about the evaluation or interpretation of what happened. This is not the same thing as reporting past disagreements (which is common, and is done by means of a joint reconstruction, with laughter); it is an actual disagreement in the course of the interview. Mr and Mrs Calder are talking about the situation since she took her evening job as a shelf-filler; he made it plain in his individual interview that he is unhappy with his regular job as a lorry-driver, because he does the same boring route everyday, and that he would be tempted to change back to agency work, or go self-employed, if it were not for her dislike of irregular earnings and uncertainty over employment. He has recently turned down the offer of another job, soon after she started her evening work.

Q:	Oh you were telling me ... in your interview about you were offered a better one.
Mr Calder:	Yeah, yeah.
Mrs Calder:	Oh ... yes. Doesn't it always happen?
Mr Calder:	Yes, with [firm's name], yeah. Never mind.
Mrs Calder:	He applied for this firm ... oh months and months and months ago. And nothing came. And ah ... soon as we get something else organised ...
Mr Calder:	They're on the phone.
Mrs Calder:	... it comes up. So ...

Mr Calder: These things happen. Something else might come up in the future that suits us, you know, suits us better. 'Cause I must admit I've ... things always, aren't always better on the other side than the, you know the grass is not always greener is it, that's the thing. I mean we found that out when we left the air force so ... [indistinct] anyway.

Q: What you think that's made you more cautious or just that ...

Mr Calder: Well ... I suppose a wee bit. I, I mean just a, just a wee bit mind because ...

Mrs Calder: [laughs]

Mr Calder: ... if she hadn't have been working at [shop's name] I would have said yes ...

Mrs Calder: He'd have taken it.

Mr Calder: ... I would have taken it there and then ... but ah. [indistinct]

Mrs Calder: Yes.

Mr Calder: But ah ... no, just one of those things.

Mrs Calder: I think if ... if he'd been really desperate to take it ... and I thought he'd been all right I'd have given up [shop's name] – I'd have given up my job. *But*, says she, and well out of arm's reach, I think he's getting too old for it.

Mr Calder: Huh!

Mrs Calder: [laughs] ... because it's general haulage work and it's ... loading and roping and sheeting and all the things he enjoys but hasn't done for a long time.

Mr Calder: You do want to go shopping today do you?

Mrs Calder: [laughs] Yes.

Mr Calder: Uh?

Mrs Calder: Yes. Yes I do. But ...

Mr Calder: Oh no.

Mrs Calder: ... you are about 10 years older than you were the last time you clambered around the top of a wagon; you've had an accident since and hurt your back; you've had another accident and hurt your knee. I don't think he'd manage it now. And it wouldn't be as enjoyable as it was first time round. So I stuck in and said ... you know ... you don't really want to go do you.
[pause]

Q: Were you happy with that?
[pause]

Mr Calder: Well I, I sup, yeah I suppose so. There was, I must admit
               there's a little bit of me thought, caw why did that have to
               happen now you know ... but on the whole I think, yeah,
               'cause ... I wouldn't mind doing distance work where there
               was maybe there was only 2 or 3 nights a week out but ...
               you were talking of 4 and 5 nights a week out you see on this
               job which ... I must admit is ... rather a lot like you know ...
               and it's sort of leaving on Monday and you might be back
               Friday night or you'll be definitely be back Saturday
               morning so ... which you had to be; you had, you gotta be
               back Saturday morning for the hours you know. But ...
               (Mr and Mrs Calder, 41–2)

This sequence starts as a joint reconstruction of the job offer, and then
briefly switches to a contested account, before finally (after two pauses)
changing to an individual account in the name of a somewhat grudging
consensus. Mr Calder finally concedes that the alternative job would not
have suited from a family point of view, though he does not agree that it
would not have suited him as a man and a worker.

DECISION-MAKING: STRATEGIES

Perhaps the most difficult issue for our whole study is the question of what
strategy (if any) is revealed through these joint interviews. In recent years,
a great deal of academic interest has focused on the issue of whether
couples can be said to pursue a household strategy in relation to labour
supply, and on attempts to capture such strategies in economic models or
sociological theories (see Chapter 2, pp. 18–22). In this chapter, our
analysis is required to establish the relationship between the couples'
attempts to provide morally adequate accounts of their decision-making in
their households, and the theoretical models of strategic decision-making
put forward by sociologists and economists (see pp. 26–30).

What is common to several of these attempts is that they are concerned
with explaining the *quantity of paid work* done by each individual at a given
wage, and conversely on the *quantity of unpaid work* done by each individual in relation to the other's paid work. Clearly the former will vary with
the income requirements of the household, and the latter will vary with its
care requirements, both depending on (amongst other things) the number
and age of children. Models and theories try to predict how much employment each partner will take at given wage rates, or explain how they reach
a certain division of labour over paid and unpaid work.

The starting point of any such analysis is a rejection of the notion that
household decisions can be treated as totally consensual (in effect, as a

decision made by the whole household, as if it was one person), and also of the notion that each partner makes an entirely separate decision, without any reference to the other's behaviour. Once these two options are ruled out the various alternatives can be set out as follows:

(a) *Contracts*: Implicit in Carling's rational choice model of household formation (see pp. 26–7, 29) is the notion of a straightforward exchange between man and woman, in which the hours of paid and unpaid work that each does are related to their wages in the labour market, and the allowance made to the person doing household tasks is treated as a wage paid by the other.[2] Couples only form households if both parties gain from an exchange of unpaid labour for the income from paid labour, as under contract.

(b) *Co-operation*: In Pahl's theory of the household division of labour, couples reach strategic decisions about how to 'get by' and 'get the work done' by the practices they adopt both over labour-market participation and in 'self provisioning'. Although much less specific in its attempt to predict and quantify paid and unpaid work, Pahl tries to explain why some households do more self-provisioning *and* provide more hours of employment than others, in terms of the possible processes and resources available, assuming common interests in maximising joint utility. Though he acknowledges that they may not consciously co-operate, and that practices may be the result of conflicts rather than agreements, he writes of households 'operating a collective strategy'.[3]

(c) *Bargaining*: Intermediate between the ideas of strict economic exchange and co-operative agreement is the notion of bargaining or conditional co-operation. This is implied in Barmby's[4] and Grift and Siegers'[5] models of household labour supply; each partner does paid work on condition the other does. This can be extended to unpaid work, or to bargains involving both paid and unpaid work. In this model, what is at stake is not an exchange of labour for money, as in the first variant, but an agreement that one partner will supply a certain quantity of labour if the other provides a certain quantity. This conditional co-operation is a version of a game outlined by Taylor,[6] who pointed out that in a small group individuals may agree to act in certain ways on condition that others perform certain actions, when without such agreements it would be in no one's interests to supply these services.

What all these models and theories have in common is the idea that couples reach some sort of agreement (contract, pact or bargain) under which their *type and quantity of work* is specified; in this sense it is a *labour strategy* that they are trying to capture. What they seek to explain is how couples decide who does what work, for what hours and for what reward. This, of course, was also our research question. But in our case, our methodology requires us first to look at how these couples construct their accounts of decision-making as morally adequate – what norm of household decision-making they are constructing as a way of legitimating their processes of deciding. This must then be related to the notion of strategy in a tight theoretical way: strategies cannot simply be inferred by looking 'through' or 'behind' the interviewees' accounts.

We have already seen (p. 20) that, even in the individual interviews, the respondents construct the norm for household decision-making as *jointness* based on discussion and agreement. This is clear in a passage in which Ms Waveney and Mr Trent, who have recently started living together (she was previously a single parent) talk about how they will make employment choices in future.

Q: Well, when you're living together would you expect to influence each other about job decisions?

Ms Waveney: Oh yeah. Yeah, I wouldn' expect him to go there and come home one day and say 'Les I've left this job 'cause I'm going for this one', 'cause it would shock me. If he come home and said, 'this [indistinct] ... ' we'd look into it together.

Q: Would you expect to influence your wife on decisions?

Mr Trent: I would, yeah. We'd talk about it and if she was unhappy you know ... but um I'd like to talk about it before. I mean we do talk about everything ... but she didn't, I mean 'twould be a shock to me I think, you know, going behind me back. But ... you know, if she, if we talked about it and she was happy I wouldn't stop her.

                                          (Ms Waveney and Mr Trent, 13)

The norm here is quite clear – decisions should be talked over and agreements reached. Yet this couple have yet to make any *employment* decisions, since they have only just formed a household. The important question for our research is how the other interviewees reconstruct their past decisions in terms of this same norm. Given that the requirement for moral adequacy is based on this norm, how are jointness, discussion and agreement achieved?

We have shown in our analysis of the individual accounts that the roles of man and woman are governed by quite different norms: these partnerships are therefore ones with segregated roles, in which the gendered division is so taken for granted that it is never questioned. Men and women, of course, have reciprocal understandings of what it is to be women and men: hence in their individual interviews, couples like the Tamars and the Wyes, where the woman is the regular full-time worker, have to do a lot of work in accounting for this arrangement according to the norms of male and female roles. Their rhetorical skill is displayed in legitimating their particular arrangements, and our analysis is able to clarify how their accounts relate to the labour markets for male and female labour respectively.

In the joint interviews, the couples start from the gendered norms already displayed, governing their segregated roles as men and women, and show how these roles 'fit together' in their partnership – a partnership whose decisions are made jointly. Their skills in the joint interviews are exercised in reconstructing segregated-role-orientated decisions in terms of jointness-in-partnership. But – as in the balancing of the different elements in their individual roles – this requires them to legitimate apparent departures from the norm of jointness, discussion and agreement. It requires them to account for occasions on which there was no discussion, and no agreement, and to show how these can be reconciled with the essentially joint and negotiated nature of their partnership. This allows us to analyse their relationships, and construct a theory of marital relations on the estate which relates to labour-market, taxation and benefit structures, by demonstrating how the couples strive to balance these aspects of their partnership.

We have seen how Ms Waveney and Mr Trent start from the strong statement that they intend to discuss and agree about their employment decisions. This implies that it should be possible to discover from them the principles or practices governing such joint decision-making, which might demonstrate the features of a strategy – a contract, co-operative agreement or bargain. But our analysis of the couples' reconstructions of their employment decisions yielded no such evidence. We therefore rejected the notion of a household *work* strategy, for the following reasons:

(i) *Absence of discussion or agreement*: If there is to be a contract, pact or bargain between the couple then there must be some discussion of its terms, in order to fix the type, quantity and reward of the work to be performed. It does not make sense to talk of a unilateral agreement; yet in the case of the men's decisions there was acknowledgement that no discussion took place. Men made their own labour-supply decisions without referring to their partners.

Of course it could be the case that a breadwinner–caregiver role division does not require discussion of this kind, since the couple have already agreed to leave employment decisions to each other within the norms of those roles.[7] However, patterns of employment in these households are far too varied and changing to be explained in these terms: such a variety of full-time and part-time, unemployed and self-employed, for men and women, could not be 'deduced' from this role division. Furthermore, unilateral decision-making was constructed as contrary to the norms of their relationships by the couples. Most couples described the process of decision-making in their household as joint or shared, and as taking the form of discussion leading (often after considerable and sometimes heated debate) to agreement. But men's decisions about employment – even those with very important implications for the whole household – were not made in this way.

Mr Calder changed his job from agency driver (involving irregular hours and earnings) to a lower hourly paid but regular job as a driver for a dairy firm.

Q: Can you remember when you were offered the job at [firm's name] did you both discuss it or was it a decision you thought that's a good job or ...?

Mr Calder: No, I just took it. Yeah. Yes. We didn't discuss it at all. I was offered, I was out there one night, I was offered the job, and I said yes. And I told her when I got home.

Mrs Calder: It isn't typical. That isn't typical is it?

Mr Calder: No. No.

Mrs Calder: It isn't typical. We usually do discuss everything. But I think he knew what I would say, I wasn't gonna argue with it [laughs]. So um ...

(Mr and Mrs Calder, 37)

Mr Ribble is a 'self-employed' building worker. Mrs Ribble describes them as a very close couple who 'share everything', and that 'it's always a joint decision, doesn't matter what'. However, when he is asked whether he discussed the decision to become self-employed when he left an employee job, he replies:

'Ah, not that one unfortunately, no. [laughs] We discuss a lot, well we discuss nearly everything [indistinct] concerns both of us ... um ... No I didn't. I ... 'cause I had a row with the boss on the phone ... um I was feeling [needled?] at the time ...'

(Mr Ribble, 33)

In the joint interview, Mrs Ribble says that she has no idea where he is working once he leaves home in the morning; there is no possibility of discussions about employment decisions because they are out of touch with each other.

Mr Plym is asked about his transfer from one civil service job to another, in a different town, involving new transport arrangements.

Mr Plym:	I said I wanted to move, didn't I? Um, as usual in the Civil Service it all happened too quick. I said I wanted to move, one week; the next week, said well – I was on holiday wasn' I? – and they rang me up at home and said, right, a job's come up in [name of town]. Do you want it?
Q:	Ah, so you have to make your mind up [indistinct].
Mr Plym:	You had to make it up there and then 'cause I had to say yes on the phone.
Mrs Plym:	Yeah.
Mr Plym:	I couldn't tell Nancy till the evening. She was working.
Mrs Plym:	[laughs]
Mr Plym:	You were working, weren't you? That's right.
Mrs Plym:	I can't remember what I was doing.
Mr Plym:	[indistinct] ... reason I was on holiday 'cause she was working ... [laughs]
Q:	And ... but you, you're quite happy with the move now?
Mrs Plym:	Oh yes. [indistinct]
Mr Plym:	Oh yes, yeah. Well I mean ... [laughs]

(Mr and Mrs Plym, 26–7)

Mr Bure puts the matter more trenchantly:

Q:	When you think about changing jobs, do you discuss it with your wife?
Mr Bure:	I lets her have her say and then I decide. If she thinks it is the right job and I don't then I don't take it. I'm one of those that believe women should have a say on where she goes and what she wants 'cos if you don't you can't get anywhere, you can't build up a relationship.'

(Mr Bure, 17)

(ii) *Discussions over women's employment*: By contrast with the responses to questions over men's employment decisions, the joint interviews emphasise that discussions did take place over women's employment decisions. However, these focus on *child care* (i.e. on arrangements for substituting for the women's role) and not on the job itself; they say that this decision was left to the women themselves. Indeed, the men told the women to decide for themselves, and disowned any say in their choice.

The same couples who said they had not discussed the man's decision had talked together carefully about this aspect of the woman's, according to their accounts. Mr and Mrs Calder were asked about the decision for her to take evening work.

Q:	Going back to the start of your job ...
Mrs Calder:	Yeah.
Q:	... did you both discuss that – starting that up?
Mrs Calder:	Yes.
Q:	So that was ... like a joint decision?
Mrs Calder:	Oh yes. Yes. We talked about it long and hard ...
Mr Calder:	Yes, because I've got the kids ...
Mrs Calder:	[laughs] ... Not just when it came but long before ... when .. well when he started this route and was home ... dinner time at 2 o'clock every day ... Um, we started talking about ... well, I suppose, you know, I could go out to work, couldn't I? Um, um, yes, well ... have to be something evenings and it would have to be, you know, between tea time and, and ... what have you ...

(Mr and Mrs Calder, 43)

Mr and Mrs Plym talked about a job offer she received for occasional work, in terms of the child-care implications.

Mrs Plym:	Yeah, I got offered another job for Saturdays, which would have been easier for us and then occasional during the week if I needed it so ...
Mr Plym:	It would mean she would be taking home about the same money, by the time you take all the money out for the childminder, weren't really losing that much were we?
Mrs Plym:	No.
Mr Plym:	But she worked 2 days a week Saturday and Monday, didn' you?
Mrs Plym:	Um.
Q:	Did you discuss it at the time or did you just decide?
Mr Plym:	We discussed it, went through it together didn't we?
Mrs Plym:	Yeah.
Mr Plym:	Realised we shouldn't be losing that much. [laughs] It's ...

(Mr and Mrs Plym, 22)

This concern with the details of child care, and the clear requirement to reach agreement over these, to satisfy both partners that the children's needs are met, and to define the husband's part in substituting for his wife's care, contrasts with the insistence on the woman's own choice over employment itself.

'Yeah, it was entirely up to me. Yeah. I ... you know ... you do what you wanna do, sort of thing. And he'll just fall in with it; I mean he falls in with anything anyway [laughs].'

(Mrs Cherwell, 26)

Mr and Mrs Nene share housework and child care, and he used to drive her to work, yet they do not discuss issues over her employment. When asked what he thinks of her likely promotion to a more senior supervisor's post at the factory, Mrs Nene replies:

'[pause] Yeah, that's a good question. I dunno what he'd think – to be honest. Because ... I don't say a lot to him about my work ... if I have a bad day and I come home [...] he says: "I don't wanna know; if you don't like it, leave". [laughs] But that's his answer to everything, like, you know, [...] I don't s'pose it would bother him one way or the other.'

(Mrs Nene, 33)

Later she adds:

'Like I say, we don't talk about our work, not really. I mean, he doesn't understand what I do and I don't understand what he does, sort of ...'

(Mrs Nene, 34)

(iii) *Men's decisions that affect child care*: Where the man is the regular earner or the main earner, decisions about his employment are made by him, without discussion, or after discussion, but with his judgement being decisive. However, where the man is the irregular or lesser earner, then discussion does take place – once again usually focused on child care, rather than the nature or extent of labour supply. This was the case for Mr Hodder and Mr Tamar, both of whom have wives in more regular employment than themselves. Mr and Mrs Wye discussed the situation which led to her taking a full-time job, and his staying at home to look after the children.

Q:	Whose idea was it? Was one of you keener on the idea than the other, or was it ...?
Mr Wye:	No, no we just sat there and talked. At the time, financially, it was, it was awkward and it was uncomfortable and we [indistinct] ...
Mrs Wye:	It was down to money again.
Mr Wye:	... and we had to sort ourselves out. That's how we come to do what we did [...].

(Mr and Mrs Wye, 30)

(iv) *Men overruling women*: Finally, when they were posed with a hypothetical clash of priorities between their employment (or their overtime) and their wives', some men said that they would simply override their partner's decision, or give her no choice.

Q:	If you decide that one of you would have to do fewer hours, workwise ...
Mr Rother:	Yeah, well that's something that she'd have to give in on.
Mrs Rother:	Yeah.
Mr Rother:	She would have to. 'Cause mine's the main job. 'Cause at the end of the day when it boils down to it, it's me and my job that gotta come first – all the way along – and that's one thing I would never give in on, no. She would have to reduce her hours.
Mrs Rother:	Yeah.
Mr Rother:	Definitely. [pause] That's one argument I would not lose.

(Mr and Mrs Rother, 51)

Although later he does modify this slightly.

Q:	If you [indistinct] and you were working and the chance came up to do another hour [indistinct] possibility of ... more hours. What would you do? What would you think you might decide?
Mr Rother:	I dunno. I don't think we, we could make that until we actually knew, could we?
Mrs Rother:	No.
Mr Rother:	... what was being offered and what was ...
Mrs Rother:	Um.
Mr Rother:	'Cause then we, we'd talk about it wouldn' us and go through it. Try and see if we could ... whatever we could work out then, as it occurred, like. If something, you know, it's pie in the sky really. I mean, you, you know, if it's off ... if something's offered ... then we'd have to sit down and work out if we could carry on as we are with the jobs that she's doing or no.
	[child comes in again: mother talking to child]

(Mr and Mrs Rother, 51–2)

Mr and Mrs Avon are asked about their anticipated future employment situation in 6–8 months' time.

Q:	Is there any change in the situation that you ... that could cause trouble for you both?

Mr Avon:	Well ...
Mrs Avon:	I don't think so.
Mr Avon:	... unless I give up, unless I lost my job ... No.
Mrs Avon:	No. Shouldn't be.
Mr Avon:	But if I lost my job then ... it would change dramatically because ... now I'm not being rude to Sandra ... I am the main breadwinner. See it, it not ... I'm not being rude to Sandra but if I never had a job and lived on what she got ... it wouldn't be, we couldn' do it ...
Mrs Avon:	Couldn' do it.
Mr Avon:	Simple as that. I would have to go out and get a say, [indistinct] part-time job, or a full-time job again. But the [indistinct], but the ah situation would be changed because ... I would be working different hours ... And also our ... Also what it would change, the fact that ... So therefore we would have to ah ... once again drop down a scale again to ah meet ... our requirements, so even though our ... Even though [indistinct] even though our ... predicaments would be the same ... we would have to stretch it out over a long period ... you see.

(Mr and Mrs Avon, 67–8)

Thus employment decisions by these couples are treated as anomalous in terms of the norms of jointness, discussion and agreement. In their individual accounts, the men construct their decisions without reference to the needs of family members (other than for income), whereas the women refer to other members' needs. In the joint accounts, men explain lack of discussion in terms of the contingencies of their working lives, while women are described as deciding ('it's up to her') after discussing child-care arrangements. This indicates that individual decision-making over employment has somehow to be constructed as consistent with jointness in household decision-making, through some process other than discussion of employment choices.

All these features of the joint interviews point to an underlying structure of social relations in which couples do not have an agreed strategy, contract, pact or bargain on *labour supply* because this is not what they discuss when they do talk about employment decisions. It is clear that they *do* discuss child care – but they also discuss other important issues, and reach agreement about these. If they do not have a *labour* strategy, what sort of strategy do they have?

DECISION-MAKING: INCOME AND EXPENDITURE

There is a good deal of reference in the joint interviews to agreements, and even to some arrangements that could be interpreted as pacts or bargains. For example:

Q:	Does that mean that you've got to continue working now?
Mrs Wear:	Oh yes.
Mr Wear:	That's an agreement made at the time. That ...
Mrs Wear:	[laughs] If we bought the house then Carla [herself] had to carry on working, yeah.

(Mr and Mrs Wear, 21)

Mr Rother:	... but it's gotta work like that; it's ... that, our family gotta work like that to do what we wanna do, to achieve what we want to achieve. Follow?
Q:	You set certain goals? What, you're saying you decide what you're going to do and once it's decided ...
Mr Rother:	Yeah, we stick to it.
Mrs Rother:	... to it.
Mr Rother:	And we help each other.
Mrs Rother:	Yeah.
Mr Rother:	'Cause it's the only way to do and to get what we want to get, and we've always been like it, all the way through.

(Mr and Mrs Rother, 40–1)

Mr Tamar:	If we ... wanna buy anything for the home or anything like that, we sit down and discuss it ... and ... work it out together. The only thing I don't discuss is the ... decorating. If Jean wants it a certain way she buys it and I do it ... And that's it. But everything else is ... talked over ... of ... together. Everything.

(Mr and Mrs Tamar, 38)

In all these households there is a detailed agreement between the partners over *expenditure* and what emerges is a strategy to cover expenditure through income of various kinds. This is quite different from a labour strategy, because there is no prior agreement on what work will provide this income; each partner is free to get the income as he or she chooses (within the norms of their roles) once they have agreed about the item of expenditure and how it will be paid for. It can therefore better be described as an *income strategy*.

The basis for the income strategy is a system of budgeting under which one partner or both manage the household's expenditure.it can be called a strategy because it is an agreed, joint system, with specifiable principles and practices, for managing risks and making messy and difficult situations more susceptible to planning and control. In most of the households, earnings are pooled (often in a joint bank account) and managed by the woman, who then allocates the man his spending money. However this is not universal; in some there are separate accounts, not for the man and the woman, but for different needs. Whether accounts are joint or separate, the couples differentiate between basic needs and 'extras' (like the Rothers' holiday, the Avons' children's clothes or emergencies like the Frome child's hospital admission). In some with only the man in employment, he pays his wife a housekeeping allowance from his wages, and keeps his personal spending money. What is universal in those households which are recognisably following an income strategy is that there is detailed, painstaking and often fiercely debated attention paid to what can be bought and how. The strategy seeks to get agreement between the partners on what items are needed, and where the income to pay for them is to be obtained. The details of how either of them acquires the necessary money are then left to the individual to choose (with or without discussion) – they are not the subject of the agreement.

There is a growing literature on systems for allocating expenditure in households, and how these relate to the labour-market status of household members. In an important paper in 1983, Jan Pahl distinguished between the pooling system we have just outlined, and those in which there is segregated decision-making. In the 'female whole wage system', the woman has sole responsibility for managing all the household finances; in the 'male whole wage system' the responsibility is solely the man's; in the 'housekeeping allowance system' the man gives the woman a fixed sum for housekeeping expenses and controls the rest of expenditure; and in the 'independent management system' the partners have independent incomes over which they make separate decisions.[8] Survey evidence suggests that the pooling system is the most common (over 50 per cent of households) followed by the housekeeping allowance system (20–25 per cent) and the female whole wage system (14–18 per cent).

In the theoretical and empirical literature, the pooling system is associated with middle-class lifestyles and more egalitarian marital roles,[9] whereas the female whole wage system is associated with poor households and segregated roles.[10] However a recent large-scale survey indicates that pooling systems are themselves very varied: Vogler's study found that only 20 per cent of her sample couples agreed that their pool was jointly managed, while in 15 per cent one or both partners thought that the man managed the pool, and in the other 15 per cent one or both thought the woman managed it.[11] In her survey, female whole wage systems and female-managed pools were associated with the lowest household incomes; households using these systems were most likely to contain a man with low earning power,[12] and men in the lowest social class were more than twice as likely to be in female whole wage system households.[13]

In our joint interviews, the couples rhetorically construct their decision-making over expenditure as joint, but they describe a variety of allocative systems, and some appear to change from one system to another when their employment situation alters. In particular, couples who practice a female-managed pool when both are in employment change to a female whole wage system when both are out of work – the woman manages the income from benefits, and gives the man some pocket money: Mr Parrett twice refers to 'going down the pub with 2 pound in me pocket' when he is out of work. Conversely, couples who have a female-managed pool when both are working may change to a housekeeping allowance system when only the man is working. This may also affect access to personal spending money.[14] Mrs Bure has given up her part-time job since she had their second child, who is 9 months old.

Mrs Bure:	I want to see if I can get a part-time job, evenings or something. 'Cos when you give up you lose a bit of money for yourself like, y'know, independence really ain't it? If I had me own money like at Christmas you can't buy presents, like for my husband it would be nice to go and buy him a jumper or something with me own money instead of he's really buying it anyway if it's his wages like ain't it?
Q:	Do you have all the money in one kitty or does he give you so much for housekeeping?
Mrs Bure:	He gives me so much first and if I do need more then, y'know.

(Mrs Bure, 1–2)

In the joint interviews, the agreement over the household's expenditure is seen as the crucial joint decision, and such agreements are described as taking place within a number of different allocation systems. Once important decisions about expenditure are taken, certain labour-market consequences flow from them.

For several of these couples, including some without a partner settled in regular work, the crucial decision which leads to the agreement is the one to buy their house. Mr and Mrs Derwent have decided to go ahead with this, and are due to start repayments soon after they are interviewed.

> Mrs Derwent: Yeah, so we've bought this one now [indistinct] so I'll have to work for the rest of me life.
>
> (Mr and Mrs Derwent, 31)

During the joint interview it becomes clear that this decision has been reached as a long-term one about their future as a family, but that both Mr and Mrs Derwent are contemplating having to change jobs in order to implement it: indeed, both are currently considering alternative jobs. The agreed decision on expenditure has been taken; the implications for jobs and hours have not.

> Mrs Derwent: ... I know it's a nice step up the ladder but it also brings problems: it's not gonna be easy. We know that don't we? Probably have to struggle for a little while but ... you know, I mean, this is the best time [talks to child] ... Yeah, so ... It's gonna be better in the end ...
>
> Mr Derwent: Yeah, it's long-term ... um insurance.
>
> Q: What, so you're looking at it as a long-term plan? So it might be quite difficult over the next few years?
>
> Mr Derwent: Next year.
>
> Mrs Derwent: Definite.
>
> Mr Derwent: Just a matter of getting used to putting back the money so ... It's like now, just putting the money back for your rent. Now we'll have to put back near double what we used to there. Only cover it by me working more overtime I expect ... or with Rachel getting another job.
>
> (Mr and Mrs Derwent, 36)

A little later in the joint interview, they are talking about the possibility of Mrs Derwent working extra hours and becoming overtired.

> Mr Derwent: It's up to her.
>
> Mrs Derwent: It's true though, he's right, I mean he's never one ... He never says to me ... if I was prepared to work 50 hours a week I think he'd let me – do you know what I mean? He's never one of these people – my friend's husband says, 'Oh Linda you're working too much, now take it easy' [...] Not him. Not him.
>
> (Mr and Mrs Derwent, 48)

Mr and Mrs Avon budget very carefully from week to week. They are asked to reconstruct the reasons why Mrs Avon returned to work at the café after having her children.

Mrs Avon: Yes I did want a job 'cause I mean ... as we were talking about, Dave's wages last week [individual interview] ... it's, it's not a lot ... so I mean I wanted the extra little bit ... so that I could go into town perhaps and ... buy 'em some shoes, you know, I mean ... or, you know, it's the things like that, it's what I wanted ... spare cash 'cause I mean time I have what you gives me Dave, time I got the shopping that's gone i'n'it [indistinct] ...

Mr Avon: Oh yeah, like I say before ...

Mrs Avon: We're still the same now.

Mr Avon: ... before Sandra got the job ... us was everlasting on HP, well you're everlasting paying out on that you see ... you never got anything in your pocket ... so by Sandra getting another job it sort of helped come, ah take off of that burden you see, we could ... like I ... we used to ah ... I got majority of things in the house on HP well now ... we, we don' hardly got anything on HP now ... you see. Because of it, you know, it, it helped a, a lot really and truly. But ah ... we had another blow, the other day – yesterday – he put us totally, back along we put a grant in for a grant for our son's uniform – we can't have it.

Mrs Avon: We can't have it [...]

Mr Avon: So we got to find the money to ah ...

Mrs Avon: Gotta find the money to buy three lots of uniform ...

Mr Avon: But that, like I say, you know, he, he needs it so obviously we got to do it, you know, so that means that I got ah do a lot more overtime order to do it. And Sandra's gotta carry on working and ... to help herself out as well, you know so ...

Mrs Avon: I mean what ... Chrissie's [daughter] not gonna be so bad ... because she's already got ... navy blue skirts up there, and she's got a couple blouses, but she's um, she's still gonna need, need new PE gear to go up there; new shoes she's gonna need; she's gonna need new plimsolls. And plimsolls is nearly 2 pound a pair now. I mean when my kids first started school I used to pay about 50 pence a pair for 'em ... now look at 'em. I mean she, the white ones she's got on tonight, I mean I paid 1.99 for they,

backalong. I mean it's, it's, it's not cheap really I mean.
We gotta get a rugby shirt for Paul [son] when he goes
[school's name] – 10 quid, that was barring a penny.

(Mr and Mrs Avon, 50–1)

After a long list of detailed expenditure on items of clothes and equipment
for the children's school and recreational pursuits, and Mrs Avon's involvement in a uniformed association, Mr Avon explains the principle behind
their strategy.

Mr Avon:	... I haven't got a bank, I got a building society [...] I could go to the building society and get a, a loan if I wanted to, but we don't do that, because ... why should I go to the building society and get a loan [...] for 5,000 pound ... right ... and we'll buy say a suite of furniture ... beds for the children, ah we'll buy a few other things for the house ... right ... possibly have a holiday out of it ... well then once all the money's gone ... right ... I have gotta work my arse off to pay that loan back. So therefore [...] at the time ... we're well off [...] but ... once that money's gone ... you still gotta pay the money back plus interest ... so therefore you're not any better off. But you still gotta pay the money back [...] Well by living the way I, I mean, living the way [...] you might think it's old fashioned, but ... ah ... living the way we are see, we're living from day to day ... ah we know what money's coming into the house ... so therefore what our bills are ... every month, so therefore if I turn round ... like this week I got me week's wages coming this week ... so that end of the week now I got, I up the shop [...] they got some trainers for sale ... 5.99. So I picks up a pair of trainers, I says to the chap behind the counter, hang onto they can you, I said and ... I'll have to pay for 'em Friday. All right, he says. So he's hanging on to they shoes now. Friday. On whatever I gets paid, I'll go up the shop, give him the money [...] Right. I turn round, I turn round to Sandra this week and say, right well we gotta pay the rent, we gotta insurance, we gotta pay [indistinct].
Mrs Avon:	Me. Gotta pay me.
Mr Avon:	Yeah, gotta pay you [...] ah ... that's it.
Mrs Avon:	That's it, yeah.
Mr Avon:	You see. Right. I look at meself, right ... what've I got left over? X amount. What do us want? Well I might be able

to say, turn round and say to Sandra, oh here you are, here's a bit extra this week ...

(Mr and Mrs Avon, 54–5)

Mr and Mrs Rother started buying their house 15 years ago; he comments that for this to be possible 'it's essential really that she did go out to work. We'd never have survived else would us?' Now she has taken an extra cleaning job to earn the money for a family holiday in Spain.

Mrs Rother:	To go to Spain. I'm determined to go to Sp...
Mr Rother:	Majorca.
Mrs Rother:	Majorca. I'm determined to go. And the only way I can do it is to get another job to pay for it.
Mr Rother:	She's paying for the holiday and I'm paying for the spending money.

(Mr and Mrs Rother, 38)

They describe the detailed agreements they have made about expenditure, and also how they help each other in the house. Then they are asked what happens when they disagree about what they want.

Mr Rother:	Oh ... well things may start flying and ...
Mrs Rother:	[laughs]
Mr Rother:	... you know, I mean.
Mrs Rother:	He's [indistinct] for days.
Mr Rother:	... don't, don't get me wrong 'tisn' ah, 'tisn' so smooth as what we're making out like, you know, ah ... I mean 'tisn' hunky dory all the time, you know. I mean, couple of the, you know, you get the odd couple of days where not a word is spoken between us like, you know, and ... you know ... she either sulks or I sulk and [...]
Mrs Rother:	Don't speak [...] and the kids do the talking ...
Mr Rother:	Tell your father, or tell your mother ... um ... you know, it goes on in every family, doesn't it? [...] But you gotta work these things out and [...] we set ourselves standards and goals I s'pose, and we're both fortunate to be in work; that's the biggest thing. We are in work. So for as long as the work lasts, we can set ourselves goals and try and achieve things and do things ... together.

(Mr and Mrs Rother, 41)

Mr and Mrs Rother make it clear that their strategy depends on them both being employed, and he has been a regular local authority worker (now foreman) for many years, with a structure allowing promotion. Their strategy for covering their expenditures, and their ways of deciding which extra expenses to incur, are long-established, Mr and Mrs Calder's strategy and their negotiation process are less secure. Mr Calder has been a regular worker for less time, and Mrs Calder makes it clear that it is her priorities over income that determine her influence on their present strategy (involving her part-time work and his regular job). This agreement is fairly tenuous, and involves friction that surfaces during the joint interview (quoted at the start of this chapter). Mrs Calder makes it clear that it is her control over expenditure that is at stake, and determines his type of employment.

Q: If you got the offer now of going back to the agency work ... would, what would both of you feel about that?

Mr Calder: Well I have, I've looked at it. I must admit I have looked at it because now there's one or two agencies give you a basic wage as well, actually pay all the time. But ah ... I don't think she'd be very keen on it mind but ...

Mrs Calder: No, I'm still not very keen on it for the, for that self same reason. I am ... so used now to a, a pay packet at the end of a week or a month as it, and knowing it's coming and being able to plan and think well, yeah out of next month's money I can do this and this and this. Not having to live by the money you've got actually now and worry about next month's when it comes. I ah, I don't like it. He knows I don't.

Mr Calder: Um.

Mrs Calder: So ... but um ... I, I know he wouldn't ... give up this job, but if this job gave him up and made him redundant or something then um ... then, if he went on to agency I would put up with it. But I would ... keep hoping and pushing ... for another permanent job. So ...

Mr Calder: Um.

Mrs Calder: But ah ... I think it's because I, I deal with the purse-strings and I'm the one who worries about the bills and the, the children's shoes and ... you know ... in a couple of months time that isn't gonna fit him any more and, and ... that kind of thing so I, I suppose I am very financially orientated. I want him to be happy in his job, yes. But I want him to bring in as much as he can, as ... often as he can. But um ... that's why I'm sort of scared of the uncertainty of well if you got a job this week, great. If you haven't next week, well ... we'll get by.

(Mr and Mrs Calder, 36–7)

Mr Wear, like Mr Calder, is a regular worker, and his wife is a part-time cleaner. She manages their budgeting – a female-managed pool.

Q: Do you have a joint account?
Mrs Wear: We have a joint account, yes.
Mr Wear: [indistinct] got a joint ...
Mrs Wear: But most of the basic everyday things I deal with, don't I? He hasn't got time for things like that [laughs].
Mr Wear: The thing is ... the thing is bills come and I'm at work and they've got to be paid usually when I'm at work. Um ... so I just leave it to her and they they [...]
Q: Do both salaries go into the same account?
Mrs Wear: They used to, didn't 'em, but mine goes into the [building society's name] now [...] Whereas what we used to do is take the money out of the bas ... the main account and put into the [building society] whereas now we take less out of the main account and put my cheque straight into the [building society]. Pay the mortgage. It just saves me putting my cheque into the [bank].

(Mr and Mrs Wear, 19)

Mr and Mrs Cherwell use a variant of the same system.

Mrs Cherwell: We've got a joint account ... his wages get paid into my account.
Mr Cherwell: But my money pays all the bills. And what she earns, she earns for the [indistinct] and the maid [daughter], like ... If I wants any money any time I just ... says to her ...
Mrs Cherwell: He goes, he comes to me for his money, his money goes straight into the bank. I get mine by cash, you see. His goes into the bank.
Mr Cherwell: [indistinct] ... it works out better like that for us. 'Cause otherwise it means ... if I have money home here as well and the wife got money home here ... then one of us could go out and spend the whole lot ... just like that [...] and so I said to her, I said, well instead of both our wages going in the bank, why don't ... you have yours in cash, just keep mine and I'll pay the bills and any money that you earn we, we can have that for housekeeping, you know, shopping, clothing, anything like that ...

(Mr and Mrs Cherwell, 47)

In their accounts of why the woman organises the budgeting, the couples construct her as a better manager. Mr and Mrs Tamar are asked how they handle their earnings.

Mr Tamar:	We just continue the two and ... and that's it, you know ... like she said, what's gotta be paid out gets paid out; what's left is left like, you know ...
Q:	Does one of you organise that?
Mr Tamar:	The wife do.
Q:	Do you?
Mr Tamar:	The wife organises all the bills that's gotta be paid.
Mrs Tamar:	You just, you just give me the money [laughs].
Mr Tamar:	I just give her the money and she pays the bills. That's what I like, you know, I mean 'cause if I got money in me pocket and I saw anything in town ... I would think that she would like or probably the maid would like ... me daughter ... I'd buy it, you know ... I could have 40 pound in one pocket and if I saw a dress. I dunno, or a skirt I thought she'd like for 25, I'd buy it ... you know [...] I'm like that [laughs].
Q:	You're more careful are you?
Mrs Tamar:	Well I've got to be.

(Mr and Mrs Tamar, 36–7)

Similarly Mr and Mrs Plym:

Q:	Do you share budgeting?
Mr Plym:	No, she does all that [laughs]
Mrs Plym:	No I do that [laughs] Yeah. I, I take care of all the ... bills and money.

(Mr and Mrs Plym, 27)

What these quotations all illustrate is that it is expenditure that is the subject of detailed negotiation, leading to joint decisions, and that the system of household budgeting has an important effect on the form of these discussions, and the influence of the partners on decisions. These joint decisions then lead to a strategy for covering expenditure, which defines the partners' roles in income generation, but leaves them to make particular decisions over employment as individuals.

NEGOTIATION: UNPAID WORK

Beyond this system of budgeting from week to week, the income strategy requires the couple to agree extra items of expenditure, which in turn need more income for the household. We have already given the most striking and substantial example – taking out a mortgage – which can require one or both partners to increase their labour supply, or change jobs to increase their earnings. However, in several households even much more modest additional expenditures meant that extra hours had to be worked. Mrs Cam is at present at home with her children, but she and her husband are asked about the time when she did some paid work, before her second child was born.

Mr Cam:	Well at ... Then she was going to stay at home but um I was on good money. Ah, 'cause it was only when the coal trade got slack and the money didn't come in that we were living on the borderline, you know. We were still doing well but we weren't doing as well as we could have been. Lucy said she wanted to go out to work, you know, sort of.
Mrs Cam:	It started off that I wanted a new cooker and he said, 'if you want a new cooker you can go out and work for one ...'
Mr Cam:	You know because I couldn't, I couldn't see my finances ...

(Mr and Mrs Cam, 40)

However, the need to reach agreement over expenditure, budgeting and income also brings with it a requirement to reach some accommodation over child care and domestic tasks, and often also transport. As was shown in the last chapter, the women's accounts describe a process of arranging substitute care for children, often involving female kin, but always requiring their partners to play some part. Help with domestic work is not regarded as essential, and women construct this as exceptional ('he's one in a million'); yet in practice, in our sample of poor households, where the woman was working the man did some housework, and where she was working full time he did substantial amounts.

The joint interviews give some descriptions of the process of negotiation over these issues – sometimes amicable, sometimes fraught. Mr and Mrs Nene both work in full-time day jobs: when asked how they manage to fit their jobs together, he replies:

'It is easy enough for us because the two children are older, so they more or less look after theirself, as such, but um ... you know if I come home lunchtime to take the dog for a walk, whatever ... hoover the carpet or do the breakfast dishes; it's no hassle.'

(Mr and Mrs Nene, 43)

Transport is an issue for them; when Mrs Nene first worked at the factory where she is a charge-hand, he took her to work in his car, before continuing to his own job. But now things are different.

Q:	Do you have 2 cars?
Mrs Nene:	No.
Mr Nene:	No. She got my car. I got a pushbike [laughs].
Q:	How did you decide that?
Mrs Nene:	[laughs]
Mr Nene:	Decided for me. [laughs] Decided for me actually. I got banned. [pause] As it come out it wasn't a bad move 'cause she ah ... it made you pass your test didn' it? [indistinct]
Mrs Nene:	I'd always said I wanted to drive but never bothered like, you know, so when he lost his licence I ... well it was 12 months before I got mine then; passed me test. So we kept the car and ... up in the garage and ... brought it out when I ... passed me test 2 years ago now. So ...
Q:	What'll happen when the ban finishes?
Mrs Nene:	Oh it's finished.
Mr Nene:	Oh it finished ... 3 years ago.
Mrs Nene:	Yeah, it was 3 years ago. Wa'n' it? 3 years ago he got banned so he ...
Mr Nene:	Still got me bike.
Mrs Nene:	So he's had his licence like for 18 months, but, I mean, the insurance is so ridiculous ... and, and I think, well while I'm paying that I could be buying something for the house like, you know, rather than sort of like insurance where you, you don't see it like that, but you see I do ... and I think to myself, well ... what do we need another car for ... that, that one's out there [pause].

(Mr and Mrs Nene, 45)

Mr and Mrs Tamar, too, construct their co-operation as harmonious. She does a full-time day job; he works nights, but with a recent interruption through illness.

Mr Tamar:	No, we share everything ... everything is shared 50–50 down the line ... you know and ... financially, housework ... cooking, everything ... is done 50–50
Q:	You share housework?
Mrs Tamar:	Yeah [pause] Well yeah [...] when he was home for 16 weeks well ... he had to have something to keep him happy didn't you? Doing the housework and ...
Mr Tamar:	Yeah, I don't expect me wife to come home from work, after a day's work, when I'm sat at home doing nothing,

	and do all the housework and cooking. When I'm quite capable ... of do, doing it meself.
Q:	Do you still share it now you're back at work?
Mr Tamar:	Yeah. Oh yeah. With the ... the girls that's home now, they ... they're quite good when I'm ... like next week when I'm sleeping they'll tidy up and dust and all that, and keep the place tidy, but I'll still get up and ... prepare the meal for me wife to come home and have a cooked one. It's unfair on her to come home ... at quarter to 5 and start cooking tea ...

(Mr and Mrs Tamar, 37)

This explicit appeal to fairness implies that the unpaid duties of the household are divided up, so as to equalise the burdens and benefits for members.[15] However, there was also plenty of evidence of this process of negotiation involving conflicts of interest, with the outcome an uneasy compromise. Mr and Mrs Wear have an agreed income strategy which enables them to budget successfully, and they are buying their council house (partly through a windfall insurance payment) when their children are still young. However, there is a good deal of tension over his child-care responsibilities.

Q:	Is it hard to switch from work to actually looking after the children?
Mr Wear:	It is 'cause [indistinct] I find work easier.
Q:	Do you?
Mrs Wear:	[laughs] There's not many men that'll admit that. [laughs]
Mr Wear:	Well it's not so much easier it's just that you don't get kids answering you back, you know ...
Mrs Wear	[laughs]
Mr Wear:	I don't get the lorry answering me back. It either starts or it doesn't, you know [laughs] ... it's as simple as that. But ah ... it's a wrench.
Mrs Wear:	Ummm.
Mr Wear:	I think ... find that when you've done a day, even now there's not so much work on you're still tired when you come home, first thoughts are 'great – thank God that day's over with'. And you get inside the door and everything ... there's kids screaming and the wife shouting at them and telling them to shut up and do as they're told, and you think, oh my God, I'll go back to work. So ah ... yeah, it can be a bit of a wrench going between the two.
Mrs Wear:	But he loves them really. [laughs]

Mr Wear:	I do now 'cause they're in bed.

(Mr and Mrs Wear, 29–30)

Mr and Mrs Calder's disagreement over his type of employment has already been analysed (pp. 192–4). Later in the same joint interview, Mrs Calder is describing how she came to be doing her evening job.

Mrs Calder:	For all he says ... about looking after the children he does it very well. He's very domesticated ...
Mr Calder:	You make it sound like a trained dog [indistinct]
Mrs Calder:	Well it is a bit like a trained dog, you know what to do and where to ... but um he's, he's not ... frightened by looking after the children – are you?
Mr Calder:	No, not now.
Mrs Calder:	Whereas ...
Q:	You're not doing it under sufferance by the sound of it.
Mr Calder:	No, no.
Mrs Calder:	No. I don't think so.
Mr Calder:	No.
Mrs Calder:	I know talking with friends of mine, I mean it's all she can do to get her husband to mind the children for an hour ... and ... he told me himself I would not do ... what Martin is doing. NO WAY. I like her about when the children are there. He's nervous of being on his own with them. But we haven't got that problem.
Mr Calder:	No. We have some nice quiet nights here sometimes when they really wind me up and they're in bed for 6 o'clock [laughs] and it's really quiet, and I think to my-self, we've cracked it tonight [laughs]. But ah ...
Mrs Calder:	That happens when I'm here so, so that's nothing out the ordinary. I mean ... they don't change their behaviour because it's Dad looking after them rather me ... they're very used to it. I mean ... I've always gone up into town or gone to my mother's for an afternoon and left them with him, so they're quite used to being on their own with Dad. It's not as though it's anything different. I think Dad putting them to bed every night was a bit of a shock to start with ...
Mr Calder:	It was a shock for me never mind them.
Mrs Calder:	... but they got used to it. And so have you.

(Mr and Mrs Calder, 44)

Some of the hours worked, by women in particular, are inconvenient and arduous, and both men and women speak of tiredness and irritability as a result of combining paid and unpaid duties. However, there is evidence of some careful planning, and detailed attention to each others' needs, in some of the arrangements they describe. Mrs Rother has found her second (evening) job very exhausting.

Mr Rother:	But as I say, it's a one-off really; she wanted to do the extra job; she said if I can do it and we can bank it every fortnight, she said, can we go? I said, well ... try it and see how you go, I said, 2 jobs plus looking after the house and the kids, I said, is a lot to take.
Mrs Rother:	Yeah.
Mr Rother:	But her've surprised me. Her's dead tired, mind you, her was dropping off in the chair just after 9 o'clock night-times, it's true.
Mrs Rother:	Sometimes [...]
Mr Rother:	... it's took it's toll, it's had an effect on you, ha'n'it?
Mrs Rother:	Yes.
Mr Rother:	And that's it. But we're, we ... see, I don't know how other people, but we've worked something pretty well together, like, know what I mean. Sundays is her lay-in, definite.
Mrs Rother:	[indistinct] he does the dinner [indistinct]
Mr Rother:	I does the dinner Sundays and I cooks it. And her gets up somewhere around about between 10 in the morning, but her gotta have one day in, see. Her gotta have one day to lay on and lay in. 'Cause it's six mornings see ...

(Mr and Mrs Rother, 39–40)

In one joint interview – Mr and Mrs Derwent – the negotiation process was actually happening at the time when Helen Kay was seeing them. This will be set out and analysed in the final chapter.

The issue of power in these 'joint' decisions is never overtly discussed.[16] The nearest it comes to being recognised and acknowledged is where two of the men with regular full-time jobs (Mr Rother and Mr Avon) imply that their status as main earner gives them the right to override their partner in decisions – Mr Rother in the issue of his overtime versus her part-time hours (see p. 202); Mr Avon in the issue of whether his wife has enough money for her needs (see p. 203). It may well be significant that these are both men with valuable 'job assets',[17] giving pensions, redundancy payment rights or holiday entitlements which their partners (and other irregular workers) lack. Several writers have related household power to such assets.[18] Conversely Mrs Bure (p. 228) and Mrs Itchen (p. 147) imply that being outside the labour market gives them less direct access to resources, and hence less influence on decision-making.[19]

Although there are specific conflicts in the joint interviews (Mr and Mrs Calder – p.193; Mr and Mrs Cam – p. 63; Mr and Mrs Derwent – p. 306), the roles of men and women are so taken for granted that the balance of power over decision-making is not directly addressed. Hence the norms of 'jointness' and 'discussion' conceal assumptions about the rights that attach to men as 'breadwinners' – to leisure opportunities and personal spending money, for instance[20] – and the duties of women to sacrifice their needs to those of children, often at the expense of any time or money for themselves. However, most of the joint interviews display the couples' concern to negotiate over the detailed implementation of their segregated gender roles, and to adjust the details of their contributions to unpaid work in line with paid working hours. This in turn means that women who contribute a large proportion of household income have more influence on 'joint' decisions.

Hence we must understand power within these households as framed within the terms of the roles of man and woman. The men define their autonomy in terms of their control over the 'spending money' that they allocate themselves (where they manage the household finances) or which is given to them by their budget-managing partners. The women define their constraints *and* freedoms over employment choice in terms of what is 'natural' for women: Mrs Nene accepted it as 'natural' that she should have to stick at her factory job to sustain household income, while her husband changed his jobs in line with his preferences for motor-cycle maintenance work. She sees it as her responsibility – in terms of her role in budgeting – to contribute income to cover household expenditure, but not to claim the job satisfaction and respect due to a man as 'worker'.

THE ROLE OF BENEFITS IN AN INCOME STRATEGY

So far almost all the couples whose strategies have been analysed are ones in which there is a man or a woman or both in regular full-time employment. The strategy is to use the main earner's income to meet the basic needs of the household, and the other (lesser or subsidiary) wage to meet other expenses, as they arise. In the case of a major regular outgoing, like a mortgage, both may have to increase their labour supply, or find better paid work. The couples in our sample who had at least one full-time regular worker well established in a job were Mr and Mrs Avon, Calder, Cherwell, Nene, Plym, Rother, Severn, Stour, Tamar, Taw and Wear. In addition, Mrs Wye and Mr Ouse had fairly recently taken jobs that seem likely to be regular and permanent, and Ms Waveney had very recently started to live with a man who is a regular worker (this cohabitation is so recent that they are just starting to develop an income strategy).

All the rest of the sample were households with no established regular full-time worker. These households had no firm basis for the kind of income strategy that has been described so far, though several were attempting to establish one. For these households of 'irregulars' – part-time or occasional, short-term or self-employed workers – benefits formed part of their income strategy. They allowed the irregularity of their earnings to be mitigated – albeit often in a frustratingly unreliable and inadequate way.

However, within this broad category of 'irregulars' we can recognise two different versions of this second income strategy. The first used benefits tactically – as a way of coping with periods of interrupted earnings, or exceptional household circumstances. Employment was expected to provide income to cover household expenditure for most of the time, but reliance on benefits for periods when work was not available, or household expenditure increased unexpectedly, was constructed as normal. This was the largest group in the whole sample, and consisted of Mr and Mrs Bure, Cam, Clyde, Colne, Derwent, Hodder, Humber, Itchen, Medway, Parrett, Ribble, Ryton, Tavy and Torridge, and Ms Otter and Mr Thames. The second group used benefits strategically, claiming for their basic needs, and doing undeclared work for the 'extras'. Here the lack of suitable labour-market opportunities for covering household needs was constructed as the reason for relying on benefits for long periods to cover household costs. This group consisted of Mr and Mrs Bow, Dart, Dovey, Exe, Frome and Spey. (It is important to note that many of the group who use benefits tactically also described doing undeclared cash work while claiming, while the partners of regular workers, and those regular workers themselves, sometimes did cash work that was not declared for tax purposes (see pp. 241–2).) Only one of the 'irregulars' – Mr and Mrs Kennet – do not use the benefits system in their strategy. We will show at the end of the chapter that the Kennets, alone among our sample, can be seen as having a *work* rather than an *income* strategy.

The role of benefits in the income strategies of the 'irregulars' helps explain the very long and detailed descriptions of benefits problems which occupy so much of the individual and joint interviews – even those who were currently in work and earning quite well. Since the benefits system is the only protection against exploitation (below-subsistence pay, or failure to pay for work done), it provides the guarantee against destitution for these households, and one to which all have resorted fairly recently, some for considerable periods. Hence its significance is comparable to the *security* that is so important to the regular workers; the irregulars are much less concerned about security of employment and earnings, but they are concerned about the unreliability and arbitrariness of the benefits system, because at times it provides for their basic weekly needs.

The hazards of irregular work are reconstructed by Mr and Mrs Ryton, talking about his last-but-one job, where his employer failed to pay him, or paid him with dud cheques. Mr Ryton describes his last few days at work, while Mrs Ryton emphasises the impossibility of managing the household expenditure in these circumstances.

Mr Ryton:	I went back on Wednesday and worked Wednesday, Thursday and Friday and then I packed it in after that, didn't I?
Mrs Ryton:	Yeah. You couldn't stand no more. I mean, Friday night ... he was gonna stick it out until longer actually ... Friday night came and um it was his wage, his pay night ...
Mr Ryton:	It was my pay night ... and I didn't get nothing ...
Mrs Ryton:	... and he came home ... he, you did; you came home with 40 pounds. 'Cause I said, what ... what's this?
Mr Ryton:	Yeah, that's right, yeah. 40 pound, that's right.
Mrs Ryton:	... you know, I said: what's this? This has got to last us for a week – 40 pound. That wouldn't even buy my groceries. I spent that 40 pound; I stocked my larder and the fridge up. And I usually do a trolley, which comes up ... I do a trolley which comes to about 38 [indistinct – child talking] ...
Mr Ryton:	Um. And then I, I didn't go in that Saturday, did I? And he phoned up and said: 'where were you today?' And I said: 'well what's the point in coming in if I'm not getting paid?'
Mrs Ryton:	That's right.
Mr Ryton:	And he goes: 'what do you mean, not getting paid?' I said: 'well I only got 40 pound this week'. And he says 'oh, well, if it's the money you want', he said, 'I can pay you, come up tomorrow' ...
Mrs Ryton:	But he ...
Mr Ryton:	... which was New Year's day. And I, I thought, well I'll go up tomorrow, 'cause he was gonna give me cash. Went up there, didn' we? And he give me a cheque.
Mrs Ryton:	Which we knew would probably bounce. So then [indistinct] ...
Mr Ryton:	It's a waste of time and I thought, well if it's gonna go on like that I'll just pack it in.

Mrs Ryton:	He, he came home that night and he was totally fed up and he said: 'right I'm not going back tomorrow and that's it. Finished.' And he, he [indistinct] ... I said, right you're not ... you know, I made sure he didn't go back. Said, right you're not going back there. And he didn't, did you? The next day Ed phoned him up and like I said, he wondered where he was and he said 'I'm not coming back to you'. And ... he didn't get nasty or anything. All he said was 'oh'. He sounded shocked, didn't he?
Mr Ryton:	Um. [indistinct]
Mrs Ryton:	And a bit ... bit fed up. He just said 'oh you could have let me know'.
Q:	Were you expecting to get another job quite quickly? Or was it just ...
Mr Ryton:	Well, I knew if I stayed in the building trade, I mean there's, there's bound to be more going somewhere; there's an awful lot of builders in Exeter like ... but ... I've actually got one now that I really wanna do, 'cause it's a trade with it, so ... plus there's training's there as well, so ... I've landed on my feet really.

(Mr and Mrs Ryton, 36–7)

In the joint interview, Mrs Ryton refers to the account she gave Helen Kay in the individual interview, where she described what happened following this, when they applied for income support (see Chapter 5, pp. 164–5 for part of this account). The full text of this part of her individual interview runs to well over 100 lines, describing how many times her husband had to make claims (including claims for crisis loans from the Social Fund), and the iniquities of trying to live on what the DSS allowed them (£32.50 a week for a couple with two children). The main thrust of her argument is that she was trying to get her husband to leave his unreliable employer for two months before he actually left, but that when he did so they found themselves in deeper trouble because the DSS refused to pay them the full rate of benefit, on the grounds that he left his job voluntarily. She concludes with a detailed account of her weekly household expenditures, and the needs of her children which she cannot afford. At the time of interview they are waiting to apply for family credit. Mr and Mrs Itchen's story is much the same (see p. 166), except that he has not found a job. Mr and Mrs Clyde also experienced a period when he lost his job and his benefit was suspended. Mrs Clyde describes the experience.

''Cause my husband got the sack, you see. And they decided that they'd suspend our money. Now the government says you need 70 something pounds to live on but they ... they worked our money out and they took another 13 pound 50 I think it was [...] away 'cause he lost his job. And with my money they used to send us 20 pound a fortnight [pause] [...] I mean we're still fighting the appeal now [...] We're still fighting for it. Not give up [...] I don't agree with this suspended money. When you've got a wife and family to keep, how can they say : you have to live on this. I mean they're quick to step in if you don't feed your kids properly ...'

(Mrs Clyde, 11)

It is of vital importance for our research to give a clear account of the part played by benefits in decisions made by irregular workers, since it is this aspect of our study that may influence the policy debate. Our analysis shows that this group – the largest in our sample – rely on benefits to fill the gaps in their income to cover basic expenditures, and construct the benefits system as integral to their strategy.

Mr and Mrs Ribble are, by their own account, a happy, close and harmonious couple; he is a 'self-employed' building worker, and enjoys the challenge of having to find his own work from one job to the next. However, their joint interview makes it clear how many times they have resorted to claiming benefits during their married life, either because of interruptions of earnings, or because of health or housing crises in the household. They lived together before they were married, but he was unemployed and they claimed separately, as single people; when they married they were living with her sister, and he claimed for them both. After their baby was born, they were living with her parents, and Mrs Ribble was in a very tense state, following a difficult childbirth. Mr Ribble describes his attitude to employment at the time.

'No, I think I needed to be there. Um ... Ah ... Well I, it's just that, work, last thing on me mind. I, I could, I had a work at the time actually; I was offered work – I just turned it down, being at home ... I thought, well, you know, what we're going through at home is more important. And I couldn't concentrate on anything anyway so ... that was it, I just stayed at home. Ah ... I think I went for a couple of weeks didn't I? [...] And it just didn' work out [...] so I just ... put work at the back of me mind and stayed off for about 6 months, wa'n'it?'

(Mr and Mrs Ribble, 47)

After this he was self-employed for a time, and enjoyed this, but then they were thrown out by her parents after a row (over his parents), and had to move into homeless families' accommodation (bed and breakfast) for 3 weeks, before being housed in their present council house. Mr Ribble is asked if he was working at that time.

'No. I weren't, no. I ... Actually I signed on because um I couldn't afford the rent of the bed and breakfast – 110 pound a week, you know, so [...] the day we went into the council all I did was, um, oh I was [indistinct – something about a mate and work] he offered some work and I just put him off, it was on the building again and um ... I just put him off because I couldn't, I couldn't bring in what I would have um ... needed to live on like. I spent 110 pound a week for one room and um ... that was bed and breakfast, that's all you got [...] on top of that you had to find ... your lunch, launderette money, anything else you needed. So really your cost of living was about 200 pound a week.'

(Mr and Mrs Ribble, 55)

About 8 weeks after they moved in, he got work again – 'it just come to me'. Meanwhile they had applied for housing benefit, which took this amount of time, and they describe a saga over the next 6 months, during which time the DSS and local authority got in a mess over their claims. So it was not until 6 months before the interview that Mr and Mrs Ribble – now a successful couple, talking of buying the house that they are busy improving – got clear (for the time being) of their tactical reliance on benefits within their income strategy. This overall strategy will be described in more detail at the end of the chapter.

Other 'irregulars' are currently using the benefits system while their situation is changing. Ms Otter is claiming income support as a single parent; her new partner, Mr Thames, works as a delivery van driver. He explains:

'we're not exactly ... living together ... I mean she is, she is claiming social and ... I will admit I, I do sleep with her occasionally but I don't ... you know I spend, I finish me job and I, I'm here then ... and I sleep in me lodgings ... you know. I go back [...] Well even, even if it was ... I mean ... there isn't anything they could do about it because she's, she's entitled and that, I'm entitled to stay here um ... up to 3 nights a week I think it is anyway. Without her losing any benefit. Which I don't ... I don't ...'

(Ms Otter and Mr Thames, 3)

His gross pay is £75 a week, he says, but he enhances it by using the firm's van for his own purposes. He has had various jobs, and says he was 'on a fiddle' in one of them; he also pays tax as a married man, though he is divorced (he thinks – the papers have not yet come through). Ms Otter claims £61.92 a week, of which £14.50 is child benefit (her children are twins). She is considering doing childminding, and Mr Thames tells her she can earn £15 a week on top of her income support. When the children are old enough to go to a nursery, she wants a full-time or part-time job.

Mr and Mrs Tavy, both previously divorced, have seven children, of whom two are still at school. She has a spastic daughter aged 27 living at home. She has not worked for several years; he was working in London as a despatch rider, until they moved to Exeter 6 months previously, since when he has done some casual agricultural work. In the past he has worked in southern Africa, been in the merchant navy, worked on oil rigs, and had his own window cleaning business. Now he is claiming benefit, but investigating the possibility of an Enterprise Allowance to set up as a self-employed fisherman.

For all these people, income support is currently, or has very recently, provided for their basic needs during gaps in a pattern of very irregular, incomplete or variable earnings or during periods of crisis or change in their housing situations or domestic lives. In Chapters 4 and 5 similar tactical uses of benefits were traced through the lives of Mr and Mrs Torridge, Mr and Mrs Humber, Mr and Mrs Parrett and Mr and Mrs Hodder – all households in which the man is an irregular worker, and the woman works only when the man is working (though Mrs Hodder and Mrs Parrett seem to have taken jobs when their husbands were doing undeclared cash work, which led to them changing their status to 'self-employed').

Another small group, many of whom have also claimed income support recently, organise their budgeting around the claiming of family credit. Whereas many other interviewees assert that the income tests associated with that benefit are unfair and arbitrary, and that it is difficult for a household to budget on the low wages which they earn, either during the processing of the claim, or after it has been refused, this group describe family credit as helpful – though with reservations about its consequences for budgeting. Their accounts reveal the tactical use of this benefit as a way of giving them income security – something that they look for from the benefits system because it is missing in their terms of employment and wage rates.

The task for the person (usually the woman) who manages the couple's budgeting in an income strategy is to cover the household outgoings each week by income from some source. Hence although low wages and benefits are a constraint, determining what can be bought, they are not a serious budgeting problem, unless they follow on from a period of high wages during which the household has committed itself to major items of expenditure. Under these circumstances, the members of an 'irregular' household will usually look for ways of making more income by extra employment, and if they are on income support this implies breaking the rules by doing undeclared work for cash. Since family credit is awarded for 6 months on the basis of 5 weeks' payslips, doing extra work for cash is not illegal under its terms. Hence at first sight family credit should not pose great difficullties for couples pursuing an income strategy.

Indeed, one couple in our sample saw the benefit as helpful and unproblematic. Mr Colne is a car valeter who has had a number of job changes, mainly through redundancy, and two periods of unemployment, each of around 8 months. In his individual interview, he describes two problems with the benefits system – the 3-week delay between losing his job, and hence his wages, and receiving income support, and the pressure from benefit authorities to take low-paid, and especially part-time work, which would not provide enough to live on. He does not mention family credit. However, Mrs Colne, whose only paid work is fostering a child, is asked whether she claims it.

Mrs Colne:	Yeah, yeah. We just got that back, haven't we? Since she [3-month-old daughter] was born. Yeah, we get um ... we get quite good family credit don't we really ... a week, which isn't a bad, bad thing [...] Yeah, I've had it ever ... we've had FIS ever since Warren was born, we been on FIS haven't we?
Mr Colne:	Um.
Mrs Colne:	Then it changed over to family credit, but year ...
Q:	And has that been easy to claim or is it difficult?
Mrs Colne:	No, it was quite easy really wasn't it? [...] Just fill in the form, didn't you? They asked for your wage slips and ... you send them away and then they work all your, your money out and ... divide it between the kids and ... everything else, and then they work out how much you're entitled to a week. So ah, it's quite nice really.
Q:	So there's no hassle about it? Was it easier than claiming social security?
Mrs Colne:	[laughs] Yeah.
Mr Colne:	Yeah [...]
Q:	Do you get housing benefit?
Mrs Colne:	No because um, because we get family credit. Whereas the family credit now um ... a part of that money is supposed to go towards helping with the rent, so you don't get the housing beneift for it, which is a bit of a nuisance but still ... you can't have it all ways ... it's like [...]
Q:	... does the family credit cover all your rent?
Mrs Colne:	No it doesn't cover all your rent; it just covers a part of the rent and um ... it covers the milk tokens for the 2 girls [daughter and foster daughter] because they're under 5

and ch ... it covers um school dinners for Warren. Because when you're, before when you're on FIS you could claim housing benefit, free school meals, and then you'd get a milk token for each child that was under 5, whereas everything ... all that's gone now. And you just get um ... the ah family credit each week which is supposed to cover all that.

(Mrs Colne, 18–19)

Mrs Colne organises the household budget – Mr Colne gives her his whole wage packet – and they work out the bills and keep the rest out for spending during the week. Their income strategy is consistent with managing on his low but steady wage, plus her fostering allowance from social services, plus family credit. Mr and Mrs Humber describe themselves as having managed on his wage from a Community Programme project plus family income supplement in much this way.

A slightly more critical note is struck in Mrs Bure's account. Mr Bure is an irregular worker who has fairly recently taken employment in an electric plating company, doing 'dangerous' and 'unhealthy' work, long hours (up to 70 hours a week) with a basic wage of £126. He is waiting to hear the outcome of the firm being taken over by another. When he started with the firm, he spent a year on a wage of £85 a week. Asked about whether he had claimed family income supplement, he replies:

'Yes. Once Jeanette [wife] had sorted it out. Paperwork I know nothing about. Figures I leave up to her.'

(Mr Bure, 15)

At the start of her interview, Mrs Bure makes it clear that she knows the rules for family credit, and has seen advertisements about it on TV.

'Yeah but I can't claim it any more because my husband's wages has gone up now so ... I used to get it when he didn't earn so much but it's just pricing what you can earn and still get it.'

(Mrs Bure, 1)

Mrs Bure seems to suggest here that, as manager of the household finances, she needs to know precisely what his maximum eligible earnings would be. Later in the interview she explains that the family income supplement has just run out, and she is saving wage slips to apply for family credit.

'I might just apply, it is worth trying even if I only get a couple of pound, y'know. I don't think we'll be able to get it but I'll try.'

(Mrs Bure, 10)

She says that his wage rise was welcome when they were still receiving £20 a month in family income supplement, which finished that week; she will miss it when it is gone. This implies recognition of a poverty trap, in which a wage increase is later all but nullified by a benefit loss, although Mrs Bure's reaction to this is one of mild disappointment rather than complaint. She is considering taking an evening job to get some extra money: 'I might go into the Job Centre on Wednesday and have a look if there's anything in there'. She says that her husband would like her to get a part-time job, to earn money for a holiday, but her children are aged 3 and 9 months, and she left the last cleaning job she had to be with the baby.

> '... we live week to week. I thought if I had a little evening job I could put so much back for Christmas and so much back for holidays on that. 'Cause we do go away on day trips while Martin is still a baby but next year he will be able to go to bed a bit later. Thought about going in a caravan somewhere.'
>
> (Mrs Bure, 10)

Mr Bure gives more priority to his wife's emotional health, but adds that the money is needed.

> 'I keep telling her to take a job because being in the house, it is all right as a house but it's hard with two kids. She's got to go out; if she doesn't go out she starts to get depressed and I don't want to go through that again. Not only that, I don't earn that much and you can't budget on one person's wages. I'll come home at half past 4 every night and she can go out till half past 7. But she's changing her mind. She says she is tired.'
>
> (Mr Bure, 17)

Two households with a regular worker, Mr and Mrs Severn and Mr and Mrs Wye, also construct family credit as useful, but with reservations. Mrs Severn tells Helen Kay in her individual interview that she receives £8 per week family credit. In the joint interview, when asked about this, she says she saw a TV advertisement, but found the process of applying humiliating; she and her husband describe the attitude of DSS staff as grudging and unhelpful. They are glad of the money, but their rent has risen by £14 a fortnight, and they can no longer get housing benefit, so they say they are no better off. Mr and Mrs Wye describe how she was getting family credit when she had two part-time jobs, but had it reduced and then lost it when she changed to full time at the warehouse, and then was promoted to the manager's job.

> Mrs Wye: When I had the two jobs and, going ... I was getting about 37 pound a week family credit ... when I went full time it dropped down to 10 pound a week, didn' it?

| Mr Wye: | Yeah. |
| Mrs Wye: | And then when I had the pay rise I didn' ah ... free dental treatment and ... prescriptions and that [indistinct]. I don't get that now. [indistinct] |

(Mr and Mrs Wye, 38–9)

Mr Wye says the form is complicated, but Mrs Wye talks about claiming again:

'you never know, you might be entitled just to 2 pound ... but if I'm entitled to 2 pound I'm saving on ... prescriptions and dental treatment [...] Yeah, it mounts up [...] I shall try again. Don't think I will be entitled but ... like I said, there's no harm in trying.'

(Mr and Mrs Wye, 39)

Here Mrs Wye describes part of what is meant by the poverty trap – she has increased first her hours and then her wage rate, yet she has lost a significant amount of benefit with each change. But neither she nor her husband (a critic of income support) express resentment about this. Furthermore, when asked about tax, Mrs Wye replies:

'Well, because David's not working, I'm claiming his tax allowances, so I only pay ... a very small amount; it's like last week ... I think the gross pay before tax was about 157 'cause I had overtime and I only paid 6 pound 75 tax on that so [...] I haven't really took much notice of it. I think next year, I don't think I'll be able to claim his tax 'cause it's all changed now ... I think it'll just be ah me own tax and I won't be able to claim his ... so I'll just wait and see [laughs].'

(Mrs Wye, 19–20)

In this household's income strategy, family credit is constructed as a way of bringing low wages up to a minimum, and saving the expense of extras like prescriptions and dental charges: hence its withdrawal as earnings rise is not perceived as unjust or a disincentive – even in combination with the impact of income tax. Mr and Mrs Wye do not seem to resent their current high 'effective marginal tax rate'; their concern is to cover their regular expenses, either through wages or through benefits.

CRITICISMS OF THE BENEFITS SYSTEM

Means-tested benefits have been extensively criticised as neither reaching those most in need, nor offering adequate incentives for low-paid workers. One of the main purposes of our study – reflected in the title of this book – was to investigate whether the 'better targeting' of the reformed system offers effective income support, or traps households like these in poverty. Hence it is crucial for us to analyse what our respondents say about these benefits, and how they construct the part they play in their decision-making. (For an explanation of the benefits system see Appendix 1.)

Because these couples follow an expenditure-orientated income strategy, which treats earnings as a way – but not the only way – of covering household expenses, their criticisms of benefits are not always the ones that are standard in the literature of the Poverty Lobby. As we have seen from the analysis of their accounts, the men are particularly critical of the delay (caused by processing of claims) between ceasing to receive wages at the end of temporary or occasional employment, and actually receiving benefit. Outgoings are not covered for these 3 or 4 weeks, and households who budget from week to week are expected to live on nothing. Both men and women are highly critical of suspensions or reductions in benefit as a result of the authorities' investigations into the circumstances of a man losing or leaving his job. Women also criticise rates of benefit as being inadequate to cover needs, especially children's needs. Several of them have found themselves in the position of bringing up children on income support after being left in debt by a husband who was an irregular worker. Ms Waveney talks about this experience.

'when I was on social with her [daughter], I was only getting 23 [...] I was only getting 19 pound on social anyway. You imagine living on 19 pound a week [...] Struggled. I used to go to my mum's and eat ... 'cause I just couldn't afford to buy food as well as paying for [...] your gas ... and your electric [...] 'cause you've gotta have heating and lighting for the kid.'

(Ms Waveney and Mr Trent, 18)

Mrs Torridge is in this position at the time of the interview.

'It's a real struggle because they give me 54 pound a week ... and I got into rent arrears so I gotta pay't, 15 pound ... out of my money every week to pay off that, so that brings it down to 41. And there's not much left by the time you pay m, put money in the meters every day [...] It's a real struggle. But ... there's nothing I can do about it unless I can get a full-time job.'

(Mrs Torridge, 23)

Mrs Taw, who was claiming for herself and her children for a time before meeting her present husband, comments critically on the change from single payments to loans under the Social Fund, especially for children's clothes.

'Mind you I liked it being on the social 'cause I used to get a clothing grant every so often ... and that used to help me get some clothes like for me, me daughter and son, me other son – 'cause I had they two living with me then. But you, you know, you gotta pay it all back now if you have the clothing grant or anything, you gotta pay every penny back now. Whereas before you didn't have to pay anything back; it's what you was entitled to.'

(Mrs Taw, 17)

All these criticisms of income support focus on the fact that, although it is nominally related to the specific needs of the household, it takes no account of their actual outgoings. Delays in payment, suspensions or reductions of benefits, no allowance for debts, and the compulsory repayment of loans, all mean that these benefits do not meet needs – as Mrs Clyde and Mrs Ryton point out in the passages quoted on pp. 20 and 165. Although these women are generally critical of the low rates of benefit for families with children (in line with the Poverty Lobby's critique) their sharpest comments are focused on the fact that a benefit which is supposed to protect people against falling below the poverty line is often delayed, withheld, reduced or deducted from by the authorities, exposing the family to a lower level of income than this official minimum, and one which does not cover their regular outgoings.

Although the four couples discussed in the last section speak of family credit as helpful, a far larger number criticise either the process of claiming, or the rules of eligibility. We have already set out the criticisms by Mrs Torridge and Mr Derwent; similar points are made by a number of couples. Ms Waveney and Mr Trent are trying to claim.

Mr Trent: ... we applied for family credit as well and it was so hard to claim, I mean we had to go to Citizens' Advice to try to find out.
Ms Waveney: Yeah but we couldn't claim that [...]
Mr Trent: No well we didn't know that ...
Ms Waveney: ... 2 pound over
Mr Trent: Yeah.
Ms Waveney: ... over the limit. And what's 2 pound?
Mr Trent: But, we tried, we, you know. But to claim it actually to c, get hold of the forms ... its incredible ...
Ms Waveney: ... forms ...
Mr Trent: It's like a book, you fill in this book and you gotta hand in 5 weeks' wage slips and you post it and you don't hear nothing for weeks ...

Ms Waveney: Yeah. And then they turn round and say no.
Mr Trent: Incredible. It's just so hard to claim anything.

(Ms Waveney and Mr Trent, 19)

Mr Taw is a bus driver; Mrs Taw does two cleaning jobs. She has considered applying for family credit:

'... that family credit thing, there's lot of people say you can get it, but you, you gotta fill in a form and ... send off these wage slips and you're not entitled to it in the end and it was a waste of time writing it all out [...] you got to have five wage slips and my old man chucks his away when he gets his. I asks him to save them but he says he forgets [...] I s'pose it might be worth trying I s'pose [pause] your face has gotta fit before you can have anything from those people.'

(Mrs Taw, 15–16)

Other couples criticise the difficulty of anticipating what their final income will be. Mr and Mrs Medway are both irregular workers; she does part-time shop work and he is working nights for a security firm earning £230 a week with overtime. Previously he had a low-paid day-time job.

Mr Medway: ... Yeah. Yes, it was about 85 basic I think. Which is terrible. That's what me last couple of jobs were ... but this one's a lot better [...] but then the thing is with the other job you used to get like ... family credit, stuff like that ...
Mrs Medway: Yeah, well it was only 18 pound: didn't work out more [laughs].
Mr Medway: Well it seemed to be, seem to be just as worse off now, don't we really?
Mrs Medway: Well yeah, you always have, the more you get the more you want, don't you?

(Mr and Mrs Medway, 4–5)

This enigmatic passage (typical of the exchanges between this couple) could be taken as a complaint about the effects of family credit being withdrawn, but we read it as a statement about the problems of budgeting without being able to anticipate how much family credit (if any) will be paid.

Mr Itchen claimed family credit when he was in his low-paid garage job, but when his wages were reduced the family's income did not cover their rent:

Mrs Itchen: family credit, yeah. We get that now from when he was ... at the garage. But see then, with that now ... now they've changed it you don't ... you're not allowed a rent rebate, see, with that, family credit now [...] 'Cause we got so far behind in our rent ... that we nearly got kicked out of here.

(Mrs Itchen, 12)

By far the most serious incident of a household not being able to budget was when Mr Cam was working for the driving agency, and the benefit authorities withheld a notional amount, equivalent to the family credit he would have received if he had claimed it (the rules require them to do this).

'I put in for a rent rebate and about 6 weeks later came back and says you're not entitled to a rent rebate. Unknown to me so I got into trouble with the rent and that and they said they was going to evict me [indistinct], they shouldn't do now because I'm paying it off so much a week now. Um but, I never knew I could apply for family credit because nobody tells you see, and when I finished with the rent rebate they [benefit authorities] automatically thought I was getting 22 pound and 4 pence from family credit.'

(Mr Cam, 14)

As a result of being unable to live on his wage plus this reduced rate of benefit, he gave up the agency work, and immediately had his income support suspended for leaving employment voluntarily. He is very angry about the system's treatment of him – both in failing to inform him of his eligibility for family credit, and for punishing him for his lack of understanding by deduction and suspension.

These couples dislike family credit, but not because of the poverty trap as it is described by academics and lobbyists. They dislike it because it is so slow to claim, and because they have difficulty knowing in advance how much benefit (if any) they will receive, and whether their earnings will remain at the same level as in the crucial 5 weeks, or fall lower (as in the case of Mr Itchen). For couples budgeting week to week, using an income strategy, these are the most unhelpful features of the system.

STRATEGIC USE OF THE BENEFITS SYSTEM

The other major policy issue in relation to labour-market decision-making in poor households concerns motivation to do paid work. The Poverty Lobby argues that households with low earning potential are trapped in unemployment: the New Right argues that they are corrupted by excessively generous or unconditional benefits, and that labour-market participation should be enforced (see pp. 24, 41–2). Hence we must analyse the role of benefits in the accounts of households who have been outside paid employment for a long time. Six couples – Mr and Mrs Bow, Dart, Dovey, Exe, Frome and Spey – are distinguishable from the other 'irregulars' by their *strategic* use of the income support system. By this we mean that they use benefits as their main source of income for basic needs, while getting extras through undeclared cash work. They construct the labour market as paying wages which are too low and too unreliable for the man adequately to fulfil his breadwinner role through employment, and the benefits system as confiscating the woman's potential earnings contribution to the household budget. We have set out the men's and women's individual justifications of their positions in Chapters 4 and 5; in this section we focus on what their joint interviews reveal about their income strategy.

Mr Exe has been unemployed for 3 years, after being made redundant from a fairly well-paid job on the railways. In his individual interview he relates his breadwinning decisions to a household income strategy:

> 'I'm looking around ... The only ... The only snag I, really is that ah ... I gotta make sure that ... that I ... earn enough ... every week ... to cover all the bills and ... everything else, 'cause otherwise [indistinct] isn' worth it, is it?'

> (Mr Exe, 1)

In the joint interview, Mrs Exe is asked if she has considered trying for a job.

Mrs Exe:	Ah, yeah [indistinct] ... Me husband said it ... yeah, I was gonna go for work but me husband says wa'n' worth it, di'n' you Gary?
Mr Exe:	Well 'ti'n' i'n'it? [...] Unless you can get what you want [...] in wages ... it ... it's a waste of time going back i'n'it? [...] 'Cause if my wife went back to work and ... if I was home, home here ... the, looking after the youngsters ... even the wife would have to bring over a hundred ...
Mrs Exe:	Oh ... ah ...
Mr Exe:	... pound a week [indistinct] ...
Mrs Exe:	[indistinct] ... manage to bring home 50 odd pound I should be pleased ... um ...
Mr Exe:	... which means if you don't get that money ... the um ... bills an' that ... won't be paid ...

Mrs Exe:	Um ... yeah ...
Mr Exe:	... which means in the long run ... we might have more to fork out ... which you haven' got ... so ... we're still back to square one aren't we?
Mrs Exe:	Um ... yeah ...
Q:	So you think it ... you'd be better off both being at ...
Mr Exe:	Where we are.
Mrs Exe:	Um.
Q:	... on social security rather than doing part-time work?
Mr Exe:	Yeah.
Q:	You're saying part-time work wouldn't be any use?
Mr Exe:	Well ... not really because if don't want ... wife done ... part-time work ... they would ... it's only ... deducted out of the benefits anyway ...
Q:	Oh right.
Mr Exe:	... so we wouldn't be no better off [pause] So you know ... how can you win?

(Mr and Mrs Exe, 12–13)

Mr and Mrs Exe describe the shortcomings of the labour market in terms of its inability to provide an income which will 'cover all the bills'. Even social security no longer does this – for example, it does not give enough for the children's shoes; since the reforms 'they've scrapped all that'. Mr Exe is about to be interviewed for employment or training under Restart, but is pessimistic:

'Well you, you gotta go down every ... 6 months, but ... it's like I said, you know ... if I'm not learning the things which I want to ... do, then it's a waste of time, i'n'it?'

(Mr and Mrs Exe, 24)

Hence Mr and Mrs Exe see no prospect of getting their expenses met through the labour market, and look to income support as the most reliable way to meet their basic needs. Mr and Mrs Dovey construct their lack of employment for the past $2\frac{1}{2}$ years as exclusion from the labour market, as a result of discrimination against people of his age. In the joint interview he explains as follows:

Mr Dovey:	... But if anybody had said to me, when I finished me contract cleaning, I had to go on the dole and you'd be on the dole for a long time, I'd have said 'No way'. Call 'em a liar. 'Cause I never been on the dole in me life and

there's no way I'd be on. I said, 'No chance whatsoever
... that happen,' but unfortunately for me 'twas the wrong
time of life it happened to me ... yeah. That's about all I
can say.

(Mr and Mrs Dovey, 28)

However, there immediately follows a revealing passage.

Q: Are there any advantages for either of you being on the
                dole?
                [pause]
Mr Dovey: The wife's medical bill from the doctors, the ... pills and
                that, that is heavy. I should think that's about the only
                advantage.
Mrs Dovey: Yeah, if I didn' have to pay, if I had to pay for that ...
Mr Dovey: Costs an arm and a leg you see, to pay for her ... pay for
                her tablets and everything every month. Apart from that.
                No. I can't see any ... to be quite honest.

(Mr and Mrs Dovey, 28)

Mr and Mrs Dovey are careful about money: he says 'we're fortunate; we
haven' got the HP [Hire Purchase] clubman knocking at the door. I think
that's the secret of how we keeping going to be honest'. Hence it is very
important to cover their weekly outgoings, one of which is prescription
charges. Mr and Mrs Dovey see an advantage in remaining on benefits as
long as this qualifies them to escape these charges; this is their version of
an unemployment trap.

Mr Dart, like Mr Exe, is under pressure from a Restart interview; he has
been unemployed long term. 'They have really slapped down. The last few
weeks I have had to sign on every fortnight that I have been for at least six
or seven jobs. I have been unemployed for 9 years, you see.' His main
concern is that his income support money would be stopped if he did not get
a job or accept a training course. He hopes to get on a course learning to
handle machinery. He helps his wife a good deal with their daughter, who
has developmental difficulties, during the interview, but she does not reply
to a question about whether she would miss him if he had a job. Helen
Kay's research notes describe the house as quite well equipped, and a van
salesman delivers two duvet covers for their daughters and a play mat for
the baby, to be paid for at £2.80 per week.

Mr and Mrs Frome construct an elaborate justification of the fact that
they are both unemployed, and have been for 9 years, despite their obvious
intelligence and ability. They criticise the conventional idea of full employment, insisting that they are doing others a favour by not seeking work.

Mrs Frome: ... it's a very strange notion that ... you know, everybody must work and yet no country could ever survive if everybody was un, in em, in employment. Because the s, that just does not work at any time and never has done and never will [...] why is it that they've got to keep on hassling people into getting jobs? Why can't they just leave them ... and if they don't want a job let them just say so. But they don't [...]

Mr Frome: ... the new world was going to be when machines were doing it all ... and people were allowed to sort of, you know, people were being trained in the schools to enjoy their free time ... and somehow, you know, we've just sort of totally reverted to the ... Victorian values of ... I mean, you know, it just looked for a while like everything was from a change [...]

Mrs Frome: It's a very strange world that says: oh well you've, you know, there are all these people who want jobs, and yet Larry, who doesn't, is being forced into having a job.

                                           (Mr and Mrs Frome, 41–2)

Mr and Mrs Frome construct themselves as very casual about money, and systematically spending more than their income.

Mrs Frome: Well ... I mean, we are the most ... dreadful spenders if we actually have money. Money is the sort of thing that burns ... holes in our pockets [...] we have both been the most dreadful spenders [indistinct] much changes ... the only thing now is that, is that we do have to make sure that our children are clothed and fed and kept warm, you know ... and a roof over their heads, but barring that [...].

Mr Frome: Well, basically we just kept getting further into debt I suppose.

                                           (Mr and Mrs Frome, 37)

They describe fending off creditors with stories, until eventually the bank closed their account. Their construction of themselves is of studied casualness over budgeting; yet when Mr Frome is talking about how he will set himself up as a self-employed antiques restorer, with an Enterprise Allowance of £40 a week, Mrs Frome makes it clear that she is concerned about maintaining what sounds very much like a careful income strategy during the transition to the new regime. Her comments about budgeting during the delay before benefit is paid sound very like those of other women in our study:

Q:	How do you see the next year then, say for yourself?
Mrs Frome:	Well I mean it's ... the first few weeks will be extra ordinarily difficult because of having to wait ... for the ... the FIS or whatever, as I say, whatever it's called – the family credit now ... um ... to come into effect ... But, you know, I mean, we've gone through difficult times before and will go through them again no doubt, so we'll survive and ... you know, the thing is, is that ... provided you realise that ... there isn't going to be, you know, a sudden boost in the financial situation and that you know there isn't going to be a profit then, you know you can do it [...]
Q:	... you're on ... Has the 40 pound a week started? No?
Mrs Frome:	No. This has to be when he decides he's gonna come off the training and then takes the 40 – this is when we have to show we've got a thousand, he gets the 40 pounds a week and we put in for family credit and wait 6 to 8 weeks for that, during which time we are forced to pay full rent ... um ... because nothing's sorted out properly and until it is of course, you know, you then bound to the council for your rent ... and ... school meals, et cetera ... But ... you know, you have to sort of fight your way through it [...] I think it's probably going to be 2 or 3 years before we ever see, you know, any real increase in our standard of living isn't it? [...]
Mr Frome:	Won't help then, we'll only spend it.
Mrs Frome:	Well that's right. I mean ... [indistinct] we'll be spending it on better things ... we'll be having better meals and [...]
Mr Frome:	Yes. Be able to have a Graves occasionally instead of Liebfraumilch. [laughs]
Mrs Frome:	[indistinct] ... that's right ... you know, you sort of ... you know ... look for the n, nicer things in life, you know ... more pleasant. I mean one of the really ...
Mr Frome:	It's normally what we do whenever we do ...
Mrs Frome:	... is that we can't take the children anywhere ...

(Mr and Mrs Frome, 44–5)

At this point in the joint interview, Mrs Frome switches from a joint construction of the couple as unconventional, unconcerned with the labour market and with budgeting, to a very recognisable account of the problems they will face in trying to sustain their current income strategy during the transition from claiming income support to becoming self-employed, followed by a construction of the future in terms of conventional aspirations for an improved standard of living. Although Mr Frome adopts a slightly mocking tone, he does not disagree with this picture. The structural difference between the Fromes and the Bows, Darts, Doveys, Exes and Speys is not in their attitude towards work and money; it is that they can borrow £1,000, and hence gain access to a regular £40 a week in Enterprise Allowance, which can provide (along with family credit) for their basic needs while he makes the transition back into work.

THE ROLE OF CASH JOBS IN A BENEFITS-BASED STRATEGY

If benefits provide the basic income for regular weekly expenses in these households, undeclared work for cash fulfils the role of income for 'extras', such as children's clothes, leisure items and emergencies; it also helps pay off debts. Those claiming long term are clear that income support benefits do not cover these items, and that there is now no scope for getting single payments to help with such expenditures from DSS, since 'budgeting loans' from the Social Fund have to be repaid through regular deductions from basic benefits. Hence cash work is the only way to cover these items in their income strategy, unless they can get substantial assistance from kin. Mrs Exe makes it clear why the latter form of assistance is unacceptable, even if it is available. Her mother and father have given them money – but also criticism.

Mrs Exe: [indistinct] ... and me mum said me hu, me husband just
               used to go out and sq, squander it on drink and I should
               say to her, it, yeah 'cause I should say, say to me mum
               that he only goes in twice a week, don't he Gary? [...]
Mr Exe: It's all right for ...
Mrs Exe: 'Cause me mum's working ...
Mr Exe: [indistinct] well you're squandering it on this and that but
               if they was out of work [...] they'd be in the same position
               as us ...
                                                       (Mr and Mrs Exe, 11)

Hence cash work provides a more acceptable way of gaining some room for manoeuvre within their budgeting. Mr Dart (unemployed for 9 years) used to be a self-employed window cleaner until he fell off a ladder and banged his head. He does odd days labouring, and is off-loading a lorry the day after the interview – 2 hours' work for £10, cash in hand. He says he could go self-employed again if he could find enough of those little jobs, but some weeks there are none, whilst this week he has had two.

Mr Bow did various kinds of short-term irregular work, but has been claiming since leaving his Community Programme Scheme 7 months pre-

viously. But for many years before he was unemployed and doing undeclared cash work.

'And then I just picked up jobs, I, you know ... I worked for, what they
call it, they call 'em travellers, they come down and they do roads and
all that lot and I do roofing for 'em. They come down and they offer me,
what, 2 or 3 weeks' work. And I go and do roads for 'em, tarmac the
roads and that lot [...] What it is, 'cause the money's there, see, the, the
money's actually there. See when they come down for me they give me
a set price at, what, how to do it and if I don't want, want it, I say no [...]
I works out, see, if it's 2 weeks' work I work out what me wife needs and
the children needs and I just double it and if they want, want me then
they say yeah. And ever since then I haven't stopped; they always comes
down see.'

(Mr Bow, 7–8)

Mr Bow is trying to get a crisis loan from the Social Fund to clear some
debts, but this has been refused.

'I'm trying to um ... get things sorted with social security; if I can't get
no different the social security, then I've gotta go out see [...] If I can't
get this crisis loan or whatever or ... I gotta go out and get it [...] Yeah,
some cash. And that's the only way I can do it see, I can get it, I ... 'Cause
with these jobs here they only last about, maybe 2 weeks, see, and it's, I
can't actually sign off the dole or ... 'Cause if I sign off the dole I'm
gonna be out of work again in another 2 weeks' time, see. And I gotta go
all through the rigmarole of signing on and all this lot and [...] that goes
on for ages and when you re-sign on ... you're like 2 week in arrears ...'

(Mr Bow, 9)

Mr Bow here clearly constructs cash work as an alternative to the recently
abolished single payments or emergency payments under supplementary
benefits, now in the form of loans. A little later in the interview, in a
passage quoted on p. 124, he makes it clear that, because income support
rates do not provide for his wife's clothes, his options are undeclared cash
work or theft – the latter leading to prison.

Mrs Bow buys her children's clothes from a club, getting a new item for
each in turn. She sometimes misses the rent in order to 'have a good spend'.
She recently had a cleaning job in a large store 'for the money', but left
when the benefit authorities were checking up.

'Well ... Shirley [friend] ... Shirley was under a false name; I was under,
I wa'n' under a false name but she was and then she ... they was looking

into her social security [indistinct] so of course [indistinct] they would
have had me up ... so she left and I left.'

(Mrs Bow, 24–5)

It may be tempting for readers to conclude from these accounts that Mr and
Mrs Bow are a specially deviant couple, for whom law-breaking is a way
of life. However, in the social relations of the estate, doing undeclared work
for cash is not seen as criminal, but as an alternative to crime, as Mr Bow
argues (see pp. 124–5). Mrs Taw (now married to a regular worker) says
with pride that she was doing *seven* cleaning jobs at once while claiming
income support *and* claiming single payments for clothing, before she met
her new husband. Furthermore, the strategy of using cash work to pay for
'extras' is not the exclusive province of those who claim for their basic
income – several regular workers or their spouses do the same, for the same
expenditures (failing to declare their earnings for tax purposes). Mr Plym,
who works as a civil servant, is one who does this. Another is Mrs Wear,
who in the joint interview talks about a job as a cosmetics salesperson.

Mrs Wear:	I mean the money ... out of it you don't make that much so ... I think it's worth it, it tops things up a bit ... Occasionally I say well that's nice, I'll have that meself, you know. [laughs] It's like Christmas stuff ...
Mr Wear:	It's money that's cash, it's there ... And you'll come to Saturday and you need a few things you just ... you just take a fiver out [...]
Mrs Wear:	So that we can sort of go out and buy fish food or food for the animals. You don't realise how it mounts up, you know. So ah ...

(Mr and Mrs Wear, 23)

Although Mrs Wear does not construct this as a job 'on the side', it is; and
the words Mr Wear uses about it as a source of income – 'it's money that's
cash, it's there' – are remarkably similar to Mr Bow's about his work for
the travellers – 'the money's there see, the money's actually there'. Mr
Wear is a respectable regular worker, buying his council house.

Mr and Mrs Dovey's cash job is the same as Mrs Wear's. Though they
went out of business as contract cleaners 2½ years ago, and see no prospect
of employment because of his age, they, too, run a clothing club in order to
be able to afford their 10-year-old son's clothes.

Mrs Dovey:	We just runs our own little club don't we ...
Mr Dovey:	Um, um.
Mrs Dovey:	... just to keep the boy in clothes. That's all.

Mr Dovey:	Yeah, we got a little club we run. One of the catalogues that we ... if he wants shoes or a pair of trousers and when it drops down a bit.
Mrs Dovey:	Get a bit more.

(Mr and Mrs Dovey, 27)

Mr and Mrs Frome's budgeting consists of him giving the DSS giro to her each week for their regular outgoings, and each working for cash for 'extras'. He says that he only drinks when he can earn the money for it.

Mr Frome:	Yeah, I just, I leave the whole of all the accounts in ... Barbara's hands um ... and then, yeah, so far as my drinking goes, it, I can, I just sort of, whatever I can make doing anything else, you know ...
Q:	If you can't make anything else does that mean you can't drink?
Mr Frome:	I always make something, somehow, somewhere ... Yeah I, well I s'pose it does, yeah.

(Mr and Mrs Frome, 69)

Her cash job is helping in the school; he does all sorts of work, from casual farm work to building, decorating and plumbing, but especially buying and selling things.

'I mean you can sort of shift records, '60s records particularly, to one shop, and another'll buy sort of cassette tapes [...] And I know a few people in the antiques who'll ... sort of buy off me [...] anything from a piece of pottery to a book [...] it's just enough to keep you sort of ticking over, you know like I say, its sort of, it's beer money, you know ...'

(Mr Frome, 22)

Mrs Frome explains that cash work is readily available on the estate.

Mrs Frome:	... if you're on social security you tend to know far more people ... um ... who have got jobs going around than if you are actually working. If you're working and trying to find a cash in hand job ... probably be far more difficult than if you were actually on social security and looking for cash in hand jobs. It's, it's ...
Mr Frome:	Yeah, I s'pose I've had plenty of cash in hand jobs. There was the ... one that I was talking about for a builder for just a couple of days a week. I mean that went, that went on sort of basically for as long as I wanted it.

(Mr and Mrs Frome, 21)

The only other ways in which these couples can gain some flexibility in their budgeting, and afford 'extras' are by borrowing, credit, bargain-hunting and charity. Mrs Spey runs up a bill in the local shop and goes to jumble sales.

Mrs Spey: We just lend off the shop if we, if we get broke at the end of the week, 'cause they, up the shop up there, they let you have food, you know like till the day, 'tis if you're getting paid the next day they let you pay it the next day like [laughs]. So ...

Q: So that helps you out a bit?

Mrs Spey: Oh yeah [pauses]. Some weeks i'n't too bad, you know, but I mean if they want – like school clothes or summat like that – well I go to jumbles a lot and 'cause I couldn' afford to buy everything new ...

(Mrs Spey, 3)

Mrs Bow has taken out loans of up to £150 to buy 'extras'.

'I can't buy it in a ... like our fortnightly money ... I can't do it ... 'cause we owes clubs, we owes rent, you know, I mean I can't do it. But with a hundred pound loan for ourselves we can do it. So I gotta get hundred pound, then I gotta buy 150 until I get another one. Ridiculous i'n'it?'

(Mrs Bow, 29)

Mr and Mrs Exe's social worker has arranged occasional assistance from charities for the family, but this will not happen again, because Mr Exe has objected to 'interference' in his affairs. All these ways of providing 'extras' have serious disadvantages for the recipients – as Mr Exe says:

'let's just ... say ... that [indistinct] social services was sticking their ... noses in ...'

(Mr Exe, 25)

RISK MANAGEMENT

What households with a regular full-time worker have in common with households who use benefits strategically is that they both have a fairly reliable source of income for their weekly needs (a main wage or income support) which is supplemented by another source for their 'extras' (a secondary wage for 'regular' households, cash work or loans, etc. for 'irregulars'). The group of 'irregulars' who use benefits tactically have no reliable source of basic income, and must therefore devise ways of managing risk – the probability that they will be without income for certain periods.

In distinguishing between these groups, we do not wish to imply that there are never transitions between them. For example, Mr and Mrs Calder were 'irregulars' until he took his present job, and he is tempted to return to this group; Mr and Mrs Frome are planning to move from using benefits strategically to using them tactically (when his Enterprise Allowance ends, in a year's time); and Mr and Mrs Dovey were irregular workers who are now unemployed and doing small amounts of cash work. However there are some households who strongly assert their commitment to remaining in their present situation if possible: Mr and Mrs Nene and Mr and Mrs Rother, for instance, among the regulars, and Mr and Mrs Ribble among the irregulars.

Mr and Mrs Ribble are an instructive study in risk management, as they are particularly articulate about the advantages of their current employment status. In the joint interview, they are asked about whether he intends to remain self-employed; both then jointly construct him as a *worker* – someone who dislikes taking orders, takes a pride in his work and likes the challenge of being his own boss.

Mrs Ribble: ... truthfully say that I could not see Steve working for anybody ...
Mr Ribble: No.
Mrs Ribble: ... again, now he's been, you know, got a bit ... of his own boss like, you know [...] He can't take orders. No chance.
Mr Ribble: No I hate 'em [laughs].

(Mr and Mrs Ribble, 67)

Mrs Ribble is then asked whether she was happy when he went self-employed.

Mrs Ribble: [pause] Well [indistinct] ... it don't bother me. I mean as long as he's happy, do you know what I mean? I mean I rather him [...] be happy than taking a job like [shop's name] for instance, I mean he was miserable as sin, do you know what I mean? I mean it ... all right so we got a wage packet at the end of the week, but money's not everything. I mean I rather him be happy in a job and do what he wants to do and then have a wage packet and I could – how to put it? – won't feel so guilty then, like ... taking the money, you know, and knowing that he's happy than taking it and knowing that he's unhappy.

(Mr and Mrs Ribble, 67–8)

Mr Ribble then describes self-employment as a challenge, especially finding work, and being able to do jobs his own way, and taking a pride in the result. He also values being able to *choose* whether or not to go to work, and to take time off – for example in a family emergency, such as illness. Mr and Mrs Ribble give the example that her mother has just been diagnosed as having cancer, and being able to go straight home to help out. Mrs Ribble sums up the advantages of self-employment.

> Mrs Ribble: Fringe benefits as well isn't there? You get a decent tax return [laughs] and higher wage [laughs]. Not just that I can have my husband home ... you know, when he wants to be home [...] it's nice ...
>
> (Mr and Mrs Ribble, 70)

Mr Ribble talks about the 'fringe benefits' of having friends on the site to 'do you a good turn', such as putting in a new bathroom in the house. Others come and borrow materials and tools – 'it's like bartering really' – on a reciprocal basis.

> Mrs Ribble: I mean, they don't sort of keep up and score, you know. I mean Gordon might come out and borrow, say, three things in one week and he might go out and like, borrow the one, you know what I mean. I mean there's no equivalent to it.
>
> (Mr and Mrs Ribble, 73)

He and Gordon help each other with improvements to their houses. Then the following exchange occurs:

> Q: Yes. Yes [pause] The only last one [question] was how the self-employment has turned out, but in fact you've told me that.
>
> Mrs Ribble: Oh, it's perfect.
>
> Mr Ribble: Yeah.
>
> Q: Right. Are there any disadvantages with it? Um ...
>
> Mr Ribble: ... yeah, if you don't work, you don't get paid ...
>
> Mrs Ribble: Simple as that.
>
> Mr Ribble: Um ...
>
> Mrs Ribble: If you're ill you don't get no sick benefit.
>
> Mr Ribble: You don't get holiday pay um ...
>
> Q: Don't you get sick pay?
>
> Mr Ribble: No, no. Like you have to be sick for ah 3 months um ... to claim any social ... um ... If I, any time in the year, I did come unemployed then I'd automatically lose me tax refund, so ... well it's, you know there's good and bad, 'cause. I mean for ...

Mrs Ribble:	It's the same in all jobs.
Mr Ribble:	You have a good year, you have a bad year; and you have a good month, you have a bad month, but um ...

(Mr and Mrs Ribble, 74)

Mrs Ribble goes on to say that if the building trade becomes slack in winter, her husband can take a temporary job in a shop. But Mr Ribble adds that he will not do that this winter, as he has some money put back, and some indoor work to do, while the housebuilding market is slack.

Q:	Is it a bit risky?
Mrs Ribble:	And there is ...
Mr Ribble:	Yeah, it is. [indistinct]
Mrs Ribble:	Can be ...
Mr Ribble:	Oh I could be out of work tomorrow you know. There's no um ... there's no fixed income has to say, well if you're out of tomorrow for 3 months there's no money. Ah I mean um ...
Mrs Ribble:	We manage. We got to.
Mr Ribble:	I mean if I fell and had an accident at work then um ... the ah firm would cover for my insurance but as far as I'm concerned I'm not covered. Ah I could buy ... you know, pay for some myself but um ... it's just a thing I don't bother with ... um ...

(Mr and Mrs Ribble, 75–6)

Mrs Ribble remarks that her husband 'loves living dangerously' and being in charge of major jobs with lots of responsibility. Finally they sum up as follows:

Mr Ribble:	... I mean it could be some ... 8, 10 weeks sometimes you're out ... um and then what money you've got in the bank you, you just have to live on and still pay the bills and still work um ... get the rent and everything else but ...
Mrs Ribble:	[indistinct]
Mr Ribble:	We do manage.
Mrs Ribble:	Oh yeah. Like I said before, we're survivors. 'Cause we've got to.

(Mr and Mrs Ribble, 80)

Unlike those in regular employment or on benefits, whose preoccupation is with securing a weekly income to 'cover the bills', Mr and Mrs Ribble place a positive value on the autonomy they gain as a couple from his irregular work, and minimise the problems of managing the risks associated with self-employment – which only emerge in response to a direct question. Yet as we have seen, the benefits system has proved a very necessary fallback for them at several times, including one quite recent occasion.

A WORK STRATEGY: MR AND MRS KENNET

Only one household among the 'irregulars' in our sample does not fit the income strategy theory we have outlined. Mr and Mrs Kennet make no reference to benefits in their account – they do not use the income maintenance system either tactically or strategically. This is surprising, since they clearly do not have a high income: Mr Kennet acknowledges that he does not earn a 'living wage' as a painter and decorator. But nor does he resort to benefits. Now 52, he was made redundant when he was just over 40, and spent 2 years 'on the dole'. When he decided to become self-employed, he applied for a grant for his tools and working clothes. He was turned down; others who had been in prison were given grants.

> 'likes of me, I like I say, I ... I, I think I'm too honest and you try and tell 'em that you need it ... and they won't listen. So ... I never bother with 'em now.'
>
> (Mr Kennet, 23)

Instead, the Kennet family have evolved a strategy in which they all 'help out' with work on various contracts and bits and pieces of work – cleaning offices and windows, painting or odd jobs. The Kennets also have Maurice, a young man of 19, living in their household: he was kicked out by his father, and is now engaged to the Kennets' daughter Valerie, aged 16. Maurice is also self-employed. Mrs Kennet explains that she became involved in an office cleaning contract taken up by Maurice, who had been previously doing some window cleaning.

> 'So he decided that he would take up the contract and roped me in for doing it.'
>
> (Mrs Kennet, 7)

Maurice takes her to work at 6 o'clock in the morning. Valerie, who has been unable to get a job or a Youth Training Scheme place, and therefore is not eligible for benefits, also 'helps out' occasionally, as does Richard their teenage son who is still at school. It seems that all these bits and pieces of earnings are pooled, to provide the basic income for the household.

> 'Just there's, there's one thing about them, they all muck in, you know, you never really go short here, because if Richard's got a few pound or she's got a couple of pound all I gotta do is say, well you know, lend us

a pound – you got it. Or a ... Maurice, you know. Now my husband's been out of work now for 3 weeks so he's down with Maurice working. So it's sort of combined operations, you know, which is really as it should be.'

(Mrs Kennet, 17)

The Kennets' withdrawal from the benefits system seems like a decision to turn their back on a possible source of income which has rejected Mr Kennet (as the employment market did when he was over 40).

'I didn't seem to be able to get a job ah ... well, when you've, when you've gone 40 they, they think you're too old.'

(Mr Kennet, 23)

Mrs Kennet says that Valerie is unable to get a job because she is too *young*.

'And she wasn't 16 till the August, and she left [school] in May. So she's nearly a twelvemonth behind all the rest. Whereas they can get jobs being as old as they are – she can't.'

(Mrs Kennet, 1)

Mr and Mrs Kennet both come from outside the area, so this may explain their lack of access to local cash jobs. They describe how for their 'extras' they rely on gifts and perks from the rich farmers who are his main customers – the relationship sounds almost feudal.

'I've got a good load of customers that ... if I was stuck I'd just ring 'em up and they'd give me even a day's work no matter what. They'd keep me going. And well ... when I first started off with them, I'd only been going about 6 months and ah the old car I had broke down and they all rung round each other and they were gonna put 30 pound apiece, buy me a second hand car so I could keep working for 'em. I would have had to sort of gone to the job and instead of picking up 100 pound, pick up a little bit less then ... they'd deduct so much each week I was there until I'd pay them the 30 pound. That's the type of customers that I've got.'

(Mr Kennet, 26)

He emphasises trust and word-of-mouth recommendation, and that in the long run it pays to price cheaply.

Mr Kennet: No, but it's like I say and some, sometimes you ... you got to start off a bit low and get your name made.

Mrs Kennet: But then they compensated really for the low wages didn't they?

Mr Kennet: Yeah.

Mrs Kennet: 'Cause I mean you ... like at Christmas he'd get duck and a chicken, hundreds of them. One of 'em would give you a chicken, another would give you a chicken. They'd give you a bag of spuds, bag of swedes, you know, ... apples, flowers. They, they are very good out there ...

(Mr and Mrs Kennet, 28–9)

Mr Kennet works for his customers' relatives, travelling far afield, to Bristol and Plymouth, for instance.

'with my customers they say, oh you don't want to use your car, take mine. So they'll take me off for the day in their car because they go up and see their daughter or whatever and ah, I just take me, me tools I need and travel in their car.'

(Mr and Mrs Kennet, 31)

Although Mrs Kennet says that the family 'never do anything without a discussion', there is no evidence in their account of agreements over expenditure. Rather the whole household is involved in work of various kinds: as Mr Kennet says, 'if you're desperate for work you'll go and get it, no matter what, like I did'. Significantly, he speaks of being desperate for *work* not money – and indeed many of the benefits he gets from work are in kind. Mr and Mrs Kennet also have 3 dogs, 72 budgies, 4 cats, 40 rabbits, 30 chickens and innumerable gerbils that take an hour to feed and clean. They are enthusiastic vegetable gardeners; Mrs Kennet again uses the term 'combined operation' in relation to their informal work activities as well as their self-employment.

Why do the Kennets not have an income strategy? Our data does not provide a conclusive answer, partly because we did not spot them as our exceptional household until the final stage of the analysis. However there are some indications in their accounts. Mr Kennet was an irregular employee who stopped being able to get short-term employment; Mrs Kennet has since 'reconstructed' him in the identity of painter and decorator, her 'family occupation' for three generations (see p. 258). Mrs Kennet also constructs Maurice as a self-employed contractor, and her offspring as 'helping out' in a 'combined operation' which replaces the employment and claiming pattern they both followed when younger. The Kennets seem to have stepped outside the employment-related system to a much greater extent than the other 'self-employed' households (for example Mr and Mrs Hodder), and their reversion to an almost pre-industrial work strategy[21] appears to be an alternative to the tactical use of benefits. This provides a morally adequate, non-economic account of their decision-making processes. This impression is reinforced by the fact that Mrs Kennet alone talks about their wish to buy their council house: no strategy for 'covering' the mortgage repayments is mentioned in the joint interview. Indeed, although Mr and Mrs Kennet construct a coherent joint account of their decision-making in their joint interview, there are several discrepancies between their individual accounts. In addition to the one over house purchase, for instance, Mr Kennet says he is never out of work for his customers, whereas Mrs Kennet says he has not had work of his own for 3 weeks, and is currently helping Maurice. This reinforces the impression that their strategy is about 'keeping busy', rather than covering expenditure.

CONCLUSIONS

In this long chapter we have reviewed the evidence from the joint interviews about how decisions are made in our respondents' households. Questioned about how their employments fit together, the couples reconstruct their individual accounts in terms of the roles of men and women, and acknowledge that they make the important decisions about these issues either separately, or as individuals after consultation over issues around care. We conclude that this is inconsistent with the theory of a household labour strategy, but that all the couples except the Kennets have a recognisable household income strategy.

This takes one of three forms, all designed to cover basic weekly needs, and 'extras' like clothes and leisure items or (in a minority of cases) buying their house. For households with a regular worker, the basic needs are covered by these earnings, while the extras are covered by those of the partner. The largest group – households with one or more irregular workers – use benefits tactically to cover basic needs when the main earner cannot cover basic needs, and overtime, cash work or a partner's earnings for 'extras'. The third group rely on benefits to meet basic needs, and do undeclared cash work for 'extras'.

We have explained how this theory covers all the households except the Kennets, and given our account of why the Kennets are exceptional. We have also shown how all the 'irregular' respondents except the Kennets constructed their decisions in terms of the benefit system as an essential fallback, and their criticisms of its functioning in this respect. When this is linked with the men's accounts of the casualisation and fragmentation of their segment of the labour market (pp. 90–1), and the women's of the effects of their partners' irregular employment patterns on their own (pp. 161–8) it indicates that most of our interviewees are following a strategy which is concerned with the management of risk.

Accounts – such as Mr Tamar's and Mr Exe's – of men who had regular employment but find themselves on the margins of the labour market, indicate an awareness of a process of exclusion from the benefits of reliable earnings, training or promotion. The joint accounts show how these couples deal with insecurity – some with relish, like Mr and Mrs Ribble, others with resignation, resentment or depression.

What is noticeable by its absence is any reference to a sense of losing status, or a place in the community, through irregularity or absence of employment. Nor is there any reference to class – either in terms of identification by 'irregulars' with organised labour, or a sense of betrayal by organised labour. Oddly, it is Mr Kennet who makes the only mention of class:

'I mean, I think that, that, the government could do something for the likes of the working, of the working class as ... if they can get a job they ought to give 'em some help, rather a pair of boots if they're going on um ... ah building site and a pair of overalls. I mean for ... for the sake of ah ... well, what would it cost? Pair of overalls about 20, 20 quid, pair of boots about 15, 10 or 15 pound. I mean, it's it's nothing to get them off the dole, really ...'

(Mr and Mrs Kennet, 42)

This seems to be Mr Kennet's acknowledgement of the moment (refusal of a grant for working clothes) when he finally left 'the working class', and adopted a new identity, as part of a household work strategy largely generated by his wife.

If there is so little sense of exclusion in these accounts, it raises some important issues about the community in which our respondents lived. To what extent is it stratified in terms of labour-market status? Is regularity of employment the major determinant of other aspects of the household's position in the community – for example, their opportunity to buy their house? And how are issues of deviance and social control constructed in the accounts? These will be the topics of the next chapter.

REFERENCES

1 E. C. Cuff, 'Some Issues in Studying the Problems of Versions in Everyday Situations', Department of Sociology, Manchester University, Occasional Paper No. 3, 1980, pp. 34–5.
2 Alan Carling, *Social Division*, Verso, 1991.
3 R. E. Pahl, *Division of Labour*, Blackwell, 1984, p. 133, where Pahl states that it is at the stage that the children go to school that 'many households may become conscious that they are *repeating* a collective strategy'. '*A household*

work strategy ... made the best use of resources for getting by under given social and economic conditions.... Households do not have to be self-conscious in the balance of work or sources of labour that they use' (p. 20 and note 7, p. 20). The notion of a *collective* strategy must, however, if it is to mean anything, imply an agreement to co-operate. Hence Pahl's concession that some patterns are the results of disagreements and conflicts ('The Restructuring of Capital, the Local Political Economy and Household Work Strategies', in D. Gregory and J. Very (eds) *Social Relations and Spatial Structures*, Macmillan, 1985, especially pp. 250–1) is damaging to his account of such strategies.

4 Tim Barmby, 'Pareto Optimal Household Labour Supply', paper presented to EMRU/Labour Study Group Conference, Loughborough University, 9 July 1990.

5 Yolanda K. Grift and Jacques J. Siegers, 'An Individual Utility Household Budget Constraint Model for Dutch Couples', paper presented at EMRU/Labour Study Group Conference, Loughborough University, 9 July 1990.

6 Michael Taylor, *Anarchy and Co-operation*, Wiley, 1976, Ch. 3. See also his *Community, Anarchy and Liberty*, Cambridge University Press, 1982, pp. 65–94.

7 See for example Jan Pahl, *Money and Marriage*, Macmillan, 1989, p. 71.

8 Jan Pahl, 'The Allocation of Money and the Structuring of Inequality within Marriage', *Sociological Review*, Vol. 31, No. 2, 1983, pp. 237–62. See also Jan Pahl, *Money and Marriage*, Macmillan, 1989.

9 G. Wilson, *Money in the Family*, Avebury, 1987; P. Hunt, *Gender and Class Consciousness*, Macmillan, 1980.

10 N. Dennis, L. Henziques and C. Slaughter, *Coal is Our Life*, Eyre & Spottiswoode, 1956; A. Oakley, *The Sociology of Housework*, Robertson, 1974.

11 Carolyn Vogler, *Labour-Market Change and Patterns of Financial Allocation in Households*, Economic and Social Research Council Social Change and Economic Life Initiative, Working Paper 12, ESRC, 1989, p. 10 and Table 3, p. 46.

12 ibid., p. 22 and Table 13, p. 52.

13 ibid., p. 38 and Table 32, p. 62.

14 Jan Pahl, 'Household Spending, Personal Spending and the Control of Money in Marriage; *Sociology*, Vol. 24, No. 1, 1990, pp. 119–38.

15 See R. F. Curtis, 'Household and Family in Theory on Inequality', *American Sociological Review*, Vol. 51, 1986, pp. 168–80; Bill Jordan, *Rethinking Welfare*, Blackwell, 1989, Ch. 8. There is considerable survey evidence that women in full-time employment get substantial help with unpaid tasks, and women in part-time employment much less, from their partners. Martin and Roberts found that 44 per cent of women in full-time employment said that they shared housework tasks equally with their partners, while 23 per cent of part-time women employees said they were equally shared (Jean Martin and Ceridwen Roberts, *Women and Employment: A Lifetime Perspective*, Department of Employment and Office of Population Censuses and Surveys, 1984, Table 8.7, p. 101 and p. 100).

16 R. O. Blood and D. M. Wolfe, *Husbands and Wives: The Dynamics of Married Living*, Free Press, 1960; H. Dreitzel, *Family, Marriage and the Struggle of the Sexes*, Macmillan, 1972.

17 Philippe Van Parijs, 'A Revolution in Class Theory', *Politics and Society*, Vol. 15, No. 4, 1987, pp. 453–82.

18 Bill Jordan, *The Common Good: Citizenship, Morality and Self-Interest*, Blackwell, 1989, Ch. 6; R. L. Warner, G. R. Lee and J. Lee, 'Social Organisation, Spousal Resources and Marital Power: A Cross-Cultural Study', *Journal of Marriage and the Family*, Vol. 48, 1986, pp. 121–8.

19 Jan Pahl, 'Money and Power in Marriage', Paper Presented to the 1989 Conference of the British Sociological Association, Plymouth.

20 Jan Pahl, 'Household Spending'.

21 See for example R. W. Malcolmson, *Life and Labour in England, 1700–1780*, Hutchinson, 1981.

7 Community, kinship and housing

Although these respondents constructed their accounts of employment decisions primarily as members of households, within their roles as men or women, they also spoke as members of a small, rather cohesive community. The estate has a clear identity, partly bestowed on it by outsiders (among many of whom it is seen as having serious social problems). But its identity is also partly a modified version of this notoriety, as reconstructed by residents – see pp. 57–60 – and partly built through the links between residents, some of which span several generations. So our interviewees spoke as people who were to some extent implicated in the estate's reputation and its 'troubles', and also as members with some commitments and loyalties to their fellow residents.

This meant that when they sought to provide morally adequate accounts of their choices, they were doing so in a wider context than that of the immediate family. Some of our questions invited them to describe helpful or problematic aspects of their relationships with others (for example over child care and transport). They therefore placed themselves in a local as well as a kinship network, and in the estate's culture and economy, describing their decisions within a system of social relations which gave a good deal of significance to friendship and community; and they also explicitly or implicitly acknowledged that their accounts were partially discredited by their residence in an area of some notoriety.

> 'It's nice here. I mean a lot of people won't come out here because it's got a very bad reputation [...] I mean there you have problems out in the street, used to have the police out here midnight [...] Never a dull moment round here.'
>
> (Mrs Kennet, 16–17)

> 'You mention [estate's name] and everybody starts turning their back on you, but it's not that bad really. It's what you make it, i'n'it?'
>
> (Mrs Ouse, 14)

'I mean we used to have a lot of rogues round the area [laughs] but [indistinct] you can get good and bad in everyone.'

(Mrs Wear, 3)

The central argument of this chapter is that the roles of man and woman, and the norms governing them, can only be understood in terms of the kinship and community systems of the estate. The men learn to be workers and providers within their networks of male relatives and friends, which in turn give them information, help with transport, and assistance with home improvements; they are socialised and sustained by kin and community. The women's employment, as much as their caregiving, is enabled by female kin and neighbours. Thus women cannot challenge the norms of their caregiving role without upsetting their networks of female support, which socialise and sustain all aspects of their lives. And membership of these same kinship and community systems define and sanction the norms of partnership and 'jointness' for couples, and the boundaries between household (private) and communal (public) behaviour and decision-making.

This takes up the theme, last developed at the end of Chapter 5 (pp. 181–3), of the relationship between individual choices and social norms. Economists and their admirers – rational choice theorists in the other social sciences – have trouble with norms. For instance, Jon Elster in his recent writings has puzzled over the glue which keeps society together, and acknowledges that – while he can offer piecemeal analyses of various kinds of moral and social behaviour – he can give no complete account of norms: 'I do not know why human beings have a propensity to construct and follow norms, nor how specific norms come into being and change'.[1]

However, as other writers have pointed out,[2] this is mainly because Elster and other rational choice theorists have a very limited notion of rationality and interests, as calculative, instrumental, and concerned exclusively with individual utility: thus norms appear as irrational rules of conduct, binding people to act against reason, preference and interest. Once it is recognised that norms are guidelines requiring judgement and discrimination for their application; that they involve negotiation and flexibility for their implementation in everyday social situations; that they are concerned with aspects of life that are inescapably shared, and resources that are inherently indivisible; and that the communities which create and sustain them also adapt and change them, then many of these puzzles start to evaporate. Roles and norms are not self-imposed straitjackets, constraining rational choice, but means of living together with others, sharing certain aspects of our lives with chosen others (as in households), and distributing the burdens and benefits of communal living with others according to standards for which we are publicly accountable, and to make sense of the world with others, in various communities. Because of this shared, public aspect of human existence, we have *common* interests, which are sustained through norms.

One of these common interests, is in predictability of public behaviour involving shared resources. For instance, it is in every individual driver's interests that all should drive on the left-hand side of the road, or all drive on the right. Even in other less clear-cut situations, the costs (in time, energy and safety) of having to renegotiate on each occasion would be prohibitive. Hence norms are collectively rational for individuals who live in collectivities.

So far we have looked at these interviews as individual and joint accounts of individual and household decisions. But collectively they represent accounts of social relations in this community: they construct its values, and its ways of sustaining them. The interviewees make many references to the wider world of kinship and community, beyond the household, and how this relates to their employment decisions and income strategies.

In this chapter we look at these accounts of wider social relations, both to see what part the interviewees described them as playing in their decisions, and also to see how economic life influenced community and kinship systems. The effects clearly work both ways: the choices open to individuals are affected by the availability of kin and neighbourly support, information and sanction (as in the examples above). But both kinship and community relations are also affected by members' economic roles.[3]

In this way we are able to construct an analysis of how the household relations we have so far demonstrated connect with these wider social relations, and how economy interacts with community. However, although all the respondents had at some time experienced poverty, this is by no means a homogeneous neighbourhood, in which all members hold the same resources, status and power. On the contrary, the social divisions *within* the estate probably increased as much in the 1980s as did the divisions between residents in the rest of Exeter and those of the estate.

So the interviewees' accounts deal in social distinctions as well as in membership and what is shared by residents. Here the estate's outside reputation is often touched upon, but mainly in order for respondents to distance themselves from what is described as a deviant minority of residents who are responsible for most of its social problems. At several points interviewees mention positive features of the community or its facilities, while acknowledging an element which has given the estate a bad name. These 'others' serve to define the morally acceptable limits to respondents' own behaviour: when describing minor (or not so minor) infractions of official regulations (on income tax or benefits, for example) they point out that most of the respectable majority do the same thing, and distinguish it from the fraudulent or criminal activities of the minority. Yet even those whom we as interviewers took to be possible examples of that minority are at pains to justify their actions by defining what they would not be willing to do, and giving examples of others who are willing to do it, and quite often do it (see accounts by Mr and Mrs Bow, pp. 14 and 240).

The significance of council house purchase, and of owner occupation generally, has been widely canvassed in both the sociological and the economic literature.[4] We address its relevance for social solidarity and social stratification on the estate. There is little doubt from our respondents' accounts that most see owner occupation as a desirable tenure, and many (including some with no obvious prospects of achieving it) aspire to this tenure. However, these people do not construct owner occupation as a rejection of their estate's community, or even in terms of opportunities for economic advantage. Rather, at a time when they consider that their situations as tenants is very precarious because of rising rents and rumours of privatisation, they see purchasing their house as the best way of securing their stake in the community, retaining their links with friends and kin, and protecting their expenditures of energy and resources on improving their council houses.[5]

FINDING AND CHOOSING EMPLOYMENT

Kinship and community emerge not as alternative but as complementary sources of information and support in our study of working patterns on the estate. This is partly because so many households had close kin (parents or siblings or both) living in the neighbourhood. In our study, 16 men and 21 women among the 36 respondent households mentioned having such kin living on the estate, and most of the rest had kin living in or near Exeter. Those with no local kin (such as Mr and Mrs Severn, Mr and Mrs Calder, Mr and Mrs Frome) were also least involved in friendship networks on the estate; they did not rely on friends for help with child care, or on friends to help do home improvements (whereas many of those with local kin did). They looked outside the immediate area for support. Others who had fallen out with their local kin (such as Mr and Mrs Spey, Mr and Mrs Exe and Mr Bow), and hence who received sporadic kinship support, or none at all, reported less involvement in community activities and in home improvements also (though in the case of Mr and Mrs Bow, more involvement with friends in undeclared cash work).

Both kinship and friendship play an important part in the men's and women's accounts of finding and choosing employment. Thus 5 men and 3 women said that relatives had told them about jobs or helped them get jobs at some point in their employment histories; 8 men and 9 women mentioned that friends had informed them of vacancies they subsequently took up (in the cases of 2 men and 1 woman these were undeclared cash jobs). Mr Derwent and Mr Kennet depended on kin for transport at some time in their working lives; so did Mrs Avon and Mrs Tamar. Mr Ribble and Mr Derwent currently rely on friends for transport to work.

Some families have followed the same occupation over two generations – Mr Ouse's father was also a signwriting employee, and Mr Rother's also worked for the local authority. In the case of Mr and Mrs Kennet, their self-employment as painters and decorators reflected a more extensive family tradition on her side – perhaps helping her 'reconstruct' Mr Kennet after his exclusion from the labour market (see p. 249).

Mrs Kennet: It, it's a family occupation really, painting and decorating. She (daughter) can do it. She can wallpaper and paint and I can do it. And my father did it for 47 years. And his father and brothers – or one brother. ... But my father did 47 years in the mental hospital. Was a foreman painter. Except for the war years.

(Mrs Kennet, 13)

Many of our respondents saw it as an advantage to have several kin in the same employment. Mr Ryton's new job as a stonemason is seen as more secure and reliable by Mrs Ryton, because of a chain of family connections, while he is glad to have a friend working there.

Mrs Ryton: Yeah, because he's got this auntie, she knows the director – well sort of from him – 'cause my, my dad – the woman he lives with – it's her son ... see my dad lives with Jan Roberts and her son's Bill Roberts and he's the director of, of the stonemasons, isn't he Ed? He's been there how long? 20 years? ...

Mr Ryton: Um.

Mrs Ryton: ... and also her younger son who's Ed's age – Jack: Jack works there as well and um ... Jack's nephew works there – Harry – so it's all sort of family. Ed's working there, Roberts i'n'it Ed? [indistinct] ... And so at least he knows people there [indistinct].

Mr Ryton: I know someone else there as well, who's, who started um yesterday, he used to ah ... I worked with him on the [...] Community Programme and um ... yeah ... we ... the same bloke he also got a job with [firm's name] [...] So I

	know quite a few people there so ... that's an added advantage ... It's better to know somebody, going to a job than going without knowing anybody.
Mrs Ryton:	Yes, yeah. So we're all feeling a lot more settled.

(Mr and Mrs Ryton, 50)

However, friends played an even larger part than kin as sources of information about employment, and also in the choice of where to work. A quarter of the women mentioned finding jobs through friends, and many saw the presence of friends at work as a positive feature of an employment opportunity.

'friend of mine, down there – she's called Elsie – she been down there, working down [...] council – for 15 years, and she asked me if I'd be interested in a morning job ...'

(Mrs Avon, 3)

'That was through a friend of mine; she [...] married a disabled person and [...] he was up there working [...] and she got a job there ... and then she got me a job there.'

(Mrs Stour, 4)

Others make close friendships at work, which form an important part of their social life; many women from the estate work at the same roadside restaurant.

'on a Friday night out there um there's about 8 of us, that we've worked together for a long time you know and ... we get on really well and really it's like a night out with the girls really more than anything. 'Cause you go out, have a yap and everything ... I mean together for 8 hours and I think if you can't sort of hit it off ... I mean I know women always, they always say don't they if you get a bunch of women together, there's always one that's got to be the bitch like. But um we do have a good night, and sometimes you can have a really good laugh and a joke, it just feels like you've been for a night out with the girls.'

(Mrs Parrett, 17)

Among the men, word-of-mouth from friends was particularly important for irregular workers who looked for short-term employment, 'self-employment' or cash work. Of the 8 who specifically said that they got paid work through friends, 2 were irregular building workers in 'self-employment' at the time, and 3 were speaking of cash jobs which they took while claiming, without declaring them to the benefit authorities (Mr Torridge, Mr Frome and Mr Bow). Similarly Mrs Bow spoke of one occasion when she was 'fiddling' the benefit authorities by working with a friend who was also 'fiddling' (see pp. 240–1).

It is also worth noting that the involvement of kin in the same employment or self-employment sometimes led to *losing* as well as finding work. Mr Humber relied on his brother-in-law for transport to work when they were doing insulation work on a self-employed basis; when his brother-in-law decided to quit, he became unemployed. Mr Wye describes two occasions on which his brother, with whom he was working, got the sack, and he left the job at the same time – once for missing work after being out drinking (already quoted, p. 96), the other when his brother got into trouble with the law.

'Ahh, no I got sacked from up there, 'cause my brother got mixed in with somebody and went up there stealing off 'em, so he got took to court with these other boys and they sacked me about a fortnight after I think.'

(Mr Wye, 6)

SUPPORT AND ASSISTANCE FOR EMPLOYMENT

As well as helping respondents find work, kin and friends gave help that enabled them to keep it. The most important element in this was child care: 16 of the households described having received help with child care from kin, and 7 from friends. As we saw in Chapter 4, most employment-enabling child care is done by spouses, but there are often occasions when this requires supplementation, or awkward gaps in the day or week which have to be filled. Here family in particular, but friends also, play an important part.

The most common pattern was for the mother of one of the couple to have the children before or after school or in the holidays, while the wife was working, and until the husband came home from work – the examples of Mrs Nene and Mrs Derwent were given in Chapter 5. Mrs Medway describes a more complex arrangement: she is a part-time shop worker.

'Well my husband works nights so ... for 3 hours he doesn't sleep or you know ... his parents would have them, or my mum or my sister ... there's alway someone there to ... have the children.'

(Mrs Medway, 1)

Mrs Clyde works at the roadside restaurant, and her husband does shift work. Her child-care arrangements are variable.

'It depends. My friend does it, up the road. Or I've got my, my brother home and his girlfriend'll do it. So it depends. If my brother and his girlfriend do it they sleep overnight. If they can't do it and I've got to do, my mate does it up the road, I have to do a late shift because I can't expect her to get up. She's got 2 children of her own; I can't expect her to get up at half past 5, make sure she's up so ... to get the kids up there sort of thing, so ...'

(Mrs Clyde, 4)

Mr and Mrs Rother talk about their neighbours, Maude and Ron (in their mid-50s) as being like kin, so longstanding has been their role in child care (see p. 191).

Mr Rother: They're only too glad to come over 'cause they like wrestling; they're wrestling freaks [...] And we've got cablevision, you see, right. And they ...
Mrs Rother: They loves it.

(Mr and Mrs Rother, 33)

Mr Rother goes on to explain that they do not pay Maude and Ron; she was a 'very, very close friend' of his (now deceased) mother, a teammate in the estate pub's darts team, and that they came to all his family's major celebrations and his family to theirs: 'they're more than what you say neighbours'. When Helen Kay remarks: 'The way you describe it, it's more like family', Mr Rother replies, 'Near enough, I should say'.

Mrs Tamar's parents live two roads away: she has grown-up children and young grandchildren living in the household, and her husband used to work with her brother as a 'self-employed' builder. Her father drives her to work in the morning, and sometimes brings her home also. Mrs Avon describes an even more interlinked system of employment and support from their families when she was working at the roadside restaurant.

'My sister used to work out there ... and um ... my brother works out there, and my sister-in-law works out there [...] Weekends [...] Mostly weekends but it was working right through the night ... so I said, well that's no problem, not really. Because when John was on night work, the same as me the Friday night, his mother had the children, they slept up their nanny's.'

(Mr and Mrs Avon, 47)

Ms Otter and her partner are still claiming income support as single people: Ms Otter has decided to set up as a childminder, with encouragement from her mother.

'Then my mum said I could do ah ... do childminding if I wanted to on top of what I'm getting off social but there's so much, ah there's so much you can't do over the ... the amount that you should get like ... for childminding [...] 'Cause I know that 'cause my mum was ... she's [...]

still a childminder, but now that there's nobody living at home she don't get [...] any money from social ... 'cause her money stops ... once we have all left home. So all she's got, and that keeps her on ... and the bills and what have you ... is from childminding. That's all she gets now. She's j, well got a little part-time job on the side as well ... but it's sort of keeping her alive.'

(Ms Otter, 19)

These accounts indicate that neither employment nor child care are treated as exclusively household issues. Women's caregiving responsibilities, in particular, are negotiated as the shared concerns of kinship and friendship networks, and hence kin and friends have a common interest – as well as a common obligation – in the proper upbringing of children. The women interviewees have helped out in looking after children, as in the above quotation from Ms Otter (see also the examples of Mrs Tavy, Mrs Ouse and Mrs Colne, pp. 182 and 226). All this explains why these women give primacy to child care over employment, and do not challenge their household role, or draw attention to male power in their partnership. They cannot do so within the terms of the public, shared standards of their female networks: to defy these norms would be to risk losing the support of kin and friends.

Hence they do not see 'putting their children first' in purely altruistic terms, or simply as making themselves at a disadvantage in the world of economy and employment, or in relation to men in the household. This is because child care is seen as a sphere in which women have a common interest in helping each other, and in sustaining a communal norm of mutual responsibility. This does not imply, of course, that it is in women's interests to take sole responsibility for this unpaid work. On the contrary, women display moral adequacy by showing how they engage their partners in supportive roles, including (in Mrs Wye's case) doing 'her' child-care work while she is in full-time employment. Furthermore, women also make it plain that – although they reject the notion of paid childminding – they welcome nurseries and other forms of public day-care for children, which they see as beneficial for their children (see p. 144). Hence the implication for public policy (for example, the Children Act, 1989) is that child care is seen as a collective responsibility in this culture, and as best supported by communal, shared facilities such as family centres.

However, despite the norms of sharing and helping out in kinship networks, not all relationships with kin are described as harmonious and helpful. Mr Cam's sister has helped with child care when Mrs Cam was working, but although they live only 5 minutes' walk away they are not 'close'. Mr Cam prefers to keep his distance from his family – 'they go and do their life and I go and do my life'. He describes his sister as liking gossip and 'exaggerating a lot', but 'she's got her uses, let's put it that way – not for a lot but for ...'. Mr and Mrs Cam continue:

Mr Cam: Well family-wise um, you know, I just keep meself to meself.

Mrs Cam: Umm.

Mr Cam: Best way 'cause there's a lot of harassment [indistinct] never got on and I don't 'spect we ever will but ... she's good for some things. She can be good hearted you know but ...

Mrs Cam: We tolerate them.

Mr Cam: So [indistinct] she helped out.

(Mr and Mrs Cam, 48)

For the irregular workers, who sometimes find themselves without income in gaps between leaving employment and receiving benefit, or with in-adequate income through wage or benefit cuts, financial assistance from kin is also an occasional form of support. Seven women mentioned receiving such assistance from kin, mainly their own parents, and two others (Mrs Medway and Mrs Frome) had received help to buy a house (subsequently sold to clear debts). However, this form of help sometimes led to criticisms and pressures – as with Mrs Exe's parents (p. 239). Mr and Mrs Ouse ran up a debt to a bank by using a credit card for their Christmas shopping 3 or 4 years previously, and she says that they have never been able to reduce it: they are taking out a personal loan to pay it off. She works part time to finance this, and says that they could not afford to pay their large bills – fuel, TV licence – without her wage.

'I mean sometimes I've got, when I haven't been working, and he had to pay it out of his money, we've had nothing for food ... so I had to go over Mum's and borrow ... not very nice that situation. Bit embarrassing, isn't it?'

(Mrs Ouse, 17)

The most disruptive and difficult part of the close network on the estate concerns ex-spouses: a high proportion of these households were re-constituted families, and hence the relationship with one or both partners' ex-spouses has to be negotiated. In some cases this means avoiding certain employments, where they or their kin are working. In others an ex-spouse has actually made trouble at work for one of the partners. Mrs Taw lost her cleaning jobs (which she was doing for cash and not declaring, while she was a single parent) because her ex-husband interfered ('put spikes in').

'Before I met Jim [present husband]. I used to clean down [name of industrial estate]; I used to clean all the factories down there [...] Yeah I had, used to have 7 jobs ... Oh I'd given them up because I met Jim ... and I was getting trouble with me ex-husband coming to me jobs all the time, so I give it up. Then I got married to Jim and that was that.'

(Mrs Taw, 14)

Ms Otter's partner got into trouble with his employers because her ex-husband reported him for using their van out of working hours to visit her.

However, the picture that emerges from the accounts is of a close-knit neighbourhood in which support from kin and friends is an important means of sustaining economic activity – especially by making it possible for both partners to do paid work. But obligations are reciprocal, and hence these hard-pressed couples are also involved in helping and supporting their kin of older and younger generations, and sometimes friends also. For instance, during the interviews with Mr and Mrs Taw, an aunt comes in to say that she has been waiting for a lift from Mrs Taw, and is locked out of her house; her mother (who is living with them) arrives with news of the doctor; and a neighbour drops by to return a strimmer he has borrowed. The impression from the interviews is of a large amount of informal activity, involving *ad hoc* negotiations over minor unforeseen events and major crises, in order to sustain long hours of low-paid employment.

HOME IMPROVEMENTS AND HOUSE PURCHASE

Another whole sphere of informal work involving kin and friends is that of home improvements. Among the respondents, seventeen had conducted major structural alterations to their houses, which they displayed with pride: others had ambitious plans for changes. Decisions about buying a house usually *followed* these structural improvements, rather than preceding them. As a building worker, Mr Ribble is particularly well placed to get assistance. He and Mrs Ribble explain that his mates have just fitted a new bathroom suite for them.

Mrs Ribble: Eric came and put the bathroom suite in for us di'n't he? [...]

Mr Ribble: Got it a lot cheaper as well than what I would have um ... if I had to pay someone ... He, I mean he was a tradesman, don't get me wrong, but if I had to pay someone I didn't know ... well I would have paid probably, what? ... 'bout 200 pound, to have it put in.

(Mr and Mrs Ribble, 71)

By his account, Mr Ribble is an energetic and radical home improver:

'Yeah. It's my complete hobby [...] I've ripped out half the bedroom and redone all that. I've ripped out the complete passageway and redone all that – well near enough [...] And ah ... dug up half the garden, chucked half of it away. Yeah. It's coming on. Take me years to do but I'll get it done eventually.'

(Mr Ribble, 24)

For materials, he deals informally with workmates. The system is one of reciprocity, characteristic of a close group, with a high degree of trust and co-operation.

Mr Ribble: Well I mean if it's something like um ... say, a couple of lengths of copper pipe, say, I've picked 'em up from somewhere and I'm not using them at the time and me mate needs them, then obviously he can have 'em. And then um this ... if I need some wood and he's got it I'll have it [laughs] ... It's like bartering really, you know [...]

Mrs Ribble: I mean they don't sort of keep up and score, you know. I mean Gordon might come out and borrow, say, three things in one week and he might just go out and like, borrow the one, you know what I mean. I mean there's no equivalent to it [...] But they sort of ... seem to even it out.

(Mr and Mrs Ribble, 73)

These home improvements are paradoxical in terms of theory about norms and social relations. On the one hand, they provide the strongest evidence of male networks which are similar to the female ones analysed in Chapter 5: groups of kin and friends who treat a sphere of activity as shared between members, with burdens and benefits shared on the basis of reciprocity and trust, without a reckoning up of what each owes the other at any point in time. These shared activities clearly consolidate and sustain male networks. Yet the outcome of their labours – enhanced value in the house – shifts the couple who benefit towards home ownership, which is often seen as the paradigm of 'privatism' and exclusive household decision-making that undermines community and kinship structures.

Our analysis is intended to show that this paradox is more apparent than real. In the first place, couples like the Ribbles treat home improvement as having priority over home purchase: they are still only thinking of buying their house. Similarly Mr Humber knocked two rooms into one and altered the stairway in his council house soon after they moved in, and long before their decision to buy: like Mr Ryton, he undertook this do-it-yourself work while unemployed. Others are doing or planning major structural work with only a faint prospect of purchase, or with no prospect at all, even though they would like to buy. Mr Hodder knocked out walls to make a large living room and is planning to build an extension with help from his brother-in-law who is a bricklayer, but he cannot foresee being able to afford to buy it. Mr and Mrs Dovey's son is building an extension to their house, but they have no prospect of buying it. Mr and Mrs Plym have knocked down a wall in their house and redecorated the whole of it, with help from her brother at weekends; they would like to buy, but cannot afford to. Mr Cherwell is hoping to buy his house after extensive improvements; if he builds an extension he will get help from two friends who are plumbers. Mr and Mrs Tamar are hoping eventually to buy their house if his employment situation improves. Meanwhile he is planning an extension to accommodate their large household (grown-up children and grandchildren), with the help of a friend who is a bricklayer and a plasterer, and his stepson who is a glazier. This list contains some households with a regular worker (Cherwell, Tamar, Plym), some with irregular workers (Ryton, Humber, Hodder) and one with no one in work for several years (Dovey).

Some of this is in line with earlier studies of public sector sales to tenants, which suggested that buyers had previously invested in their houses.[6] However, our interviews were conducted in the period immediately following the 1988 Housing Act and reflected a sharp increase in anxiety about the future of council housing in general, and of the estate in particular. Among our respondents, 5 were already purchasing and 13 expressed a desire to buy their houses: this compares with a survey of a large sample of council tenants by the British Market Research Bureau in 1986, which found that 39 per cent would 'most like' to own their house in 2 years' time.[7] Given the characteristics of our study estate – which might be regarded as typical of those considered most likely to become a residual 'ghetto' of welfare housing[8] – our figure is high, in relation to the wider survey of tenants from desirable and less desirable estates. This suggests that the pressure to buy was mounting at the time of our interviews.

Our sample survey of houses on the estate (see p. 58) suggested that there were no sales on the estate prior to 1980 (in fact Mr and Mrs Rother bought their house in 1975, which indicates that they were among the very first to do so). From 1980 to 1987, 11 per cent of houses on the estate were sold, and from 1988 to 1989 another 9 per cent – a considerable quickening of the pace of sales during our interview period.[9]

This was reflected in the reasons the respondents gave for purchasing or wanting to purchase. Those who had started to buy before 1988 were (as in other research studies of purchasers[10]) older, more securely employed and more long term in their residence than the average among our interviewees (Mr and Mrs Rother, Nene and Stour). Their reasons for buying were expressed primarily in terms of liking the area and having roots in kinship, friendship and community (see quotes pp. 58–9). Among those who had recently become purchasers, the emphasis was on uncertainty about the future – fear of privatisation and of rising rents.

Q: Can you remember the reasons you had at the time for changing to a mortgage?

Mr Wear: Um. Probably the talk that it was gonna go private or the possibility of it going private. I've heard some of the rents that are round from private landlords.

(Mr Wear, 13)

'Well I mean ... they reckon that the rents are going up so much more and then they were being privatised and you know, sort of, the other people were talking over which would mean that the rent went up so much. It really just paid us to buy it.'

(Mrs Derwent, 3)

Mr and Mrs Cam had decided to buy their house; when he was made redundant they quickly changed their decision. Their reason for wanting to purchase was similar.

Mrs Cam: We'd heard a rumour that they were ...

Mr Cam: They're gonna ...

Mrs Cam: ... going to be taken over by a private landlord.

(Mr and Mrs Cam, 53)

These fears, combined with a desire to protect their investment in home improvements, a desire for more control over their living environment, and a wish to give their children more security, were the main reasons given for wanting to buy. As we shall show in the next section, these reasons do not imply a desire to retreat into privatism or a rejection of community networks, but a desire to secure and strengthen them.

However, there was a somewhat paradoxical relationship between job security and house purchase. Of those in regular employment, the Avons, Plyms, Calders and Severns, while seeing purchase as desirable, considered it was too risky because they could not rely on keeping their current jobs or because their wages were too low. For example, when asked whether they had thought of purchasing, Mr Avon replies 'No [pause]. Because it's so unpredictable', and goes on to describe the danger of redundancy at the job where he has been for 15 years. Mrs Calder says she feels more secure as a tenant because of rising interest rates. Mr and Mrs Wye expressed a wish to buy, but probably not their present council house. On the other hand, several very irregular workers expressed a strong desire to buy their house (the Rytons, Colnes and Cams, for example) and others who knew they could not afford to spoke wistfully of this tenure as the most desirable.

HOUSING AND COMMUNITY

Theory on home ownership links it with privatism, mobility and the break-up of close-knit communities. Some authors have argued that owner occupation has given working-class households opportunities for upward social mobility in the 1980s, even when economic activity was depressed.[11] Conversely, renting from the council has been portrayed as desirable mainly in terms of security and affordable rents for those in work, and housing benefits for clients: the latter tend to trap tenants in unemployment,[12] and hence reinforce the polarisation between the two tenures.[13] Increasing purchases of council houses have been portrayed as evidence of individualism and consumerism among those with an employment-based share in the prosperity of the late 1980s, while legislation on public-sector housing is seen as marking out some estates as 'one class estates of less popular dwellings'.[14]

There is limited support from our interviews for the notion that council house tenants are becoming more orientated towards private property, savings and bequest. A few give the chance to make money on the housing market as a reason for buying, but this is almost always qualified by a comment about liking living in the area and having friends there. Mr Ribble is keen to use his building skills to economic advantage, eventually moving out of the area in order to follow a 'housing career', by doing up old houses while living in them.

> 'It's not that I've got nothing against [area]; I mean, I might even move back into, you know, might even be [...] private houses nearby. [...] I like it, as an area – [estate's name] I think is great, personally. I mean ... I've got on with all the neighbours and ... you know, they're really good. But ... it's not the ah fact the community I want to move out of it so ... it's ... well it's just better, the property circumstances, I think [...] Yeah, basically it's to make money and ah ... be able to live comfortably and have something to leave my son or whatever children.'
>
> (Mr Ribble, 25)

Mr and Mrs Rother talk about moving into 'a little bungalow' in their old age, and Mr and Mrs Derwent 'a little flat somewhere'; two other intending purchasers talk of leaving the house or capital to their children (Ryton, Cherwell). Mr Wear says that buying their house means 'you can always move if you want to'. But several others recognise that moving off the estate would be impossible, even if they wanted to.

'We couldn't afford to move. What else can you buy? ... You know, with three bedrooms and whatever ... I mean, you'm talking a lot of money, isn't you? 70, 80 grand. Just can't do it, can you?'

(Mr Nene, 55–6)

However, the predominant theme of these accounts is the desire to remain in the community. The overwhelming bulk of references to the estate as a place to live are positive; they refer to its bad reputation in order to rebut or qualify it.

'I mean the area now is so different to what is was when we first moved in. I mean we used to have a lot of rogues around the area [laughs] but [indistinct] you can get good and bad in everyone. It's quite good here [indistinct] you probably know?'

(Mrs Wear, 3)

Only one respondent expresses direct dislike of the area; Mr Torridge says: 'I hate the area' but then immediately adds 'that's a [sounds like "lie"]'. This is said with some bravado in front of his estranged wife's sister. His wife would like to move (to get away from him) but adds:

'It's not the area. The area's a nice area, even though people's got ... keep saying "Oh I wouldn't live out there, its awful." But you've gotta live here to actually know; it's not as bad as some of the other housing estates that's around.'

(Mrs Torridge, 24)

Mr and Mrs Wye express mixed feelings about the area (gossip and some rowdy neighbours, but good school and facilities); they would like to transfer to nearer her workplace, to make transport easier. On closer questioning this turns out to be the next council estate, which is so contiguous to the study estate that many outsiders regard it as one neighbourhood. However, Mrs Wye grew up there, and distinguishes between it and the study estate, where Mr Wye's family all live.

Apart from these, no respondent criticises the neighbourhood in which they are living, and many praise it (see quotes on p. 58, all by purchasers). Mr Rother is among the strongest enthusiasts for the community:

'... the area suits me: we got our friends here; um ... how can I say? I don't, I don't wanna ... lose ... the roots ... It doesn't appeal to me to go and live up on ... let's say Nob Hill then, all right ... we got a lot going for us here, alright. If promotion comes tomorrow and I go up about ten places in the league, you know, I still wanna live here; I still wanna have me mates; I don' wanna change it.'

(Mr Rother, 72)

What purchasers and would-be purchasers seem to be seeking is a stake in this community – both in the sense of securing their position as residents in a period of economic uncertainty, especially over rents, and for the sake of intergenerational continuity, which is such a feature of the estate. The decision to buy is a reaction to the threat of housing insecurity, rather than a rejection of their former values or of public provision. They are critical of some aspects of the council as landlord. Mr Cam says the council workmen 'come to paint the windows, then they painted half the garden as well'. Mr Humber says the council wouldn't let them exchange houses when his wife had a miscarriage – 'not good enough reason at all'. But they are much more fearful of private landlords. Their concern is to protect both the support from the community that is such an essential assistance for their economic participation, and their investment of time, energy and resources in improving their council houses. Thus their priorities are very similar (in terms of continuity, security and affordability) to those which led their parents' generation to prefer council housing. It seems to be this enhanced sense of belonging to the community as a purchaser that Mr Wear is refering to when he says, 'I s'pose you feel ... a bit more part of society actually'.

ECONOMIC CHANGE

The processes of economic change in the 1980s – the shedding of unskilled and semi-skilled workers from manufacturing industries, the restructuring of firms into 'core' and 'peripheral' functions, the growth of part-time employment, subcontracting and self-employment, the 'feminisation' of the workforce, mass unemployment – have caused economists and sociologists to look outside Britain and Western Europe for comparisons. Deprived communities in the advanced countries have been compared with parts of cities in the Third World. In the latter, the industrial sector has failed to absorb the rapid influx of rural population into regular employment. Hence the poor have resorted to 'alternative survival strategies' – hawking, street trade, petty commodity production, reciprocal kin-based exchange and service activity.[15] To what extent have the households in our study been marginalised in similar ways by economic change?

The notion of marginalisation implies that households have little or no access to mainstream services and infrastructure, and resort to informal and casual ways of producing and exchanging, outside the officially defined labour force and officially recorded economic activity. Such ways of life are characterised by poverty and insecurity. In practice, even in Third World countries, research has shown that it is difficult to identify the boundaries of such economic sectors or communities.[16] Where such identification and demarcation have been claimed, studies have shown that the 'marginal' areas are linked to the mainstream economy in many ways. 'Households themselves are difficult to categorise along sectoral lines, making use of multiple strategies to ensure survival',[17] which are differentiated by gender and stage of the domestic cycle.

In both the activities pursued, and the complex links with the rest of economic and social activity, these studies of Third World marginal communities do seem to provide useful comparisons with our interviewees' descriptions of their activities in terms of kinship and friendship networks and care work. As well as relying on reciprocity between female kin and friends over child care, and between male kin and friends over home improvements, our respondents describe themselves as willing to sustain a wide variety of informal service and 'self-servicing' work (animal breeding and selling, vegetable growing, casual farm work, leafleting, door-to-door selling), and some 'petty commodity production'. As well as his bird, fish and animal breeding, Mr Humber has considered producing garden gnomes on his premises:

> 'made some garden gnomes, didn' I? [...] Yeah. Us went to the bank and all this for a loan. So I could try and start it they wanted [...] proof that you could sell between – I dunno – it was 5 or 7 hundred quid's worth of gnomes before they'd even look at the bloody application, didn' 'em?'
>
> (Mr Humber, 32)

But the major difference between Third World and advanced countries lies in the relative importance of kinship and state welfare systems in sustaining households with little or no economic activity, either formal or informal. Clearly in the advanced countries, income maintenance systems form a much more important part of household strategies for covering expenditure, whereas in the Third World there is greater reliance on kinship networks, including income transfers from city-based branches of the extended family in 'good' times, and withdrawal of whole city-based households to the rural area as a last resort in 'bad' times.[18] There is also differentiation in all types of economies between categories of household over use of any welfare services available. 'Low-income female-headed households may utilise welfare benefits and kin-based reciprocity, without resident males, because they are already deprived of access to forms of work with a higher return to labour',[19] or for other reasons. But exchanges through kin are a crucial part of all studies of survival strategies in Third World 'marginal' urban communities.

However, other studies in the 'marginal' areas of advanced countries report *resistance* to 'informalisation'. The poor in Naples, for example, have organised to hold out for regular employment and adequate wages, seeing the return to the traditional 'informal' practices of the 'street-corner economy' as associated with unacceptable levels of poverty.[20] Our study suggests that on the estate, households both adopt and resist informal practices. They describe themselves as doing cash work and casualised 'self-employment' (informal) yet they rely on benefits for their main income, either tactically or strategically, and insist on the availability of 'suitable' employment (resistance to informalisation). This applies to households in all the three groups of strategic responses we have identified. Those in regular employment do undeclared cash work (Rother, Nene, Plym), but all strongly resist and fear redundancy and the insecurity of becoming an 'irregular'. Those which use benefits tactically have minimum requirements for acceptable employment (see pp. 120–1) in terms of male earnings. Those who use benefits strategically legitimate undeclared cash work to cover household expenditure (Bow, Dart, Dovey) and insist on a 'family wage' as a condition of return to employment.

Hence what needs to be understood are the links between the formal and the informal economies,[21] how kinship exchange and state income support interact,[22] and the effects of economic change on the culture of communities.[23] These interviewees provide new evidence, and our analysis draws out new hypotheses, about these links, interactions and effects, by showing how casualisation and informalisation reinforce reliance on *both* kinship assistance (as the New Right would wish) *and* benefits (as the New Right fears). But economic change also alters the relative positions of households in the community, strengthening the security and giving new property assets (in their jobs and their houses) to some, while making others' labour-market position more precarious. In this sense our study provides evidence of the consequences of polarisation of employment security and wage levels, even in this relatively deprived community.[24]

Even though we have argued that the rapid increase in purchases of their council houses by tenants, and in the desire to purchase (even or especially among irregular workers) does not reflect a fundamental change in social relations on the estate, economic change has certainly altered the relative life-chances of the households in our study. We have no way of knowing how homogeneous the estate's social structure was in the past, but it is clear that the fortunes of – for example – Mr and Mrs Spey and Mr and Mrs Rother, or Mr and Mrs Exe and Mr and Mrs Ribble, have radically diverged during the 1980s. The intriguing question – and one which we have not attempted to answer in this chapter, but which deserves more research – is to what extent this divergence reflects the better kin and friendship support available to some families, and the relative isolation (often owing to family quarrels) of others. Certainly some of the most economically marginal households (Bow, Exe, Spey) report that they have quarrelled with their parents, or that their parents are so poor and oppressed that they can offer no support. On the other hand others (Dart, Torridge) are almost equally marginal economically, even though they have close relations and plenty of links on the estate. Conversely, others with few or no links (such as Calder and Severn) are among the households with a regular worker.

Quarrelling with kin is certainly not specific to the three households mentioned above: for example, Mr and Mrs Ribble, who at various times lived with her sister and his parents, describe at great length quarrels with both of these (which involved moving in one case, and being homeless in the other) and with her mother. However these quarrels were patched up: perhaps the important skill is not sustaining harmony (which no household seemed to achieve) but keeping open the possibility of reconciliation after rows. Marriage break-up was another common occurrence, but here again it seemed important to retain the support of close kin: Ms Otter and Ms Waveney had done so; Mrs Spey had not.

It is also difficult to gauge how serious the consequences of community disapproval are for those whose behaviour is perceived as transgressing the norms of the estate. By his own account Mr Bow was in an approved school and had recently been to court for social security fraud, but it seems unlikely that a criminal record is in itself enough to marginalise individuals or households: Mr Wye's brother, for instance, retains his links with him. Mr and Mrs Dart include his brother, who has just come out of prison, in their joint interview. Mrs Taw's daughter was removed under a court order because of physical cruelty (which Mrs Taw denied), but she retains responsibility for her (hyperactive) son, and a large number of kinship and community links, as well as her marriage to a regular worker. Although interviewees use 'others' to define the limits on their own behaviour in terms of what is unacceptable as well as what 'everyone does', it is unclear whether this means that sanctions are applied to those who break these rules.

Another distinction which we did not pursue in the study was made by Mrs Spey. She disliked living on one side of the estate, and much preferred the street to which she had been transferred.

'Nobody stays there, you know. It was the type of avenue that ... the kids were [...] terrible, you know. Chuck stones at you out the windows and ... everything, you know. Hated it [...] oh it's much better here [other side of the estate] yeah. They always seem to stick the same sort of people in the avenues you know [...] army type of people, break into your houses and everything [...] Yeah I like it here. Well I was born and brought up here, you see. I lived in the front, was brought up in the front – you know, where the school is.'

(Mrs Spey, 11)

Mrs Spey's reference to 'the front' is to the main thoroughfare of the estate: 'the avenues' are the roads that fan off from this, a couple of minutes' walk away. The notion of 'army people' must refer to discharged service families (there is a barracks nearby). She was married to a soldier who left her, and was a single parent for a time before meeting Mr Spey (who had come out of prison). There were several of our respondents who had been in the services (for instance, Mr Calder, Mr Ryton, Mr Kennet) but nothing else differentiates them as a group from the rest.

Much more overt in a few accounts, however, are the distinctions between those households who proclaim their dedication to hard work and thrift and the 'others' who are seen as workshy and spendthrift: these emerge, not in discussions about employment or community, but in reply to questions about benefits. Mr and Mrs Avon are resentful about the fact that they have been refused both family credit and housing benefit, on the grounds of earning too much, despite the fact that his wage is well below that of the man in the government's TV advertisement for family credit.

Mr Avon: Well, 'cause in their, their opinion I'm earning too much money. The money I'm earning I should be well off. Yet I can, I can give you ah ... a list of 9 or 10 people in this [estate's name] – right – who go abroad every year for holiday; who drive a nice new car; and they've never worked a day in their, never worked a day in their life [...]

Mrs Avon: Yeah, I knows a few like that.

(Mr and Mrs Avon, 23)

But equally, the few who acknowledge that they have been in trouble with the benefit authorities insist that they have been wrongly identified as the main culprits – that their accusers in the community have pointed the finger at them when 'others' are far more guilty. Ms Otter's friend Ms Clyst had been prosecuted.

'Someone reported me to social security 'cause I was [indistinct] 'cause I earned 6 pound a week ... but according to their law they said that anything over 5 pound you earnt you're supposed to notify them of [...] They said I was earning a lot of money but I wasn't, I was only earning 6 pound, and it was 2 hours work. And they fined me 124 pound for that, and they made me pay 124 pound because I, I earned a pound more than what they said that, you know, was the going rate. And yet other people [...] you know I could have looked out of the window and I could have named loads of 'em what were going ... having 60 or 70 pound social money and then going out earning another 40 or 50 pound ...

(Ms Clyst in Ms Otter, 24)

Does this imply a 'divided community', with hostilities between those couples struggling to buy their houses (or just to meet living costs) by both working long inconvenient hours at low wages, and others claiming, doing undeclared work and spending recklessly? Not in any very obvious way to us as outsiders, either from observation or from our respondents' accounts – references to community loyalty and solidarity far outnumber these references to divisions and resentments. Furthermore the community 'activists', such as Mr and Mrs Avon (bowling, guides), Mr and Mrs Kennet (children's band) and Mr Wye (captain and stipendiary secretary, sports club) are a diverse group of regular, irregular and very irregular workers, all council tenants, not purchasers. Indeed someone who was on her own account an extensive practitioner of undeclared cash work while she was a single parent (but who insists others were far more unscrupulous than herself), Mrs Taw, is now married to a regular worker and at the centre of a network of neighbourly and kinship mutual support. All this seems to point to a community whose close ties of interdependence, leading to both assistance and quarrelsomeness, have endured the changes of the 1980s.

CONCLUSIONS

Our analysis of decision-making in the interviewees' households has shown how this was constructed within clear norms of segregated gender roles, and how particular decisions were justified by reference to a balancing of the various elements in these roles. Jointness in decision-making referred primarily to issues over household expenditure, and income strategies reflected household systems for financial management. In this chapter we have shown how household members also accounted for their decisions in terms of membership of kinship and friendship networks, and a close-knit community, which provided information, support and sanction for labour-market activity, both formal and informal.

This picture of the normative construction of labour-market decision-making fills out our analysis, by showing how the interviewees' versions of morally adequate employment choices were related to the norms of this small community. These norms place economic calculation and the striving for individual and household advantage in a moral and social framework of how members of such a community should behave; like Mr Rother, even individual success, training and job security should not disrupt relationships with kin and friends, and home ownership should not lead to desires to move out and live on Nob Hill. This is because of the nature of the community itself, and the way in which the good life for members is constructed as lived within a community.

'it appeals to me, like most of the people are genuine people, around here salt of the earth. You get a lot of slagging off in the papers and things and that about [estate's name] area, but it's only again ... the minority spoiling it for the majority around here, because a lot of people are salt of the earth around here. ... New people that haven't lived here, p'rhaps they can't handle it and that's why they slag it off like they do, but I mean ... everybody towards us are friendly.'

(Mr and Mrs Rother, 74)

For Mr and Mrs Derwent, a distressing aspect of their striving to buy their house, and the extra hours of work it has entailed, is their loss of contact with friends.

Mrs Derwent: 'Cause we've lost a few really, through that, haven' we?
We used to go out or ...
Mr Derwent: Yeah.
Mrs Derwent: ... Socialising. We lost all them.

(Mr and Mrs Derwent, 59)

In all this, the interviewees' accounts contrast with – for example – Bellah and his colleagues' data from their study in California, which shows Americans constructing their activities in terms of 'finding themselves', and their relationships in terms of therapeutic encounters. Bellah *et al.* criticise individualism and therapeutic modes of relating as demanding a great deal of time, energy and awareness, adding that

it is the moral content of relationships that allows marriages, families, and communities to persist with some certainty that there are agreed-upon standards of right and wrong that one can count on and that are not subject to incessant re-negotiation. It is that third element of the classical idea of friendship, common commitment to the good, that allows traditional relationships to persist coherently even when the 'giving-getting' balances shift, as they inevitably do.[25]

However, the normative structure of our study's interviewees' accounts was not one of absolutism or dogmatism. Standards of behaviour for men, women, neighbours and friends were 'normative guidelines', whose detailed implementation had to be negotiated.[26] Although gender roles were constructed as non-contestable, their performance called for flexibility: indeed, moral adequacy lay in the ability to adapt, improvise and renegotiate arrangements between partners, with kin and friends, and in the community. 'Jointness' in household decision-making required skills of listening, awareness, consideration and sensitivity, and although women were constructed as doing such things 'naturally' (Mrs Nene), *good* men did them also (Mr Ribble). Not all issues were successfuly negotiated, of course, and quarrels were commonplace. Decisions about house purchase were particularly demanding in terms of negotiation[27] – for a further analysis of such a decision's implications, see the final chapter, pp. 303–7. This shows that such decisions can bring to the surface the hurts and resentments in partnerships.

This chapter has also shown how analyses of the development of employment as a separate sphere, away from household and community,[28] may miss important features relevant to labour-market decisions. Recent research suggests that the relationship between labour markets and communities was always more complex and interwoven than such accounts suggested.[29] On our study estate, casualisation of employment and the prevalence of cash work reinforce these linkages, and make neighbourhood information through word-of-mouth networks a very important part of employment finding.[30] Mr Parrett and Mr Ribble both say that work 'becomes available' through contacts, and Mr Frome that he doesn't find jobs, they find him.

Finally, the normative framework of the estate's culture provides social sanctions on employment behaviour in formal and informal economies. It defines what kind of employment it is acceptable for men and women to take, and how much cash should be earned without declaration to the authorities. It also provides status for those – both regular and irregular workers – who make good decisions, and opprobrium for those who do not. Among men and women, it gives rise to a system of stratification as well as one of solidarity, derived from the playgroup,[31] the clinic and the adult learning centre as well as the workplace, on what it is to be a morally adequate man or woman.

At the start of this chapter, we addressed the question of whether this normative framework is a 'rational' response to these people's situation. Following Garfinkel, we would suggest that reasoning about how to behave is a practical activity by which members of a community make sense of their world – of the circumstances in which they collectively find themselves.[32] Hence in these accounts of labour-market decisions, rationality is a practical accomplishment of this group of social actors in their current situation:[33] it is how they reason together about the choices available to them, and how each respondent conveys this reasoning to the researcher in an interview. To apply a standard of rationality from economic individualism, or from natural science, to these accounts would be to misunderstand what the accounts are about – members of a community, constructing their individual versions, within a shared framework for making sense of their common situation. In the final chapter we will turn to some examples of how key decisions are negotiated within this framework, and to the policy implications of our findings.

REFERENCES

1 Jon Elster, *The Cement of Society: A Study of Social Order*, Cambridge University Press, 1989, p. 125. See also his *Solomonic Judgements: Studies in the Limitations of Rationality*, Cambridge University Press, 1989; and *Nuts and Bolts for the Social Sciences*, Cambridge University Press, 1989.

2 See for instance Martin Hollis, 'Why Elster is Stuck and Needs to Recover his Faith', *London Review of Books*, 24 January 1991, p. 13; Bill Jordan, *The Common Good: Citizenship, Morality and Self-Interest*, Blackwell, 1989; Amitai Etzione, *The Moral Dimension: Towards a New Economics*, Free Press, 1988; and Adrian Oldfield, *Citizenship and Community: Civic Republicanism and the Modern World*, Routledge, 1990. It should be noted that not all economists embrace the view of rationality criticised by these authors. For example, Thorstein Veblen wrote, 'The hedonistic conception of man is that of a lightning calculator of pleasures and pains, who oscillates like a homogeneous globule of desire of happiness under the impulse of stimuli that shift him about the area, but leave him intact ... When the force of impact is spent, he comes to rest, a self-contained globule of desire as before.' (Why Economics is Not an Evolutionary Science', in *The Place of Science in Modern Civilisation*, Harcourt, Brace & World, 1961, pp. 73–4.

3 On kinship, see Janet Finch, *Family Obligations and Social Change*, Polity, 1989, especially Chs 6–9.

4 See for instance Peter Saunders, 'Beyond Housing Classes: The Sociological Significance of Private Property Rights in the Means of Consumption', *International Journal of Urban and Regional Research*, 8, 1984, pp. 202–25; V. Karn, J. Kemeny and P. Williams, *Home Ownership in the Inner City: Salvation or Despair?*, Gower, 1985; Pahl, *Divisions of Labour*.

5 Simon James, Bill Jordan and Helen Kay, 'Poor People. Council Housing and the Right to Buy', *Journal of Social Policy*, Vol. 20, No. 1, 1991, pp. 27–40.

6 Alan Murie, 'The Sale of Council Houses', *University of Birmingham Centre for Urban and Regional Studies*, Occasional Paper No. 35, 1975.

7 British Market Research Bureau, *Housing and Savings*, British Market Research Bureau, 1986.

8 J. English, 'Must Council Housing Become Welfare Housing? Part 1: Council Housing at the Crossroads', *Housing Review*, 31, 1982, pp. 154–6; R. Forrest and A. Murie, 'Residualisation and Council Housing: Aspects of the Changing Social Relations of Housing Tenure', *Journal of Social Policy*, 12, 4, 1983, pp. 453–68; R. Forrest and A. Murie, *Selling the Welfare State: The Privatisation of Public Housing*, Routledge, 1988.

9 See Appendix A in James, Jordan and Kay, 'Poor People, Council Housing and the Right to Buy', for a fuller account of this survey.

10 R. Forrest and A. Murie, 'Monitoring the Right to Buy, 1980–2', *University of Bristol School for Advanced Urban Studies*, Working Paper 40; M. B. Foulis, *Council House Sales in Scotland, 1979–83*, Scottish Office Central

Research Unit, 1985; N. J. Williams, J. Sewel and F. Twine, 'Council House Sales and Residualisation', *Journal of Social Policy*, 15, 3, 1986, pp. 273–92.

11 Saunders, 'Beyond Housing Classes'; Pahl, *Divisions of Labour.*

12 J. Black and D. C. Stafford, *Housing Policy and Finance*, Routledge, 1988.

13 M. Murphy and O. Sullivan, 'Unemployment, Housing and Housing Structure among Young Adults', *Journal of Social Policy*, 15, 2, 1985, pp. 205–22.

14 Forrest and Murie, *Selling the Welfare State*, p. 167.

15 N. Redclift and E. Mingione (eds), *Beyond Employment: House- hold, Gender and Subsistence*, Blackwell, 1985, Introduction, p. 2.

16 B. Garcia, H. Muñoz and O. de Oliveira, *Hogares y Trabajordes en la Ciudad de México*, UMAM, 1982.

17 Redclift and Mingione, *Beyond Employment*, p. 3. See also R. Bromley and C. Gerry (eds), *Casual Work and Poverty in Third World Cities*, Wiley, 1979, for a critique of dualism and the marginalisation thesis.

18 Liselotte Wohlgenannt, comment on first draft of this book. We are grateful for her perspective, derived from work and research in African cities.

19 Redclift and Mingione, *Beyond Employment*, p. 3. See also Garcia, Muñoz and de Oliveira, *Hogares y Trabajordes.*

20 Gabriella Pinnarò and Enrico Pugliese, 'Informalisation and Social Resistance: The Case of Naples', in Redclift and Mingione, *Beyond Employment*, pp. 228–47.

21 R. Edwards, D. Gordon and M. Reich, *Segmented Work, Divided Workers*, Cambridge University Press, 1982; M. Paci (ed.), *Famiglia e Mercato de Lavoro in una Economia Perificata*, Angeli, 1980.

22 Didier Cornuel and Bruno Duriez, 'Local Exchange and State Intervention', in Redclift and Mingione, *Beyond Employment*, pp. 165–88, argue that state 'intervention' takes over from and replaces kin and community informal exchange, undermining social cohesion. Our study provides contrary evidence of families using both systems as part of household strategies – see Ch. 6.

23 Francis Godard, 'How Do Ways of Life Change?', in Redclift and Mingione, *Beyond Employment*, pp. 317–37.

24 Department of Employment, *Employment Gazette*, April 1990, Table 4, p. 202 (1989 Labour Force Survey preliminary results). Between 1984 and 1989 the number of employees in employment grew by 2,575,000 (counting government training schemes). Of these, the largest components were full-time women employees (773,000) self-employed men (586,000) and part-time women employees (499,000). Full-time male employment grew by only 209,000. Meanwhile, bottom decile male earnings fell from 66.0 per cent of median male earnings in 1979 to 58.5 per cent in 1989, and bottom decile female earnings from 69.4 to 63.1 per cent of median in the same period (*New Earnings Survey*, 1979 and 1989). See Hermione Parker (ed.), *Basic Income and the Labour Market*, BIRG Discussion Paper No. 1, Basic Income Research Group, 1990. For increasing poverty among the self-employed as the second largest new element in poverty in 1987, see Paul Johnson and Steven Webb, *Poverty in Official Statistics: Two Reports*, Institute of Fiscal Studies, 1990, p. 25.

25 Robert N. Bellah, Richard Madsen, William D. Sullivan, Ann Swidler and Steven M. Tipton, *Habits of the Heart: Individualism and Commitment in American Life*, University of California Press, 1985, pp. 139–40.

26 Janet Finch, *Family Obligations and Social Change*, Polity, 1989, Ch. 6.
27 C. Whan Park, 'Joint Decisions in Home Purchasing: A Muddling-Through Process', *Journal of Consumer Research*, Vol. 9, 1982, pp. 151–63.
28 H. Braverman, *Labour and Monopoly Capitalism, The Degradation of Work in the Twentieth Century*, Monthly Review Press, 1974.
29 Richard Whipp, 'Labour Markets and Communities: An Historical View', *Sociological Review*, Vol. 19, 1985, pp. 768–91.
30 Alan McGregor, 'Neighbourhood Influence on Job Search and Job Finding Methods', *British Journal of Industrial Relations*, Vol. 21, 1983, pp. 91–9.
31 Janet Finch, 'Dividing the Rough and the Respectable: Working-Class Women and Pre-School Playgroups', in N. Garmarnikow (ed.), *The Public and the Private*, Gower, 1983, pp. 106–17.
32 H. Garfinkel, *Studies in Ethnomethodology*, Prentice Hall, 1967, p. 4.
33 ibid., pp. 4 and 283.

8   Lone-parent households

As a comparison with the two-parent households which formed our main sample, Helen Kay also interviewed 7 lone parents (all women) with dependent children, during the period of our study. As explained in Chapter 3, 4 of these were contacted through the mother and toddler group run by the health visitor on the estate, another 2 were contacted through the Adult Learning Centre, and one through the Community Centre. This meant that a high proportion of the lone-parent interviewees were members of organisations, compared with our sample of two-parent households. This should be borne in mind when making comparisons, especially over voluntary work (see pp. 291–2).

There are several ways in which the lone-parent interviews can complement and fill out our theory of decision-making in two-parent households. First, does the lone parent construct herself as a 'breadwinner', as someone with primary responsibility for child care, neither (something else) or both? Second, what is their attitude towards labour-market participation – do they see it in similar terms to the women with partners, as a way of contributing to household income, and of fulfilling their personal needs for a 'break' and self-development? Third, it is widely suggested in the social policy and economic literature that lone parents face fewer disincentives to part-time work than the spouses of unemployed men do, but greater disincentives to full-time work than one-earner two-parent households, because of childcare costs.[1] Is this how these interviewees see it? Fourth, how does their budgeting and income strategy relate to those of the couple households, and what influence does a former marriage, its break-up, and subsequent financial arrangements with an ex-spouse have on this?

However, in attempting to compare these interviews with those of the couples, we run the risk of distorting them. It is important that we do not analyse the lone parents' accounts solely in terms of the theoretical framework that we developed for understanding couples' accounts: they may be about quite other issues. In this respect it is perhaps fortunate that Helen

Kay did almost all these interviews *before* the ones with couples – though this meant that some issues of interest for comparison were not fully explored. But it is also important that we do not fall into another trap which is common in looking at women's accounts of employment decisions. We should not consider them solely in terms of the interviewees' family situation, at the expense of their labour-market situation. It may be that factors in the labour market, reinforced by the benefits system, influence their decisions as much or more than the fact that they are single parents. Finally we must bear in mind that these women's quest for moral adequacy in their accounts of their employment choices was not constructed with determinate alternative accounts of partners in mind.

Of the 7 lone parents interviewed, 3 (Ms Axe, Ms Dee and Ms Taff) were divorced. Ms Welland and Ms Yeo were separated; Ms Fowey and Ms Usk were single parents. Each of them lived in rented council houses, though in the case of Ms Dee it was her mother's council house. Ms Welland had 4 children; Ms Axe, Ms Dee, Ms Taff and Ms Yeo 3 children; and Ms Fowey and Ms Usk one each. All had children aged less than 16 except for Ms Yeo, but her family consisted of 3 teenagers including a 16-year-old daughter with her own baby living at home and a 17-year-old son who was unemployed and not receiving benefits. At the time of the interviews 4 had part-time employment and 3 had no regular paid employment.

IDENTITY AND ROLE

Whereas the partners in couple households adopted roles, as men and women, which were supported, normalised and sanctioned by the culture of the estate, the role of the lone parent was – despite the prevalence of such households – anomalous. In seeking a morally adequate account of their decisions, these women were conscious of the need to legitimate their situation in relation to employment, and some also commented on their situation in relation to men and partnership.

Ms Welland is separated, has four children (7, 4, 3 years and 18 months), and works part time as a shelf-filler. She went to college after school, and later worked as a nursery nurse and in a catering firm, in the personnel department, leaving when she became pregnant. She indicates her positive attitude towards employment.

'No, I'm all for single mums working; I'm all for mums working, married or not, working, as long as they feel comfortable. I mean I don't think I'd feel comfortable until my children were at least 6 months old, to go out to work and leave them. But I think that is because my youngest one was so ill last year that I could have lost him and if I had been working I think I would have felt guiltier than I feel already.'

(Ms Welland, 3)

This statement indicates a strong orientation towards employment, qualified by a strong statement about children's needs. It is echoed by Ms Taff, who is divorced, and has three daughters aged 15, 11 and almost 7. She conveys a clear identity as a worker before marriage.

'I wanted to be a car mechanic before I left school. And I tried in a few garages, and they wouldn't employ me being female. So I couldn't get a job as a car mechanic so I worked with machines. I always worked with machines. I used to be able to prepare them as well. Don't know whether I could now, mind ...'

(Ms Taff, 5)

She goes on to give a detailed account of her employment history ('I was never out of work. I am now [laughs]') up to her marriage, and a description of short-term, part-time work she did during her marriage – she left employment when she moved to be near her husband, a soldier, and returned to Exeter after her divorce. She has recently bought a typewriter, and does part-time voluntary work as a typist at a social centre, as well as going to typing classes.

A third lone parent, Ms Usk, gives an account of being a regular worker throughout her adult life (she is a single parent – see below pp. 287–8), and a fourth, Ms Yeo (whose children are all teenagers) has worked – first part time and then full time – as a care assistant at a residential home for many years, and has only given up this job (where she was earning over £100 a week) because her 16-year-old daughter has had a baby.

The other three lone parents – like many of the women with partners (see p. 149) – had done various very short-term jobs, or had no employment at all, before falling pregnant. Ms Axe 'hasn't bothered' with seeking employment since having children, but Ms Dee has done voluntary work and now does part-time paid work as a nursing assistant (she lives with her mother, who looks after the children), and Ms Fowey has just started voluntary clerical work as part of an attempt to train herself for employment, and also does some cosmetics sales.

Hence all but one of these women are or have recently been employed, voluntarily or on a paid basis, and show a strong orientation to work, both rhetorically – in their construction of their identities in these accounts – and in their behaviour. Furthermore, three of them – Ms Usk, Ms Yeo and Ms Welland – display a debate with themselves and the interviewer about full-time employment, describing it as more advantageous than part-time. In the latter two's accounts, this is framed in terms of the benefits system.

'Like I say, a lot depends on whether you're part time or full time doesn't it? Really. Say if it was full-time you'd want about 60 to 70 pound a week, to cover. 'Cause like I say by the time you take the rent ... and all your bills out of it you still want to be left with some, don't you? But if it's part time, not ...'

(Ms Yeo, 7)

'it would be more beneficial if I did it full time than if I did it part time [...] Mm. But they (social security officers) advised me against doing it because I had four small children [...]'

(Ms Welland, 5)

As in this last quotation, the lone-parent women emphasise the need to reconcile employment with their responsibility for child care, which makes the strongest claims on them. And because they have no spouse to help with child care, the problems of 'fitting it all in' are accordingly greater.

Ms Dee is a part-time nursing assistant for two evenings a week and alternate Saturday nights. When asked whether she wants full- or part-time work, she replies:

Ms Dee: Part-time work. I wanted work that would em ... make it sort of fit in with looking after the children so that I wouldn't have to find anybody to look after the kids. That would make life a bit easier. That's why I've got evening work at the moment. I mean I could do days which is 8 until 1 but it means that I would have to find someone to take my little one to school so that is a bit awkward and they don't do anything from 10 till 2 which would be better still 'cos she would be out at school. So I can't do that.

Q: But you have someone to look after them of an evening?

Ms Dee: Well the oldest daughter, she is 13, she can look after them anyway until I get back from work which is half past 9 and every alternative Saturday night when I've got to work overnight my mum is there anyway. So it doesn't matter.

Q: Your mum lives in Exeter?

Ms Dee: My mum lives in Exeter. I've got three kids and all three go to school.

Q: And they are quite happy when Granny comes to ...

Ms Dee: We all live together in the same house. So it's no problem.

(Ms Dee, 2)

Ms Fowey also says she wouldn't want to work full time because 'I feel Sean needs me at home more than the amount of money that I could earn'. On being asked the advantages of her part-time work selling cos- metics, Ms Fowey says:

> 'I could do it when I wanted to. I could do it while Sean's at school and if he is ill I don't have to do it. I don't have to go out.'
>
> (Ms Fowey, 6–7)

She does however face difficulties if she goes out in the evenings as she has to find a babysitter. This is worthwhile financially when a friend's daughter does it occasionally 'for a couple of pounds' or a relation helps out, but it would not be worth employing a 'proper babysitter'. Working full time also presents problems because:

> 'I don't think I can go out to work full time 'cos I, the training I haven't got, I wouldn't earn enough money to pay for the babysitter I'd need in the summer holidays.'
>
> (Ms Fowey, 6)

Several stress the importance of looking after their own children them- selves. Ms Dee says she has never used childminders to look after her children. She feels it is wrong to pay someone else to look after her children; as it was she who brought them into the world it is up to her to bring them up. Ms Fowey is also reluctant to leave her son with a 'proper childminder', who would also be too expensive.

> 'I do think I need to be at home for him. Apart from that I don't like leaving him with people. I don't think it is right for a child to be brought up by somebody else really. 'Cos em ... y'know, to have to pay a proper childminder is just extortionate. I wouldn't mind working Sunday, 'cos he goes down to see his grandparents on Sundays. So I've got a reliable good babysitter every Sunday but you can't get jobs just for Sundays. I think I must be the only person who wants to work on Sunday.'
>
> (Ms Fowey, 4–5)

Ms Welland has a similar view:

> 'I wouldn't like to leave my children with just anybody. My kids would have to know the person I left them with. I mean OK, tax is only one side of it but you can always get an income tax rebate whereas you can't get a childminding rebate.'
>
> (Ms Welland, 3)

However in her case, she also feels some conflict between looking after her children and following a career, and to illustrate the position that lone parents can find themselves in, it is worth quoting from her interview at some length:

'I could get a better job, this sounds awful and I wouldn't want to wish it, I could get a better job if I didn't have four children. And I could have a career whereas I had a career before I started having children, y'know. But I know that when my children are old enough then I can go back.'

(Ms Welland, 4)

'I'd be better off getting a job. It's getting the people to look after the children plus you've got to get over this guilt trip where you think I'm leaving my kids, I'm leaving somebody else to bring up my kids, even though I brought them into world and I've loved them. Somebody else is having to bring them up because I'm having to work to keep them and it's a vicious circle and it is a guilt trip. I mean even working Wednesdays I feel guilty and I mean that is just one day a week, it's 5 and a half hours a week but I feel that y'know especially with the younger two 'cos he is at school and the other one is at nursery. When I come home there is a rush of arms and "Missed you, Mummy" and I miss them when I'm working but at the same time I need it, even though I'm thinking about giving it up I need it, y'know I need it for me, disregard the kids I need it for me.'

(Ms Welland, 5)

Nevertheless such work is necessary:

'I mean I love my little job, it is only a little job, I mean, it is only filling flipping shelves but it gets me away from here, it gets me away from the children, it sounds awful but it gets me away from the children, but at the same time as I'm saying that all I want to do is to stay at home, and if I gave up the job then I think I'd go right back, I wouldn't get out at all. I wouldn't, I think things would become worse in the family if I gave the job up. That's why I stuck with it. I don't know how much longer it is going to last 'cos I don't know how strong I really am. The first week I said I am going to go this week, I'm not going to go or whatever. I've phoned him up before with a head, to say I'm not coming in and I felt guilty for the next week and gone in the next week. That is just, I think really due to family pressures; it's not due to the actual job or the money involved and if you do work there are more family pressures. I mean I work one day a week but people tend to forget that I need that for me for one thing and I also need to get away from family pressures, might be only just a few hours but I think if I didn't I'd be in [name of local psychiatric hospital] right now. I do, honest I really do. And I think all these people that have got kids, and some of them have only got two or three kids and I mean I've got four and they say "oh no I won't go to work until my kids are in proper schooling" and they make me so mad "how can you leave your children?" and it makes me think they've got such a good life, such a good family relationship and atmosphere that maybe they don't need that, but they can't see past that, they can't see that other people need that, y'know.'

(Ms Welland, 6–7)

However, Ms Usk, a single parent with a 9-year-old son, describes herself as having given priority to employment – but as regretting this. She has been continuously employed since leaving school: 'you had people on the dole saying there was no jobs. There was jobs'. She went to work for a bus company (for some years she was a bus driver) ''cause all my family worked there'. She returned to work 11 weeks after her son was born. But she regrets this:

'if I had it all over again I wouldn't go back. I'd have had ... as it's turned out you don't bring 'em up, it's other people's ah, that's bringing your ... you're just looking at 'em, i'n'it?'

(Ms Usk, 4)

Her life was 'all work and no play'. She never had enough money to choose.

'I never had no choice. Never had enough money. I tried ... before I went back to work I tried to ... tried on the social [indistinct], only done it for 2 weeks. God knows how many people ... how they survive on social 'cause when I went down there it was only 28 pound. That's all you got.'

(Ms Usk, 5)

She regrets her working life, and says she wouldn't do it again. 'Been working since I was 15. That's enough, don't you reckon?' She went sick 2 years ago with a 'nervous breakdown' for 3 weeks, and is off sick from work again at the time of the interview. She dislikes the Department of Social Security, 'because you got to wait before you get any money off them'. Her present job is in the canteen. She had to give up driving when minibuses replaced the older vehicles because the shifts were now too long (11½ hours instead of 6 hours) and she would not have seen her son at all. Her pay has fallen sharply.

Ms Usk: Slashed in half. In fact slashed in a quarter. On the buses now it's what? £130. Yeah £130 now. I bring home what? £50, £58. And that's ... that's to claim everything else off. Trouble is I can't claim everything else with all this new system changing. So to be well off now I'd have to go in

	... back in for a full-time job again. No chance. I wouldn't do a full-time job again now.
Q:	Why is that?
Ms Usk:	I'm getting too old. Can't put up with the pressure.
Q:	How old are you? You're telling me a story [laughs].
Ms Usk:	Good though i'n'it [laughs].
Q:	Good story. I have a picture of this little grey-haired lady sitting ... [indistinct]
Ms Usk:	Well it is. Enough's enough though i'n'it? It does get enough. It'd be alright for the ones that ah ... that's never worked 'cause they won't know any different. The ones that's always worked. No. I don't think they should have to work on. Should have somebody here to keep me.

(Ms Usk, 11–12)

She describes the difficulties of trying to reconcile full-time work with her child-care commitments.

'I used to take all your middle shifts – 12 o'clock to about 8–9 o'clock. So I used to run over to [place name], drop him [her son] off, run into work, do my work, run back, pick him up and run back home. Trouble is you don't get no time for socialising then.'

(Ms Usk, 4)

Ms Usk is a single parent who has never been married: she constructs women as the real workers, in a way none of the women with partners do. Speaking of men, she says:

'Home from work, sit on their asses and you do the meals and that's all. They have got it easy and do you kow something? All the men I know, that's what it is like. They've got it easy. It's the women that's got to do all the work.'

(Ms Usk, 12)

BEING ALONE AND RESPONSIBLE

Ms Usk and Ms Fowey have not been married, but all the other women refer to the time of their lives when they lived as partners, and to decisions made during this period concerning employment. There is not enough detail in the interviews to analyse what kind of budgeting or income strategy they followed during those periods, but there is plenty of evidence that the financial arrangements around the break-up of their marriages has a great influence on their ways of managing money, their actual resources, and their decision-making at the time of the interviews.

Ms Taff was married to a soldier and their marriage broke up when they were living away from Exeter. The divorce was very stressful, but Ms Taff now receives maintenance of £320 per month for herself and the children, and she got £2,500 in capital as a settlement. Her description of the income she receives from her ex-husband is similar to the accounts of women married to regular workers, in that it represents a usually dependable source of income for basic household needs. She says that he has a good job and is reliable, though there was a 2-month period recently when he was unemployed and she had to claim income support. But she got a grant from supplementary benefits for furniture, carpets and curtains when she moved back to Exeter with the children. Extras like children's clothes are expensive, and she is grateful to her ex-husband and his new wife that they help with these.

> 'yeah, she's all right. And now, you know, when the kids, you know – 'cause he has the kids now – um, couple of times a year, you know, sometimes just for a long weekend. Summer holidays he can have them like for 2 weeks in the summer holidays and whenever they come back they always come back with new shoes and new clothes so it helps you know because it's maybe the wrong stuff [...] but it tides me over till I'm able to get them shoes so it does help, it does help.'
>
> (Ms Taff, 16)

Ms Welland's husband also pays maintenance regularly, but unlike Ms Taff she gets no advantage from this: the amount of her regular weekly payments is determined by her entitlement to income support. She resents this, especially in relation to the expense of 'extras'.

> 'It's ridiculous really, because my husband pays them maintenance every month, and we don't see a penny of it because what he pays them they pay me each month and that's it. I'd be better off getting a job.'
>
> (Ms Welland, 5)

Ms Welland's account reflects the notion that her part-time earnings could supply the 'extras', as in the income strategy of households with a regular worker. However, being alone and responsible for her children, she faces dilemmas over this.

> 'I mean even working Wednesdays I feel guilty and I mean that is just one day a week ...'
>
> (Ms Welland, 5)

While the interviews were not, of course, directed at the particular stresses of lone parenthood it is worth noting that two of them, Ms Taff and Ms Usk, said that they had had nervous breakdowns and Ms Axe's mother said that she [Ms Axe] had been 'on the way to a nervous breakdown'.[2] Ms Taff's account is the most detailed in this respect. She is asked how long the cleaning job she had had the previous year had lasted:

'About ah ... about well ... 5 or 6 months. Um [...] we done um 'cause it was 4 o'clock every afternoon um 4 till 6.30. And my sister used to have ... The kids used to go to my sister's straight after school but there was a lot of aggro you know and my kids start playing her up and of course when I was coming home they were kicking up to me and [child's name] was kicking up to me and .. and then course by the time they got into bed I mean it was 8, 8–9 o'clock by the time they got into bed which was late for them. And it was just chaos, it was just total chaos. And then of course I ended up having a breakdown. I still carried on with work and trying to do it a different way ... My friend had um one of the children so that it would be easier on my sister; that I didn't get the aggro from the kids and my sister and ah didn't work ... didn't work. And of course I had a breakdown and ah [indistinct] well they kept the job open for me and, and a woman that worked there that only lives up the road, she was pretty good. She sort of used to do overtime and that so that they didn't have to employ anybody else to take my place. But I just give up. Just said, no I didn't want to do it [indistinct]. I'll stay at home with the kids [indistinct].'

(Ms Taff, 18)

WORK AND EMPLOYMENT

Only two respondents, Ms Axe and Ms Yeo, had no form of work outside the home at the time of the interviews. However both were involved in the care of small children. Ms Axe has not worked since she had the children, who are aged 5, 3 and 18 months:

Ms Axe: I haven't bothered, No. When they are old enough, when they go to school all day I shall get myself a job then.

Q: Do you do any selling or catalogues?

Ms Axe: No I do nothing at the moment, No. All my time really is put on the kids.

(Ms Axe, 4)

Ms Yeo also does not work outside the home. Although her own children are aged 18, 17 and 16 (all unemployed), Ms Yeo has given up her full-time job a few months previously when she discovered that her 16-year-old daughter was pregnant and her husband left her. At the time of the interview, however, the baby has arrived and Ms Yeo was 'looking out for another job'.

Ms Taff has had part-time jobs but gave them up not only for the reasons alluded to above but also because, when she received maintenance payments they were taxable and absorbed her personal allowances; any further income she received was subject to tax. She also says that a babysitter would have cost too much and although her sister had looked after the children, the arrangement was not a satisfactory one.

Apart from Ms Axe, all of the lone parents felt the need for some form of activity outside the home for reasons additional to pecuniary reward, though that was usually important as well. In Ms Axe's case the reason for staying at home is because she has three young children. Although Ms Taff does not have paid employment, she gives a change of activity as one reason for taking on her last paid job. She also has two voluntary jobs:

Ms Taff:	Yeah I like a change. Ah on a Friday now I go up the school to help at [name of school]. I was up there at what – about quarter to 11 – half past 10 until 2 o'clock, right. And it was great. Time just flew past. And I was on everything. I was on the electric stapler and um copy machine and – photostat copying – folding machine, I was on four different things altogether.
Q:	What was this for?
Ms Taff:	Just to help the teachers out. So ... it was all right. [...]
Q:	That was just voluntary ... ?
Ms Taff:	Yeah. Voluntary. Yeah.
Q:	You didn't get paid for it?
Ms Taff:	No. It's not bad though, not bad. Something to do eh? 'Cause I can't work.

(Ms Taff, 2–3)

She also helps at another institution, where she might be paid if one of the regulars is absent:

Q:	You also help at ...
Ms Taff:	At [name], yeah.
Q:	Do you get paid for that?
Ms Taff:	No. I get a free dinner. And ... But now if Jan's not there I get paid that day. I get paid for that day. [indistinct] Just when Jan's not there.

(Ms Taff, 3–4)

In addition to her part-time paid job Ms Dee helps out at a school:

'Yeah, then we moved [...] and I worked at the nursery down there for a little while and I still do afternoons Wednesday afternoons down the school now. I done cookery with the kids last term, one afternoon a week. It's all volunteer work, y'know just something to do. An' I'm doing numbers and maths this term with the others, with the little ones, 5–6-year-olds.'

(Ms Dee, 6)

Although Ms Yeo is currently without employment she says she is:

'... looking out for another job now actually 'cause I'm getting so fed up staying home, but, you know I dunno how some of these people can sit home there and not do anything ...'

(Ms Yeo, 3)

Both Ms Dee and Ms Fowey think it important to go out to work although they have a lot to do at home:

Ms Dee:	I'd like to be classed as employed, not unemployed and ... useless. [laughs]
Q:	Do you feel that?
Ms Dee:	Yeah, you do. You do feel useless even though you know yourself that you are a full-time mum, and that is a full-time job anyway. It's still nice to be able to do something different.

(Ms Dee, 3)

Ms Fowey expresses similar feelings:

Q:	Do you think it is important to go out to work?
Ms Fowey:	Yes, it is really, isn't it? Everybody else is working. If you can work I think you should work but ...
Q:	Do you feel lazy if you don't?
Ms Fowey:	Not really, I do enough here. You know I'm not a lazy person.

(Ms Fowey, 2)

Ms Welland, who works part time filling shelves at a local shop, also presents non-pecuniary reasons for working:

Q:	The research is about how you decide when to take a job and how you decide between jobs.
Ms Welland:	That's quite a leading question, quite a difficult question. I mean right now I'll take a job not because of the money but because I need time away from the home for myself. It's just one day a week, $5^1/_2$ hours a week.

(Ms Welland, 1)

So all the respondents either are or intend to be (Ms Axe when the children go to school) involved in work outside the home. However, for all the lone parents the children are an important constraint which lead the women to choose either not to work at all (Ms Axe) or to limit their labour-market activity in some way. In their accounts, both employment and child-care responsibilities impose stronger moral imperatives, and the conflict and stress in reconciling them – in 'fitting it all in' – is stronger than among the women with partners.

TAX

Relatively little was said about taxation, probably because the lone parents usually earn too little to be affected by it. However, Ms Taff, in addition to her awareness of the tax implications when she received maintenance payments, is also aware of that sometimes tax can be avoided by relating periods of work to different tax years. In recalling her employment history she said:

Ms Taff: Left there and moved to [name of city]. And I couldn't get a job there 'cause ah I'd filled in a form that, then if ... I went down to the tax office here in Exeter to find, you know – I found out which one I belonged to – and I went down there and they ... I had all my tax back for that year. But it meant that I couldn't work for like the 12 months 'cause it wasn't in a 12 months my tax year and everything. But I couldn't work until the tax year the following year.

Q: Really?

Ms Taff: Well it's something to do um ... you know the tax year is April to April. Well I packed in work ... I think it was ah about the June. I think it was about the June. So I got my tax back sort of for those months ... I, I know it's the same with a baby. If you're pregnant and that and have a baby, at certain times of the year you get a tax rebate don't you, certain times of the year. Well it was the same with when you're working. When you give up work depend ... Well anyway I couldn't work. So I didn't work. And then of course when I went to get work I couldn't 'cause I was pregnant. So ... that knocked that up. That was the end of that.

(Ms Taff, 8)

In discussing her employment history Ms Yeo is asked if she had ever turned down overtime because of tax:

> 'No. No. It didn't worry me like that. I think, whatever overtime come up, I was always there to take it on. Mainly, like I say, for something to do. You know, and I had a ... 'cause the money wasn't too bad anyway, so ... tis'n as if I wanted the money as that, like that, that, not then anyway.'
>
> (Ms Yeo, 8)

The lack of reported effects of taxation, apart from those of Ms Taff, does not, of course, prove that it is not an influence on decisions. It might have an effect in other circumstances and can combine with other factors, in particular the costs of child care and the costs of going to work, neither of which are tax deductible, to present some severe obstacles to financially worthwhile employment.

> 'Yeah, if I had a baby now I'd like to go back to full-time work. Obviously I'd wait until the baby was a few months old, like I intend to do with all my kids. But the only problem really facing us as single parents now is the fact that we are paying out more than what we earn in babysitting fees. When you get a childminder or a babysitter in, they are charging you over 2 pound an hour, so you are paying out more than what you earn in the end, after the tax, y'know. You get your wages basic then you get the tax taken out which I don't because I earn less than I'm supposed to anyway. But if I was earning enough to work, say I was on a 40-hour week and I was earning so that my tax would be taken out, then I would lose almost over half of what I earned on babysitting. So I wouldn't be any better off than I am now. But I would like to go back to work.'
>
> (Ms Welland, 2–3)

Nevertheless, the constraints of the social security system in the form of the withdrawal of income related benefit is much more immediate than is the tax system for some lone parents.

BENEFIT SYSTEM

For three of the lone parents, Ms Axe, Ms Usk and Ms Taff, the benefit system does not appear to affect directly the amount of work they do. Ms Axe is aware that she can earn up to £15 a week without penalty but wishes to devote all her time to her children. Ms Usk tried claiming when her son was born but found that she could not survive on benefits and has not claimed since except in short periods of sickness. Ms Taff gets most of her income from maintenance payments from her estranged husband; she is constrained by income tax, but not by the benefits regulations, in her labour supply.

However, benefits provide the main income for all the other lone parents. Following the family crisis, Ms Yeo is currently without paid work but is hoping to get another job.

Q: Has it been easier then on social security than you expected?

Ms Yeo: Um ... No. It's, it's harder than what I thought; the money's, like I say, there's not a lot of money and we're still struggling through each fortnight. Wouldn't be so bad if it was paid weekly, but with it paid fortnightly, one week you get the things you got some money, and next week you haven't got nothing.

(Ms Yeo, 7)

Both Ms Usk and Ms Yeo are used to earning a wage and, if anything, the low level of social security support provides an incentive towards paid employment. For the other four, however, the low disregards operate a powerful adverse effect to paid employment in that anything earned in excess of £15 per week is deducted in full from the benefit payable. The choice is therefore to remain with earnings below this level unless a parent is able and willing to work for many more hours. This is illustrated by Ms Dee's position. After some discussion about being allowed to earn only up to £15 a week, Ms Dee is asked about her hours of work:

'That's from 9 till 8; it's only alternative Saturdays, y'see and they class it on a weekly thing which is only 11 hours a week but I'm only just doing, I'm doing tonight and Friday which is two evenings which is 5 till 9 so that'll be an extra 8 hours this week but it works out every alternative week so it's still sort of evens out at less than £15 a week. But what I want to do eventually is to try and do it full time or to get over the 24 hours which means I won't have to claim social security anymore, that makes it a lot easier.'

(Ms Dee, 3)

If she worked for over 24 hours, Ms Dee would then be able to claim family credit (see p. 334).

Ms Fowey had irregular earnings and as a result suffered from uncertainties in the level of benefit received; this was also experienced by other groups in the sample.[3] Combined with low basic levels of benefits such uncertainty seems to provide disincentives to her taking work.

Q: What advantages did you think the job would bring?
Ms Fowey: Just that I would be going out to work. I hoped, I thought
                it would bring in some extra money but by the time it
                worked out I was actually worse off. The social were
                messing me about because I wasn't earning a regular
                wage, it was a different wage each week. It was only part
                time and then by the time I got it all sorted out I had spent
                the money on things that I expected to use. I just couldn't
                sort my money out, it was different all the time.
Q: What made you take the job in the first place?
Ms Fowey: To get a bit extra money, and to be going out to work ...
                [indistinct] ... it's just not worth it.

                                                               (Ms Fowey, 1)

As with Ms Welland the combination of factors including expenses of
babysitting and travelling to and from work can make paid employment
financially unattractive:

Ms Fowey: Yeah. I wasn't earning the same wage each week. When
                you start work, they take your average wage for 5 weeks,
                divide that up yeah your average wage and you get that
                taken out of your money but then they changed the rules
                anyway, saying that you earned 15 pound and that was it,
                'cause before you could earn 4 pound and half of any-
                thing between 4 pound and 20 pound plus expenses but
                then they changed it so you could just earn 15 pound
                which made it awkward as well. It changed it so it just
                kept ... I never held my book while I was at work which
                meant I never had regular money coming in. Some weeks
                I was only getting 8 pound for working and I was
                supposed to live on it.
Q: And your benefit was not making up the difference?
Ms Fowey: They were making it up. I was getting the right money
                when I hassled for it, I had to hassle for it. They back-
                dated it all and everything but unless I hassled them for it
                I didn't get it.
Q: So they stopped paying you altogether?
Ms Fowey: No they didn't stop paying me but I had to keep ringing
                them up to make sure they were paying me. It was so
                awkward not knowing when you were getting your
                money. 'Cause I was still getting more money from social
                than I was work.

Q: You told them you were going to start work?
Ms Fowey: I started work and then I sent my book in. And they
              stopped ... I had giros each week after that or each week
              or fortnight or whatever they decided to send it.
Q: So you could not rely ...
Ms Fowey: On the social, no. I couldn't rely on my wages either
              because, like I said, they would be different each week.

(Ms Fowey, 3)

And again:

'By the time you have paid the bus fares out of the 15 pound you are
allowed to earn you are getting about a tenner. You've got to be working
in the school hours. It's not worth working in the holidays because you
are paying more to go out to work. If you were working 5 hours, it's
about 1 pound an hour, isn't it for a childminder so that's 5 pound. You
wouldn't be working more than about 5 hours part time, would you? You
would be paying to go to work, that really is a waste of time. The job I'm
doing now down there (at Open Learning Centre) is just 3 hours a week
and it is more for the work experience than the money.'

(Ms Fowey, 4)

Ms Welland is also very aware of the £15 limit and earns just £12.
However;

'I earn 12 pound now but out of that 12 pound I am really only earning 6
because I pay the babysitter 6 so for $5\frac{1}{2}$ hours work I'm getting, well it's
longer than that it's 6 hours work I'm getting 6 pound and she is getting 6
pound just over for sitting with the children and I've still got to come home
and do all the housework, the washing and cleaning and cook their meals
and everything.'

(Ms Welland, 6)

Many of the criticisms of the system are similar to those made by women
with partners. Several lone parents describe situations in which they got
into debt through delays, mistakes or misunderstandings with the benefits
authorities. Ms Fowey says that when she started work she could not rely
'on the social, no. I couldn't rely on my wages either because [...] they
would be different each week'. Ms Yeo describes her first benefit claim:
'Took them about 4 weeks before I had any money at all'. This made
budgeting difficult. Ms Taff found that, with the new benefit arrangements
in April 1988, she was responsible for her whole rent.

'So anyway he [benefits officer] looked into it and of course it took a
couple of months to do – well it does now. And by the time it come

through I ended up in arrears [...] owing a hundred and odd pound.'

(Ms Taff, 15)

Living on benefits, lone parents do not – unlike some of their counterparts with partners – mention undeclared cash work. Instead they speak of debts, incurred to catalogue firms, for 'extras' like clothing. Often it is a choice between paying these or spending on basic needs.

> 'I haven't got enough food in the fridge or the cupboards or anything ... but the grand debt is going down [...] Yeah, I bought a load of catalogue stuff. You can't afford it any other way ...'

(Ms Fowey, 8)

Mrs Yeo has the opposite experience:

> 'you've gotta stop and watch every penny [...] just buys the necessary things mainly, you know, like food and ... 'tisn' as if you can go out on an evening or anything 'cause you haven't got the money left over once you've been shopping.'

(Ms Yeo, 3)

Perhaps the final word on the social security system should go to the otherwise articulate Ms Welland: 'I'm really confused by it'.

CONCLUSIONS

In the lone parents' accounts, women sought moral adequacy in terms of a willingness to undertake some form of paid or unpaid employment outside the home; in their rhetoric and their actions, this was stronger than among women with partners. As women on low incomes and with child-care responsibilities it may seem surprising that two of the seven lone-parent respondents undertook voluntary work. However voluntary work is a means of 'getting out of the house', and confers the status of working but does not disturb the security of regular benefits payments or require deductions from wages above the level of disregarded income. It may also offer some useful work experience. It does not, of course, remove the constraints of child care and both the volunteers worked only during school hours. We saw in Chapter 5 that the women with partners also expressed a need to take breaks from child care but saw the route to this through paid rather than unpaid employment.

There are several reasons contributing to this outcome. One obvious factor is that the benefit system with its low disregards can penalise paid employment particularly harshly in these lone-parent households. Another is that lone parents may have a greater need to spend time away from children and with other adults. But these interviewees place most emphasis on employment as inherently satisfying and worthwhile. However, in their accounts the women with partners express a stronger requirement on them (in terms of moral adequacy) to make a *financial contribution* to their households than do the lone parents to theirs. The exception to this is Ms Usk, but she now regrets having sustained her household from her earnings, and claims no moral credit for having done so.

Thus the accounts by these lone parents contain strong appeals to an identity of worker, but much less to one of provider. Employment is a high priority, but they also see their employment as having to be 'fitted in', though without the need to fit in with a spouse. It is important to them that they attend to their children themselves, particularly in their younger years and if a babysitter is required, a relative is much preferred to a paid stranger.

However, even so, the low disregards of the social security system emerge, unsurprisingly, as a powerful potential disincentive to paid employment. In addition, because of the restrictive nature of the UK tax system in not allowing the deduction of many expenses necessarily but not 'wholly and exclusively incurred in the performance of the duties' of the employment (see p. 325), further financial obstacles are placed in the way of such parents seeking paid employment.

REFERENCES

1 See for example J. F. Ermisch and R. E. Wright, 'Employment Dynamics of British Lone Mothers', Discussion Paper 302, Centre for Economic Policy Research, 1989; S. P. Jenkins and J. Millar, 'Income Risk and Income Maintenance: Implications for Incentives to Work', in A. Dilnot and I. Walker (eds), *The Economics of Social Security*, Oxford University Press, 1989; S. P. Jenkins, 'The Probability of Working Full-Time: A Multivariate Analysis of the 1989 Lone Parents Survey', University of Bath, 1990.
2 For the relationship between unemployment and psychological wellbeing see John T. Haworth and Stephen T. Evans, 'Meaningful Activity and Unemployment', in D. Fryer and P. Ullah (eds) *Unemployed People*, Open University Press, 1987, pp. 241–67; P. Warr, 'Job Loss, Unemployment and Psychological Well-being', in V. L. Allen and E. van der Vliert (eds) *Role Transitions*, Penum, 1984.
3 See Sarah Buckland and Patrick Dawson, 'The Claiming Process: From Here to Eternity', Paper Presented to the British Sociological Association, Annual Conference, Loughborough University, March 1986.

9 Conclusions: trapped in poverty?

One of the paradoxes of the subject we chose for our study is the gap between the intimate nature of the phenomena, and the grandiose theories they inspire. Labour-market decisions in low-income households are intrinsically small-scale and humble, yet – as we set out in the second chapter – they have given rise to theorising by the major social thinkers of the modern age. A question we never satisfactorily answered is why there have been so few empirical studies of these decisions, despite their acknowledged importance for social policy formation.

Starting from the grandiose, we have been driven further and further back into the intimate in the course of our analysis. In Chapter 6, we came to the conclusion that the clue to the labour-market decisions in the respondents' households lay not so much in the wider public world of wage rates and benefit levels, as in their discussions about spending patterns, and the income they needed to sustain these. We outlined a number of income strategies, based on the way these couples budgeted to cover their basic expenses and 'extras', such as clothing, leisure items, and (for some) the attempt to buy their own council house.

This is in line with recent economic and sociological theory about household decision-making, which has questioned the assumptions behind their respective disciplines' analyses. As Jan Pahl comments, economists 'have created a black box in the space between earning and spending'[1] – though as we have seen recent work has tried to penetrate the box.[2] What our study offers is a glimpse inside, and (as suspected by several writers on decision-making in the household) the way in which household expenditure is managed turns out to be of crucial significance for other aspects of behaviour.

Most of our data consist of interviewees' retrospective reconstructions of their past decisions, within the normative framework of how men and women who are parents of children should behave. As part of their accounts, they describe their reasons for decisions in terms of the economic advantages they produce: they display rhetorical skills in reconciling these with the moral requirements of their roles. Yet in the final analysis, this attempted reconciliation only makes sense in the context of the expenditure decisions they have already committed themselves to, and which emerge in their joint accounts as the determinants of their choice of work. These in turn must be understood in relation to their positions as regular or irregular workers, roles which are largely structured by employers' demand for labour, and by the way the benefits system sustains the incomes of people who do not have regular employment.

In this chapter we make our final analysis of the process of decision-making by concentrating in detail on the joint interviews with two couples in the process of change. Mr and Mrs Derwent have very recently decided to buy their house, and are about to start repayments of their mortgage: both are considering changing their jobs to facilitate this. Ms Waveney and Mr Trent have only recently formed a household, and are in the process of evolving their system of budgeting, and hence their income strategy. Hence both these situations allow us to look at what underpins the particular decisions accounted for in our interviews, at the dynamics of the relations between the couple. Mr and Mrs Derwent are, in effect, negotiating about how they will fulfil their roles in their new situation. Ms Waveney and Mr Trent are constructing the consequences of deciding to live together. These two joint interviews should allow us to see how couples handle the immediate consequences of a joint expenditure decision (the missing link in our theory that such decisions are followed by individual employment adjustments), and how they decide to become couples (the missing starting point in our theory of the roles and norms of 'man' and 'woman' in these accounts).

Having thus completed our analysis of the interviews, we then return for the last time to the theoretical issues of our study. Are employment decisions to be understood in terms of calculative or social/moral considerations? The analysis shows how labour-market decisions are located within normative structures but that these are derived from productive and administrative categories. The 'social forms'[3] available to the interviewees for the construction of their versions of their decision-making are part of the repertoire of ways in which actions have to be done in contemporary British society to be properly accomplished.[4] Moral adequacy is therefore attainable only in terms of the stock of social forms. These forms are structured through employment and government administration, which systematise, standardise and normalise behaviours, defining what constitutes 'work', and what is recognised as 'initiative' or 'enterprise' (and what in turn as 'crime' or 'dependence') and what is 'normal'.[5] The analysis of roles in terms of officially sanctioned social forms should be read as complementing our analysis of norms in terms of the shared culture of the estate (Chapter 7).

We have shown in our analysis of the individual interviews with men and women that the normative framework of their accounts – the roles which they produce and reproduce, and in terms of which they seek to give morally adequate versions of their decisions – is structured by the social forms characteristic of the politically organised subjection of poor people in British society. Through the official categorisation and regulation of unemployment, poverty and low-paid work, our interviewees are provided with 'an expected set of connected ways' of doing things which, as Philip Corrigan points out, supplies a range of social identities which are 'coercively encouraged', but also establishes enlarged human capacities and new forms of love and solidarity.[6] This paradox of state administrative power – that it structures both the subordination and the freedom of subjects – has been demonstrated in each of the chapters.

Inevitably, because of the research questions we set ourselves, our study, too, has been structured around the requirements of that process of government administration and regulation. We have tended to focus on our interviewees' accounts of their decisions in terms of the tax and benefits system and the structure of labour market, at the expense of other features of their versions. We included Mr and Mrs Cam's accounts of their problems with employers and the benefit authorities, but not of their house fire. Yet – as we shall briefly indicate in this chapter – even their descriptions of autonomous activities, their private pains and pleasures and their yearnings for alternatives to their current work roles (Mrs Parrett's poetry, Mrs Cam's art, Mrs Bow's panic attacks, Mr Calder's ambitions) are constructed within the social forms that provide the available elements in the identity of a poor person in British society today.

This has important implications for our final attempt to draw together some policy conclusions to the book. It is easy enough to string together a series of criticisms of the tax and benefits system. Our findings on these are not particularly original: they largely echo those of McLaughlin, Millar and Cooke, for example.[7] It is much more difficult to consider how alternative proposals for radical changes in these systems can be assessed in the light of these findings – and hence to contribute directly to the debates about whether the tax and benefits system should be integrated, for example, or whether benefits should be made more universal and unconditional, or more 'targeted' and conditional.

This is because our respondents' accounts are structured by the present systems, in just the ways we have been analysing. Hence perhaps the furthest we can go, beyond pointing out the ways in which these systems are failing in their own terms, is to draw attention to the ways in which our interviewees are – in constructing their own amendments to the current rules and regulations (for example, over undeclared cash work) – actually creating an alternative system, which is more workable for them. We will argue that this alternative system has many of the features of a Partial Basic Income scheme[8] – a small unconditional income for each adult member of the household, allowing them to cover certain basic household expenses while doing part-time or irregular work.

A HOUSEHOLD IN TRANSITION: MR AND MRS DERWENT

We argued in Chapter 6 that the income strategies characteristic of these households take the form of joint decisions on expenditure, and individual decisions about work as a means to provide the income to cover this expenditure. However, we have also shown that women – because they construct themselves, and are constructed by their partners, as holding primary responsibility for caregiving – have to negotiate substitutes for themselves when they enter paid work, and that a good deal of give and take is required to allow couples to fit their hours together when they are both in employment. We pointed out that negotiation is about unpaid work – how it is to be shared – rather than paid work.

Mr and Mrs Derwent provide a case study in these processes, because they decided to buy their council house just before their individual interviews took place, and were negotiating about the changes that they needed to make in order to finance this, around the time of (and even during) their joint interview. Hence they give an insight into the forms of negotiation that take place between couples over how their employment can fit together so as to cover their outgoings (the mortgage repayment 'works out nearly double what the rent is') and allow the household tasks to be done.

After explaining about buying the house, Mr and Mrs Derwent tell Helen Kay that they are both contemplating changes in their employment. Mrs Derwent has applied for a nursing auxiliary post:

Mrs Derwent: ... Yeah, I mean whether I get it ... It's at [hospital's name] but it's half past 3 till 9 ... in the evening [...]
Mr Derwent: Yeah, 'cause I been offered [indistinct]
Mrs Derwent: Oh yeah, he's been offered another job.
Q: Have you?
Mrs Derwent: It's the same place but he starts at 2 in the morning. Isn'it? 1 in the morning?
Q: What, you actually start in the night?

Mr Derwent: Yeah. Instead of working all evening like in there as well
                as the night, I'm starting in the morning and work till the,
                till the daytime like.

                                                        (Mr and Mrs Derwent, 33)

His new job would be driving, and he has to pass his HGV (Heavy Goods
Vehicle) licence to get it – he is in the middle of a course. They are unsure
about whether it will be more money, but it may have other advantages.

Mrs Derwent: I dunno what the money'll be like, nothing like that. But
                at least it means we got the evenings together [...]
Q: If you get the hospital job you won't see each other in the
                evenings?
Mrs Derwent: I'd be home by 9...
Mr Derwent: Yeah.
Mrs Derwent: ... so I mean it's not ... I mean ... [indistinct] like, I mean
                I wouldn't stay there, I mean it's just like really sort of
                say, oh do the house and everything up isn't it? I mean, I
                wouldn't, I wouldn't plan on staying there for the rest of
                ... you know, years ahead. It's only [indistinct] a year so
                we do everything like [...] I just wanna make sure there's
                enough money ... of doing it, you know, till we get sort of
                in, into it.

                                                     (Mr and Mrs Derwent, 34–5)

Mrs Derwent says that she gets tired in the evenings, and he says that he
sometimes goes without sleep in the day. He finds it very hard when he has
to be responsible for all three children all day, and they are glad when he
goes back to work. Later Mrs Derwent criticises him for working excessively long hours on some occasions when he is asked to do so, and for not
standing up for himself against the management. She gets very angry when
he drives after working all night: 'well it's too long. He'll kill himself like
that [...] I was fuming ... wasn't I?'.

Q: So you would give your husband advice on his job?
Mrs Derwent: He won't take it. I might try ... put me penny's worth in
                ... but ...

                                                        (Mr and Mrs Derwent, 45)

However, Mr Derwent immediately contrasts this with their joint decisions
over spending. He says 'I never [indistinct] ... I won't buy nothing unless I
ask you will I?' and she agrees: 'Oh yeah, we, we discuss it ...'. She points
out that he used to be very different, before they had the children, and when
they were both working full time, and she was earning more than him; then
they both spent more on themselves, especially on clothes:

Mrs Derwent: No, I used to be different mind you, didn't I? [laughs] ...
I used to be ... oh [indistinct] when I used to come home
I used to ... long as I had the chequebook on me it was ...
well away.

Mr Derwent: [indistinct] not one shirt – four shirts ... yeah.

Mrs Derwent: Then I'd get, say, three pairs of jeans to go with 'em
[indistinct]. Oh you grow up, don't you, in the end
though.

(Mr and Mrs Derwent, 46)

Hence the contrast is drawn between a previous pattern of individual, undiscussed spending, and their present system – a joint-managed pool – established once the children were born. They acknowledge that their system is still rather haphazard:

Mr Derwent: I always just ... we just chuck the money together and ...
well, when it's gone it's gone i'n'it? I mean we don't ...

Mrs Derwent: We've always got mine to fall back on.

Mr Derwent: We work out our bills, like, put back for them, but the
money that's left we don't ... actually budget out for
different things. We just draw on it when we want it don't
we?

Mrs Derwent: That's right, I mean my money we know is always there.
Like in the bank, you know, but I mean we had like a
driveway and that put in – we was a bit skint this [laughs]
last couple of weeks.

(Mr and Mrs Derwent, 54)

This joint-pool system requires them to discuss and decide together in a way which causes disagreements which they jokingly rehearse. But it is contrasted with decision-making over employment, which is made by them as individuals. Her present choice – whether or not to expand her working hours by taking an extra part-time job – is seen as hers to make. She comments that 'if I was working 50 hours a week – be truthful – and the, and the kids were fine you wouldn't say nothing, would you? You wouldn't'. He acknowledges that 'it's up to her' but points out that 'if I earned enough money you'd stay at home'. Here they both construct his role as ideally the one of providing enough income to cover the whole of family expenditure, but hers as making a contribution which is necessary in their particular circumstances over household outgoings. This contribution is hers to organise and choose, subject to discussions over arrangements for child care and domestic tasks.

At this point the practical complications of their job changes become explicit, and their conflicts over unpaid work overt. As she says:

Mrs Derwent: that's the only time where we row where we can't, and if
              he's truthful we cannot agree on ... is what should be done
              and who should do it. 'Cause I mean ...
Q: At home?
Mrs Derwent: Yeah at home ... that ... Oh no ...
Q: Not about jobs, but jobs at home? [...]
Mrs Derwent: I mean it's a shame on him. I know I've nagged him. This
              room here has taken – what? [...] this has taken him a year
              and a half ... about that [...]
Mr Derwent: Rome wasn't built in a day.
Mrs Derwent: Yeah, precisely, it was built in a ... under a year I 'spect.

                                            (Mr and Mrs Derwent, 55)

They say they have plenty of rows (considering that they hardly see each other) about work in the house. But it emerges that, with the proposed changes in working hours, that is not their only problem.

Q: Do you manage to share the car without any [indistinct]?
Mrs Derwent: This new job is gonna cause a problem.
Mr Derwent: Yeah, she'll have to walk.
Mrs Derwent: How can I walk?
Mr Derwent: [laughs]
Mrs Derwent: I benefit 'cause I gets paid all me petrol. I can't, I need the
              car. I mean without the car I couldn't get the job.
Mr Derwent: I'll get a pushbike.
Mrs Derwent: But he starts work at 2 and I ain't getting up to drive
              anybody to work at 2 in the morning.

                                          (Mr and Mrs Derwent, 56–7)

This is left unresolved. They go on to say how both of them have had to give up their weekly night out (her Wednesday, his Thursday) at darts, and how they have lost friends through not having time to socialise. She dislikes being on her own in the house, and is nervous at night when he is away.

Mrs Derwent: I mean it gets to a point where I've had it. I w, and I mean
              ... It's, I know it sounds daft and that but I mean it, it's not
              like being married really, ... the amount of time we spend
              together i'n'it? [...] It just seems I spend all my time on
              my own. I mean I get really depressed occasionally, don't
              I? And I really gets worried. And I thinks, well I'm on my
              own all the time, all I ... My life reverbs round work and

the kids ... and the ironing, dishes. I know I keep bringing
that up but that really bugs me you see.

(Mr and Mrs Derwent, 61)

She talks about their son being ill when he was young – 'I mean it was
always me that had to cope'. She has limited help from her parents, because
they, too, work long hours – her father a shiftworker, her mother a nurse.[9]
By the end of the interview Mr Derwent's contribution has become mono-
syllabic.

This joint interview gives a picture of the stresses endured and sacrifices
made in households striving to improve their material standard of living[10]
in the face of low wages and what Mr Derwent identifies (p. 129) as the
poverty trap. In order to buy their house, both are giving up a good deal of
their social support and recreational activities, they are largely living
separate daily existences, Mrs Derwent feels anxious, lonely and depressed,
and they find it very difficult to agree about a fair division of labour over
unpaid tasks. The jointness of their planning of consumption expenditure is
in stark contrast with the separation of their working lives, and it is difficult
for them to negotiate the detailed domestic preconditions for their labour-
market participation. We expect to find that higher-income households
working these hours employ childminders, home helps or even *au pairs*.

It also helps explain the high rate of marital breakdown on the estate –
how the struggle to escape from poverty can itself precipitate the break-up
of households. This seems to have happened in the first marriages of Mr
Tamar, Mrs Cherwell and Mrs Medway, two of whom owned their houses
during their first marriage. However, couples that split up do usually form
reconstituted families, and it is to this process of household formation that
we now turn.

HOUSEHOLD FORMATION: MS WAVENEY AND MR TRENT

Ms Waveney was a single parent, bringing up her daughter with some
support from her mother, until the winter of the interview: now she and Mr
Trent are engaged and living together, and she is expecting his child. She
has come off income support and his earnings support the household. He
has a regular job as a meat-cutter, and earns just too much for them to claim
family credit. Hence they are in the process of organising their new household budgeting system and planning their future pattern of expenditure and
employment when the interview occurs. It provides an opportunity to see
how a couple see their relationship at its outset, and how administrative
systems influence the income strategy they adopt.

After she left school, Ms Waveney worked in a shop on a YTS (Youth
Training Scheme), was unemployed for a time, did some factory work and

some work in an old people's home (which she enjoyed), married a soldier, left work when she became pregnant, and was deserted by her husband soon afterwards. Mr Trent (who is now 31) got his job soon after leaving school, and has been in it for 15 years. He used to work short hours and spend his money on drink and leisure, but all that has changed. Asked whether he ever turns down overtime he replies:

Mr Trent:	Occasionally, but not very often – not now. I used to turn it down all the time [laughs] before I met Les [laugh] but ah ... [child speaks]
Q:	Why's that? How's that changed?
Mr Trent:	Well before I used to work and I used to leave and I used ... well weather like this I'd be straight to the beach. [laughs]
Ms Waveney:	When he was single.
Mr Trent:	Yeah when I was single, or to the pub ... playing pool, you know [pause]. But I'm more committed now. So I try to pick up as many pennies as I can [laugh] [...] Well I come and just hand me wage packet straight over, don't open it.
Q:	Do you?
Mr Trent:	Yeah. I just get me little pocket money. [laughs]
Ms Waveney:	Yeah. [indistinct]
Q:	So what, you give it, you organise the money [...]?
Ms Waveney:	I do all the bills and that because he's not used to it, see. 'Cause he's just come into the family like [indistinct] ...
Mr Trent:	I mean, compared to what I was doing before, I was earning the money and spending it straight away ...
Q:	And that works out reasonably well?
Ms Waveney:	'Cause I've learnt to control money and ... pay the bills and what was ever left we could spend. As long as all the bills, and you got the food and the house and ... we're clothed ... then all the rest is just spending money ...
Mr Trent:	Yeah, we're quite happy with it. It's enough, if I've got money I want to spend it but if I haven't got it in me pocket I can't spend it so it do'n' really affect me that much [...]
Q:	[indistinct] ... that's all changed has it?
Ms Waveney:	Yeah. [indistinct]
Mr Trent:	Yeah, well we met last August and since then everything's gone topsy-turvy for me [laughs] ...

Ms Waveney: [laughs] Very ... very strange to start with. I'm b, I'm getting used to it now ... sort of since Christmas I've been settling down.

(Ms Waveney and Mr Trent, 8–9)

Mr Trent, until so recently the carefree and pleasure-oriϵntated single man, is already constructing himself as a regular worker and provider of family income. Asked about promotion he replies:

Mr Trent: Um [pause] well there would be, I mean ... if I, if I really did want promotion, you know backalong then I probably could have got it. But I was quite happy with what I was doing and just finishing and no overtime and ... but now I'll be looking for promotion; there is a chance of promotion ... so that was only for the money ... now.

Q: What you need more money now?

Mr Trent: Well the more money I can get, the better for the family ...

(Ms Waveney and Mr Trent, 10)

He sees the tax system as helping in the process of transforming himself into a new social identity. He still pays income tax as a single man, so it is still not very advantageous to do overtime:

'if I do 5 or 6 hours overtime and then they say, right, would you work Saturday morning, I'd turn it down because I know most of that would go on tax so I'd only be going in for about 10 or 15 pound, whereas I'd be earning 30 and that, half, at least half of that would be going in tax [...] I mean, being single, I am not in married man's tax; we're just living together. But if, if we were married then p'raps I wouldn't because I'd be getting, wouldn' be paying so much tax ... but I don't know that until it happens [laugh] ...'

(Ms Waveney and Mr Trent, 10)

Mr Trent has considered changing his job in the past and more recently but now – like Mr Calder, Mr Avon and Mr Rother – he is very aware of the importance of security:

'I've thought about changing me job, yeah, but where I am now I think more of the security 'cause I've been there so long ... with living with a family like I've gotta think more of security than another job. I could start another job tomorrow and be made redundant 6 months later – as, where I am now I'm, I know I'm in a secure job.'

(Ms Waveney and Mr Trent, 10)

At this early stage of their relationship, Ms Waveney and Mr Trent expect to discuss their employment decisions, and construct joint decision-making as the norm in their relationship.

Ms Waveney: Yeah, I wouldn' expect him to go there and come home one day and say 'Les I've left this job 'cause I'm going for this one', 'cause it would shock me. If he come home and said, 'this [indistinct] ...,' we'd look into it together.

Mr Trent: We look into everything together sort of you know, well I do [laughs].

Q: Would you expect to influence your wife's decisions?

Mr Trent: I would, yeah. We'd talk about it and if she was happy then I'd be happy you know ... but um I'd like to talk about it before. I mean we do talk about everything ... but if she didn't, I mean 'twould be a shock to me I think, you know, going behind me back. But ... you know, if she, if we talked about it and she was happy I wouldn't stop her.

(Ms Waveney and Mr Trent, 13)

They have already discussed the possibility of buying the council house, but the mortgage would be too much for them: repayment would put them under a lot of strain, and 'the children would suffer'. Ms Waveney anticipates problems for her in getting back into the labour market because her skills will be rusty and out-of-date (for example with computers).

In the final part of the joint interview, they explain the process of changing from her status as single-parent claimant of income support to being treated as a household unit. The benefit authorities were prompt in taking away her money when notified they were living together. This was done far more quickly than adjustments in the other direction: they had to get advice on income tax from the Citizens' Advice Bureau.

Ms Waveney: When you owe them money they'll ... they're there in about 2 days but [indistinct] ...

Mr Trent: ... but if I can get my tax code sort of highered so that I can earn more before tax [...] if I hadn' have gone there and looked into it then ...

(Ms Waveney and Mr Trent, 20)

Similarly, they are now paying full rent (£46 a fortnight) because of his earnings (£110–20 per week); they have claimed family credit but were turned down as £2 over the limit – they may be eligible when the new baby is born. They were very disappointed to be turned down.

Ms Waveney: ... it really does annoy you. You can't win either way.
Mr Trent: [indistinct] 2 quid less a week we could have been picking about 30 quid extra on top so ... so we're [...] Catch 22 [indistinct] i'n'it?

(Ms Waveney and Mr Trent, 21)

Ms Waveney and Mr Trent are thus seen in the process of constructing themselves as a couple, who budget by means of a female whole wage system, providing for all household expenditure through his secure, if low-paid, job. Already they are describing the perils of redundancy and fears of time spent on the dole: ''Cause I think it would be very hard to get another job if I ever did, was out of a job' – Ms Waveney adds especially at his age (31). Like other households with a regular male worker (Taw, Avon, Calder) they are cautious about buying their house, seeing renting as safer. Although they are not yet married, the timing of the process of their household foundation is largely dictated by the administration of state systems. First they have to declare themselves as living together, and get their benefits adjusted to take account of this, resulting in a very substantial loss of income. Next they try for family credit, wait for it to be processed, and find they are not eligible – in the meanwhile trying to budget on his earnings. Finally, their marriage decision will be influenced by the availability of an extra tax allowance against his earnings (see pp. 326–7).

ROLES AND IDENTITIES

The last two sections have been about the respondents constructing transformations in themselves in the interviews. Mr and Mrs Derwent, who very much enjoyed the 18 months that he was unemployed, and both did undeclared cash jobs during that period (see p. 102 and p. 164) are changing their employments in order to become owner occupiers. Ms Waveney and Mr Trent are changing from being impoverished single-parent claimant and leisure-orientated bachelor respectively, into a careful, responsible couple – he a regular worker doing overtime and seeking promotion, she the manager of the family's finances.

These transformations raise some fundamental issues for economic and social theory: they also raise questions about the explanatory status of theoretical models. Clearly no economist would claim that a micro-economic model of choices made according to preferences under constraint can *explain* the processes of decision-making that we described in these two sections. Economic models are not explanations in this sense – they are *models* of behaviour, which function rather like decoy ducks.[11] The latter do not really look very much like ducks, and certainly do not behave like ducks (except that they float). Yet despite their wooden and unrealistic features, real ducks 'adopt' them as if they are ducks. In much the same way, people who conduct their lives in markets adopt economic discourse to legitimate their actions, and use it selectively within their accounts of decision-making. For instance, Mr Derwent says that when they are in their early 50s they will be able to sell their house, cash in on their discount as tenants, buy a flat and take early retirement; Mrs Derwent adds, 'He's worked it all out he has'.

Yet many of the same issues arise in relation to sociological theory, and especially its analysis of behaviour in terms of roles and norms. Are we really to suppose that people embrace such constructions as constituting the whole of their identities, and exhausting all their potentialities? If so, how can we explain changes like the ones described in this chapter, and the endless variation in these accounts? Social theory needs to be able to account for the way in which people occupy different, and often apparently contradictory, roles from one hour to the next, and how they handle the tensions and incongruities between them.

This becomes possible through the use of a concept of *identity*. Outside simple societies, human beings are preoccupied with the question 'Who am I?', and aware of the multiple, confusing and contradictory nature of social roles. Modern psychological literature is reflected in a popular pre-occupation with identifying 'the real me'. Mr Trent seems to be recognising the disorientating effects of changing his role when he says 'since then everything's gone topsy-turvy for me'. But the idea of a more mobile, malleable identity[12] is also attractive to him, and he uses the market-orientated, consumerist discourse of 'freedom of choice' and escape from state interference to express this. He is considering joining a private health insurance scheme:

'I think national insurance ... I pay a lot of that as well, and I'm sort of thinking ... with all the hospital charges they're doing now, I mean why should I be paying that when I could sort of go into it, sort of de, independently ... [indistinct] go on a private scheme [...] I mean I hardly ever get ill or anything and to me I've ... it seems a waste of time ... for what, they offer me now. And they're on about going private.'

(Mr Trent, 12)

Though he is quick to say that he knows the NHS (National Health Service) is very good, he is worried about the changes being made, and thinks he may not be getting value for money in the state system. But he adds:

'I mean I'm not blaming ... the health service at all ... I think it's more the government.'

(Mr Trent, 12)

A great deal of the talking done in all the interviews is about the construction and management of identities, through balancing and reconciling the many aspects of roles, and the norms of different spheres of social life. This talk is conducted within the repertoire provided by social forms – the approved and administratively reinforced and regulated ways of doing things properly in society. Hence moral adequacy is sought by reference to norms which are structured by these forms, and the motives and behaviours that they systematise and normalise. Mr Ribble, as an irregular worker, constructs himself as 'self-employed', 'independent' and a 'risk taker' within the social grammar of the enterprise paradigm, according to the standardised form of an entrepreneur.[13] Yet it is only months ago that he was a homeless claimant. Mrs Calder constructs herself as a woman who is simultaneously contributing to the household income and exercising her brain in her part-time job (as a shelf-filler), having previously legitimated this activity by demonstrating that she has made satisfactory arrangements for the care of her children. Yet she really wanted to be a soldier or a police officer.

Philip Corrigan has forcefully reminded us that role performance is not necessarily role compliance, and compliance is not necessarily a sign of commitment. 'People have cognitive, affective, and above all somatic senses, perspectives, longings, hopes, desires, which cannot be fitted into the ways in which they are coercively encouraged to behave'.[14] People need to adopt social forms, and to survive by behaving themselves, but this compliance is often tactical. Despite the networks of female support described in Chapter 7, many of the women in our study (who emphasise 'putting children first') are constructing their identities through repressing their desires. In Mrs Derwent's case, the strain on her shows in her anxiety about being alone, and morbid preoccupations.

'You know I think my house could go bang. You know, if I step out that gate that's it. This is up in flames. Oh I hate it. Terry says, well you'd be safe. I says, yeah, but I wouldn't have the kids. If we gotta go I wanna go together. You know, I panic.'

(Mr and Mrs Derwent, 60)

Mrs Bow has panic attacks too. Hers, however, take a rather different form. Mrs Bow mobilises her panic attacks as part of her identity, and as rather congruent with her role as the partner of an irregular worker, in a household that uses benefits strategically, and in which both partners do undeclared cash work.

'Gets on me nerves, housework every day [...] It's hard work i'n'it? Annoys you really. I was told, mind you, I could have, go in for a pension, um a thing, 19.50 a week, I haven' looked into it yet because I just ... can't be bothered to go right into it actually. 'Cause I suffers from me nerves very badly so ... nerves can stop you doing a lot of things ... like what you wanna do ... 'cause I can't enjoy me life 'cause I got this nerve trouble ... you know ... Panic attacks [indistinct] ... Can't breathe and ... funny heads and ... I had an illness I couldn't go out for 12 months, that sort of thing. I've had it now for 4 years [...] It's a, it makes your relationship very hard, 'cause I'm always leaving see, running away from it. My husband ... accepts it but ... when I'm in a panic attack no one can stop me doing what I'm going do, you know.'

(Mrs Bow, 18–19)

Both Mrs Derwent and Mrs Bow use the same word to describe their experiences, but their accounts have very different flavours. Mrs Derwent's has about it the feel of 'the hidden injuries of class'[15] – the wounds inflicted, partly by herself, in the name of striving for security and a measure of comfort. Mrs Bow's version is altogether more active and purposeful – her 'attacks' are just that, ways of getting things done. Yet both construct their versions of their feelings within the same social form, that of a woman with anxiety problems about her domestic role.

As with so many other lengthy passages in the interviews, Mrs Derwent and Mrs Bow are explaining why their situations are apparently divergent from the norm, and justifying them in terms of the norm – as exceptions that prove the rule. In their case it is the norm of 'jointness' that is breached by Mrs Derwent's feelings of isolation and depression, and Mrs Bow's periodic desertion of her husband. In both cases thay deploy medical, psychological and therapeutic knowledge to achieve moral adequacy, by showing that they understand their behaviour in terms of the officially sanctioned discourse about such emotions.

Transformations, such as the Derwents' and the Waveney-Trents', are possible because these interviewees do not have strong or singular role commitments. Like others', their talk is rehearsing and experimenting with alternative identities. This is very explicit in Mrs Parrett's account of herself as 'spreading her wings' and re-experiencing some freedom in going for typing lessons and sports activities, after bringing up six children.

'So it was a while ago that I ... sort of breaking away from it all [laughs]. Not breaking away from it all anyway. Spreading my wings [...] it's nice to know that once the kids are off to school in the morning the day is my own. I can choose what I want to do, and I don't have to think oh, will I be able to get the buggy on the bus, you know, all these little things [...] I can ring up a friend and say, "Do you want to go swimming, do you want a game of badminton?" or whatever. It's it's really great [...] But just knowing that ... you've got to be home by half past 3 that's it. A bit like Cinderella [laughs]. But it is nice. Forgot what it [indistinct] well I'd completely forgotten what it was like.'

(Mrs Parrett, 15)

Yet this 'freedom' is itself constructed within social forms. As Corrigan points out, society is held together by norms (coercive encouragements) which provide a set of approved expressive behaviours. These in turn are sustained by official (and hence legitimated) authorities which standardise and normalise activities. For instance, Mrs Parrett goes to English classes, where there is a teacher who is authorised to say what poetry should be like. The teacher has asked her to write a poem about November, and suggested how she should do it:

'she says words like um, you know, "blustery" and "auburn leaves" an' oh God [...] that's her thoughts on November i'n'it? It's not mine, see.'

(Mr and Mrs Parrett, 41)

Mrs Parrett is able to draw on a different repertoire of words and feelings for her poem, which reads:

November
Worry, worry, worry, worry,
Worry, worry, worry,
Christmas.

(Mr and Mrs Parrett, 41)

Her poem expresses both vividly and creatively the way in which the celebration and festivity of Christmas is linked with anxiety over finding the money to pay for it. In all the accounts, freedom, autonomy and pleasure are constructed within the frameworks supplied by economy and state administration. Identities are confirmed and sustained through practices which reflect and reproduce power relations.[16] It is because they give freedom and pleasure as well as constraint and pain that they are a source of meaning and identity for those who participate in them.[17] Mr Bow's identity is constructed around claiming and doing undeclared work: his pleasures are constructed around freedom and illegality. Hunting with his dogs

'That's the only, that's me, you know that's the enjoyment I get [indistinct] it's the only enjoyment I get really ... going out with 'em [...] Rabbits, hares, foxes, deer or you know that's ... well it's ... ain't s'posed to some of the things but ... most of it I, I get it all.'

(Mr Bow, 16)

He then constructs an ingenious legitimation of his hunting and selling of the catch (which he says earns about £20 a week, but has sometimes earned £100). He acknowledges that he does not pay tax, and that the social security authorities might disapprove if they found out, but manages to show how it falls within their regulations.

> '... if I go out rabbiting [...] it's me dogs do the work, see ... And that money don't go into me wife's ... or me, it actually goes back into food for the animals.'
>
> (Mr Bow, 16)

In a brilliantly creative move, Mr Bow thus shows that his dogs, which are not claiming benefit, are both the workers and the beneficiaries of his hunting activities and hence he is blameless. This discourse conjures up a vivid image of a kind of hunting which is constructed within the social security regulations, taking place at night (and hence not during normal working hours), and involving neither effort nor reward for the hunter, who merely observes his dogs earning their keep – and enjoys it.

TRAPPED IN POVERTY? POLICY IMPLICATIONS

Which (if any) of the couples discussed in this chapter is trapped in poverty? Are the Derwents and the Waveney-Trents, with their earnings just outside the limits for family credit, and their difficulties in increasing their income? Are the Parretts, with their six children, and their irregular work patterns – such that he gives up paid work when she leaves her part-time job, and she gives up her employment when he is made redundant? Are the Bows, in trouble with the benefit authorities, but both with access to undeclared cash work?

Our analysis makes us very cautious about trying to answer these questions. All of these couples describe occasions when they have felt excluded from the labour market, from benefits, or from both. Yet their accounts of decision-making are constructed within the social relations of that same labour market and benefits system. Their identities are negotiated and made significant by their skills in handling the roles derived from those structures of power-knowledge – the Derwents and Waveney-Trents as hard-working and independent, responsible as workers and as parents; the Parretts as versatile, flexible and adaptable, surviving despite adversity and insecurity, and still learning new skills and new freedoms; the Bows as ingenious and subtle but principled manipulators of the state's welfare systems, with a special talent for breeding and killing animals. Although they all talk at times of traps, vicious circles or 'Catch 22', their accounts describe themselves as forging their identities within these same structures.

Hence none of them analyses or criticises the labour market or the benefits system from the detached stance of an academic or a politician: they speak as insiders, experienced in the arts of living within the regulatory constraints of both. It is very difficult, for instance, to relate their accounts to Lawrence Mead's prescriptions for 'reintegrating' the poor into society.

> If society seriously wants more of the disadvantaged to work regularly, to achieve goals like integration, then it must require them to. Merely to offer the jobless freedom and opportunity to work will not suffice, at least under current conditions. Work must be treated as a public obligation, akin to paying taxes or obeying the Law.[18]

This pronouncement – which has been echoed by British politicians such as Michael Heseltine – reads oddly in the context of our interviews. It is difficult to imagine someone saying this to the respondents: the Derwents and the Waveney-Trents do not need to be reminded of their obligations, and the Parretts and the Bows would be unlikely to see its relevance to their situation. Yet the claims of the opposite school of thought read equally strangely:

> Poverty spells exclusion from the full rights of citizenship ... and under-mines people's ability to fulfil the private and public obligations of citizenship ... The exclusion of millions of our fellow citizens from the enjoyment of the full fruits of citizenship that a wealthy society like ours can provide is an issue for public, not private, morality.[19]

These couples certainly do not construct themselves as excluded from society, nor as members of an underclass. They describe themselves as active in pursuit of their purposes within a framework of roles and norms which they assume others (such as the interviewer) share – hence perhaps their frequent use of expressions like 'you know' and 'i'n'it?'. Hence they would find very strange such comments as:

> the least well-off in our society are being detached from the mainland of general prosperity in such a way as to mock the idea of belonging to one another, or a shared citizenship.[20]

We have emphasised throughout our analysis that interviews are a particular context for interactions, and that interviewees' descriptions of their decisions are constructed for this particular context. However, within the interviews, respondents display a range of interpretative practices which – although not necessarily the full range available to them – are more variable and less internally consistent than some analyses might suggest.[21] Thus although Mr Tamar's account of his attitudes towards men's and women's employment roles is probably different from the one he would give in the pub (see pp. 77–8), he also gives rather different versions in his individual and joint interviews, and modifies his statements under questioning and in response to comments from his wife. Because the interviewer was interested in pursuing respondents' reasoning about decisions, and the role of benefits in these, she was free to ask questions and request clarification, and – particularly in joint interviews – to bring in the partner's perspective. Since all versions of decision-making and all accounting practices were relevant for our study, she was not seeking one 'true' or 'standard' account, and this allowed a range of interpretative practices to be displayed.[22] Our analysis then allows us to show the range of such practices, and how they are used to achieve moral adequacy. This range enables us to generalise about a topic such as benefits, first showing which elements in the accounts are context-specific (for example, Mr and Mrs Dart think that Helen Kay is a health visitor) and which emerge as part of the normative structure of social relations.

We have been at pains in our analysis to locate comments on benefits in the normative structure of employment decisions by individuals and households. At this stage of our argument it therefore feels safe to generalise – to lift them out of this context, and examine them more closely for the relationship between working and claiming that they construct, and the interpretative range that the descriptions of such decisions display.

Although they produce many of the critical comments on benefits to be found in other qualitative studies of poverty,[23] the interviewees do not display a *theory* of poverty, how to prevent it or even how to alleviate it, nor do they make social policy prescriptions. Speaking as insiders, they display their knowledge of the system and how to get by within it, the absurdities and arbitrariness of certain aspects, and how the very behaviours it pretends to encourage are actually frustrated or blocked by it. But they say little or nothing about how it might be reformed, or reconstructed according to new principles. (The exceptions to this are Mr and Mrs Frome, see p. 163.)

Yet something rather important for policy can be gleaned from their accounts, and especially from those of the irregular workers who are in and out of employment – the women as well as the men. Although they display quite detailed knowledge of the regulations, even those respondents who display exceptional commitment in their accounts to the ethic of hard work and family responsibility do not keep these rules. Mr and Mrs Derwent both did undeclared cash work when he was unemployed: in this they followed the norm for irregular workers on the estate, because it is generally agreed among the respondents that the earnings rules on benefits are unfair. Cash work is constructed as legitimate, given the unreliability and short-term nature of much employment and 'self-employment' in this sector of the labour market, and the delays in implementing claims for income support and family credit. But all the respondents also constructed limits (self-imposed) on what it was legitimate to earn on undeclared cash jobs (i.e. above which claimants should come off benefits, and 'self-employed' workers declare their earnings to the tax authorities). Indeed, their accounts of 'others' who cheated and fiddled the system, were mainly descriptions of people who overstepped these limits of fairness, by earning much more, or much more regularly, yet remaining on benefits.

The system of 'rules' described by the interviewees is a response by poor people to the particular combination of employment casualisation and benefit system failure that they face: on this estate it has become a cultural response, reinforced by sanctions of disapproval and even 'grassing' to the authorities. It is part of the taken-for-granted understanding of social relations of residents, not a policy proposal. However, what our interviewees *actually describe themselves as doing* corresponds rather closely to a specific policy proposal. They say that they treat their income support benefits as an entitlement, which allows them to earn up to a certain amount (usually about £30–50 per week) without any deduction: in other words, they give themselves an 'earnings disregard' well above the DSS regulation of £5 per week. In this way, they make part-time, short-term cash work worth taking. If they stuck to the official rule of £5, they really would be trapped in poverty *and* unemployment, because most available work would simply make them worse off, certainly in the short term, and probably in the long term (through a combination of deductions and/or delays in payment of benefits). If their earnings rise above their limits, or their partners return to work, the (male) claimants then change their administrative status to employed or self-employed, but grant themselves an additional tax allowance of about the same amount, by not declaring small cash jobs to the tax authorities. In this way they compensate themselves for the disincentives of benefit withdrawal and the impact of income taxation as they leave the claimant status.

This is almost exactly how the schemes for Transitional and Partial Basic Incomes, proposed by Atkinson and Sutherland,[24] Parker,[25] Rhys Williams,[26] Walter[27] and Vince[28] (amongst others) would work. For instance, Atkinson and Sutherland put forward a scheme for 'cashing out' income tax allowances (which would be abolished) by introducing a Partial Basic Income of £10 per adult in the household. This would mean that a couple with two children on child benefit of £7.25 per week would get an unconditional weekly sum of £34.50 per week. Using a new and refined computer model (TAXMOD) they show that – with a disregard of the first £16.60 of earnings for tax purposes – the largest net gainers are couples with one earner and single parents. High-income households are losers, most householders gain very small amounts, but the bottom group of earners gain most.[29] In Hermione Parker's scheme Transitional Basic Incomes would give the same amount to claimants and their partners as in the previous scheme, but allow them to opt into it or remain in the old income support system, thus giving those with access to part-time or irregular employment a choice.[30] The scheme described by Vince would introduce a unified income tax of 34 per cent (consolidating National Insurance Contributions into income tax) and make other minor benefits changes, before introducing a £10 'Citizen's Income' for all adults, with a tax disregard on the first £20 of earnings. This scheme, in combination with a means-tested Low Income Benefit, redistributes £2,000 million to the poorest households.[31] Both the scheme Vince describes and Parker's anticipate the Partial Basic Income rising to £25–7 per week at 1988–9 prices. In Parker's calculations (excluding housing costs) a single-wage married couple earning £80 per week would get £114.80 per week in final income (compared with £75.81 in the actual 1988–9 tax-benefit system), and one earning £150 would get £160.30 (compared with £123.04).[32]

It is quite likely that the couples we interviewed would be puzzled by the thinking behind these schemes, or might reject them altogether – as 'helping scroungers' or 'something for nothing'. However, their proposers – while sometimes making grandiose ideological claims on their behalf – are trying to suggest practical ways forward from the tax-benefit muddle that is so graphically described in our study interviews. If it were pointed out to them that these schemes simply made official the rules under which almost all of them operated their lives, these interviewees might be more readily persuaded of their merits.

Of course, claims that a policy innovation implements the expressed wishes or implicit needs of service users, or gives them more 'choice', should be treated with caution. Reforms which claim to 'liberate' or 'include' state beneficiaries deal in the same power-knowledge as the systems that they seek to replace, and can be used to legitimate benefit cuts and increased regulation.[33] Reformist knowledge is, like administrative practice, always implicated in power, and service users are always required to construct both their autonomy and their constraints in its terms. Thus it may be that the most that can be claimed for a reform – even a radical restructuring – is that it can extend the repertoire of poor people's interpretive practices, allowing them new ways to describe and legitimate their actions, and add to their already diverse, complex and contradictory range of accounts and rhetorical skills.[34]

One of the features of the present situation on the estate is that the similarities between the norms espoused by Mr and Mrs Derwent and Mr and Mrs Bow are obscured. To a casual reader of the two accounts, the former are exceptionally hardworking and responsible, the latter workshy and devious. In the culture of the estate, the couples themselves would be unlikely to make these distinctions, and might indeed be close friends (members of the same darts teams, for example). In making the regulations correspond to the actual practices on the estate, the authorities would not only be decriminalising undeclared work and providing a more rational structure of incentives; they would be recognising the culture of the estate as a sensible, shared response to changed economic circumstances.

Perhaps the last word should go to Mr and Mrs Frome, the only respondents who actually framed their criticisms of the benefits system in terms of this proposal. Mr Frome is scornful of the 'full-employment' aims of government in a post-industrial economy, and openly prefers the work he does 'on the side'. Mrs Frome concludes her interview quite specifically:

'I think they'd find then ... that a high ... a lot of the fiddling would stop because, you know, people who are earning less than that, you know, aren't declaring it and then it, the government has to take them to court and all the other hassles ... and watching them and everything else. Whereas if they were just to pay it out then ... a lot of it would stop.'

(Mrs Frome, 10)

REFERENCES

1 Jan Pahl, 'Household Spending, Personal Spending and the Control of Money in Marriage', *Sociology*, Vol. 24, No. 1, 1990, p. 120.
2 Yolanda K. Grift and Jacques J. Siegers, 'An Individual Utility Household Budget Constraint Model for Dutch Couples', and Tim Barmby, 'Pareto-Optimal Labour Supply', both papers presented to EMRU/Labour Study Group Conference, Loughborough University, 9 July 1990. See also Lydia Morris with Sally Ruane, *Household Finance Management and Labour Market Behaviour*, University of Durham, 1987.
3 Philip Corrigan, *Social Forms/Human Capacities: Essays in Authority and Difference*, Routledge, 1990, especially pp. 199–220.
4 ibid., p. 199.
5 ibid., p. 206–13.
6 ibid., p. 199.
7 Eithne McLaughlin, Jane Millar and Kenneth Cooke, *Work and Welfare Benefits*, Avebury, 1989.
8 Hermione Parker, *Instead of the Dole: An Enquiry into Integration of the Tax and Benefit systems*, Routledge, 1989, especially Chs 14 and 20; A. B. Atkinson and Holly Sutherland, *Integrating Income Taxation and Social Security: Analysis of a Partial Basic Income*, London School of Economics Number TIDI/123/July 1988.
9 In an interesting paper delivered to the EMRU/Labour Study Group at Loughborough University on 9 July, 1990, Professor Joseph Altonji argued that parental work hours are a very important determinant of the work hours of their offspring. His econometric modelling of work patterns showed that the work preferences of young men and women were strongly correlated with

those of their parents. See J. G. Altonji and T. A. Dunn, 'An Intergenerational Model of Wages, Hours and Earnings',loc. cit. For a study of stress on women through working long hours in the informal labour market and the household, see Enzo Mingione, 'Social Reproduction of the Surplus Labour Force: The Case of Southern Italy', in N. Redclift and E. Mingione (eds), *Beyond Employment*, Blackwell, 1985, pp. 14–54, especially p. 49.

10 See for comparison Richard Sennett and Jonathan Cobb, *The Hidden Injuries of Class*, Cambridge University Press, 1977, pp. 125–6.

11 We are indebted to Walter Van Trier of the University of St Ignatius, Antwerp, for this analogy.

12 Raymond Williams, *Towards the Year 2000*, Chatto & Windus, 1983.

13 Corrigan, *Social Forms/Human Capacities*, pp. 199 and 216–17.

14 ibid., p. 219.

15 Sennett and Cobb, *The Hidden Injuries of Class*.

16 David Knights and Hugh Willmott, 'Power and Subjectivity at Work: From Degradation to Subjugation in Social Relations', *Sociology*, Vol. 23, No. 4, 1989, p. 550.

17 Michel Foucault, *Power/Knowledge*, Harvester, 1980.

18 Lawrence Mead, *Beyond Entitlement: The Social Obligations of Citizenship*, Free Press, 1986, p. 82.

19 Ruth Lister, *The Exclusive Society: Citizenship and the Poor*, CPAG, 1989.

20 J. Kennedy (ed.), *No Mean City: A Methodist View of Poverty and Citizenship*, Methodist Church Division of Social Responsibility, 1989. It should be added that one of the authors of this book, Bill Jordan, has expressed similar ideas, albeit in less metaphoric language.

21. Jonathon Potter and Michael Mulkay, 'Scientists' Interview Talk: Interviews as a Technique for Revealing Participants' Interpretive Practices', in M. Brenner, J. Brown and D. Canter (eds), *The Research Interview: Uses and Approaches*, Academic Press, 1985, pp. 247–71, especially p. 248.

22 ibid., p. 269.

23 For example, McLaughlin, Millar and Cooke, *Work and Welfare Benefits*.

24 Atkinson and Sutherland, *Integrating Income Taxation and Social Security*.

25 Parker, *Instead of the Dole*.

26 Sir Brandon Rhys Williams, *Stepping Stones to Independence: National Insurance after 1990*, Aberdeen University Press, 1989.

27 Tony Walter, *Basic Income: Freedom from Poverty, Freedom to Work*, Marion Boyars, 1989.

28 Philip Vince, 'Citizen's Income', *Basic Income Research Group Bulletin*, No. 11, 1990, pp. 20–1.

29 Atkinson and Sutherland, *Integrating Income Taxation and Social Security*.

30 Hermione Parker (ed.), *Basic Income and the Labour Market*, BIRG Discussion Paper No. 1, Basic Income Research Group, 1990; see also Parker, *Instead of the Dole*, Ch. 20.

31 Vince, *'Citizen's Income'*.

32 Basic Income Research Group, *Basic Income*, BIRG, 1989, p. 4.

33 David Silverman, 'The Impossible Dreams of Reformism and Romanticism', in J. F. Gubrium and D. Silverman (eds), *The Politics of Field Research: Sociology Beyond Enlightenment*, Sage, 1989, pp. 30–48.

34 ibid., pp. 43–5.

Appendix 1 The taxes and benefits system in 1988/89

Throughout the book, repeated references are made (by the interviewees and in our analysis) to the systems of income taxation and social security benefits. The interviews took place in late 1988 and early 1989, when the reforms introduced by the 1986 Social Security Act were being implemented, and the names of certain benefits were being changed. For example, interviewees sometimes talk about family income supplement (FIS), which was replaced by family credit in April 1988; or about supplementary benefit, which was replaced by income support at the same time.

Hence it seemed helpful to provide a background guide to the system as it operated then (it has been changed again in several ways since). This is not an exhaustive account, but is meant to indicate some of the main principles underlying income taxation and social security benefits and how they were applied in the fiscal year 1988/89.

Perhaps the most striking aspect of the system in relation to work incentives is the extent to which it embraced the population. In the UK in 1988/89, counting married couples as one, there were about 21 million paying income tax and about 18 million receiving benefits. Many were both paying tax and receiving benefits at the same time. The estimated total number of individual taxpayers was some 25 million. These included some 3.9 million wives who were paying tax on earned income.[1] This compares with a total population of those aged 18 and over of some 43 million.

Such a large number of taxpayers is not, perhaps, surprising since thresholds for income tax were, in historical terms, very low. For example, a person entitled only to the single person's allowance would, in 1988/89, have begun to pay tax as soon as their income exceeded £50 a week. A married couple could have incurred income tax if their weekly income was as low as £78 per week. The result is that relatively poor people are swept into the tax net by such low tax thresholds.

This can be illustrated by taking an example of a couple with two children both less than 11 years old, and where the husband is in paid employment but the wife is not. Suppose also that the only tax allowance to which they are entitled is the married man's allowance (as it then was). In 1988/89 they would have started paying National Insurance Contributions as soon as the husband's weekly wage exceeded £41 and, as already stated, income tax as soon as the wage exceeded £78. Yet at these levels of income the family would have been considered to have insufficient to live on and would have qualified for payments of family credit. For instance if their income (after tax and National Insurance Contributions) were £95 a week they may have been entitled to a weekly family credit payment of about £18.

Not only are many low-income households subject to tax and National Insurance Contributions but the additional withdrawal of income-related benefit payments as income rises can lead to incentive problems. Despite the reforms introduced in 1988, such interaction between the tax and benefit systems could still create circumstances in which financial incentives to earn more, or to work at all, were severely impaired or even, in some circumstances, wiped out altogether – the 'poverty and unemployment traps'. The poverty trap describes the situation where the effects of income tax and National Insurance Contributions on the one hand, and the withdrawal of income-related benefits on the other, offset extra earnings. The unemployment trap describes the situation in which there is little or no financial benefit to be gained from taking a job at all.

Such problems are compounded by a further issue which was raised by the respondents but which is normally given little if any consideration in the academic literature, and indeed much of the rest of it as well, and this relates to the administration of the system. It is clear from the respondents' accounts that delays, complexities and uncertainties associated with the system, together with possible ignorance on the part of claimants or potential claimants, can also affect the willingness of individuals to take paid employment. For example, when an unemployed person takes a job they may lose income support but, if the job is low-paid, they may qualify for family credit. However, they can be worse off taking a job if the income support is lost while they have to accumulate the requisite number of wage slips in order to claim family credit and perhaps face a further wait before the claim is processed.

To deal with these issues this appendix begins by examining income tax and National Insurance Contributions as they were operated at the time the interviews were taking place (1988/89). The appendix then turns a similar account of the social security system. It is certainly true that a number of major attempts to reduce disincentive effects in the tax and benefit systems as it affects low-income households have been made in recent years. Some of these, such as modifications to unemployment benefit and the main forms of cash help for people on low incomes are discussed below. Nevertheless, as will become clear, disincentives remain. The next section therefore describes the interaction of the tax and benefit system and poverty and unemployment traps as they applied in 1988/89 and some of the administrative aspects which can also affect labour-market decisions.

INCOME TAX

Like other tax systems, individuals are granted certain allowances before they become liable to tax and those applying for 1988/89 are shown in Table A-1. In addition some other payments, such as, (within certain limits), mortgage interest payments in respect of a person's home may be claimed.

With regard to work expenses for employees, the UK system is, partly for historical reasons, extremely restrictive. In order for an employee to successfully claim work expenses they would normally have to be incurred '*wholly, exclusively and necessarily in the performance of* ' the duties of that employment.[2] This is much more restrictive than the rules applying to self-employed taxpayers and is often interpreted literally. Thus the costs of travel to or from work is not allowable because they are not incurred *in the performance* of the employment. The costs of training for a job may likewise be disallowed on the same grounds. Although this arrangement considerably simplifies the tax system and limits the potential for fraudulent claims, it may also produce disincentive effects since the costs of employment (including training and so on) usually fall in full on the employee.

One expense particularly relates to this study and that is the costs of child care for working parents. This clearly does not fall within the allowable range since the costs of child care are not wholly, exclusively and necessarily incurred in the performance of a job. Indeed, until April 1990, if an employer provided child-care facilities or assistance with child care, the value of such support was considered part of the taxable income of the employee and subject to income tax. This is because another principle of income tax law is that an employee should not escape tax if he or she is paid in kind rather than in cash. However, from April 1990, the value of workplace nurseries provided by employers became exempted from tax, though this exemption still does not include, for example, a situation where an employer provides a cash allowance for child care or pays an employee's bills for child care. Still less, of course, does it cover the vast majority of cases where parents pay for their own child care. None of our respondents received any form of assistance with child care from employers.

Table A-1 Allowances against gross income in 1988/89

	£
Single person's allowance	2,605
Married allowance	4,095
Wife's earned income allowance	2,605
Additional personal allowance	1,490
Widow's bereavement allowance	1,490
Age allowance – single person age 65–79	3,180
Age allowance – single person age 80 and over	3,310
Age allowance – married couple age 65–79	5,035
Age allowance – married couple age 80 and over	5,205
Blind person's allowance (each)	540

The Taxation of Husband and Wife

In 1988/89 the UK income tax code contained some curious arrangements which were only finally abolished in April 1990. Nevertheless these arrangements had implications for a number of the respondents, as is demonstrated in Chapters 4, 5 and 6 and particularly in the discussion of Mr and Mrs Wye (pp. 175–8).

The relevant recent legislation appeared in Section 37 of the Income and Corporation Taxes Act 1970: 'A woman's income chargeable to income tax shall ... [for any year] during which she is a married woman living with her husband be deemed for income tax purposes to be his income and not to be her income'.

In 1988/89, when two people married they lost their single person's allowances, each of £2,605, but the husband would gain the married man's allowance of £4,095. In addition, if the wife were in paid employment, she could benefit from the wife's earned income allowance of £2,605. If both husband and wife worked they received both the married man's allowance and the wife's earned income allowance. Together these were worth more than two and a half times the single allowance. If only one spouse worked the value of their allowances depended on whether the single earner was the husband or the wife. If the wife worked but the husband did not, the couple still received both the married allowance and the wife's earned income allowance. If the husband worked but his wife did not, the couple just received the married man's allowance. This was worth about one and a half times the single person's allowance. If only one partner worked, the tax position clearly provided an incentive for that partner to be the wife.

The reason for this curious arrangement was that the husband and wife were treated as one person: the husband. Therefore if only the husband has paid employment he could claim only the married allowance. However if he did not have paid employment but his wife did, then he could claim both the married allowance and his wife's earned income allowance. One couple in our study, the Wyes, benefited from this situation: Mrs Wye was able to earn a total of £6,700 in 1988/89 before becoming liable to income tax.

The Rates of Tax

The rates of tax as they affect most taxpayers have been considerably simplified during the past two decades. From April 1973 the standard rate income tax and surtax were formally unified, with the standard rate becoming known as the basic rate and surtax as higher rate tax, though many commentators still refer, mistakenly, to the basic rate as the standard rate of tax. In addition, in 1973 the two-ninths earned income relief which had previously existed was abolished.

An additional lower rate of tax on the first £750 of taxable income was introduced in 1978 which may have improved work incentives for those on low incomes, but it was abolished in 1980. Furthermore the number of higher rates of tax was reduced from nine to five in 1979, and the range of income covered by each of the remaining bands widened considerably. Finally all the higher rates except one were abolished in 1988, leaving the UK income tax with two rates: the basic rate on the first £19,300 (in 1988/89) and one higher rate of 40 per cent on the excess.

The long basic rate band is the appropriate rate for the vast majority of taxpayers. For instance it was estimated that for 1988/89 out of some 25 million individual income taxpayers only 1.4 million paid tax at the higher rate. In other words, over 94 per cent of taxpayers paid tax at the basic rate.[3] The long band has the advantage of simplicity. However the main reason for its existence is that it allows tax to be deducted at source very accurately from the investment income and any second and subsequent employments of most taxpayers. All that has to be done is to set the rate at which tax is deducted from these sources of income to that appropriate to basic rate taxpayers. The only adjustments then required after the end of the tax year are those for the relatively small proportion of individuals who do not pay tax at the basic rate.

However, one of the disadvantages of the long basic rate is that it can create disincentive effects at the bottom end. As we have seen, people on relatively low incomes are subject to income tax, but with the long basic rate band, they start paying at the full 25 per cent straight away. In combination with National Insurance Contributions and the withdrawal of income-related benefits, this can pose severe financial disincentives to individuals wishing to earn more.

NATIONAL INSURANCE CONTRIBUTIONS

There are four classes of National Insurance Contributions. Class 1 relates to employees, Classes 2 and 4 to the self-employed and Class 3 is voluntary.

The Class 1 contribution is paid partly by the employee and partly by the employer and the rates applicable to employees who are not contracted out of the state earnings related pension scheme are shown in Table A-2. Employees pay contributions on their weekly earnings (or monthly or yearly equivalents) between the 'lower earnings limit' and the 'upper earnings limit' (£41 and £305 respectively in 1988/89). The rate of contribution shown in Table A-2 applied to *all* earnings and not just the amount in excess of the relevant threshold. For example someone earning £60 in 1988/89 would pay National Insurance Contributions on the entire £60 and not just the amount over £40.99. However there is a limit on the employee's contribution so that no further contributions are required on earnings over the upper earnings limit. The same arrangements apply to employers except that there is no upper earnings limit on the employer's contribution.

Where employees are contracted out of the state earnings related pension scheme both employees and employers pay a lower rate of contribution on earnings between the lower and upper earnings limits.

Table A-2 National Insurance Contributions from 6 April 1988

Employee's weekly earnings	Employer rate of contribution	Employee rate of contribution
£	%	%
0–40.99	0	0
41–69.99	5	5
70–104.99	7	7
105–154.99	9	9
155–305.00	10.45	9
over 305	10.45	9 (of £305)

Note: The above figures apply to employees who were not contracted out of the state earnings related pension scheme. Lower rates apply where employees were contracted out, except for the employer contribution on earnings in excess of £305.

The role of National Insurance Contributions in influencing labour-market decisions should not be underestimated. It might be thought that, given their title, they are of a fundamentally different nature to income tax and could not, therefore, be expected to have the same sort of effects on labour-market decisions. Such a view is hard to substantiate. Indeed in many ways National Insurance Contributions are a tax in everything but name. A definition of taxation from the Organisation for Economic Co-operation and Development (OECD) suggests that 'the term taxes is confined to compulsory, unrequited payments to general government'. For reasons described by Messere and Owens[4] the OECD classifies compulsory social security contributions which are levied on an income tax base as income taxes.

National Insurance Contributions (the relatively unimportant Class 3 aside) would fit such a definition closely. There is no strong link on normal commercial principles between the contributions paid in and the benefits received. Indeed Class 4 contributions, which are paid by the self-employed, do not attract any benefit at all. Even for the other classes of contribution the link is a feeble one since lack of entitlement to national insurance benefits does not disqualify anyone from qualifying for other benefits such as income support and family credit. In the 1980s only around half of social security spending came from National Insurance Contributions: the rest came from general taxation. The 'National Insurance Fund' is not a reservoir of accumulated contributions from which future claims will be met. Rather the Fund is run on a 'pay-as-you-go' basis and what tomorrow's claimants will get will depend on what tomorrow's tax-payers are willing to pay.

This line of reasoning has led to a number of suggestions that the personal income tax and National Insurance Contributions should be merged into a single direct tax.[5] The administration of the two levies appears to have considerable scope for rationalisation. By far the largest type of contribution is Class 1, which relates to employees and is paid by both the employees and their employers. It is, however, withheld at source from salaries and wages and the Inland Revenue is responsible for collecting it as well as income tax. In 1988/89 the Inland Revenue collected over £29 billion in contributions from employees and employers on behalf of the Department of Social Security.[6] In the same year the Inland Revenue collected over £43 billion in income tax, most of it from employees through the PAYE machinery. The two 'taxes' are normally paid by the same taxpayers, and collected by the same revenue service, yet they are administered on a completely different basis. Income tax is subject to the cumulative PAYE machinery, National Insurance Contributions to a non-cumulative arrangement. So far as administrative costs are concerned the bill for maintaining contribution records is about £100 million a year and about 10,000 civil servants are involved.[7]

The main argument used by the government against such a move seems to be that it believes that it is right to retain a link between the contributions paid in and benefits received'.[8] Yet the link is often no stronger for individuals than is the link between income tax and public expenditure generally. It has already been pointed out that Class 4 contributions do not attract any benefit at all. It might also be noted that a small step towards integrating income tax and Class 4 contributions has been made in that, from 6 April 1985, 50 per cent of the contribution may be deducted from total income for the purposes of income tax. Possibly it is thought that individuals might be more willing to pay taxes which are called contributions than they are to pay taxes which are called taxes. Perhaps the income tax should be merged with National Insurance Contributions, rather than the other way round, and the result called the social contribution or even the national community charge!

BENEFITS

The benefit system consists of a variety of different components. National insurance benefits are payable only to those who qualify on the basis of their National Insurance Contributions record, and who fall within other eligibility requirements. These benefits include unemployment benefit, sickness benefit, the basic state retirement pension and maternity allowance. In addition there are means-tested benefits which are payable according to a person's circumstances rather than their contributions record. In 1988/89 these benefits included income support, family credit, child benefit and housing benefit.

Some benefits, such as unemployment benefit are taxable (providing of course that an individual has enough income to exceed his or her personal allowances). Other benefits, such as income support, family credit, housing benefit and child benefit are tax-free. Some benefits are of little direct relevance to work incentives. This is most particularly true of child benefit since it is payable at a fixed rate and does not vary according to the parents' earnings. Most of the other main benefits can influence labour-market decisions and require some further description.

National Insurance Benefits

The main national insurance benefit of direct relevance to the study is unemployment benefit. A person in receipt of unemployment benefit is permitted to earn up to £2 a day before their benefit is reduced. It therefore affects the unemployment trap and is discussed further below.

In principle a person who has paid sufficient Class 1 National Insurance Contributions is entitled to unemployment benefit when they are out of work. Since 1979 there have been a number of major modifications to the benefit. Previously there had been an earnings-related supplement but this was first reduced and later abolished altogether by the Social Security (No. 2) Act 1980. In 1982, unemployment benefit became taxable and any tax rebates arising from unemployment were no longer payable until after the individual returned to work or after the end of the tax year.

The administration of the benefit also became more stringent. This took place in several stages and entitlement to unemployment benefit now depends on the claimant being capable of, and available for, work on every day for which they make a claim. In 1988/89 this was established by means of a questionnaire for all claimants.

There were also changes to the maximum disqualification period which may be applied when a person refuses to take work or training which was considered suitable. The disqualification period also applies where a claimant leaves a job without good cause or as a result of misconduct. In 1986 the period during which unemployment may be withheld on any of these grounds was increased from 6 to 13 weeks. From April 1988 it was increased to 26 weeks. A further significant change came in 1988 when the contribution conditions for unemployment benefit were tightened. In particular, the arrangement that entitlement was dependent on the claimant's contribution record of the tax year before the 'benefit year' was changed so that it became dependent on the *two* tax years before the benefit year. The two conditions a person has to meet are now considerably more stringent than before. The first is that they must have *paid* (credits do not count for this condition) Class 1 contributions on earnings of at least 25 times the lower earnings limit in one of the two relevant tax years. The second condition is a requirement to have been paid or credited with Class 1 contributions on earnings of least 50 times the lower earnings limit in both of the two relevant tax years.

Means-Tested Benefits

In the second half of the 1980s the means-tested assistance scheme was also subject to some signifant changes. In its White Paper *Reform of Social Security* (1985) the government gave five reasons for proposing change. Three of these were of direct relevance to this study: that the social security system was too complex, that it failed to give effective support to many of those in greatest need and that it left too many people trapped in poverty or unemployment. The fourth may well be relevant to future job decisions: namely that there should be fewer obstacles to the transfer of pension rights when individuals change employment. The final concern of the government related to the funding of the state pension scheme but this is not of direct relevance here.

Following the White Paper the arrangements relating to income-related benefits became subject to the Social Security Act 1986, and the required changes were subsequently phased in, with most of them operating from 11 April 1988. Some assessment of the implications of these changes will be considered later, but the first task it to describe the system as it affected the respondents.

In brief, the main changes were that income support replaced supplementary benefit and family credit replaced family income supplement (FIS). The old system of 'one-off' payments for exceptional needs was replaced by grants and loans from the new social fund and changes were made to the way housing benefit was calculated.

Income Support

Income support is payable to people who are considered to have insufficient money to live on and who are unemployed, or aged 60 or over, single parents, too sick or disabled to work full time, or required to stay at home to look after a disabled relative. Income support is not normally available to anyone who works for 24 or more hours a week (or who has a partner who works for 24 hours or more a week) though there are exceptions for individuals who work at home as a childminder or who are so disabled they cannot earn very much.

Income support is worked out on the basis of how much a person is considered to need to live on. This is calculated in terms of *allowances* and *premiums* The rates applying from April 1988 are shown in Table A-3. A person's allowances depend on age, whether they are single or not and the age and number of any children, and claimants should receive all the allowances they qualify for. Premiums are extra weekly amounts for people with special needs. If a person qualifies for more than one premium he or she will normally only get the premium which is worth the most. However, family premium, disabled child's premium and severe disability premium can be paid in addition to other premiums.

Income support can provide assistance towards mortgage interest. Furthermore, a person on income support is entitled to help with their rent and rates (subsequently replaced by the community charge) from housing benefit (see below). People receiving income support also benefit from items such as free prescriptions and dental treatment.

The potential effect on incentives, of course, arises as income support is withdrawn as individuals earn more. After the total amount of allowances and premiums has been determined in each case, the total is reduced by the amount of other income a person receives. For this purpose, if the individual or his or her partner has part-time earnings, it is the amount after tax,

Table A-3 Allowances and premiums applying from April 1988

Allowances	£ per week
Single person aged 16 or 17	19.40
Single person aged 18 to 24	26.05
Single person aged 25 or over	33.40
Single person 18 or over with a child	33.40
Couple both under 18	38.80
Couple with at least one over 18	51.45
Each child under 11	10.75
Each child aged 11 to 15	16.10
Each child aged 16 or 17 in education	19.40
Each child aged 18 or over in education	26.05
Premiums	
Family premium – at least one child	6.15
Disabled child's premium	6.15
Lone-parent premium	3.70
Disability premium – single person	13.05
Disability premium – couple	18.60
Severe disability premium	24.75
Pension premium– single person	10.65
Pension premium – couple	16.25
Higher pension premium – single person	13.05
Higher pension premium – couple	18.60

National Insurance Contributions and half of any pension contributions which is counted. No allowance is made for work-related expenses such as fees for child minding, fares to work and so on.

In 1988/89 the first £5 of earnings made no difference to the amount of income support paid. For single parents entitled to a lone-parent premium and disabled individuals in receipt of a disability premium, the first £15 of earnings were disregarded. The £15 limit also applied to couples who were under 60 and had been unemployed and receiving supplementary benefit or income support for 2 years or more. The £15 disregard normally applied to couples as well as single people. In other words, respondents on income support would lose benefit equal to all of their earnings in excess of the relevant disregard. They therefore faced severe financial disincentives to taking employment unless they were able to find and keep a job which paid enough to take them out of benefit altogether.

Income support was also restricted if the claimant's savings exceeded £3,000 but this was not a factor that was mentioned by any of the respondents.

Family Credit

In April 1988 family credit replaced the old family income supplement. It is payable to anyone (married or single) who has one or more children and who works for at least 24 hours a week. It is available both to people who are employed and to those who are self-employed.

Like income support, for the purposes of family credit, earnings are those received after deduction of tax, National Insurance Contributions and half of any pension contributions. Child benefit, housing benefit, mobility allowance and attendance allowance are not counted at all. If a family's income falls below a certain threshold, which depends on the number of children and their ages, then family credit is payable.

For 1988/89 the threshold for family credit was calculated as follows. For the claimant the relevant amount from April 1988 was £96.50. This amount applied whether the claimant was single or had a partner. A further £8.50 was added for each child under 11; £16.00 for each child between 11 and 15 and £21.00 for each child aged 16 or 17. If there was a child of 18 following a full-time course of education which was not above A level or OND standard, an extra £30.50 was added. If the family's income fell below the threshold then the full amount of family credit was payable. If the income was greater than the relevant threshold, the amount of family credit payable was the full amount less 70 per cent of the excess income. Although this appears much more favourable to work incentives than the arrangements for income support, when this operates together with other income-related factors, financial incentives can still be largely wiped out, as we shall see later.

The Social Fund

The social fund, also introduced in 1988, replaced single payments for exceptional needs and urgent needs payments for specific needs. The new fund provides loans and grants for people with exceptional needs which they find difficult to meet from their income. If claimants meet certain financial criteria, maternity and funeral payments can be made and there are also three types of discretionary payment: budgeting loans, crisis loans and community care grants.

Budgeting loans are for people receiving income support who cannot afford to pay for something they need, such as furniture, at the time that they need it. To be eligible for a budgeting loan a person or their partner must have been receiving income support for the previous 26 weeks, although one break of 14 days or less is disregarded. These loans are usually repaid by deductions from the recipient's social security payments and still have to be repaid if a person stops receiving benefit. Crisis loans are available to anyone, whether or not they are receiving any social security benefits. They are only available if a claimant has no other way of avoiding a serious risk to the health and safety of their family.

Community care grants are to help people to return to the community rather than being in 'care' in places such as hospitals, nursing homes and residential care homes. They are also available to help someone stay in the community rather than going into care and to cope with difficulties such as disability, long-term illness or problems following the break-up of a marriage. Community care grants are for people who are receiving income support or who are entitled to income support when they move into the community. They do not have to be repaid, except where a person does not receive income support when they move back into the community.

The amount of money in the social fund for these payments is limited and Social Fund Officers have to decide which of those applying shall receive help.

Housing Benefit

Housing benefit is administered by local authorities and is to help people on low incomes with their rent and rates. It is available to individuals whether or not they are in work and whether they pay rent or own their own home and may be payable even to those in receipt of other social security benefits.

In 1988/89 housing benefit covered all or part of the rent and up to 80 per cent of the rates (since replaced by the community charge). For this purpose rent did not include any payment for fuel for heating, lighting and cooking and suchlike. If a person was receiving income support and paid rent or rates, they automatically qualified for housing benefit. If they did not get income support they may still have qualified for housing benefit, depending on their circumstances. Both housing benefit and income support are calculated on a similar basis.

THE POVERTY AND UNEMPLOYMENT TRAPS

As indicated earlier in the appendix, the poverty trap is said to occur where an individual incurs high effective marginal tax rates when he or she earns more. This is made up of increases in income tax and National Insurance

Contributions combined with the effects of the withdrawal of income-related benefits. Before the social security reforms were introduced in April 1988 it was even possible for a person to make themselves worse off by earning more.

The unemployment trap is similar to the poverty trap, but refers to a different set of benefits. It exists when there is little or no financial incentive for an unemployed person to take paid employment. One useful way of describing the unemployment trap is to refer to the 'replacement ratio':

$$\text{Replacement ratio} = \frac{\text{income when unemployed}}{\text{income when employed}}$$

If the ratio exceeds 1, individuals would actually make themselves worse off by taking employment and, like the poverty trap, this could occur before the 1988 changes. However, with the unemployment trap it is more likely that the individual incurs high marginal tax rates as his or her earnings rise.

One of the aims of the 1986 Social Security Act was to ensure that there was always some net return to increased earnings, even if it were only a small one. In other words the combined effects of taxation and benefits should not produce marginal effective rates of taxation in excess of 100 per cent. The way this was done was to change the basis on which the main income-related benefits were calculated from gross income to net income. If benefits are always tapered in relation to net income there should always be something left over.

Strictly this is true, but it can be a very small amount. It should be borne in mind that individual cases differ for all sorts of reasons; some of the complications will be described below. However, let us look at a stylised example of a low-income worker who is claiming both family credit and housing benefit and is faced with an offer of a job which pays an extra £10 a week. The first loss is the 25 per cent marginal rate of income tax and 9 per cent rate of Class 1 National Insurance Contributions which would take £3.40, leaving the worker with £6.60. The family credit and housing benefit calculations must then be taken in turn. Family credit is withdrawn at a rate of 70 per cent on the net amount and so is reduced by £4.42 (£6.60 x 0.7), which leaves £1.98. Housing benefit comes next and if the worker were entitled to rebates for both rent and rates (as it then was, now community charge) this is withdrawn at a rate of 80 per cent of the net amount (£1.98 x 0.8 = £1.58), which leaves the individual with a net gain from the extra £10 gross pay of just 40 pence. The effective marginal rate in this case is therefore 95.8 per cent.

There are, of course, some qualifications to this stark calculation. Family credit is awarded for 26 weeks at a time. Permanent changes in earnings will not, therefore, affect the level of family credit until the end of that period. Temporary changes will not affect the level at all unless they happen just before the end of the period in which case they *might* result in a reduction of benefit for 26 weeks. Another factor is that many individuals do not, for one reason or another, take up their entitlement to family credit and other benefits. Clearly if they are not taken up they cannot be withdrawn again. The estimated take-up for family income supplement, which family credit replaced, was thought to be only about 45 to 55 per cent of those eligible.[9] Our study thus throws light on some of the reasons for low take-up, especially those relating to the time it takes from coming off income support to receiving the benefit and the effect this has on budgeting in households.

In considering the unemployment trap, the situation is further complicated by the near certainty that taking a job will impose work-related expenses such as travel to and from work and costs related to child care. In such cases, even where effective rates of tax are less than 100 per cent, a person could still find themselves worse off as a result of taking a job. As can be seen from the repondents' accounts these factors are particularly important for respondents who are lone parents.

If an unemployed person has sufficient National Insurance Contributions they may be entitled to unemployment benefit. The earnings rule applicable here was that an individual may earn up to £2 a day without losing unemployment benefit provided they are still available for and seeking full-time work as an employee. Unemployment insurance staff check the claims of all who register as unemployed for their eligibility under the conditions.

Some Administrative Considerations

The adverse incentive effects of the poverty and employment traps can be worsened by administrative delays and errors, as some of the respondents found. If a person is unemployed and receiving income support, that benefit is stopped when the person takes a job and the household can be financially worse off while the worker has to accumulate the requisite number of wage slips in order to claim family credit. There will also be a further wait before the claim is processed.

As was shown in Chapter 4, a further administrative practice reinforcing the unemployment trap is the investigation of the reasons why an employee left his or her previous employment, which can take several weeks. This is particularly difficult for irregular workers who have to resort frequently to benefits, and for household budgeting in their families because this means being without any income for several weeks while a claim is processed. The consequence may be that claimants see the offer of short-term employment, or a job of uncertain duration as too disruptive of their household budgeting to be worthwhile.

In a report by the Comptroller and Auditor General[10] it was acknowledged that claimants and their representative organisations had identified delays in receiving decisions on family credit as a problem. There had been an improvment in the time taken by the Department of Social Security to deal with these applications, but delays still exceeded targets, apparently because of the time taken for employers to reply to enquiries about claimants' earnings. The target average clearance time for each claim for family credit was set at 18 working days for 1988/89 but in that year an average of 21.2 working days was achieved. About 100,000 claims took twice the target period to clear (some 25,000 of these were from self-employed claimants).

Some improvements have been made. For example, the fast family credit arrangements operated so that unemployed people about to start work can receive family credit straight away have been extended from the North Fylde Central Office dealing with family credit to the local office network.

However, there is still room for improvement. For example, despite a major advertising campaign, many unemployed people on income support still appear to have little knowledge of family credit, let alone fast family credit. The report by the Comptroller and Auditor General cited above included the results of surveys of 1,040 income support recipients and 782 family credit recipients carried out for the National Audit Office by Market and Opinion Research International (MORI) and National Opinion Polls Market Research (NOP). Of the income support recipients, 88 per cent had heard of family credit, mostly through advertising, although 8 per cent said that they had heard about it from the Department of Social Security and 1 per cent from the Department of Employment. However, 22 per cent of those who had heard of family credit had no firm idea as to what it was, or how it worked, and only 13 per cent said that they had actually received any advice or explanation about family credit.

Apart from ignorance relating to family credit and delays involved in claiming it, there is a significant number of errors in payments, which adds to uncertainty. In 1990, and for the second year running, the Comptroller and Auditor General qualified his certificates of the appropriation accounts relating to benefit payments.[11] His examination of a sample of awards of income support showed that some 14.4 per cent of the cases looked at contained errors and some 22 per cent of family credit awards were wrong. Of course, ensuring a higher level of accuracy would increase delays in the system, some of the errors were very minor and there were both overpayments and underpayments, but the net effect is to increase the uncertainty surrounding decision-making in low-income households.

REFERENCES

1 *Inland Revenue Statistics*, London, HMSO, 1989.
2 For further discussion see S. James and C. Nobes, *The Economics of Taxation*, 3rd edn, Philip Allan/Simon & Schuster, 1988.
3 *Inland Revenue Statistics*, London, HMSO, 1990, Table 1.5.
4 K. C. Messere and J. P. Owens 'International Comparisons of Tax Levels', *OECD Economic Studies*, Spring 1987, pp. 93–119.
5 See for example S. James, 'The Reform of Personal Taxation: a Review Article', *Accounting and Business Research*, No. 66, Spring 1987, pp. 117–24.
6 Board of Inland Revenue, *Report for the Year Ending 31 March 1990*, HMSO, London, Cmnd. 1321.
7 A. W. Dilnot, J.A. Kay and C. N. Morris, *The Reform of Social Security*, Oxford University Press, 1984, Ch. 1.
8 *Reform of Social Security: Programme for Action*, HMSO, 1985, Cmnd. 9691.
9 Nicholas Barr, *The Economics of the Welfare State*, Weidenfeld & Nicolson, 1987.
10 National Audit Office, *Support for Low Income Families*, HMSO, January 1991.
11 National Audit Office, *Report of the Comptroller and Auditor General, Appropriation Accounts, 1989/90*, HC 632–VIII, HMSO, 1990.

Appendix 2

HOUSEHOLDS IN COUPLE SAMPLE: PSEUDONYMS AND FAMILY STRUCTURE

Man *Employment status*	Woman *Employment status*	Children at *home and ages*
Mr Dave Avon Labourer (foodstuffs) (Ft*)	Mrs Sandra Avon Cleaner (Pt*)	Chrissie (11), Paul (10) and son (7)
Mr Bow Unemployed	Mrs Bow Housewife	8, 6, 2^1/$_2$
Mr Martin Bure Metal finisher (Ft)	Mrs Jeanette Bure Housewife	3 and 9 months
Mr Maurice Calder Lorry driver (Ft)	Mrs Calder Shelf-filler (Pt)	4 children (2 at school and 2 under school age)
Mr Cam Roadsweeper/driver (Ft)	Mrs Lucy Cam Housewife	Emma (6) and Luke (4)
Mr Cherwell Café supervisor (Ft)	Mrs Alison Cherwell Café worker (Ft)	daughter (1)
Mr Clyde Labourer (Ft)	Mrs Clyde Café worker (Pt)	5 and 4 months
Mr Colne Car valeter	Mrs Colne Housewife/foster parent	13, 8, 5 and Warren (3 months)
Mr Dart Unemployed	Mrs Dart Housewife	son (5), Monica (3) and Martin (4 months)
Mr Terry Derwent Warehouseman (Ft)	Mrs Rachel Derwent Care assistant (Pt)	Teresa (6) and 2 others aged 4 and 2
Mr Dovey Unemployed	Mrs Dovey Housewife	son (10)
Mr Gary Exe Unemployed	Mrs Exe Housewife	5 and 3

Man *Employment status*	*Woman* *Employment status*	*Children at* *home and ages*
Mr Larry Frome Unemployed	Mrs Barbara Frome Housewife	Natasha (8) and son (6)
Mr Tom Hodder Painter (S/E*)	Mrs Hodder Chambermaid (Pt)	17, 15 and 10
Mr Humber Unemployed	Mrs Humber Housewife	daughter (8) and son (5)
Mr Nigel Itchen Unemployed	Mrs Itchen Housewife	4 and 1
Mr Kennet Painter (S/E)	Mrs Kennet Cleaner (Pt)	Valerie (16) and Richard (14)
Mr Medway Security guard (Ft)	Mrs Medway Shop worker (Pt)	3 and 1
Mr John Nene Motor-cycle mechanic (Ft)	Mrs Gill Nene Factory supervisor (Ft)	Emma (16) and Stephen (13)
Mr Thames Van driver (Ft)	Ms Otter Singe parent/housewife	twins (3)
Mr Ouse Labourer (signwriting) (Ft)	Mrs Ouse Cleaner (Pt)	4 and 2
Mr Parrett Unemployed/ self-employed	Mrs Parrett Café worker (Pt)	6 children (17–5)
Mr Plym Civil servant (clerical) (Ft)	Mrs Nancy Plym Shelf-filler (Pt)	6 and 4
Mr Steve Ribble Plasterer (S/E)	Mrs Sheila Ribble Housewife	Michael (1)
Mr Rother Council foreman (Ft)	Mrs Rother Cleaner (Pt x 2)	14, 12 and 4
Mr Ed Ryton Stonemason (trainee)	Mrs Ryton Housewife	4 and 18 months
Mr Severn Gardener (Ft)	Mrs Severn Housewife	2
Mr Spey Unemployed	Mrs Spey Housewife	11, 8, 6 and 2
Mr Arnold Stour Shop manager (Ft)	Mrs Stour Machinist (Pt)	daughter (16)
Mr Tamar Factory machinist	Mrs Jean Tamar Factory machinist	daughter (14)
Mr Tavy Unemployed	Mrs Tavy Housewife	14 and 12

Man Employment status	Woman Employment status	Children at home and ages
Mr Jim Taw Bus driver (Ft)	Mrs Taw Cleaner (Pt)	son (3)
Mr Torridge Warehouseman (Pt)	Mrs Torridge Housewife/single parent	12 and 10
Mr Trent Meat cutter (Ft)	Ms Lesley Waveney Housewife	son (3)
Mr Wear Council labourer (Ft)	Mrs Carla Wear Cleaner (Pt)	7, 5 and 2
Mr David Wye Unemployed	Mrs Linda Wye Warehouse manager (Ft)	5 and 3

Note: *Ft = full time; Pt = part time; S/E = self-employed.

Name index

Subject index